Ecologies of Inception

Responding to increasing levels of planetary pollution, waste generation, carbon dioxide emission, and environmental collapse, *Ecologies of Inception* rethinks potentiality—an object's ability to change—in architecture and design.

The book problematizes the still-prevailing modern paradigm of design practice: the technical *tabula rasa*, a tendency to begin from scratch and use raw, amorphous, and obedient materials that can be easily and effectively manipulated, facilitating a seamless and faithful embodiment of intentions. Instead, the philosophy of design developed in the text prompts—through a variety of case studies, thinkers, and disciplines—a collective reconsideration of value, dissociating it from the projects and signatures of any one author or generation. Whereas the merits of upcycling and circular design are canonically defined vis-à-vis status-quo economic and socio-cultural orthodoxies, this project unpacks the theoretical assumptions that underpin these practices, showing that they perpetuate the same biases and exclusions that generate waste in the first place. As an alternative, the book introduces a nodal and exaptive paradigm for design: a conceptual and methodological toolset for engaging the durational and anthropocenic materiality of the third millennium, and for radically prioritizing practices of maintenance, reuse, care, and co-option. This approach, which is inspired by (and builds upon) evolutionary biology, technological disobedience, queer use, adaptive reuse, experimental preservation, and improvisational practices such as collage, adhocism, bricolage, and kit-bashing, refuses to reduce pre-existing material substrates to abstract lists of properties or featureless lumps, encountering them on their own terms—as situated individuals and co-authors.

Ecologies of Inception will appeal to undergraduate and postgraduate students, educators, and professional architects and designers interested in sustainable design and seeking to develop conceptual and design tools commensurate with the magnitude and urgency of the climate emergency.

Simone Ferracina is the founding director of Exaptive Design Office (EDO) and a Lecturer in Architectural Design/Detail at the Edinburgh School of Architecture and Landscape Architecture (ESALA), The University of Edinburgh.

Ecologies of Inception
Design Potentials on a Warming Planet

Simone Ferracina

Routledge
Taylor & Francis Group

LONDON AND NEW YORK

Cover image: Superuse Studios, *Wikado Playground*, Rotterdam, 2007. Photograph by (©) Denis Guzzo.

First published 2022
by Routledge
2 Park Square, Milton Park, Abingdon, Oxon OX14 4RN

and by Routledge
605 Third Avenue, New York, NY 10158

Routledge is an imprint of the Taylor & Francis Group, an informa business

British Library Cataloguing-in-Publication Data
A catalogue record for this book is available from the British Library

Library of Congress Cataloging-in-Publication Data
Names: Ferracina, Simone, 1978- author.
Title: Ecologies of inception : design potentials on a warming planet / Simone Ferracina.
Description: Abingdon, Oxon ; New York : Routledge, 2022. | Includes bibliographical references and index.
Identifiers: LCCN 2021043371 (print) | LCCN 2021043372 (ebook) | ISBN 9780367858759 (hardback) | ISBN 9780367858766 (paperback) | ISBN 9781003015444 (ebook)
Subjects: LCSH: Sustainable design. | Sustainable architecture.
Classification: LCC NK1520 .F47 2022 (print) | LCC NK1520 (ebook) | DDC 745.2—dc23/eng/20211022
LC record available at https://lccn.loc.gov/2021043371
LC ebook record available at https://lccn.loc.gov/2021043372

ISBN: 978-0-367-85875-9 (hbk)
ISBN: 978-0-367-85876-6 (pbk)
ISBN: 978-1-003-01544-4 (ebk)

DOI: 10.4324/9781003015444

Typeset in Adobe Garamond Pro
by codeMantra

This book is dedicated to my father, who would have been proud to hold it in his hands.

Contents

Introduction

Tampering with Design Potentials on a Warming Planet

The planet is warming. Human-induced changes in the climate system are increasing the frequency and intensity of extreme weather events, from deadly hurricanes in the Caribbean and Atlantic, to unprecedented wildfires in the Bolivian Amazon, Canada, and western continental US. Between September 2019 and January 2020, wildfires in New South Wales and Victoria destroyed about 5.7 million hectares of broadleaf woodland—one-fifth of the continent's forests. Ocean acidification from the absorption of anthropogenic carbon dioxide in the Bering Sea and northern Indian Ocean threatens the survival of marine organisms and ecosystems. Coral bleaching is under way along the coasts of Queensland, having already halved the number of living corals in the Great Barrier Reef. Anthropogenic emissions are responsible for droughts across the global map, from the Iberian Peninsula to Southern Africa; from Indonesia to New Zealand. As temperatures continue to rise above preindustrial levels, more extreme heatwaves, heavy precipitations, tropical cyclones, coastal flooding, and multi-meter rises in sea level are forecasted, with catastrophic effects on human and natural systems (e.g., human health, water resources, food security, ecosystem diversity, biodiversity), particularly for the regions and populations exposed to the exacerbated effects of compound climate-related events.[1] The Intergovernmental Panel on Climate Change (IPCC), in a special report on the impacts of global warming, warns that the remaining "CO2 budget available for emissions is very small," demanding "large, immediate and unprecedented global efforts to mitigate greenhouse gases,"[2] and underscoring the need to urgently and "strongly limit the demand for land, energy and material resources."[3] Philosopher and ecofeminist Val Plumwood further warns that "[a]s the free water we drink

1 IPCC, *Special Report: Global Warming of 1.5°C*, 2020.

2 IPCC, "Chapter 3: Impacts of 1.5°C of Global Warming on Natural and Human Systems," in *Special Report: Global Warming of 1.5°C*, 2020, 177.

3 Ibid., 180.

DOI: 10.4324/9781003015444-1

4   Val Plumwood, *Feminism and the Mastery of Nature* (London: Routledge, 2003),13–14.

5   In the text, *design* is used as shorthand for a broad set of practices. That is because, as will become clear, my use of the term refers to the purposeful potentializing of objects towards one another—to the emergence of ecologies of inception—and can therefore apply to a diverse range of contexts, ones that need not coincide with strict professional labels or disciplinary nomenclatures. That said, I tend to refer to practices that modify the material world, and the ability to act and interact within it. And while each case or example must contend with specific sets of constraints and parameters—and my own professional and academic trajectory pertains, as will be evident, to architectural design—this book approaches cupcakes, buildings, electric toasters, marble sculptures, undersea cables, and sidewalks *equally* as instances of design.

6   UN Environment and International Energy Agency, "Towards a Zero-Emission, Efficient, and Resilient Buildings and Construction Sector," Global Status Report 2017.

7   European Commission, "Eurostat: Waste Statistics," 2021. This figure refers to the 2,337 million tons of waste generated in 2018 (source dataset: ENV_WASGEN), of which construction and demolition contributed 35.9%, and mining and quarrying 26.6%.

8   Aristotle, "On the Soul," in *The Complete Works of Aristotle: The Revised Oxford Translation*, ed. Jonathan Barnes, trans. J.A. Smith (Princeton: Princeton University Press, 1984), 24.

from common streams, and the free air we breathe in common, become increasingly unfit to sustain life, the biospheric means for a healthy life will increasingly be privatised and become the privilege of those who can afford to pay for them. The losers," she continues, "will be (and in many places already are) those, human and non-human, without market power."[4]

What is the role of design[5] in the efforts to stave off environmental collapse and mitigate a looming future characterized by soaring levels of extinction, biodiversity loss, climate injustice, desertification, hunger, poverty, and forced migration? If the construction industry is responsible for an astonishing 39% of global carbon emissions,[6] and the construction and demolition of buildings, alongside mining and quarrying, account, in Europe, for over 60% of all the waste generated by economic activities and households,[7] what forms of environmental stewardship might transform the protocols and practices that contribute to these figures? Or, more broadly: how can the designers of buildings, toilet rolls, sofa beds, parks, cargo ships, window frames, and bicycles rise to the challenge set by the IPCC? How do we begin to forswear our contributions to ecocide, and decouple design potentials from ecologies of extraction, exploitation, obsolescence—and from the imperative of economic growth?

In the following pages, I will begin to address these questions by investigating the still-prevailing modern paradigm of design practice: the technical *tabula rasa,* a tendency to begin from scratch and use raw, amorphous, and obedient materials that can be easily and effectively manipulated, facilitating a seamless and faithful embodiment of intentions. As I will argue, this predominant *modus operandi* is grounded in the hylomorphic philosophy of Aristotle, which associates matter with potentiality (the wet clay's malleability) and form with actuality (the fired clay's fixity), thus foreclosing the ability of formed/individuated objects to change.[8] By reappraising potentiality—understood broadly as the ability to change—I will establish a theoretical framework for neutralizing such a view and, more generally, for reconsidering how design generates and maintains potentials in space and time. This will lead to the introduction of conceptual and methodological tools for, on one side, fusing designed objects with their political and environmental effects and, on the other, finding value in embodied materials and intergenerational collaboration (rather than novelty, authorial signatures, or individual projects).

The gargantuan challenges posed to designers by the climate emergency and its associated crises and injustices, I claim, cannot be addressed with targeted technological fixes, or even with decarbonization alone, but must call into question the disciplinary value systems and forms of professional practice that continue to produce and sustain them. Yet, this does not suggest a relinquishing of creativity, or the adoption of strictly corrective measures. Rather, the *exaptive design* approach proposed here might encourage the emergence of new collective imaginaries and modes of evaluation and invention.

The central concept of this book—ecology of inception (EoI)—describes the networks of tools and actors woven together by design scripts:[9] their edges, temporalities, and the mechanisms according to which potentials—the languages objects use to communicate—are progressively unlocked, both within and across system boundaries. As moving constellations of objects, and as emergent bodies tethered to (but physically and temporally removed from) design aims and intentions, EoIs rearticulate, combine, adopt, and modify a number of established philosophical terms and concepts (equipment, individuation, assemblage, network, hyperobject, et cetera). Across the chapters, I use these and other terms—and lean on (and gain insights from) a variety of thinkers and disciplines (architecture, environmental psychology, anthropology, discard studies, etc.)—to iteratively redefine and study EoIs, progressively adding and shifting perspectives, examples, and levels of nuance. The resulting investigations cluster around three key threads—the blank slate as a figure of potentiality in Part I ("*Tabula Rasa*"), materiality and material potency in Part II ("Hypermaterials"), and design intentions in Part III ("Authorship").

If EoIs set the boundaries within which potentials can be actualized—enclosures that tune objects towards one another, finding value in their cooperation—the same boundaries also exclude or reject noncommunicative or unproductive elements, in the same way that, as anthropologist Mary Douglas has shown, dirtiness and impurity are only identifiable in relation to specific systems of classification.[10] In this sense, ecologies of inception are valuing and devaluing machines, and may—as conceptual tools—help shift the focus of design from the configuration and celebration of outputs (be they Philippe Starck's lemon squeezer; Frank Gehry's buildings; Dunne & Raby's robots; or Madelon Vriesendorp's paintings) to the tracing and untracing of the borders that assign them roles.

While, on one side, EoIs curate and implement protocols of purification and improvement that increase (and simultaneously conceal) violence, oppression, and injustice, they may also reclaim the ability of design to power *other* (postcapitalist, nonanthropocentric, pluriversal, feminist, antiracist, queer, anticolonial) valuing engines. Whereas, in conservation theory, art historian Alois Riegl could neatly separate memory values

9 Throughout this book, the use of the term *script* broadly follows the one proposed by Madeleine Akrich, as the end product of the work through which designers *inscribe* their "vision of (or prediction about) the world in the technical content of the new object." Madeleine Akrich, "The De-Scription of Technical Objects," in *Shaping Technology/ Building Society: Studies in Sociotechnical Change*, ed. Wiebe E. Bijker and John Law (Cambridge: MIT Press, 2010), 205–24.

10 Mary Douglas, *Purity and Danger: An Analysis of Concepts of Pollution and Taboo* (London and New York: Routledge, 2002), 45.

11 Sebastiano Barassi, "The Modern Cult of Replicas: A Rieglian Analysis of Values in Replication," *Tate Papers*, no. 8 (Autumn 2007).

12 Alois Riegl, "The Modern Cult of Monuments: Its Character and Its Origin," *Oppositions* 25 (Fall 1982): 21–51.

13 Michael Thompson, *Rubbish Theory: The Creation and Destruction of Value* (London: Pluto Press, 2017). Thompson also theorizes a third socially determined category (rubbish, with zero and unchanging value), through which dynamic transfers (from transient to durable) become possible.

14 The point being, of course, not that maintenance and repair are bad (they may be, depending on what is being maintained, for whom, etc.), but that obsolescence appears to be the only alternative to them. For an overview of scholarship on maintenance and repair, see Shannon Mattern, "Maintenance and Care," *Places Journal*, November 2018.

15 The term *deep* here refers both to the consideration of longer time spans that cut across individual ecologies or outputs (with a metaphorical nod to the *deep time* of geology), and to the philosophy of deep ecology, which rejects "the man-in-environment image" of a *shallow* ecological movement that fights pollution and resource depletion with the "health and affluence of people in the developed countries" as chief objective, and proposes instead a platform according to which "[t]he flourishing of human and non-human life on Earth has intrinsic value" and "[t]he value of non-human life forms is independent of the usefulness these may have for narrow human purposes." Arne Naess, *Ecology, Community and Lifestyle: Outline of an Ecosophy* (Cambridge: Cambridge University Press, 1998), 28–29.

16 Throughout the book, I avoid using the pronoun *we*, with its clumsy undertones of objectivity and universality, unless *who* that refers to is (directly or implicitly) qualified. When the pronoun is italicized, however, I am deliberately pointing to the violence of what Donna Haraway calls the "god trick of seeing everything from nowhere." Donna Haraway, "Situated Knowledges: The Science Question in Feminism and the Privilege of Partial Perspective," *Feminist Studies* 14, no. 3 (1988), 581.

(towards psychological and intellectual needs) and present-day values (pertaining to both practical and aesthetic needs),[11] and confidently list the corresponding subcategories (age-value, historical value, and intentional commemorative value in the former; use-value, newness-value, and relative art-value in the latter),[12] and Michael Thomson's *Rubbish Theory* could distinguish between objects that are transient (declining in value over time) and durable (increasing in value over time),[13] EoIs demand a higher degree of openness, fluidity, and contingency, attributing or naming values only as a function of ecological demarcation.

Now, if objects were coextensive with the roles assigned to them by EoIs—if they merely embodied or performed equipmental scripts—the associated potentials would necessarily abide by—and be funneled into—the target outputs and actualizations, or be relegated to ecologies of enforcement, maintenance, and repair.[14] If, however, one were to admit that the ontology of objects vastly exceeds ecological functions or the ways in which *we* encounter them (that the reality of a bicycle exceeds its bicycle-ness for us, even as we designed and manufactured it), unscripted, de-scripted, and over-scripted potentials may begin to emerge, as well as practices that radically expand revaluation, care, reuse, and repurposing. That is: whereas ecologies of inception weave objects into relational networks, holding them in position and confining potentiality to their ability to produce effects or communicate, I follow Giorgio Agamben (inoperativity), Sara Ahmed (queer use), and Graham Harman (nonrelationality) in understanding objects as openable to *other* uses and users, and as always partially withdrawn or held in reserve.

Here, the notion of ecology of suspension (EoS) begins to account for these withdrawals from the perspective of design, both requiring a shift in the spatial and temporal adjudication of powers (from the relationality of a *tabula rasa* to the plasticity of a *rasura tabulae*) and pointing to *deeper* modes of valorization,[15] which are affirmed in excess of use values, functional scripts, and molecular obedience, and in defiance of established measurement and justification protocols. Refusing to consign potentials to ecologies of inception (to ends, knowledge, and control; to *our* ability to detect and quantify them;[16] to a dispositional interior), and deferring the attribution of values or functions, EoSs negotiate a measure of worth in suspension, in the lack of productive relation. In the context of design, this doesn't only concern the decoupling of value from purposeful scripts, or the delaying of actualizations or use (impotentiality). Ecologies of suspension are also deployed to negotiate the gaps between EoIs: facilitating transfers and exchanges (e.g., the migration of materials and components); establishing localized temporalities (e.g., the slowness of acts of deconstruction, disassembly, and reconditioning as opposed to the careless speed of the wrecking ball); and preserving a stock of existing (co-optable) parts.

A term borrowed from evolutionary biology—exaptation—will guide my understanding of suspension, prompting a re-articulation of design authorship and practice that embraces vestigiality; allows for cross-generational collaboration; and welcomes a lack of certainty and control.[17] By dismissing the *tabula rasa* and endorsing a paradigm of radical reuse and repurposing, the nodal and exaptive approaches to design proposed in this book[18]—and illustrated throughout with exemplary precedents and case studies—begin to offer a conceptual toolset for engaging the durational and anthropocenic materiality of the third millennium, renouncing the imperatives of growth and extraction, and refusing to consign *value* to economic or functional orthodoxy. This approach, which is inspired by (and builds upon) practices like adaptive reuse,[19] superuse,[20] technological disobedience,[21] deconstruction,[22] design for disassembly,[23] and experimental preservation,[24] as well as improvisational methods such as collage, adhocism, bricolage, frottage, and kit-bashing, does not reduce pre-existing material substrates to abstract lists of properties or to featureless lumps, but encounters them on their own terms—as situated individuals and coauthors.

The two chapters in Part I ("*Tabula Rasa*") expose the enduring and damaging legacy of Aristotle's theory of substance, and develop a philosophy of design and value that, while being grounded on the notion of potentiality, refutes its narrow association with matter.

Chapter 1 ("Ecologies of Inception: Orientation of Designed Objects") introduces the notions of "technical *tabula rasa*" and "ecology of inception (EoI)," beginning to investigate how design and fabrication unlock potentials and negotiate exchanges between—and translations across—objects. The chapter also develops an ontological meditation on waste and wasting, understood as corollaries of design, and begins to consider how reuse, repurposing, and hoarding (in the sense, following Jane Bennett and Sylvia Lavin, of inorganic sympathy and animation)[25] return objects to spatiotemporal ecologies of care and value.

Chapter 2 ("Hylomorphism Reconsidered: Matter, Form, and the Ability to Change") traces the origins of the technical *tabula rasa* back to Aristotle's philosophy of substance, which associates matter (*hyle*) with potentiality, and form (*morphê*) with actuality, and, by so doing, deprives formed objects (e.g., wind turbines, car tires, videotapes, buildings, and glass bottles)

17 Stephen Jay Gould and Elisabeth S. Vrba, "Exaptation—A Missing Term in the Science of Form," *Paleobiology* 8, no. 1 (1982): 4–15. See also Simone Ferracina, "Exaptive Architectures," in *Unconventional Computing: Design Methods for Adaptive Architecture*, eds. Rachel Armstrong and Simone Ferracina (ACADIA Conference, Toronto: Riverside Architectural Press, 2013), 62–65.

18 By *nodal design*, as will be explained in Chapters 2 and 4 in relation to linear and circular fabrication processes respectively, I mean design that does not take the objective roles of *matter* and *form* (or of *material* and *object*) seriously.

19 See, for example: Duncan Baker-Brown, *The Re-Use Atlas: A Designer's Guide Towards the Circular Economy* (London: RIBA Publishing, 2017); Liliane Wong, *Adaptive Reuse: Extending the Lives of Buildings* (Basel: Birkhäuser, 2017); Graeme Brooker and Sally Stone, *Rereadings: Interior Architecture and the Design Principles of Remodelling Existing Buildings* (London: RIBA Publishing, 2017).

20 Ed van Hinte, Césare Peeren, and Jan Jongert, *Superuse: Constructing New Architecture by Shortcutting Material Flows* (Rotterdam: 010 Publishers, 2007).

21 Ernesto Oroza, "Technological Disobedience: From the Revolution to Revolico," *Technological Disobedience Archive* (blog), March 30, 2016.

22 See, for example: Michaël Ghyoot et al., *Déconstruction et réemploi: Comment faire circuler les éléments de construction* (Lausanne: Presses Polytechniques et Universitaires Romandes, 2018).

23 See, for example: Michael Braungart and William McDonough, *Cradle to Cradle: Remaking the Way We Make Things* (New York: North Point Press, 2002); Elma Durmisevic, *Green Design and Assembly of Buildings and Systems: Design for Disassembly a Key to Life Cycle Design of Buildings and Building Products* (Saarbrücken: VDM Verlag Dr. Müller, 2010).

24 Jorge Otero-Pailos, "Experimental Preservation," *Places Journal* (September 2016).

25 Jane Bennett, "Powers of the Hoard: Further Notes on Material Agency," in *Animal, Vegetable, Mineral: Ethics and Objects*, ed. Jeffrey Jerome Cohen (Washington: Oliphaunt Books, 2012), 237–69; Sylvia Lavin, "Architecture In Extremis," *Log*, no. 22 (2011): 51–61.

of the ability to change. The text also develops, in conversation with the philosophies of Giorgio Agamben and Gilbert Simondon, a detailed analysis of potentiality (the ability to do), impotentiality (the ability to *not* do), and individuation (the coming-into-being of individuals), neutralizing hylomorphism and demonstrating that all physical objects are entitled to powers.

Having established a framework for recognizing and defeating the dualistic structure of potentiality in Western thought, the two chapters in Part II ("Hypermaterials") turn to the analogous divisions that are operative in the manufacturing of materials, and in discourses concerning their circulation as technical nutrients.

Through the work of Bruno Latour, Katie Lloyd Thomas, and others, Chapter 3 ("Purity beyond Nature and Culture: Wildfires, Hypermaterials, and Co-option") describes the technical *tabula rasa* as an apparatus for translating nature into culture (for enforcing their separation), and for transforming situated objects into smooth and ubiquitous *hypermaterials*. Against the abstract materiality of the global economy, and in addition to a *design context* that informs local environmental, socio-political, and economic considerations, the chapter foregrounds the *material context* of the bricoleur and her treasury, which precedes intentions and steers design decisions and goals. The chapter ends with a discussion of reuse, architectural bricolage, and boundary objects in the work of the Brussels-based firm Rotor/Rotor Deconstruction.

Chapter 4 ("Circularities: Technical Nutrients, Hyperobjects, and Rooms") employs three designations of purity—teleological, energetic, and hypermaterial—as well as perspectives from the fields of discard studies and industrial ecology, to reassess upcycling and the circular economy, advocating reuse and repurposing as more serious and radical design stances. Furthermore, if the circular economy still relies on the matter/form dualism, privileging the former's ability to change (technical nutrients), the *nodal* economy proposed in this chapter is predicated on the interchangeability of their roles, and on the dissolution of hylomorphism. The chapter also borrows from Jane Hutton (materials as "fragments of other landscapes"),[26] Kiel Moe (buildings as "processes of urbanization"),[27] and Timothy Morton (hyperobjects as "massively distributed in time and space")[28] to redefine—and extend the scope of—EoIs.

Finally, the five chapters in Part III ("Authorship") consider how powers may be detached from EoIs (from teleological and authorial scripts), and investigate nonrelationality and suspension as supplements for an ethical reformulation of design methods, values, and objectives.

26 Jane Hutton, *Reciprocal Landscapes: Stories of Material Movements* (Abingdon and New York: Routledge, 2020), 5.

27 Kiel Moe, *Empire, State & Building* (New York: Actar, 2017), 242.

28 Timothy Morton, *Hyperobjects: Philosophy and Ecology after the End of the World* (Minneapolis: University of Minnesota Press, 2013), 1.

Chapter 5 ("*Rasura Tabulae*: From Formats to Media") follows Alexander of Aphrodisias in privileging—as a figure of potentiality—the thin layer of wax covering the writing tablet over its blankness or lack of inscriptions.[29] The resulting shift (from the absence of content to the plasticity of a medium) is used to study how EoIs broadcast messages, and how they promote exchanges between formats and media, both in the context of secondary uses (Charles Jencks and Nathan Silver's adhocism; Ernesto Oroza's technological disobedience; and Alfred Sohn-Rethel's philosophy of the broken)[30] and in conversation with Keller Easterling's formulation of "medium design" and "infrastructure space."[31]

Chapter 6 ("Ecologies of Suspension: Potentiality without Intentions/Relations") turns to Bataille's *formless* and Melville's scrivener Bartleby,[32] among others, to investigate de-formation, suspension, silence, and refusal as forms of ecological unravelling and diversion. To temper a relational model of design (ecologies of inception) that, with Marshall McLuhan, privileges background scripts over surface effects, I introduce a non-relational supplement (ecologies of suspension) that, following Graham Harman's object-oriented philosophy, regards all possible contact between objects as superficial. Whereas EoIs confine objects to specific networks, communication protocols, roles, and uses, EoSs allow them to move across enclosures, scripts, meanings, generations, and projects.

Chapter 7 ("Exaptive Design: Radical Coauthorship as Method") interrogates the senseless demolition of TWBTA's Folk Art Museum in New York City, demonstrating that, paradoxically, it was the value attributed to the architects' project—to the integrity of their intentions—that sanctioned the building's demise. The notion of *exaptation*, introduced by Stephen Jay Gould and Elisabeth S. Vrba in a 1982 paper entitled "Exaptation—A Missing Term in the Science of Form,"[33] offers an antidote against the authorial obsolescing of objects, and an effective paradigm for articulating suspension in design—for decoupling function and form, value and utility.

Chapter 8 ("Authorship vs. Withdrawal: OOO and Architecture") imagines an alternative trajectory for the engagement of object-oriented ontology (OOO) with the field of architecture. Here, the notion of *withdrawal* is not used to claim disciplinary autonomy (architecture as the object), to increase the authority of architectural authors (the architect as object), or to justify a lack of empathy and responsibility (the building as object), but as grounding an ethos of uncertainty and not knowing. Following Harman's rejection of an ontological separation between humans and nonhumans (onto-taxonomy),[34] and Val Plumwood's understanding of nature (nonhumanity)

29 Giorgio Agamben, *Potentialities: Collected Essays in Philosophy*, trans. Daniel Heller-Roazen (Stanford: Stanford University Press, 1999), 245.

30 Charles Jencks and Nathan Silver, *Adhocism: The Case for Improvisation* (Cambridge: MIT Press, 2013); Oroza, "Technological Disobedience;" Alfred Sohn-Rethel, "The Ideal of the Broken Down: On the Neapolitan Approach to Things Technical," *Hard Crackers: Chronicles of Everyday Life* (blog), February 15, 2018.

31 Keller Easterling, *Medium Design: Knowing How to Build the World* (London: Verso, 2021). Keller Easterling, *Extrastatecraft: The Power of Infrastructure Space* (London and New York: Verso, 2014).

32 Georges Bataille, "Formless," in Yve-Alain Bois and Rosalind E. Krauss, *Formless: A User's Guide* (New York and Cambridge: Zone Books, 1997), 5; Herman Melville, "Bartleby," in *The Piazza Tales* (New York: Dix & Edwards, 1856), 31–107.

33 Gould and Vrba, "Exaptation."

34 Graham Harman, *Dante's Broken Hammer: The Ethics, Aesthetics and Metaphysics of Love* (London: Repeater Books, 2016).

35 Val Plumwood, *Feminism and the Mastery of Nature* (London: Routledge, 2003).

36 By *cultural archive* I mean the "official" and monolithic sanctioning (and making stable) of value by privileged actors, often from within institutions or governments. Notably, the phrase is used by Edward Said to denote the site "where the intellectual and aesthetic investments in overseas dominion are made." Edward W. Said, *Culture and Imperialism* (New York: Vintage Books, 1994), xxi.

as a political category,[35] I explore four detaxonomizing scenarios: metaphorical (the object as Land), ecological (the non-human as inhabitant), humansnail (the object as inhabitant), and mereological (the object as parts).

The last chapter ("Conclusion") reviews, summarizes, and weaves together the book's main contributions and arguments, synthesizing its parallel discussions, challenges, and discoveries. By comparing the central features of ecologies of inception and ecologies of suspension with related philosophical terms (equipment, assemblage, and hyperobject), and by identifying some of the trajectories along which the text has bent or modulated these terms, the chapter argues that the tensions and apparent contradictions between the relational/nonrelational and synchronous/diachronic accounts of potentiality developed in the book, rather than being at odds with one another, contribute to an expanded philosophy of design—and may give rise to novel imaginaries, protocols, and forms of practice. Ultimately, this book argues that, in order to address the climate emergency, the design disciplines must become able to articulate value as existing beyond commodities and cultural archives[36]—and beyond the projects and outputs of any one generation or author.

Part I
Tabula Rasa

Chapter 1

Ecologies of Inception: Orientation of Designed Objects

1.1 What Is an Ecology of Inception (EoI)?

A blank sheet of paper lying on the floor of an otherwise empty room does not possess any intrinsic potentiality. It becomes capable of change, and charged with powers, only if it participates in a relational ecology that names, defines, and limits them. A paper–rain assemblage defines the sheet of paper as something that can be wetted and reduced to a pulp. A paper–dust assemblage turns it into a surface for the deposition of atmospheric particles. A paper–hand assemblage defines it as something that can be crumpled or folded; in a paper–hand–pen assemblage, it becomes a support for drawing or writing.

An ecology of inception (EoI), understood as the definition of the potential orientation of a physical system,[1] is the prerequisite of any technical operation aiming to intentionally change an object. The word *orientation* recognizes the necessarily directional nature of potentiality; the fact that a *telos* (a purpose or aim) becomes apparent as soon as a potential can be identified and named. To have powers is to be able to do something (and not anything).

The orientation of a system accounts for the possible outcomes stemming from the interaction of its component parts—its horizon of possibility. Even if one upholds the notion that powers are inherent in a thing, regardless of context—that the sheet of paper's ability to be folded or wetted precedes the encounter with the hand or the rain—potentials can only be unlocked relationally, in the interaction with an external agent or actor, which the EoI subsumes and internalizes. Indeed, the aim of any ecology of inception is to unlock the powers of an object in the context of a specific, more or less closed, system of relations. [**Figure 1.1**]

Gilles Deleuze and Félix Guattari entrust social or collective "machinic assemblages" with this function, suggesting, in the "Treatise

[1] My use of the term *system*, often interchanged with *assemblage*, *constellation*, and *network*, simply denotes an arrangement of objects or parts.

DOI: 10.4324/9781003015444-3

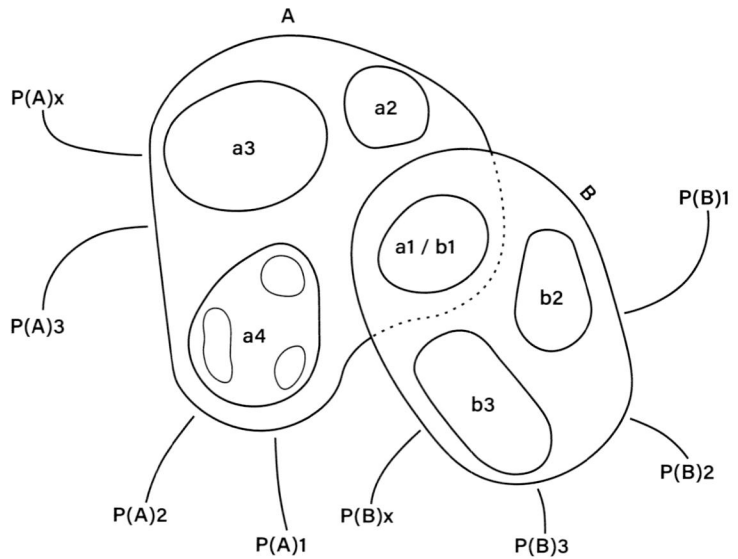

Figure 1.1 Ecologies of inception (A, B) are assemblages that unlock the relative potentials (P) of their components (aX, bX). Membership in EoIs can be temporary and nonexclusive, and objects might play, in different contexts or at different scales, the simultaneous role of component (part) and ecology of inception (whole).

2 Gilles Deleuze and Félix Guattari, *A Thousand Plateaus: Capitalism and Schizophrenia*, trans. Brian Massumi (Minneapolis: University of Minnesota Press, 1987), 397–98.

3 André Leroi-Gourhan similarly writes that "the technological definition of an instrument is of little interest, as the term responds to a notion of common usage. […] The distinction between *tool* and *weapon* does not have a technological value: the same knife, used in the same percussive fashion, becomes tool or weapon according to the nature of the processed object." André Leroi-Gourhan, *L' homme et la matière: évolution et techniques* (Paris: Éditions Albin Michel, 2013), 112. My translation.

4 Manuel DeLanda, *Assemblage Theory* (Edinburgh: Edinburgh University Press, 2016), 72.

on Nomadology," that technical elements, and even technical machines, lack the ability to affirm their own autonomous orientation.[2] A knife, for example, cannot be identified as either a tool or a weapon without resorting to associations with a corresponding "work-" or "war-machine."[3] While this is consistent with assemblages having emergent and immanent properties (with wholes not being reducible to the sum of their parts), Manuel DeLanda notes that the authors seem to (uncharacteristically) privilege relations of interiority, reducing parts to the whole they compose.[4] However, the screw holding together two sheets of plywood can be unfastened and reused elsewhere. Screw-ness, that is, can be expressed and effectuated apart from specific pieces of furniture or millwork arrangements, spanning EoIs.

Even if processes of disassembly and reassembly rely on established woodworking ecologies and tools (on carpenters; on assembly instructions; on screwdrivers and drills), choosing to join parts with a threaded fastener—rather than with glues—also increases the potential redeployment of the parts being fastened, strengthening their relations of exteriority.

What is at stake here are two terms—reuse and repurpose—that, in the English language, are often considered interchangeable. Instead, this book will follow the more precise definition of the French words *réemploi* and *détournement*.[5] By *reuse* I will refer to ecological changes (that is, changes pertaining to ecologies of inception) that maintain the formal and functional orientation of an object, as in the case of the screw, which is used recursively in subsequent assemblages. [**Figure 1.2**] I will instead speak of *repurposing* to denote ecological changes that largely maintain formal features but divert them toward new functional orientations, as in the case of the plywood sheet that, after being detached from a bookshelf, might enter a new partition, desk, or flooring assemblage. In some cases, the two approaches are combined: in the *Officina Roma* project, built in 2011 by the German collective Raumlabor in Rome, Italy, reclaimed

5   I am referring in particular to those proposed by Michaël Ghyoot et al. in *Déconstruction et réemploi: Comment faire circuler les éléments de construction* (Lausanne: Presses Polytechniques et Universitaires Romandes, 2018), 8. These are consistent with the nine Rs adopted by the Ellen MacArthur Foundation, and defined in José Potting et al., "Circular Economy: Measuring Innovation in the Production Chain," Policy Report (The Hague: PBL Netherlands Environmental Assessment Agency, January 2017), 5.

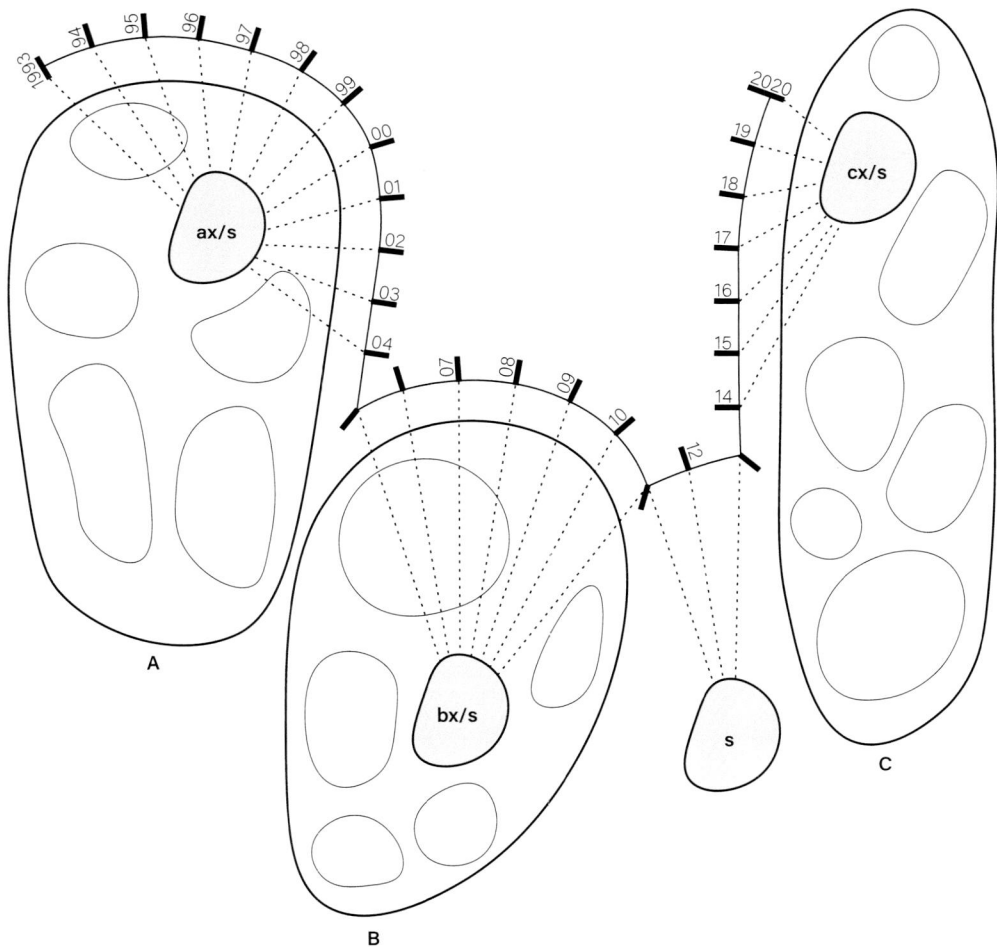

Figure 1.2 An object, for example a screw (s), can contribute to subsequent ecologies of inception (A, B, C), surviving their eventual demise. By considering disassembly, designers can refuse to consign the attribution of value to specific ecological scripts or relations of interiority.

Figure 1.3 Raumlabor, *Officina Roma*, Rome, 2011.

Figure 1.4 Raumlabor, *Officina Roma*, Rome, 2011.

6   DeLanda, *Assemblage Theory*, 73.

wooden windows and old furniture represent instances of reuse (they maintain their role as windows, chairs, and tables), whereas discarded glass bottles, car doors, dry wall profiles, and oil barrels are repurposed—becoming bricks, windows, and roofing structures respectively. [**Figures 1.3 + 1.4**] But let us return to DeLanda.

Adjusting Deleuze and Guattari's "macro-reductionist" approach in the passages referred to above, and reaffirming relations of exteriority between parts (their relative autonomy from the whole of the assemblage), the philosopher proposes the distinction between *properties* and *capacities*.[6] Properties are relatively stable, can be easily enumerated (the sharpness, length, and weight of the knife) and emerge from the interactions between the object's own components; capacities are variable and dependent on encounters (for instance, between the knife's ability to cut and an apple's cuttability). Accordingly, design links properties with capacities, either by tuning the latter to the former, or by modifying the former in view of the latter. The difference between these two approaches will be central to the arguments of this book. In any case, an ecology of inception might be described, in the language of assemblage theory, as a machine whose assemblages effectuate transformations that change the properties of technical objects in order to consign them to specific relations and capacities. And it might also be described as the assemblage whose internal relations maintain and enable such capacities.

An ecology of inception defines the orientation based upon which a system may actualize its potentials—its teleological orbit. From the Latin *incipere* (to begin) and *capere* (to be receptive, to grasp, to seize), it rehearses relationships that may set in motion (originate) new performances, interactions, and functional sympathies. In addition, *in-capere* (to capture in, to enclose) also alludes to the violence implicit in annexation, appropriation, and inclusion; it suggests the drawing of boundaries, and a compulsion to make things fit.

Before being included in a system, each component undergoes a series of transformations that progressively increase its ability to interact within that system. A tree and a printer, for example, cannot form an effective assemblage because they are unable to communicate: not only do they belong to different territories, the forest and the office; their configurations and *modi operandi* are incompatible. A long series of technical operations is required to find a common language between tree and printer, a ground for their interaction. A tree (and not *any* tree) must undergo several alterations before becoming the white sheet of paper that so aptly fits the printer's paper tray and receives the ink released by its cartridges. Firstly, it must be felled, logged, debarked, and chipped. The wood chips are then moved to a pulp mill, where organic polymers such as lignin and hemicellulose are separated from the cellulose fibers through chemical, mechanical, and thermal processes, or combinations thereof. The resulting pulp is bleached, dried, baled, and transported to a paper mill, where it is mixed with water, refined, and blended with coloring agents and fillers. Then, it enters the paper machine, where it is progressively pressed, drained, dried, sized, coated, and finally cut into printer-ready sheets.

The processing of the tree relies on an emergent condition of hybridity, on alliances—permanent or transitory as they may be—forged with other actants: the saw, the wood chipper, and the various rotating wires, rollers, and calenders in the paper-making machine; the caustic soda or sulfurous acid in the chemical digester; the calcium carbonate, clay, and talcum powder added to the pulp; the starch or latex coating the surface of the paper. Even a working interaction between printer and paper depends on other components of the assemblage, such as the electricity required to power the printer, the RIP chip that communicates raster images to the printer's laser, and the ink, which effectively embodies the information and transfers it onto the sheet of paper. With each subsequent phase, the processing of raw matter narrows its focus toward a specific kind of ecology, catering to the particular interactions within it. This increases the material's compatibility within the target system and decreases its compatibility without it. For instance, a log can be altered along many potential orientations and undergo a variety of transformations—becoming chair, flooring plank, sheet of paper, and so forth. The sheet of paper, instead, has a more limited range of possible uses and alliances, which tie it to a specific set of writing, drawing, folding, and printing ecologies. Furthermore, the last stages in the making of paper were specifically geared toward optimizing its interaction with the printer and its ink: increasing its smoothness and sizing it with starch to ensure that the printing ink will dry on its surface rather than be absorbed into it. The hybrid pulp-calcium carbonate-starch assemblage resulting from these processes is foreign to (and very different from) the original tree, or pure lumber.

Indeed, the potentiality of a lump of matter is determined not only by the intrinsic properties, implicit structures, and self-organizing potentials so vividly described by Gilbert Simondon (e.g., the colloidal microstructures of clay, the "slow undulations" of wood fibers),[7] but also by progressive encounters with (and assimilations to) other materials, tools, and orientations, during which greater internal potency is acquired. While an artisanal approach to individuation would seem to follow a linear and incremental trajectory of specialization, along which relations of interiority are progressively emphasized over relations of exteriority, a contextual definition of potentiality does rather forbid such a view, which would entail the existence of a latent potency patiently waiting at the heart of an object, being progressively deployed through technical actualizations, until it is exhausted or depleted—and the object has become stable, or dead. In fact, a plywood sheet on the shelves of Home Depot might be more susceptible to interaction—more "talkative"—than the log is, even though the log precedes it in the technical chain of tree modifications, and has a purer implicit structure and chemical composition.[8] Similarly, lacking the tools or expertise to fell and process a tree, a carpenter may find a chair easier to carve and rework. The blending, merging, and mixing of tree derivatives with other components—starches, clays, waxes, resins, fibers, and glues—disproves the account of a linear history played out between intrinsic and extrinsic properties, because no such properties exist for long; "inside" and "outside" are provisional states in the encounters between things.

The preparation and staging of an ecology of inception operate at four levels: deterritorializing/reterritorializing (from the forest tree to a log in the timber lorry), decoding/recoding (from "wood" to a "plank" or "bowl," from copper and zinc to "brass"), hybridizing (from the continuous roll of veneer peeled off by the rotary lathe to the sheet of plywood), and de-forming/con-forming (from a shapely trunk to a usable lump of cellulose pulp or lumber). The first operation, *deterritorialization*, refers to the plucking of a tree out of a forest assemblage and to the undoing of its natural and contextual identity, severing linkages to its active metabolic and symbiotic networks. Once the tree is felled and stops contributing to the forest's emergent relations, as well as to

7   Gilbert Simondon, *L'individu et sa genèse physico-biologique; l'individuation à la lumière des notions de forme et d'information* (Paris: Presses universitaires de France, 1964), 52. Quoted in (and translated by) Léopold Lambert, "Simondon/Episode 03: Topological Life: The World Can't Be Fathomed in Plans and Sections," *The Funambulist* (blog), accessed April 14, 2019.

8   Here and throughout the book, I follow Gilbert Simondon in using the term "technical chain" to describe sequences of technical operations. This is also largely consistent with what André Leroi-Gourhan calls *chaîne opératoire* (operational sequence).

its own individual relations of exteriority, the log is reterritorialized (assigned to a new assemblage): the orderly stack of logs in the lorry.

Another process borrowed from assemblage theory—*coding*—converts these changes to a discursive format. At every stage in the processing of the tree, language re-appropriates the materials attained by coupling them with sets of nouns, definitions, practices, discourses, and norms, facilitating either their cultural reintegration or their progression into the next step in the technical chain (the next deterritorialization). [**Figure 1.5**] The third operation, *hybridizing*, refers to the tendency to mix heterogeneous materials and objects into assemblages like steel, paper, or blueberry pie that, through their emergent properties, overcome previous limitations vis-a-vis a particular ecology or goal. [**Figure 1.6**] The fourth operation, *de-forming/con-forming*, casts an individual (a tree, a grain of salt, water, an ingot of gold) into a new process of individuation. It does not denote the in-forming of a raw material that previously

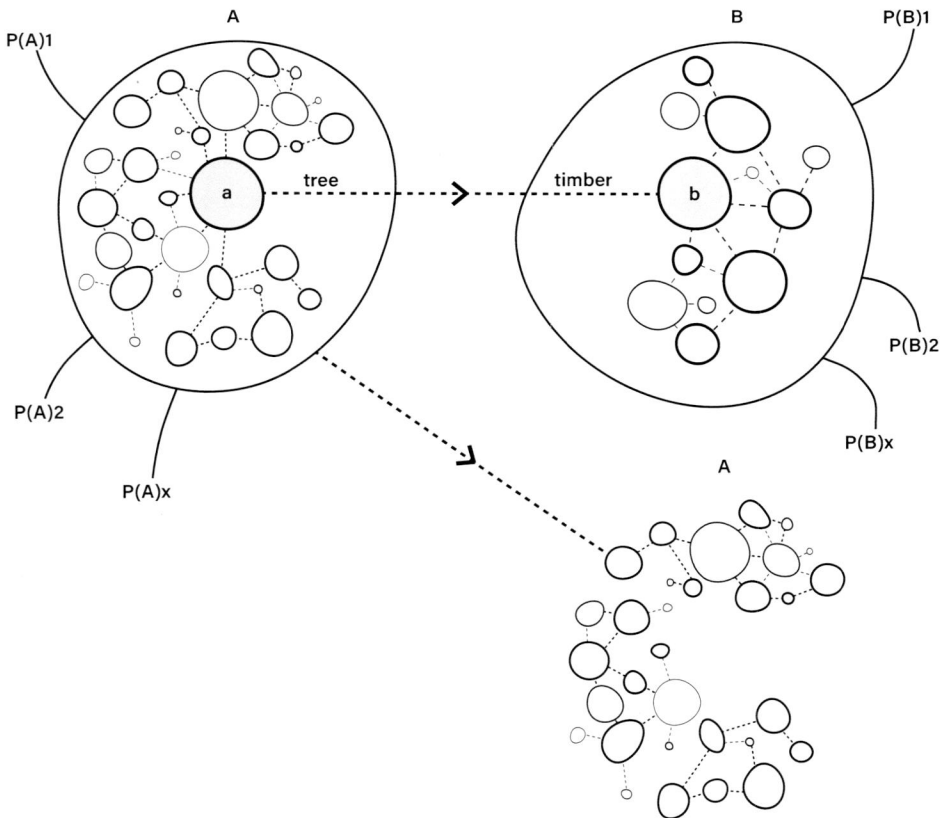

Figure 1.5 Territorialization and coding. When a tree (a) is felled and its metabolic links within the forest (A) severed, it is inscribed in a new ecology (B, the lumber industry) and rebranded as timber (b). Unlocking the powers of ecology B diminishes those of ecology A. In this sense, the establishment of an ecology of inception corresponds with a transfer of powers.

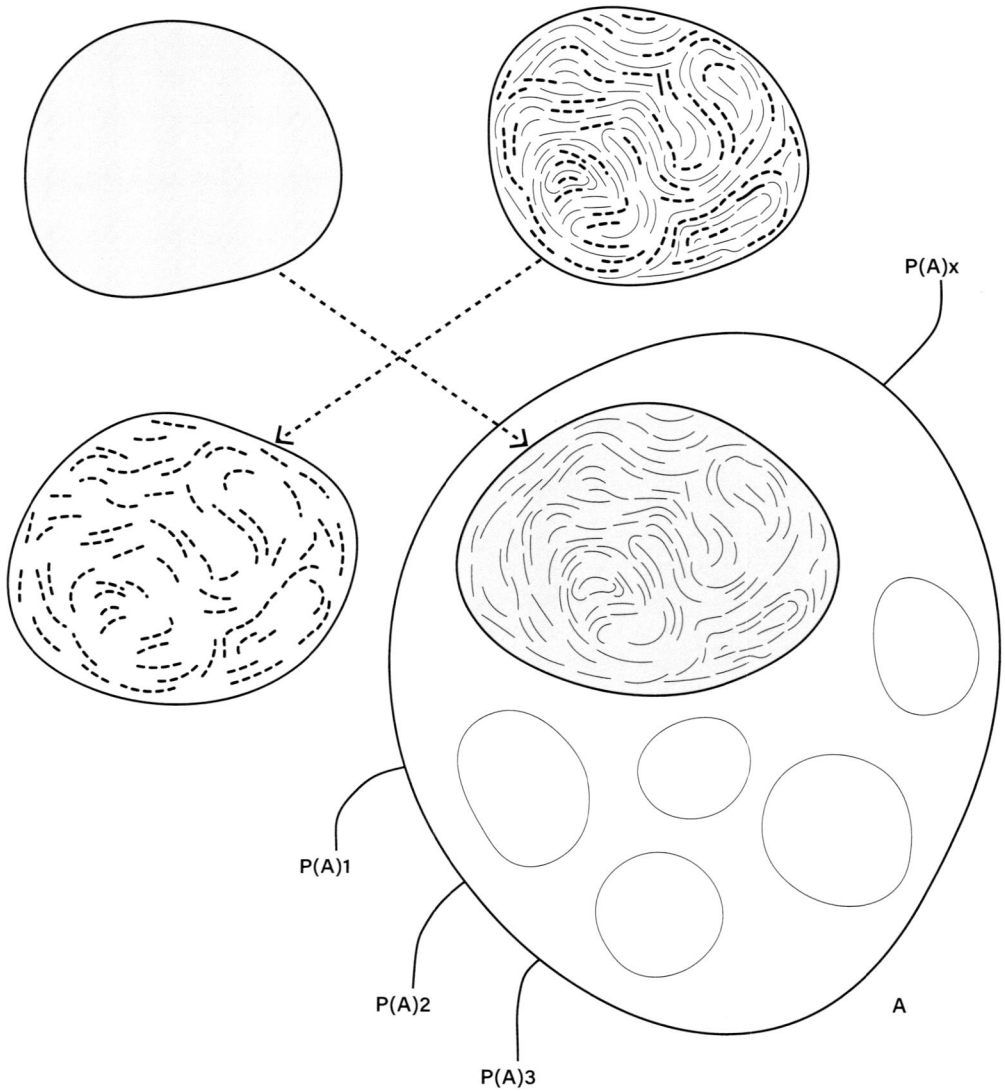

Figure 1.6 Hybridity can be viewed as the simple combination of two ingredients (for example, flour and water) to form a new composite object (dough). However, if one considers a longer material trajectory (one that, for example, includes the milling of wheat, or the bleaching of flour), hybridity involves as much mixing as it does separation and removal.

lacked form, but rather a metamorphosis, a state transition, from one ac-tualized form to another (from water to ice, from the ingot to a bracelet, from bauxite ore to aluminum extrusions), at different scales and with varying degrees of autonomy, integrity, and purity. [**Figure 1.7**]

The processes described above, and the environmental damage and social injustices upon which they depend, are usually removed or ex-cluded from the point of view of the action and actors empowered by them (the users or inhabitants of the resulting outputs). Moreover, the components of an ecology of inception, whose "content" was at the receiving end of a chain of technical operations during the preceding phase, become content-less once the system has reached maturity—once they have successfully unlocked new content-forming interac-tions. This inversion (from form to matter, and vice versa) corresponds to a *tabula rasa*, understood as the set of technical operations whereby an ecology of inception is produced, reaching its target potentials.

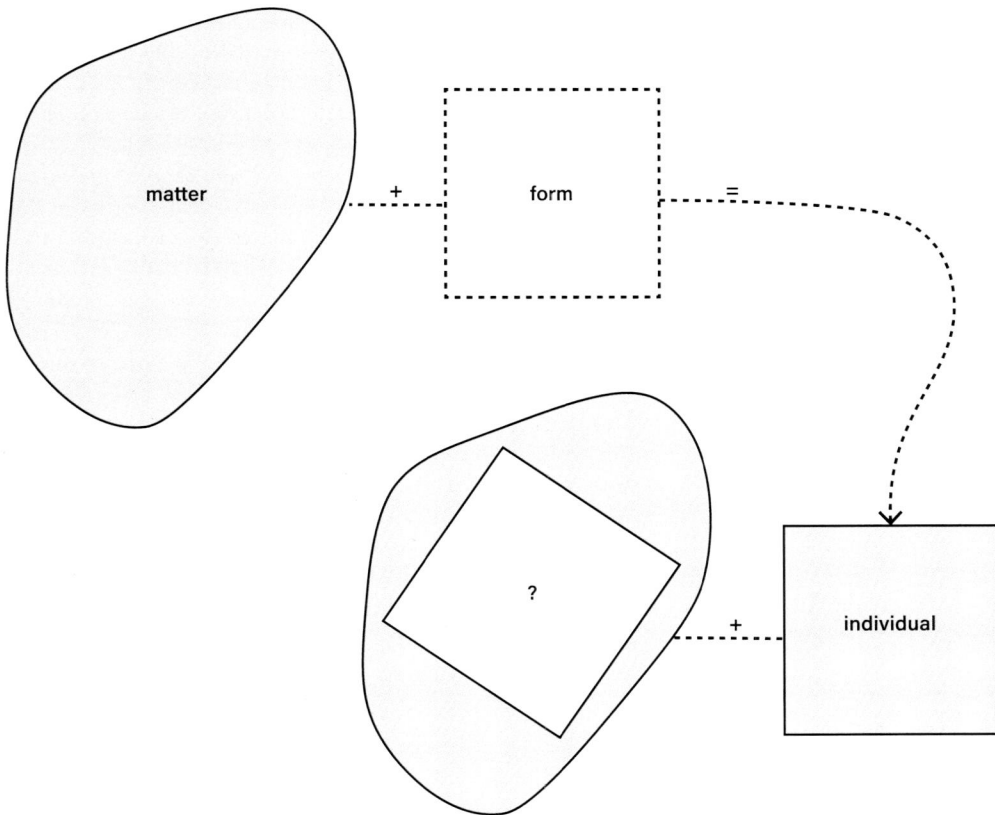

Figure 1.7 The hylomorphic cookie cutter. Deforming and conforming processes assign the role of *matter* to objects, thus stipulating their lack of form and, subsequently, endowing them with one.

1.2 Technical *Tabula Rasa*

The writer's blank sheet of paper, the painter's empty canvas, the cook's finely sliced and minced ingredients, and the builder's mortar and bricks do not support or substantiate the claim of a creation *ex-nihilo*, an emergence out of nothing, yet they stem from a transaction with nature whereby a measure of *nihil* is actively pursued and attained.[9] The Latin term *tabula rasa* indicates not a blank slate, but a *blanked* slate, an erasure—a wax tablet whose content has been actively and purposefully scraped prior to writing. The Latin verb *radere* (to scrape) is still employed in modern Italian to denote shaving, and shares with *rodere* (to gnaw, to corrode) and the English "rodent" the Sanskrit root of the verb *radati* (to bite, to dig, to cut) and the noun *radanah* (tooth). Therefore, one could describe the technical *tabula rasa* as an operation whereby culture masticates (and appropriates) nature. The gnawing and chewing image, however—a grinding that breaks down particular foods into a digestible sludge—cannot be taken literally.

One should not fall into the trap of believing that such operations are necessarily marked by a progression toward less difference, more homogeneity and (more or less temporary) reductions in scale. It is however true that the irregularities found in natural resources such as rocks, trees, soils, and grains undergo purification procedures whereby they are washed out and progressively removed, and that the countless forms found in nature tend to be reduced to a handful of quasi-formless primary typologies—powders, liquids, blocks (ingots), sheets, and glops—each proposing a different interpretation of the verb *radere*, encompassing mechanical, thermal, and chemical abrasions; pressing, distilling, and melting processes; drying, cutting, grinding, et cetera. The underlying goal of these operations is one and the same: to purify and pre-pare[10] matter for human use. Even when combined and supplemented, and regardless of scale, the early alterations in the technical chain towards an ecology of inception replace a formed thing with one that is *de-formed*—a material, from which a thing is or *can* be made. The verb *de-form* is used here with emphasis on the Latin prefix *de-*, with its function of inversion and reversal, and it is taken to mean not only the modification of form, but its undoing and de-actualization— its return to a shapeless, preindividual state. In the transformation from tree to wood, from cow to beef, and from wheat to flour, the *rasura* rejects and erases formal attributes, reverting an actualized form into a potential (and often standardized) lump of matter.

1.3 Waste Regimes

> Mining denies that death carries in its womb a new birth. Instead, mining proceeds on the assumption that the birth of the new requires the death of the old.
>
> Zygmunt Bauman, *Wasted Lives*[11]

[9] In this context, I would adopt Kate Soper's definition of nature as the "material structures and processes that are independent of human activity (in the sense that they are not human-created products), and whose forces and causal powers are the necessary conditions of every human practice and determine the possible forms it can take." Kate Soper, *What Is Nature? Culture, Politics, and the Non-Human* (Oxford and Cambridge: Blackwell, 1998), 151. Quoted in Kiel Moe, *Unless: The Seagram Building Construction Ecology* (New York: Actar Publishers, 2020), 32. In Chapters 3 and 8, I will instead emphasize the use of *nature* (or *Nature*) as a social and political category.

[10] Interestingly, the verbs prepare (to make ready) and pare (to trim, to reduce in size) share the same etymological root in the Latin verb *parare*.

[11] Zygmunt Bauman, *Wasted Lives: Modernity and Its Outcasts* (Cambridge: Polity, 2011), 21.

Deformations are rarely of the topological kind, like the many shapes a child impresses on Play-Doh, a liquid poured into different vessels, or aluminum billets neatly heated and extruded into mullions. With few exceptions, the transformations imposed upon matter by technological *rasurae* and the associated production processes (from the extraction of resources to the many labor- and energy-intensive operations involved in their reorganization) are messy, trigger separations and informational losses, and generate byproducts. Purifications operate by introducing selective parameters and removing noncompliant elements; by discarding anything in excess of their reductive intents.[12] André Leroi-Gourhan notes that "to wash a mineral is also, in some measure, to soak it and to dissolve the light materials that coat it" (*les matériaux légers qui l'enrobent*), and that "boiling rice is to dissolve a part of its chemical components."[13] Similarly, as also articulated in the quotation at the beginning of this section, Zygmunt Bauman couples modern creation with waste: "The vision of a perfect form hidden inside the formless slab of raw stone precedes its birth-act. Waste is the wrapping that conceals that form."[14] Indeed, purifying entails the removal of impurities (from gold ore to pure gold), but also the removal of that which obstructs access, of that which stands between (the material excavated to reach a gold-bearing vein). An externality is precisely that which, in a system, can be destroyed to unlock a potential. Therefore, purification is also a license to violate and pollute—to leave behind and to leave elsewhere. Gabrielle Hecht writes that a "typical 14 karat gold chain leaves one tonne of waste rock in South Africa."[15] Accordingly, one might find a different way of answering Buckminster Fuller's question about the weight of a building.[16]

As Jennifer Gabrys points out, remainders may also take insidious and hazardous forms. "Much of the rhetoric around waste management and recycling assumes that remainders may be recuperated in some way," she writes,

> [b]ut electronics do not simply dissolve into raw materials ready to take on a second life. [...] Waste pickers who salvage the remains of dead electronics recycle these devices into various forms of raw materials and reusable parts. But in the process of salvaging, the expanded materialities of these devices become detectable in the form of contaminated environments and bodies.[17]

In any case, the digestive rumblings of the technical *tabula rasa* include both nutrition (the compacting of oneself, in the etymological sense of adjoining, fastening together) and discharge (the expulsion of the other, or of what in the individual has become other). Design consolidates matter around forms and ideas by generating—by establishing—waste.

> [I]t is not the difference between useful products and waste that begs and plies the boundary. Quite the contrary, it is the boundary

12 Lefebvre writes: "walls, enclosures and façades serve to define both a *scene* (where something takes place) and an *obscene* area to which everything that cannot or may not happen on the scene is relegated." Henri Lefebvre, *The Production of Space*, trans. Donald Nicholson-Smith (Malden: Blackwell, 2011), 36.

13 Leroi-Gourhan, *L'homme et la matière*, 76.

14 Bauman, *Wasted Lives*, 21.

15 Gabrielle Hecht, "Human Crap," *Aeon*, March 25, 2020. In this context, it is meaningful to note that, according to Jonathan Chapman, "[t]here is more gold in a tonne of phones than a tonne of rock from a gold mine." Jonathan Chapman, "Product Moments, Material Eternities," in Duncan Baker-Brown, *The Re-Use Atlas* (London: RIBA Publishing, 2017), 163.

16 Carlos Carcas and Norberto López Amado, *How Much Does Your Building Weigh, Mr. Foster?*, documentary, 2011.

17 Jennifer Gabrys, "Salvage," in *Depletion Design: A Glossary of Network Ecologies*, ed. Carolin Wiedemann and Soenke Zehle (Amsterdam: Institute of Network Cultures, 2012), 137–38.

that divines, literally conjures up, the difference between them—the difference between the admitted and the rejected, the included and the excluded.[18]

The same is true for affirmations of identity and selfhood in the everyday context of garbaging. Indeed, Italo Calvino describes the daily habit of taking out the domestic rubbish as a "rite of purification," an unburdening that allows his being to "identify completely (without residues)," day after day.[19] "If this is true," he writes,

if the gesture of throwing away is the first and indispensable condition of being, since one is what one does not throw away, then the most important physiological and mental gesture is that of separating the part of me that remains from the part I must jettison to sink away into a beyond from which there is no return.[20]

Waste, it would appear, is not just a residue, something left over and tossed aside, but the condition whereby a project is possible, be it the mining of coal, the manufacturing of plywood, the keeping of a domestic interior, or the construction of subjectivity. It is a surgical removal that both scars and engenders survival.

Successive splits and bifurcations along the chain of technical operations either funnel matter inside an ecology of inception or push it out into a wasteland of nonecological landscapes. Once an output is ready for consumption, however, these rifts and material separations are no longer required, and entire objects can be turned into waste without changing or shedding at all—just notionally. Discursive practices, and the corresponding reterritorializations (tossing something out), allow for a blurring of the object that deforms it without actually affecting its physical structure. The concrete properties that a discarded object retains, regardless of its eventual state of degradation, are subsumed under the terms *trash*, *garbage*, and *rubbish*, and concealed behind the opacity of a thick polyethylene bag; its objecthood is revoked, and any tie to previous purposes or meanings is severed. While, in lumbering, a chaotic nature was supposedly improved and organized into culturally viable artifacts,[21] garbaging proceeds in the opposite direction, by digesting devalued outputs and excreting them back into the realm of the profane. In this respect, the presumed lack of qualities that forecloses the usability of refuse—that prevents it from re-entering productive ecologies—is purely ideological.

In any case, as Calvino's *poubelle agréée* demonstrates, it would be wrong to assume that no split takes place in everyday garbaging, as it does in extractive and manufacturing processes; here too, discarded objects are the shavings peeled off a larger object (a landscape, a house, a room, a subject). Jumping across scales and perspectives, rubbish does not emerge autonomously, but in relation to something else—as an object A cut off from a larger (mutilated) object B.

18 Bauman, *Wasted Lives*, 28.

19 Italo Calvino, "La Poubelle Agréée," in *The Road to San Giovanni*, trans. Tim Parks (Boston: Mariner Books, 2014), chap. 5, E-book.

20 Calvino, *The Road to San Giovanni*, ibid. See also Brian Thill, *Waste* (New York: Bloomsbury Academic, 2015), chap. 2, E-book. I should note here that, of course, waste is also the flip side of consumption. Nicki Lisa Cole and Alison Dahl Crossley warn against the conflation of expression and empowerment with acts of consumption, particularly in a feminist context. "[F]or most women today," they write, "as with most consumers of any gender, consumption is hardly an act of empowerment, but rather an act that creates debt and further binds one to the exploitative system of global capitalism and finance." Nicki Lisa Cole and Alison Dahl Crossley, "On Feminism in the Age of Consumption," *Consumers, Commodities & Consumption* 11, no. 1 (December 2009).

21 John Locke writes: "God and his reason commanded him [man] to subdue the earth, i.e. improve it for the benefit of life, and therein lay out something upon it that was his own, his labour." John Locke, *Political Writings*, edited and with an introduction by David Wootton (Harmondsworth, 1993), 276–77, quoted in John Scanlan, *On Garbage* (London: Reaktion Books, 2005), 24.

While the definition of *tabula rasa* given above re-ferred to the orientation of an object toward a higher degree of formal specificity and interactivity, the *ra-sura* effected by garbaging erases differences, demotes objects to an amorphous goop, and sanctions their ex-clusion from further ecological engagement.[22] A pile of garbage does not amount to a proper Deleuzian or DeLandian assemblage precisely for this reason: while, technically, it is a "multiplicity which is made up of heterogeneous terms,"[23] these are not held together by specific *teloi* or cofunctional orientations. But more importantly, the identity of garbage is conceptual: it does not emerge from, nor is it maintained by, the re-lations between its parts. The discarded objects in the garbage dump are not parts relating to a whole, with their own properties and therefore relations of exteri-ority, but mere aggregates of post-individual matter. For the identity of a pile of garbage, it is irrelevant whether plastic bottles, rotting apples, or a rusted car chassis compose it. Anything goes—garbage is the prince of nonemergent wholes. [**Figure 1.8**]

Discarding objects virtually separates them from their material properties, as well as from their ability to interact and communicate. Of course, this does not consign them to actual inertia or lack of character—nu-clear wastes continue to emit hazardous ionizing radia-tion, epoxy resins persistently leach bisphenol A (BPA) and, indeed, landfills are active sites of methane and carbon dioxide production through chemical reactions and processes of volatilization and bacterial decomposition. Furthermore, these processes pose serious health risks that are disproportionately foisted on low-income communities, as well as racial and ethnic minorities.[24] While garbage might be said to lack fixed and durable properties,[25] one must also acknowledge the continued physical persistence and biochem-ical agency of the individual discards within it, and their cumulative ef-fects. To this end, it is useful to expand DeLanda's definition of capacity so as to qualify two possible families of relations: objectual and molecular.[26]

Objectual capacities depend on interactions at least partially af-forded by the shape of the interacting objects—for instance, a cup be-ing filled with water, or a hinge connecting a frame with the moving leaf of a door. Molecular capacities, on the other side, depend on in-teractions that occur at the atomic or molecular scale, and, while they may change the overall (macro) shape of an object, the latter does in no way afford (or even contribute to) the interaction. The rusting of a poorly galvanized steel railing is one such example: for the production of iron oxide, little does it matter if the vertical posts are orthogonal, slanted, or shaped like *art nouveau* branches and leaves. A wide range

Figure 1.8 The pile of discarded items in a skip, Newcastle-upon-Tyne, 2020. Photo-graphs by the author.

22 The word "ecological" is used throughout to indicate some degree of membership in (or affiliation to) EoIs.

23 Gilles Deleuze and Claire Parnet, *Dialogues*, trans. Hugh Tomlinson and Barbara Habberjam (New York: Columbia University Press, 1987), 69.

24 Kate O'Neill, *Waste* (Cambridge and Medford: Polity Press, 2019), 11.

25 John Scanlan claims that, at least metaphorically, garbage is formless and lacking concrete properties; that it is "neither one thing nor another," but a "jumble of inexactness." Scanlan, *On Garbage*, 16.

26 While my use of these terms resembles Deleuze and Guattari's use of the terms "molar" and "molecular," it does not carry the

same associations (of an increase in segmentation towards the molar; of an increase in dynamism towards the molecular). Deleuze and Parnet, *Dialogues*, 124–25.

of configurations will indeed promote differences in surface area and, therefore, in the overall number of oxidations. However, at the molecular level, rust is not concerned with the shape of the object—at least not as it is perceived by human senses. Whereas both objectual and molecular capacities are active in ecological exchanges (both the shape and rigidity of a fork contribute to its equipmental fitness), active interactions between discards are largely confined to the molecular realm and to simple relations of contiguity or proximity.

As argued above, the kind of *de-formation* applied to discarded objects neutralizes form, making it indifferent and inactive, and causing it to be subsumed into matter; into a generic waste material. The resulting shift in scale and resolution is consistent with what Graham Harman calls the "undermining" of objects: a tendency, in both science and philosophy, to explain objects away by subordinating them to the ontological primacy of something deeper and more fundamental, such as atoms or being.[27] In Harman's metaphysics, instead, objects regain center stage as the building blocks of philosophy, and cannot be reduced downwards (to more primary entities) or upwards (to their effects and relations).

27 Graham Harman, *The Quadruple Object* (Winchester and Washington: Zero Books, 2011).

In everyday experience, certainly one way to undermine technical objects is to throw them away—downgrading them and renouncing their objecthood and objectual capacities. But garbaging doesn't only limit the kinds of interactions and changes discarded objects can participate in or undergo; it also subsumes their properties and identities under the abstract and materially indifferent category of Garbage. In this sense of absorption and undifferentiation, the garbage dump is the ontological equivalent of the Greek *apeiron*; that infinite primordial substance of which, according to Anaximander of Miletus, everything is made and to which everything must return. The *apeiron* substitutes the definite objects fallen into it (or emerging from it) with an indefinite, unifying substance that erases and washes over singularity and individuation. Nietzsche eloquently sums up the Greek philosopher's invention:

> Wherever definite qualities are perceivable, we can prophesy, upon the basis of enormously extensive experience, the passing away of these qualities. Never [...] can a being which possesses definite qualities or consists of such be the origin or first principle of things. That which truly is, concludes Anaximander, cannot possess definite characteristics, or it would come-to-be and pass away like all other things. In order that coming-to-be shall not cease, primal being must be indefinite.[28]

28 Friedrich Wilhelm Nietzsche, *Philosophy in the Tragic Age of the Greeks*, trans. with an introduction by Marianne Cowan (Washington: Regnery Publishing, 1998), 47.

Anaximander, in other words, invents the eternal and indeterminate *apeiron* to subdue and arrest the passing of time evidenced by the progressive degradation and wasting away of all things; to guarantee that the source of all individual beings will not also decay and perish. Following Nietzsche, according to whom the key to *apeiron* is a lack of definite qualities, eternity is invented by Anaximander to prevail over, but also to negatively establish, obsolescence.[29] With it, the modern notion of garbage—not as

29 Nietzsche, *Philosophy in the Tragic Age*, 47.

the collection of definite discards, but as the ontological overcoming (and occlusion) of their definite qualities—is born. In this context, undermining consists of the simultaneous consigning of objects to their mere molecular capacities and to their absorption into the indefinite, nonemergent whole of Garbage. Here, discarding is a coping mechanism, and a way to navigate and master the (unruly) temporality of objects.

According to Jean Baudrillard, objects help us to make time discontinuous, classifiable, and reversible. The function of collecting—a limit case of everyday possession and consumption—is the "resolving of real time into a systematic dimension," or the abolition of time as continuous and uncontrollable.[30] And it is in this same sense that Gastón R. Gordillo describes the abstract notion of ruin as predisposed to highlighting "the object's *pastness*" and a separation from modernity.[31]

In the case of rubbish, this imaginary mastery relies on decisions, on the design of thresholds that are either established in advance (as is the case in the industrial practice known as planned obsolescence) or imposed *ex tempore*.[32] These decisions and thresholds are not objective or validated by universal and unequivocal parameters, but dependent on context.[33] Accordingly, value is not constitutional or intrinsic, but a function of relative (ecological) positioning. [**Figure 1.9**] Before being

30 Jean Baudrillard, *The System of Objects*, trans. James Benedict (London and New York: Verso, 1996), 95.

31 Gastón Gordillo, *Rubble: The Afterlife of Destruction* (Durham: Duke University Press, 2014), 8.

32 By *planned obsolescence* I mean the three strategies identified by Vance Packard: obsolescence of function (products becoming outmoded when better-functioning ones are introduced); obsolescence of quality (products breaking down or falling apart after a set amount of time); obsolescence of desirability (products that are still performing becoming undesirable due to changes in style and trends). Vance Packard, *The Waste Makers* (New York: Pocket Books, 1969), 46–47. For a history of obsolescence in the built environment (in the North American context), see Daniel M. Abramson, *Obsolescence: An Architectural History* (Chicago and London: The University of Chicago Press, 2016).

33 A "context" can range from specific cases and situations to more systemic mechanisms, such as the "periodical depreciation of existing capital—one of the means immanent in capitalist production to check the fall of the rate of profit and hasten accumulation of capital-value through formation of new capital." Karl Marx, *Karl Marx: A Reader*, ed. Jon Elster (Cambridge and New York: Press Syndicate of the University of Cambridge, 1986), 119.

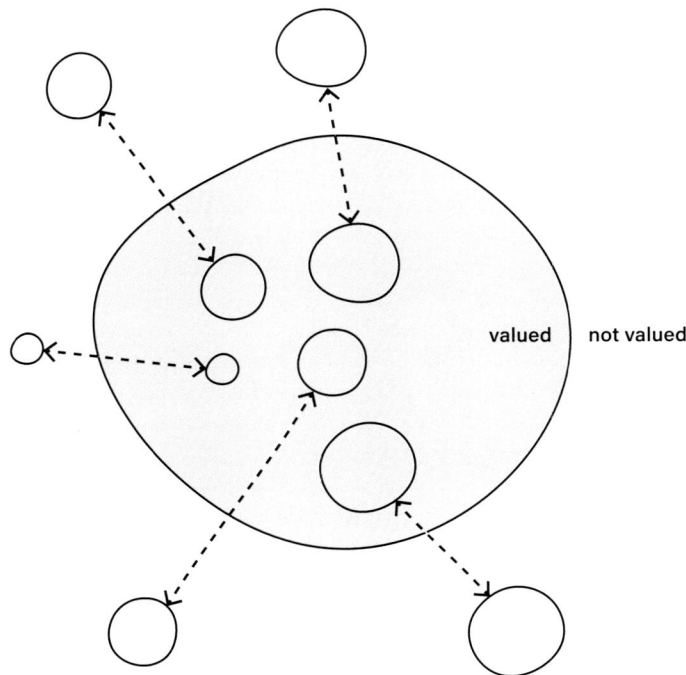

valued | not valued

Figure 1.9 As objects enter an ecology of inception, they gain value. As they exit it, they lose value. Yet other ecologies always exist or can exist, and ecological boundaries can be moved, ignored, erased, and redrawn.

34 "[Dirt] is a relative idea. Shoes are not dirty in themselves, but it is dirty to place them on the dining table [...]. [O]ur pollution behavior is the reaction which condemns any object or idea likely to confuse or contradict cherished classifications." Mary Douglas, *Purity and Danger: An Analysis of Concepts of Pollution and Taboo* (London and New York: Routledge, 2002), 45.

35 Douglas, *Purity and Danger*, 44.

36 For a more nuanced exploration of these dynamics, see Jonathan Chapman, *Emotionally Durable Design: Objects, Experiences and Empathy* (London and New York: Routledge, 2015). For a historical account of how household habits in the US changed around the turn of the twentieth century, see Susan Strasser, *Waste and Want: A Social History of Trash* (New York: Owl Books, 2000).

discarded and subsumed into the garbage heap, out-of-fashion, broken, and unused objects are, in the words of Mary Douglas, simply "matter out of place."[34] Becoming garbage, that is, necessarily implies a reference system, a normative order based upon which inappropriate elements can be identified and plucked away.[35]

This reference system coincides with the emergence of the ecology of inception within which the object is inscribed, and with the pursuit of its proper and continued operation. A pen is discarded once it breaks and ceases to effectively perform its role within an ecology of writing; a clothing item is tossed out when it no longer works towards an ecology of "being fashionable" or "signifying good taste," or when a hole exposes the skin to the elements, compromising an ecology of "keeping warm."[36]

To be sure, garbage is not, strictly speaking, "matter out of place." Douglas specifically writes that "rubbish is not dangerous" and "clearly belongs in a defined place, a rubbish heap of one kind or another."[37] However, what I am interested in is not waste per se (an ecology of rubbish heaps, or the global waste economy) but *wasting*—the negative relation between an EoI and an object or part that was previously affiliated with it; or the dissolution of a relation of interiority.

Figure 1.10 Raumlabor in collaboration with Refunc, *Vortex*, Den Haag, 2012.

While material deterioration and decay—the slow erosion of underwater caves, the molding of wet gypsum board, the burning of forests, the animal digestion of food, the oxidation of brass, and so forth—require no human intercession, the *apeiron* and its subsequent translations make it possible for culture to claim (and profess control over) the designation and sanctioning of waste. In order to last within this paradigm (to avoid being undermined downwards), an object must continually sustain and prove its functional membership in an ecology of inception, ongoing or latent, technical or symbolic as it may be (that is, it must be undermined upwards). The survival of objects—the preservation of their objectual capacities—thus depends on the renunciation of some degree of autonomy in the name of "higher" ecological scripts.

In architectural design, the heap (John Scanlan's "jumble of inexactness") can also be a figure of material affirmation and recalcitrance; a protocol for resisting the top-down ordering of matter and its reliance on precise geometrical principles, gendered joints, and strict relations of interiority—one according to which parts are radically detachable and roles remain tentative and interchangeable. In *Vortex*, built in The Hague by Raumlabor and the Dutch/German collective Refunc, diverted timber pallets and other locally sourced discards are temporarily

Figures 1.11 + 1.12 Raumlabor, *The Big Crunch*, Darmstadt, 2011.

arranged in the shape of a whirlwind, and used as a meeting point for a local arts festival. [**Figure 1.10**] A dynamic (and seemingly random) accretion of materials also features in Raumlabor's earlier *The Big Crunch*, which combines discarded objects—an heterogeneous "swarm" of chairs, windows, refrigerators, scrap, and timber—to construct a gathering space and public forum in Darmstadt, Germany. [**Figures 1.11 + 1.12**] Here as in the whimsical huts built by Richard Greaves on a piece of land in rural Beauce County, Canada, the misuse of parts (their noncompliance with standard functional roles; the renunciation of predetermined relations and designs) produces architectures that embrace a state of instability and precariousness, and a degree of chaos. [**Figure 1.13 + 1.14**]

37 Douglas, *Purity and Danger*, 197–98. See also Max Liboiron, "Waste Is Not 'Matter out of Place,'" *Discard Studies* (blog), accessed May 23, 2020.

Figure 1.13 Richard Greaves, *The Three Little Pigs' House*, Beauce County, 2001. Photograph by Richard-Max Tremblay.

Figure 1.14 Richard Greaves, *The Round House*, Beauce County, 2001. Photograph by Richard-Max Tremblay.

38 Jane Bennett, "Powers of the Hoard: Further Notes on Material Agency," in *Animal, Vegetable, Mineral: Ethics and Objects*, ed. Jeffrey Jerome Cohen (Washington: Oliphaunt Books, 2012), 244.

39 Bennett, "Powers of the Hoard," 246.

40 Ibid., 259.

41 Ibid., 253.

The figure of the garbage heap is similarly operative in the hoard—in the piles of junk compulsively accumulated, stacked, stored, and lived-with by hoarders. [**Figure 1.15**] Moving beyond psychopathology and the medicalization of disposophobia, political theorist and philosopher Jane Bennett ascribes to the differently-abled bodies of hoarders a "special sensory access to the call of things."**38** According to Bennett, rather than being susceptible to the subtractive model of perception described by Henri Bergson, which is "biased toward instrumentality rather than vibrancy," hoarders are captivated by (and attuned to) the shapes, colors, and textures of things, affirming their vitality and worth beyond use value or even aesthetic appreciation.**39**

If the disposal of domestic rubbish allowed Calvino to confirm and reaffirm his own identity (to recognize and remove otherness), the hoarder's body is porous and guided by "inorganic sympathies"—a relational weakness that allows it to merge (and become con-fused) with the animal/vegetal/mineral nonhumans in the hoard.**40** The rising mounds of clutter in a hoarder's home often compensate for a personal loss—for the traumatic event that triggered the person's hoarding habits. Bennett writes that "the hoarder desperately clings to things because metal/plastic/glass/ceramic/wooden objects […] *last longer* than human flesh. Their relatively slow rate of decay presents the reassuring illusion that at least *something* doesn't die."**41**

While garbaging and hoarding share similar features (the weakening of mereological and ecological scripts; the attenuation of objectual capacities; the additive—rather than emergent—character of their properties), Bennett's account of the latter depicts a vastly different temporal relation between things and human beings, one that overcomes mortality not by obsolescing objects (by delivering them to an invisible and universal *apeiron*; by attempting to master them), but by keeping them close. The hoarder prototypes new temporalities not by concealing the decay of objects, but by borrowing its pace; not by rejecting material corruption in general, but by living alongside (and caring for) aging things.

In a short essay entitled "Architecture in Extremis," critic and historian Sylvia Lavin considers hoarding as a form of perturbation against (and "critical resistance" to) the modern architectural regimes of propriety, functionality, structural stability, and hygiene, and as a prompt to "engage systems of instability and participation" that may help redefine and radicalize architectural design.**42** By hindering conventional modes of circulation and inhabitation—by filling and congesting living spaces—hoarding defeats ecological protocols, programs, and scripts, permitting "the interior as such, not its use value, to become an architectural material."**43** In addition, Lavin notes that the hoard is not (only)

42 Sylvia Lavin, "Architecture In Extremis," *Log*, no. 22 (2011): 61.

43 Lavin, "Architecture In Extremis," 60.

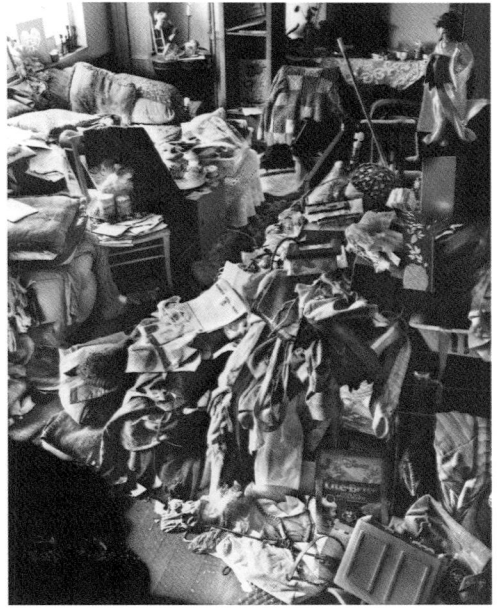

characterized by vertical processes of accumulation (the laying of objects on top of one another; the formation of piles), but subject to "churning"—an active and recursive process whereby hoarders move items across the hoard, from one place to another. This "constant state of rotation" animates architecture, endowing the interior with a "temporal flow."[44] Lavin writes: "Churning, or the recognition that objects do not merely function to produce architectural ambiances but operate to keep them fluid, offers buildings a measure of durational variation that the typical definitions of architecture lack. Hoarding, in other words, gives to architecture a field of animated effects."[45]

Unlike the chairs and refrigerators cladding *The Big Crunch*, or the shoes lining Greaves' *Three Little Pigs' House*, where animation and instability remain on a metaphorical plane and misuse (or the interruption of use) attains a measure of provisional stability, the rotational practices that characterize hoarding (understood not only as processes of accumulation, but as ones of cohabitation) promote fluidity and the changeability of interior spaces, constructing a temporality that is not predicated on the unlocking of potentials—on the implementation or preservation of uses and values—but on the bond between hoarder and hoard.

Figure 1.15 Everitt Clark, "I want a before and after" (*Churn Sequence*), silver gelatin contact prints, 4" x 5," 2016.

44 Ibid.

45 Ibid.

1.4 Encrustations

Let's consider reuse and repurposing, understood as the practices that allow discarded or discardable objects to regain a measure of ecological value (to sustain or rejoin ecological alliances). Can they, like garbaging, revalue objects by dint of stories, codes, and decisions? After all, if the focus is shifted from wasting (the crossing of a threshold) to waste management (the collection, transport, treatment, and disposal of garbage), one is no longer discussing value judgments, intentions, and conventions, but ecologies of garbage trucks, energy recovery facilities, rubbish heaps, waste pickers, global corporations, toxic fumes, and geosynthetic liners.

In his philosophical exploration of waste, William Viney emphasizes the temporal dimension of use, and the role of narration in producing and distributing a time for objects. The "diverging temporalities we associate with things," he writes, "energize and are energized by the shape of our narrative descriptions."[46] Yet, while Viney stresses the personal associations with things, and Deleuze and Guattari underscore the "very general primacy of the collective and machinic assemblage over the technical element,"[47] one cannot overestimate the role of a discursive or cultural "post-tuning," or its ability to override and adapt objects.

Indeed, raw materials undergo considerable transformations (coding, territorialization, hybridization, and forming), and the resulting manufactured objects are far from programmatically vague. Their common names, properties, and capacities consign them to an incontrovertible teleology of use. In the case of shoes, for example, one might agree that, as Viney writes, "I construct a story for these things long before I put my feet into them. The stories I tell about my shoes," he continues, "anticipate and inform their use."[48] Yet, more importantly, by the time one purchases a pair of shoes, the large majority of the narratives that will ever be associated with them have already been embodied in their materiality and inscribed in the language that describes them. Borrowing Lorraine Daston's memorable characterization of quotidian objects, one might describe the shoes as possessing "the self-evidence of a slap in the face."[49]

Once the shoe-object detaches from a given ecology (of running, of hiking, of looking like Michael Jordan, and so on), it is this material embeddedness of purpose (or, paraphrasing Jacques Rancière, this partitioning of the sensible)[50] that reuse and repurposing must face and conquer—narratives can only go so far. In addition, Viney's suggestion that a pair of worn-down shoes could be repurposed as a "doorstop, ornament or plant pot"[51] seems to indicate not that objects can be narratively diverted, but that a thing's material history and original *telos*—the shoe's shoeness—can never be entirely overcome. However, finding a new ecology for a shoe does not only involve discursive labels and instructions (the shoe-as-pot), but the physical and unapologetic transformation of the shoe into a working plant pot (for example, the piercing of drainage holes, or the removal of permeable insoles). In other words: one can slap back.

Designer Helen Kirkum uses a variety of techniques (the separation of layers and materials; the cutting of zippers, logos, and other

46 William Viney, *Waste: A Philosophy of Things* (London and New York: Bloomsbury Academic, 2014), 5.

47 Deleuze and Guattari, *A Thousand Plateaus*, 398.

48 Viney, *Waste*, 6.

49 Lorraine Daston, ed., *Biographies of Scientific Objects* (Chicago: University of Chicago Press, 2000), 2.

50 Jacques Rancière, *The Politics of Aesthetics: The Distribution of the Sensible*, ed. trans. Gabriel Rockhill (London: Bloomsbury, 2013).

51 Viney, *Waste*, 10.

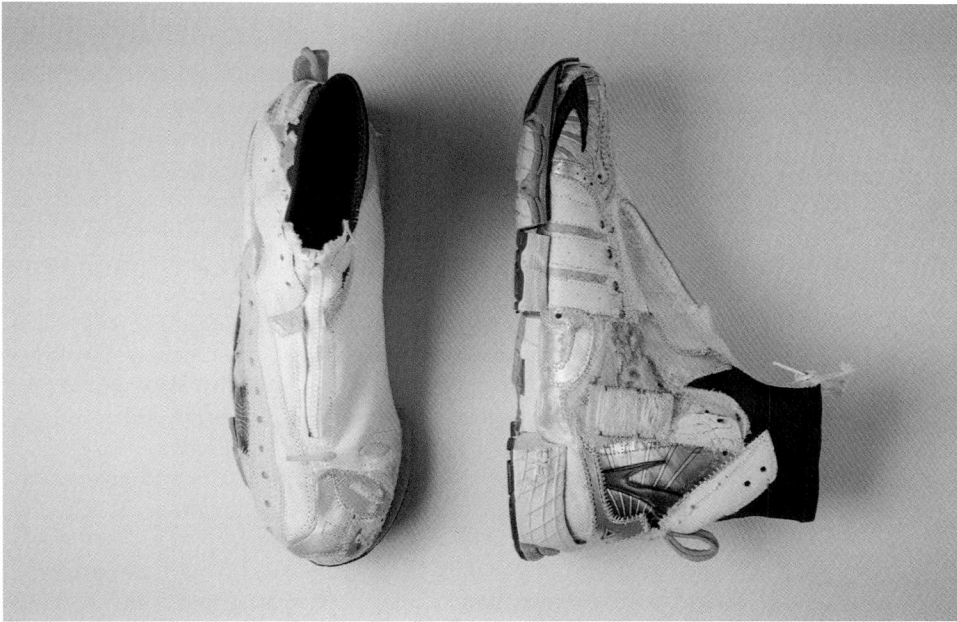

Figure 1.16 Helen Kirkum, *Spliced Sneakers*, London, 2016. Photograph by Rachel Dray.

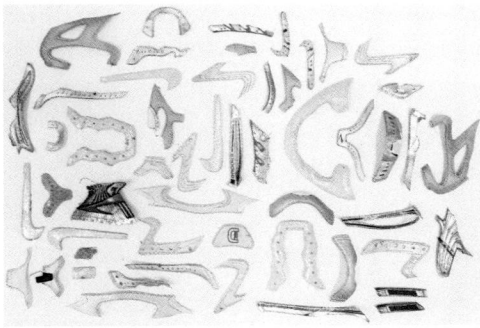

Figure 1.17 Helen Kirkum, *42 x Deconstructed Pieces*, London, 2016.

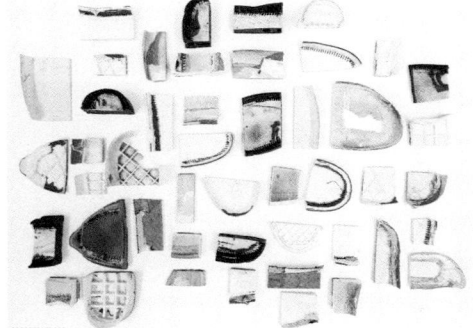

Figure 1.18 Helen Kirkum, *44 x Deconstructed Soles*, London, 2016.

features) to disassemble discarded sneakers, taxonomize their parts, and re-mix the resulting fragments into novel, and surprisingly appealing, pairs of shoes. [**Figures 1.16–1.18**] Architect Greg Lynn develops furniture and bespoke fountains that utilize, as building blocks, robotically cut children's toys. [**Figures 1.19–1.21**] And in *Salvaged Landscape*, architect Catie Newell of Alibi Studio deconstructs a house damaged by arson in Detroit and recombines its timber fragments into a room, turning the house's scarred surfaces (the charred wood) into raw textural and atmospheric spatial qualities. [**Figures 1.22–1.24**] Following Sara Ahmed, one might say that "queer use," understood as "how things

52 Sara Ahmed, *What's the Use? On the Uses of Use* (Durham: Duke University Press, 2019), 199.

53 Ahmed, *What's the Use?*, 229.

54 Siri Hustvedt, "A Woman in the Men's Room: When Will the Art World Recognise the Real Artist behind Duchamp's Fountain?," *The Guardian*, March 29, 2019.

55 Octavio Paz, *Marcel Duchamp: Appearance Stripped Bare*, trans. Rachel Phillips and Donald Gardner (New York: Arcade Publishing, 2014), 24.

56 Martin Heidegger, *Being and Time*, trans. John Macquarrie and Edward Robinson (Oxford: Basil Blackwell, 1962), 97.

57 Heidegger, *Being and Time*, 97. Interestingly, and unlike Scanlan's garbage, equipment is specifically not experienced "as a jumbled heap of things." Martin Heidegger, *The Basic Problems of Phenomenology*, trans. Albert Hofstadter (Bloomington and Indianapolis: Indiana University Press, 1982), 163.

can be used in ways other than for which they were intended to be used or by those other than for whom they were intended,"[52] requires "more than an act of affirmation: it requires a world dismantling effort."[53] But let's return to changes of the discursive and conceptual kind.

The readymade, from Marcel Duchamp onwards, epitomizes the ambivalence and ambiguities at stake in narrative repurposing. *Fountain*, a porcelain urinal turned work of art—whose actual author reliably appears to have been Baroness Elsa von Freytag-Loringhoven[54]—would at first seem to be an exemplar of repurposing: a modest object upsurging in value, rising from the profane realm of plumbing fixtures and urination to that of museum-going and the cultural archive, leaping from a temporality of use and progressive decay to the controlled environment of the display case and the eternal inscription into the History of Art. However, the new status acquired by the object is not justified by either physical or conceptual changes: neither does it undergo major modifications, becoming an altogether new object, nor does it signify or denote new meanings. The readymade clings to its identity and history, pointing to an absent (and provocatively extra-cultural) ecology of use. It is not converted, as Octavio Paz claims, "into an object existing in a vacuum,"[55] but is rather experienced as one component in a larger (albeit missing) system of references; in what Martin Heidegger would call a "totality of equipment."[56]

According to the German philosopher, an object is defined by its equipmentality; by its being "in-order-to" do something (assignment) or "in terms of" other equipment (reference).[57] Objects are so enmeshed in referential networks and so absorbed in productive and purposeful

Figure 1.19 Greg Lynn FORM, *Fountain*, Los Angeles, 2010. Photograph by Brian Forrest.

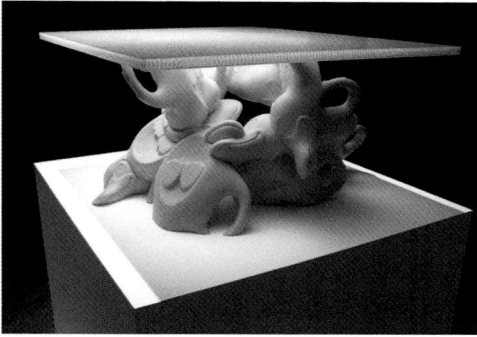

Figure 1.20 Greg Lynn FORM, *Toy Furniture*, Venice, 2008. Courtesy of Greg Lynn FORM.

orientations ("work"), that they withdraw from access.[58] What one typically encounters in experience is the readiness-to-hand of things, their networked usability. It is only when an object breaks and stops performing its function, and when it becomes unusable, that equipment—in its solitude—"becomes conspicuous," and appears as present-at-hand.[59] Yet the readymade is not present-at-hand as much as disconnected and inaccessible. A pen continues to point towards an ecology of writing even if the totality of writing equipment is momentarily out of sight, or dispersed; if there is no paper, no desk, and nothing to be written. And so does *Fountain*, now an iconic work of art, continue to allude to public restrooms and, as contended by Pierre Pinoncelli and others, to invite urination.[60]

As much as it relativizes the difference between a work of art and ordinary objects, and trivializes the notion of inherent artistic truth ("innovation," writes Boris Groys, "is an act of negative adaptation to cultural tradition"),[61] and while furthering Duchamp's agenda against "retinal" and manual art and towards an artistic practice of making acts rather than crafting objects, the readymade also demonstrates the stubbornness of things vis-à-vis the artist's discursive overlaps (e.g., names, performances, signatures)—the refractory core objects oppose to human concepts and meanings. As René Magritte might be forced to admit, *ceci est une pipe.*

Returning to Deleuze and Guattari's difficulty in tracing a clear boundary between weapons and tools—in delineating the intrinsic weapon-ness or tool-ness of a knife without the intercession of machinic assemblages—the philosophers nonetheless admit that "certain secondary adaptations" develop.[62] No knife is alike: spatulas, butter knives, granton knives, bread knives, steak knives, paring knives, and cleavers are very different from one another. Inside the kitchen alone, blades range from clip points to sheep's feet, from forked to rounded, from sharp to blunt or serrated, curved to straight, wide to slim, long

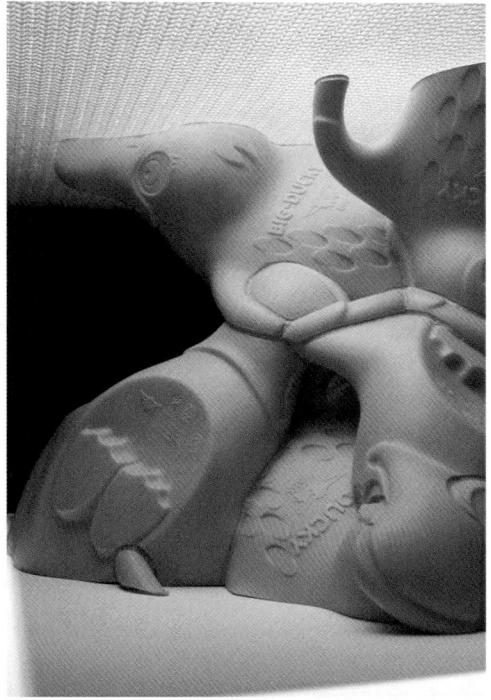

Figure 1.21 Greg Lynn FORM, *Toy Furniture*, Venice, 2008. Photograph by David Erdman.

58 Heidegger, *Being and Time*, 99.

59 Ibid., 102.

60 On August 24, 1993, Pierre Pinoncelli urinated in a replica of *Fountain* exhibited at the Carré d'Art in Nîmes, before striking the sculpture with a hammer. He later defended his actions stating that the "invitation to urinate is offered *ipso facto* by the object." Leland de la Durantaye, "Readymade Remade: Pierre Pinoncelli and the Legacy of Duchamp's 'Fountains,'" *Cabinet*, Fall 2007.

61 Boris Groys, *On the New*, trans. G. M. Goshgarian (Brooklyn: Verso, 2014), 16.

62 Deleuze and Guattari, *A Thousand Plateaus*, 395.

Figures 1.22, 1.23 + 1.24 Catie Newell (Alibi Studio), *Salvaged Landscape*, Detroit, 2010.

to short. The handle, cutting edge, tip, heel, and bolster of a knife speak of specific ecologies—of chopping and dicing vegetables, of removing meat from bones, of peeling fruit, of slicing bread, of carving pumpkins, of filleting fish, of cutting steak, and of spreading jam. A butter knife cannot be used for stabbing, and neither can a saber, which is designed to cut sideways, along the tapering length of the blade.

There is no doubt that design, through technical operations and processes of extraction and manufacture, affects the reality of the objects it modifies. Yet as soon as our intentions are encrusted into their bodies, objects begin to betray our volatility, to exceed our goals, and to degrade—and can no longer be easily overridden. As Heidegger writes, "The jug is a vessel whether we represent it in our minds or not."[63] This is compounded by the disproportionate resilience and obstinacy of objects (the longevity of the plastic bag, or the unambiguous affordances provided by the shape of *Fountain*) vis-à-vis the limited foresight of design ambitions, and by the infinitesimal scope of human history and experience vis-à-vis deep geologic changes and temporalities. The primary flaw in the technical *tabula rasa*—in the idea that technology can master nature (can chew it into cultural availability and submission)—is therefore the assumption that technical individuation matches objecthood, or that the two exist on compatible or comparable ontological planes. Instead, not only do objects not need individuating (they are objects all along), but as soon as they emerge from processes of individuation, even as they continue to fulfill an equipmental or ecological mandate, they recoil into extra-equipmental isolation. In other words, the teleology of use and ecological roles associated with manufactured objects, enabled by physical reconfigurations as they may be, exist not as objective and universal ontologies but at the level of human perception, culture, and psychology.

"To refer to something as a postbox," writes Ahmed, "is to refer to a use of a thing or even a use not a thing. […] Just because something comes to exist for a purpose, we should not confuse what it was intended for with what it is or can be."[64]

A bicycle or wheelchair cannot be (or emerge as) a bicycle or wheelchair in a world without human beings—without our understanding of the turning of wheels, our prehensile hands, our knees and elbow joints, our leg and foot size, bodily coordination, and muscular memory. The bicycle–object is not defined or exhausted by human names, aims, and purposes, or even by the relation to our limbs or to bells and air pumps, to which it is, at least in part, indifferent. Rather, following Harman, the bicycle exists "in a permanent autonomous zone where objects are simply themselves."[65] Or, in Donna Haraway's words, it has an "independent sense of humor."[66] As much as designers imagine them to fully adhere to their intentions and connotations, something is always left in reserve; despite the various transformations we put them through, objects continue to silently ignore us—in Harman's words, to "withdraw." This does not mean that objects (products and byproducts) are inert, but that they act in their own terms; in contingent, unexpected, and utterly extra-cultural ways. Or that one can separate their existence from the ability to detect its effects. Realism, Harman says, means precisely that objects cannot be replaced by knowledge.

This is a provocative proposition for designers, who still predominantly envisage their role in terms of the translation and embodiment of intents.[67] We (architects and designers) must negotiate a balance between the pertinacity of individuated forms and the realization that no technical individuation or system of relations actually coheres with (or provides full access to) the reality of objects; between orienting matter and understanding our orientations as necessarily partial, collaborative, and fluid.

63 Martin Heidegger, "The Thing," in *Poetry, Language, Thought*, trans. Albert Hofstadter (New York: Perennial Classics, 2001), 167.

64 Ahmed, *What's the Use?*, 35.

65 Graham Harman, "The Third Table," in *Documenta: 100 Notes–100 Thoughts*, ed. Katrin Sauerländer (Documenta, 2012), 10.

66 Donna Haraway, "Situated Knowledges: The Science Question in Feminism and the Privilege of Partial Perspective," *Feminist Studies* 14, no. 3 (1988): 593.

67 The relationship between Harman's ontology (object-oriented philosophy) and design will be further elaborated on in Chapters 6 and 8.

Chapter 2

Hylomorphism Reconsidered: Matter, Form, and the Ability to Change

2.1 Potentiality

As the proverb goes, one man's trash can be another man's treasure. While throwing something away may seem to foreclose future uses or to strip objects of their value, booming formal and informal waste economies across the globe show that value doesn't actually wash away, but is merely reformatted. The commodification of trash fuels a vibrant industry, with profits reaching over four hundred billion dollars worldwide.[1] Hence, if garbage necessarily depends on a loss of resolution and value, this loss remains confined within a limited perspective and context—within the shadow of the ecologies that generated it. What enrolls a wide range of material discards under a common "garbage" banner is therefore not an objective and shareable lack of value, but a voluntary and locally determined release—the act of garbaging.

Garbaging is performed in either a magical or active capacity. The former designates the ideological changes that objects undergo upon being discarded; their sudden vanishing from ecologies of use and value, and the stipulation of a distant and invisible spatiotemporal reality (out of sight, out of mind).[2] The latter describes instead the phased and energy-intensive operations required to collect, transport, sort, process, and dispose of solid waste. While magical garbaging erases objects by removing them from a given context, active garbaging reduces them to bundles of raw materials to be recovered, recycled, resold, shipped off, burnt, and buried. Both modes of garbaging undermine objects in Harman's sense, either by sacrificing them to the greater outlines of an all-encompassing (yet elusive) Garbage, or by separating their matter (molecular properties) and form (objectual properties) from one another. While the invention of Anaximander's *apeiron* discussed in the previous chapter can be seen as founding magical garbaging, the theoretical basis for active garbaging can be traced back to the philosophical tradition that first separated objects into matter (*hyle*) and form (*morphé*): Aristotle's theory of substance.

[1] Kate O'Neill, *Waste* (Cambridge and Medford: Polity Press, 2019), 59.

[2] "Of course we know well enough how our excrement leaves the house, but our immediate phenomenological relation to it is more radical: it is as if the waste disappears into some netherworld, beyond our sight and out of our world." Slavoj Žižek, *Living in the End Times* (London and New York: Verso, 2011), 260.

DOI: 10.4324/9781003015444-4

For the Aristotle of *Categories*, a primary substance (an individual) is that which is one, selfsame, and "neither predicable of a subject nor present in it."[3] An individual maintains its identity while admitting a variety of changing qualities and affections;[4] John remains John whether he is wearing a white or a yellow shirt; whether he is in a good or a bad mood, healthy or sick, at home or in the middle of the desert. A box is a box whether it is filled with diamonds or empty, wet or dry, on the table or under it. Such durability places substances on a higher ontological ground with respect to the other categories, yet it doesn't prevent them from changing or ceasing to exist altogether— or one would incur in the Megarian impasse whereby "that which is standing will always stand, and that which is sitting will always sit."[5] Rather, the salient feature of substances is precisely their ability to last through modified incarnations. Aristotle accounts for such changes by introducing the concepts of potentiality and actuality and, more importantly, by coupling them with matter and form respectively.

At the beginning of Book Theta of the *Metaphysics*, Aristotle defines potentiality (*dynamis*) as the principle of change that can be internal or external to the thing changed, or both, combining the patient's ability to be acted upon—e.g., the flammability of oily stuff—with the agent's ability to act—the burnability of fire.[6] Actuality (*energeia*), on the other hand, designates something that is already present—e.g., fire actually burning an oil-soaked cloth.[7] Actuality stands to potentiality as building stands to the ability to build; and "that which is seen to that which has the eyes shut, but has the power of sight; *and that which is differentiated out of matter to the matter; and the finished article to the raw material*."[8] The distinction between differentiated, formed matter on one side and undifferentiated, raw material on the other is presented by Aristotle as analogous to the opposition between actuality and potentiality. On one side are particular things (e.g., a wooden box), which are already formed, and on the other definite materials (e.g., the "wooden material"), which have the ability to attain form, becoming something else.[9] In *De Anima*, the philosopher goes even further and collapses the analogy into a definition: "the word substance has three meanings—form, matter, and the complex of both—and of these matter is potentiality, form actuality."[10] Potentiality is therefore contingent on a degree of formlessness, and, inversely, form is that which hinders change. According to this paradigm, the burly trunk of a tree, as well as the complex geometries of its limbs, branches, and twigs, is too rich in actualized forms to welcome change; potentiality is progressively gained only through a process of de-formation: by felling, delimbing, bucking, debarking, hewing, and so on. The same goes for discarded glass bottles, old newspapers, and all manner of ecologically loose objects: the restoring of formlessness and rawness (or, in common parlance, recycling) is the forced gateway to entering new processes of individuation (from the bottle to glass cullet to a differently shaped bottle).

Yet formlessness is not an absolute attribute or principle, but always defined relationally; it does not only entail the ability to change (to be formed), but also the capacity not to prevent a particular agent from

3 Aristotle, *Categories*, trans. E.M. Edghill, The Internet Classics Archive, accessed April 14, 2019, sec.1, part 5.

4 "[I]t is a distinctive mark of substance that, while remaining numerically one and the same, it is capable of admitting contrary qualities, the modification taking place in the substance itself." Aristotle, *Categories*.

5 Aristotle, *Aristotle in Twenty-Three Volumes. 17: The Metaphysics: books I–IX*, trans. Hugh Tredennick (Cambridge: Harvard University Press, 2003), 437.

6 Aristotle, *The Metaphysics*, 431.

7 Ibid., 447.

8 Ibid., 447. My emphasis.

9 Ibid., 453.

10 Aristotle, "On the Soul," trans. J.A. Smith, in *The Complete Works of Aristotle: The Revised Oxford Translation*, ed. Jonathan Barnes (Princeton: Princeton University Press, 1984), 24.

enacting that change. There is a direct correspondence between the way capitalism masticates natural resources and the sharpness of its teeth; between the potentiality attained by processing a thing (from the tree to lumber) and the tools employed to do so—saw, axe, log jack, skidder, and the like. In this sense, the *rasura* no longer involves scraping something, but rather tuning it to something else—paraphrasing a thing in the language of the tools and practices that will alter it. There is potentiality in the standard wood plank on the shelves of Home Depot not because it was simplified and geometricized, but because its flatness, rectangular shape, and overall dimensions allow for it to be easily transported, stacked, laid on a table saw, sanded, nailed, glued, drilled, and used for paneling. In the technical *tabula rasa*, potentiality is engendered not by a degree of blankness, but by attuning a form—new or preexistent, simple or complex as it may be—to technical tools and cultural apparatuses; the tighter the fit, the higher the degree of potentiality attained. As Gilbert Simondon demonstrated, in its actual manifestations the cultural reordering of matter is not platonic (in-forming it through ideal geometries) but technical (steering objects towards, or pitting them against, one another).[11]

In these encounters and collisions, not all objects are equal. While the withdrawal of objects discussed in the previous chapter implies a flat ontological plane (a degree of reciprocal indifference), an ecology of inception manipulates the points along the plane into three-dimensional topographies, pushing and pulling to generate bumps, berms, and depressions. This entails the existence, in its standard poietic make-up, of at least three distinct types of components, which I will call *herders*, *shearers*, and *sheep*.[12] Herders name the modifications that will occur within the system and establish the physical and operational status required of other system components. They are teleological engines, located on the outside and on the receiving end of poietic processes upon which they exercise a normative function, discriminating based on their own goals or material biases: the weight and flatness of the hammer head; the sharpness and length of the knife; the net dimensions of the shipping container; the regulatory standards governing the height of speed bumps; and so on.[13] They are external to the production theater but, unlike in the case of abstract forms, their energetic engagement is not necessarily revoked—only postponed.[14] The other two kinds of components, shearers and sheep, actively interact; the former effectuates changes that the latter receives and translates (the saw and a log, the 3D printer and a spool of PLA filament, the squeezer and a lemon). Sheep exit the interaction upon becoming (or releasing) the intended output or product.

The rules of engagement in the linear manufacturing process thus described are such that herders are removed from the interaction (they remain at a distance), they precede sheep, and sheep undergo the bulk of material modifications. Repurposing undermines and confuses these parameters, sequences, and relative positions in favor of the sheep, which fold upon themselves to partially assume, from the inside, a herding role. [**Figure 2.1**] No longer are sheep mere passive receivers of

[11] Gilbert Simondon, *L'individuation à la lumière des notions de forme et d'information* (Grenoble: Millon, 2005).

[12] My use of the term "poietic" simply refers to making. However, I am not impartial to the difference between the Greek words *poiesis* (production in the sense of a bringing into being, of a bringing-forth) and *praxis* (in the sense of willed and creative action). See Giorgio Agamben, "Poiesis and Praxis," in *The Man without Content*, trans. Georgia Albert (Stanford: Stanford University Press, 1999), 76. See also Martin Heidegger, "The Question Concerning Technology," in *Basic Writings: From Being and Time (1927) to The Task of Thinking (1964)*, ed. David Farrell Krell (San Francisco: HarperSanFrancisco, 1993), 311–41.

[13] The latter example is a nod to Bruno Latour's discussion of speed bumps in *Pandora's Hope*. Latour writes: "The speed bump is ultimately *not* made of matter; it is full of engineers and chancellors and lawmakers, commingling their wills and their story lines with those of gravel, concrete, paint, and standard calculations." Bruno Latour, *Pandora's Hope: Essays on the Reality of Science Studies* (Cambridge: Harvard University Press, 1999), 190.

[14] To future encounters, which may occur in new productive transformations, couplings, and recombinations; in testing and verification regimes; or in mere use.

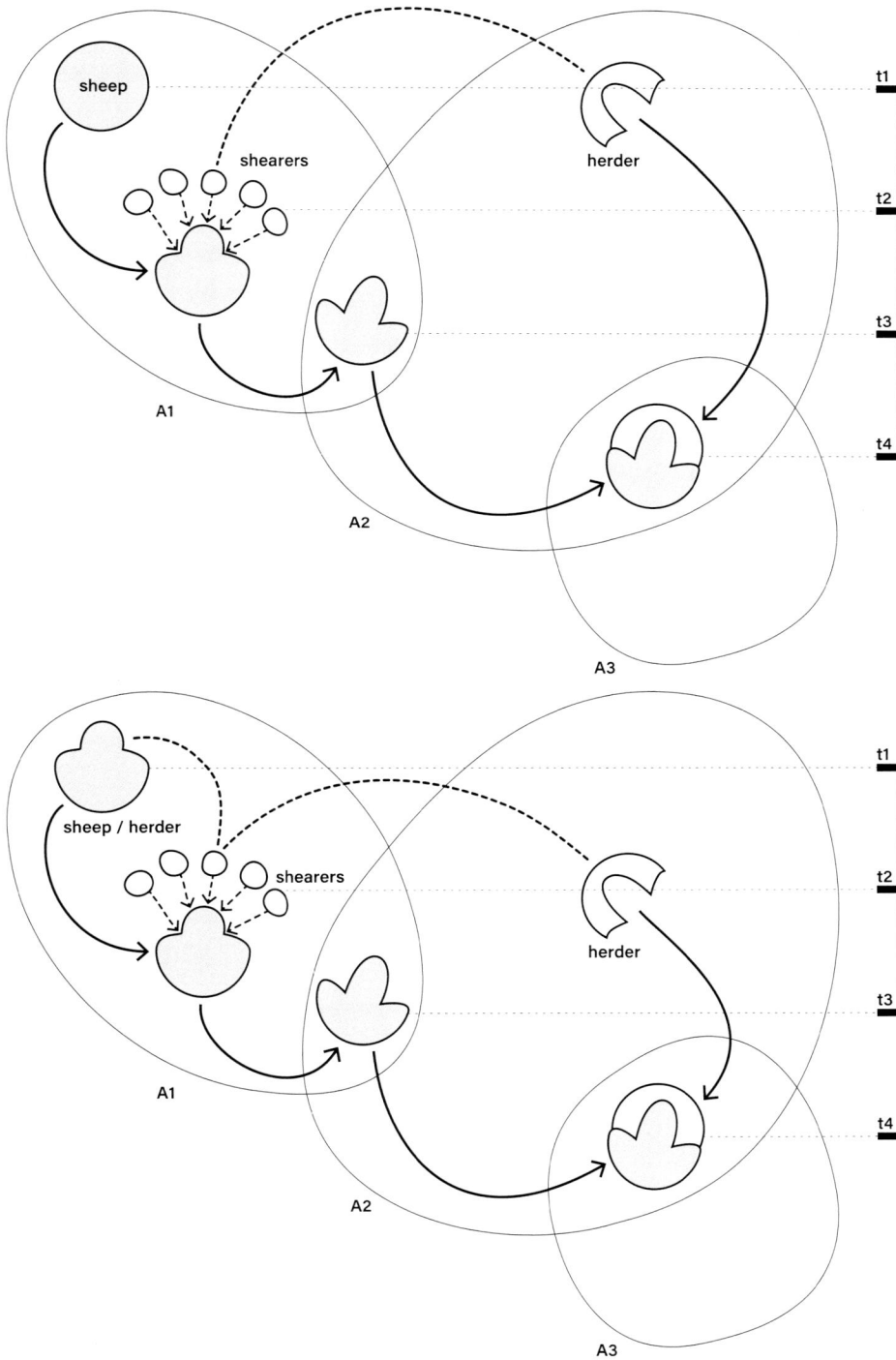

Figure 2.1 The preparation and modification of objects towards an ecological interior, illustrating the relative spatial and temporal positions of herders, shearers, and sheep in subecologies A1, A2, and A3. In linear manufacturing (above), sheep are subordinated to herding commands, whereas in repurposing (below) they partially assume a herding role.

external cosmetic pressures (in the etymological sense of the Greek *kosmos*, the act of ordering and arranging), or only active in the translation and distribution of (or resistance to) inputs, but they themselves orchestrate modifications and attunements. Here, sheep are both agents and patients, designers and designed, at once *teloi*, points of departure, and results.

Let's take for example the rotor blades in a wind turbine, which are manufactured by lining molds with layers of plastic and fiberglass reinforcement, and by injecting them with resin via a process known as vacuum infusion. Indeed, the technical chains associated with their production (the selection and preparation of materials; the fabrication of molds; the calibration of recipes; the fine-tuning of chemical reactions and curing times; the streamlining of steps; and so forth) establish internal parameters for the development and optimization of the blades over time, either in the context of a specific model or, following Gilbert Simondon, alongside a longer trajectory of concretization—the progressive evolution of a technical essence, usually involving simplifications and "functional condensations for synergies."[15] Despite this, herding commands are largely imparted from the outside—sparked by the desire for increased reliability, efficiency or power capacity; and aiming to aerodynamically translate wind pressure into rotational energy, and to withstand dynamic loads, centrifugal forces, and changing wind conditions. These inputs, and the associated testing regimes, write the ecological scripts performed by shearers in the manufacturing of rotor blades.

Whereas other parts of decommissioned wind turbines can be recycled, rotor blades cannot be returned to their virgin components, they are difficult to crush or transport, and end up buried in landfills.[16] [**Figure 2.2**] Yet one exemplary project demonstrates not only that these large carbon fiber-reinforced plastic objects can be persuasively and poetically repurposed—it also illustrates how repurposing shuffles ecological roles, endowing sheep with the ability to herd (or rather, pointing to the fact that such roles are temporary and precarious). The *Wikado Playground* designed by Rotterdam-based architects Superuse Studios (formerly 2012 Architects) transforms discarded rotor blades into architectural structures. [**Figure 2.3-2.5**] Remarkably, it is impossible to reduce the project to herding intents or decisions—to requirements satisfied by (or to ideas wrought into) a relatively passive matter. Instead, the project's materials (the discarded rotor blades), while performing the role of sheep—while being sawn, perforated, welded, and fastened—also take on a decisive (herding) role in the design, suggesting forms and configurations that would be otherwise unthinkable, and inventing, in the context of a playground, novel uses and affordances. The tip of the blade becomes a surface to climb and walk on, but also one for eating, drawing, or leaning against. The root of the blade becomes the mouth of a tunnel—of a secret room for hiding, gathering, and playing with friends. Other upside-down blade sections fashion

[15] Gilbert Simondon, *L'invention dans les techniques, Cours et conférences* (Paris: Seuil, 2005),169, quoted in Andrew Iliadis, "Two Examples of Concretization," *Platform: Journal of Media and Communication* 6 (2015): 86–95.

[16] Chris Martin, "Wind Turbine Blades Can't Be Recycled, So They're Piling Up in Landfills," *Bloomberg Green*, February 5, 2020.

Figure 2.2 January 9, 2020: Pieces of wind turbine blades are buried in the Casper Regional Landfill in Casper, Wyoming. Photograph by Benjamin Rasmussen/Reportage Archive via Getty Images.

Figure 2.3 Superuse Studios, *Wikado Playground*, Rotterdam, 2007. Photograph by (©) Denis Guzzo.

Figures 2.4 + 2.5 Superuse Studios, *Wikado Playground*, Rotterdam, 2007. Photographs by (©) Denis Guzzo.

towers, with perforations identifying windows and escape routes, and supporting nets and slides.

In repurposing, the functional combinations that activate capacities across objects are no longer read or computed like predetermined sequences or punch cards, like sentences or strings of code, from left to right or from the periphery towards the center, but in every possible direction, and jumping across a rich mesh of nodes and actors. In this sense, these practices shift the poietic focus from the individual object to the whole system or network; or, more precisely, from changing one object according to established cultural, economic, and technical paradigms, to redesigning the paradigms—their methods, values, and boundaries—altogether. While traditional fabrication and manufacturing tools strictly require the input of (or interaction with) purified formats such as blocks, filaments, and sheets, or a progression towards increased optimization, repurposing resets the horizon of technological invention to admit of more open-ended and unpredictable scenarios, overcoming biases between old and new, intentional and unintentional, internal and external, prepared and unprepared. Beyond any given project or output, the true goal of repurposing might be to design from within a democracy of objects.[17]

The fundamental difference between the two approaches discussed— linear and nodal—is the amount of agency afforded to the modified object. In the linear process from log to timber beam, only the "implicit" molecular forms and energetic capacities of the wood fibers are at work, chiefly adopting responsive behaviors and defensive postures—chemical reactions, mechanical friction, resistance to forces, modulation of received inputs. The carpenter learns to "listen" to the material biases of the wood, and to embed them with purpose, preferring, for instance, wedge cutting to saw-cutting in the making of structural timber beams.[18] The modified object has no individual voice; it merely translates, with some modifications, the herder's inputs or intentions—it is a mere material. Instead, a nodal approach to design and making allows for the explicit forms and capacities of the object to also play a role, and to impart herding commands. While linear *poiesis* is acted upon (or, at most, transmitted across) matter, reuse and repurposing are performed and codesigned with forms.[19]

Aiming to transform a wooden box into a figurine of Zeus, one of two approaches might be followed. An intransigently hylomorphic one would trust the Aristotelian bias against forms, and believe that the box's ability to change—its potentiality—is contingent on a re-becoming matter, on a decrease in actuality and resolution (the tablet has to be scraped clean so that something new might be written on it). This approach will aim to de-actualize the box, reverting it to a raw state, one capable of attaining new forms. The wooden box (the sheep) is not examined or surveyed, but ignored, obliterated, and atomized— cut into identical cubes of about five millimeters each, reassembled in the image of Zeus (the herder), and sanded down to the intended

17 This felicitous phrase is borrowed from OOO philosopher Levi Bryant. See Levi R. Bryant, *The Democracy of Objects* (Ann Arbor: Open Humanities Press, 2011).

18 See Simondon, *ILFI*, 52–53.

19 I will further develop the implications of this nodal approach to materials (particularly as compared to a circular one) in Chapter 4.

20 Max Liboiron, "Modern Waste as Strategy," *Lo Squaderno: Explorations in Space and Society*, no. 29 (2013). In this text, Liboiron refers to both disposability and recycling as strategies for the externalization of the costs associated with the industrial production of waste.

21 Franz Kafka, "The Cares of a Family Man," trans. Willa and Edwin Muir, in *The Complete Stories*, ed. Nahum N. Glatzer (New York: Schocken Books, 1988), 469–70.

shape. According to this view, having powers and having the power to be formed are the same thing. That is: what is at stake are not really the potentials of the box, but a conflation of potentiality with the herder's ability to impart commands, with the shearer's ability to execute the herder's commands, and with the sheep's ability to receive and distribute the shearer's inputs.

Recycling rehearses a similarly hylomorphic refrain, assuming that discarded objects—PET bottles, palladium circuit boards, glass panes, and aluminum extrusions—cannot be transformed or revalued unless stripped of their historical specificity and formal (objectual) integrity. If recycling extends (more or less successfully) the lifespan of matter, it does so by confirming the formula that makes garbage possible in the first place—by endorsing the idea that objects, upon losing their ecological membership, are actually void of potentials, and can only be re-potentialized if reduced to an amorphous, formless goop, or shredded into tiny pieces. "Recyclables," writes Max Liboiron, "are just disposables by another name."[20]

Figure 2.6 In the manner of Giuseppe Arcimboldo, designed or engraved by Giovanni da Monte Cremasco, *The Instruments of Human Sustenance (Humani Victus Instrumenta): Cooking*, engraving, Venice, after 1569. The Elisha Whittelsey Collection, The Elisha Whittelsey Fund, 1977.

A nonhylomorphic design approach would instead set out from an archeology of the box, survey and analyze its configuration and composition—its shape; the thickness of its sides; the orientation of wood grains; its superficial finishes; the way pieces are joined to one another—and study possible alterations based on existing material properties and affordances. The ensuing figurine would mediate between the ideal form of Zeus in its classical representation—the muscular body, softly draped himation, curly beard, and lightning bolt—and the current structure of the box—its sharp angles, doweled connections, and veneered surfaces. The resulting Zeus would be a hybrid figure, more akin to Kafka's Odradek than to the sinuous marble statues of the ancient Greeks.[21] Or it might resemble a figure painted by Giuseppe Arcimboldo, a sculpture by Nancy Rubins, or the strange creatures in Max Ernst's *Natural History*. [**Figure 2.6**] Its angular profile would challenge a strict substantialist doctrine and admit of more fluid and democratic exchanges between matter and form, herders and sheep. The box could no longer be compelled to attain an infinite number of forms, solely limited by such attributes as quantity, size, and implicit molecular constitution; nor would it seem reasonable to assume that it could (or, indeed, should) perfectly reproduce or embody a foreign, abstract idea.

If, as argued, the hylomorphic scheme corresponds with the opening up of a space wherefrom the idea of trash and its active implementations become conceptually viable, the first task of a philosophy of reuse and repurposing—a philosophy that grounds the radical recirculation and recombination of objects—must be to neutralize and deactivate hylomorphism. The hybrid Zeus, with its restricted compositional palette, represents a step in this direction, moving towards a design and fabrication *ethos* that partially renounces herding privileges to embrace and pursue flatness, horizontality, and a measure of uncertainty.

Following Jane Bennett, one shall not "posit a subject as the root cause of an effect," but "see human intentions as always in competition and confederation with many strivings."[22] Bennett's distributed understanding of agency "does not deny the existence of that thrust called intentionality, but it does see it as less definitive of outcomes."[23] Accordingly, the very conception of design could be revised to include not only drawing and making, but also listening and finding.

[22] Jane Bennett, *Vibrant Matter: A Political Ecology of Things* (Durham: Duke University Press, 2010), 31–32.

[23] Bennett, *Vibrant Matter*, 32.

2.2 Impotentiality

In discussing the industrial processing of an actual tree, I have mentioned growing, or at least varying, degrees of potentiality. The transformations described imply that, albeit opposite, potentiality and actuality are not separate and mutually exclusive, but rather imbricated and coextensive, like the full and empty halves of a glass of water: whether you pour into the glass or drink from it, you will simultaneously affect both. One intuitively understands that something similar occurs between matter and form, as matter continues to exist "*in* the form,"[24] and the wooden material, after having been carved, continues to be identifiable in the statue of Zeus.

[24] Aristotle, *The Metaphysics*, 459.

Yet things do get more complicated with potentiality and actuality. These notions, as described thus far, are decided in different arenas: *dynamis* in the constellation of possible relations that can define it, *energeia* in the actualization of one such relation. In order to communicate to (and eventually pass into) actuality, potentials must narrow their scope and focus on one specific *telos*—on the potentiality to do or to be something specific. But this is not enough; if potentiality were only "potentiality to be," there would be nothing to stop it from automatically passing into actuality, as the Megarians believed. However, if being able to build a house does not necessarily result in the construction of a house, or if it is possible to be a piano player without constantly playing the piano, it is because being capable of doing something entails a capacity to both do it and not do it, to act and to withhold action. Aristotle writes that "[e]very potentiality is at the same time a potentiality for the opposite. For whereas that which is incapable of happening cannot happen to anything, everything which is capable may fail to be actualized. Therefore that which is capable of being may both be and not be."[25] Giorgio Agamben considers this internal relation to privation, this "welcoming of non-Being," to be the essence of *dynamis*.[26] But the dual nature of potentiality also introduces a new problem: what happens to the

[25] Ibid., 461.

[26] Giorgio Agamben, *Potentialities: Collected Essays in Philosophy*, trans. Daniel Heller-Roazen (Stanford: Stanford University Press, 1999), 182.

potentiality to not-be (*adynamia*) when the potentiality to be (*dynamis*) passes into actuality?

Agamben reads an excerpt from *Metaphysics* in which Aristotle describes the passage of potentiality into actuality as one whereby "there will be nothing impotential"[27] to mean not, as is usually thought, that *adynamia* is discarded in order for *dynamis* to rise and pass into being, but rather that *adynamia* is preserved in actuality and "passes fully into it as such."[28] He concludes:

> Contrary to the traditional idea of potentiality that is annulled in actuality, here we are confronted with a potentiality that conserves itself and saves itself into actuality. Here potentiality, so to speak, survives actuality and, in this way, gives itself to itself.[29]

The conservation of potentiality within actuality would seem to refute the latter's presumed lack of potency—a lack that, as discussed, underpins garbaging practices (the operative logic being: "formed matter cannot change—it cannot be reassigned to new ecologies—and must therefore be discarded"). But how is potentiality conserved in actuality, exactly? By granting formed objects the ability to undo their own actualized potentials. Just as impotentiality (the piano player's ability to not play) ensured the existence of potentiality (her ability to play), preventing it from automatically passing into actuality (music being played all the time), so does it guarantee the reversibility or changeability of actualized forms—the rotor blade's propensity for becoming tunnel, tower, or drawbridge.

Yet, if one intuitively understands impotentiality in association with human faculties, what this term refers to when applied to inanimate objects is less clear. A lump of wood can be wrought into a variety of functional objects: a chair, a table, a statue of Zeus, and so on. In the lump of wood, the potentiality to be chair is coupled with the potentiality to not-be chair, or, in other words, with the potentiality to either not change or to change into something other than a chair (e.g., a table, a stool, a mask). Following Agamben, when the carpenter works the lump of wood into a chair—when the potential to be chair passes into actuality—the potentiality to not-be chair is preserved in the actual object. The lump of wood has therefore not been stripped of the ability to change by acquiring the shape of a chair; inside of it still reside—though muted—the potentialities (and impotentialities) to be table, Zeus, bowl, and so on.

Even if actual forms continue to have powers (if their powers are not exhausted by processes of actualization), it is not likely that the impotentiality thus preserved would remain unchanged, or result from a translation in the mathematical sense—a repositioning that does not alter what it moves. The impotentialities carried over in a chair and in a statue of Zeus, both hypothetically made out of the same lump of wood, would hardly be identical. Firstly, the impotentiality preserved

27 Agamben, *Potentialities*, 183.

28 Ibid.

29 Ibid., 184.

is, by definition, not a potential privation in general, but one tied to the particular actual form attained. That is, the potentiality to not-be chair cannot reside within the statue of Zeus, because the statue of Zeus is (already) not a chair. And if it could, it might still include a potentiality to be Zeus, with the aporetic effect of something simultaneously being potential and actual. Secondly, based on the relational definition of potentiality I have tentatively provided—one according to which potentials are unlocked by tuning objects toward one another, thus forming ecological bonds and enclosures—it is clear that the tools, designs and operations required to alter a chair will be different from those needed to transform a wooden Zeus.

In light of Agamben's reading of Aristotle, the relational definition of potentiality proposed in the previous chapter must therefore be revised, for it is now clear that it is not only the passing of potentiality into actuality that is played out in the theater of relations within which an individual actor is situated, but also a transformation from an impotentiality to do *x* to a potentiality to do *y*, or a potentiality to not do *y*. In other words, it seems necessary to discriminate between two types of impotentiality: the impotentiality to do *x*, as used above, refers to an utter lack of specific (targeted) potentials—the inability of the tree to interact with the printer. I will call this an *external impotentiality*. The potentiality to not do *y*, instead, refers to a privation within the potentialized network of relations in an ecology of inception—the stack of paper inside the printer tray, while the printer is off. I will call this an *internal impotentiality*.

It would seem that the impotentiality discussed by Aristotle and Agamben belongs to this latter type, because, as outlined above, their philosophies employ it as a mechanism to delay and withhold specific actions—actions that, in order to be possible at all, must have already been identified and named within an ecological interior. This prompts two observations. On one side, I can now describe ecologies of inception not only in terms of their equipmental orientation (of what they can do), but also as the interior landscapes held together by their impotentialities; as the bodies engendered by sets of temporarily suspended relations.[30] [**Figure 2.7**] On the other, one might consider how—or rather, if—the reciprocity between potentiality and impotentiality also animates external impotentialities; whether a lack of specific powers (a broad inability to communicate) establishes the ground for their emergence. Doesn't recognizing the tree and the printer as unrelated establish

Figure 2.7 Eols, represented with the dashed lines in the image, can be understood as sets of temporarily suspended relations (between the scissors and paper, the coffee and sugar, the pencils and the pencil sharpener, et cetera).

30 I don't mean something like a phenomenological body, which mediates a reality for a subject, but rather an ecological body: an assemblage whose component parts are attuned to and capable of affecting one another. Little does it matter whether something like a skin holds it all together as one physically contiguous entity. A body is understood here as a map of attuned organs (objects), be they organic or inorganic, in apposition or separated by several miles; as the system within which (real) coordinated changes can occur.

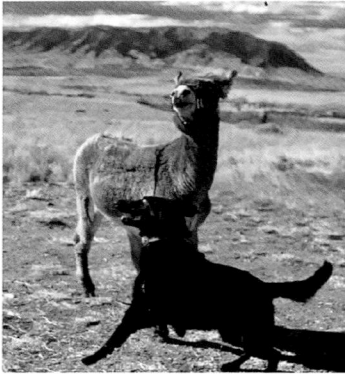

Figure 2.8 Greetings and play: friendship between the dog Safi and the donkey Wister. Photograph by Barbara Smuts.

a form of relation between them? Doesn't uttering the words *rotor blade* and *playground* in the same sentence already suggest a horizon for their encounter? In this sense, an external impotentiality, as soon as it comes into focus, is no longer a mere lack of communication, but the beginning of (or a desire for) a dialogue.

In any case, if Agamben focuses on internal impotentiality, it is because, for him, what is at stake in the notion of potency is our very humanity—the ability to transform one's capacities into "faculties," to suspend and withhold possible action and, therefore, to be free. Furthermore, the distinction I have suggested resonates with the one Agamben draws between humans and nonhumans. For the philosopher, this distinction hinges on two different types of internal impotentiality: "inability to do" on the side of things and animals, and "ability to not do" on the side of humans. He writes that

[i]t is not only the measure of what someone can do, but also and primarily the capacity of maintaining oneself in relation to one's own possibility to not do, that defines the status (*rango*) of one's action. While fire can only burn, and other living beings are only capable of their own specific potentialities—they are capable of only this or that behavior inscribed into their biological vocation—human beings are the animals capable of their own impotentiality."[31]

When speaking of "biological vocation," Agamben might be thinking of the predatory instinct of a cat chasing a mouse, or of a lion devouring a gazelle. Yet, growing evidence of interspecies friendships, including between predators and prey, demonstrates that such instincts can indeed be overridden or, rather, that the abilities associated with them can be diverted towards other relational modes, such as play. Following Donna Haraway, it is because "the kind of predators dogs are know how to read in detail the kind of prey donkeys are and vice versa" that dogs and donkeys might be well suited to becoming friends.[32] [**Figure 2.8**]

For Agamben, impotentiality preserves a faculty—a latent ability—and not intentionality. It is not about the pianist's decision to not play at a particular time, but about her very ability to play and withhold playing. It is, however, in the confusion between an ability to do something and the intent or impetus to do (or to not do) that lies Agamben's bias toward humans. Certainly, while a pianist seated in front of a piano can decide not to play, a ball set on a sloped surface cannot avoid rolling. But that said, on what basis does one assume that the pianist's ability to play is ontologically superior to the

31 Giorgio Agamben, *Nudities*, trans. David Kishik and Stefan Pedatella, Meridian (Stanford: Stanford University Press, 2010), 44.

32 Donna Haraway, *When Species Meet* (Minneapolis: University of Minnesota Press, 2008), 233. The specific case Haraway refers to is that of the dog Safi and the donkey Wister as described by Barbara Smuts. See also Barbara Smuts, "Encounters with Animal Minds," *Journal of Consciousness Studies* 8, no. 5–7 (May 2001): 293–309.

ball's capacity for rolling? The former is undeniably more complex, but both are equally impotential—both can either do or not do. The ball doesn't always roll: sometimes it rolls, sometimes it doesn't. The pianist doesn't always play: sometimes she plays, sometimes she doesn't. Intentional action is not determining of the inherent ability to play or to roll. Rather, it implements it, either by choice (in the case of the pianist) or interactively (in the case of the ball on a slope, or kicked). What defines and maintains both abilities are not decisions or actions, but sets of individuated forms.

Without falling into a neural reductionist position, this conception admits that physical changes in the brain—for instance, the electrochemical pathways associated with playing the piano—can be assimilated to the spherical shape of the ball; that, after all, the abilities of both brain and ball similarly depend on and are structured by mere actualized forms.

This view radicalizes Agamben's claim that impotentiality is conserved within actuality, or, better, that the latter *preserves* the former. Coupling potentiality with actuality (with the roundness of the ball or the firing of neural networks) marks an overlap between them—a temporary fusion or zone of indistinction that is pressed into existence by relational linkages and transitory alliances (with the piano; with the slope). The actual and potential states of an object thus intermittently collapse and coalesce into one another. In this sense, to relate is to temporarily fuse an object to its powers.

The differential distance between matter and form appears to have shortened, so much so that the two terms occasionally merge. In fact, one might have no reason to claim that matter ever exists apart from form, in a truly amorphous state. Whether matter is described as formed or formless is merely a function of who does the describing (or presumes to do the forming), and dependent on scale and context. Raw and formed matter are defined oppositely and relatively, as the beginning and end points in a technical operation, or in a chain of technical operations. As matter is transformed along a teleological vector, each step is marked by a reassignment of roles. To the lumberjack, the tree is raw matter and the log is formed matter; to the sawyer, the log is raw matter and the board is formed matter; to the carpenter, the board is raw matter and the chair is formed matter; and so on. [**Figure 2.9**]

Matter and form are the roles performed during processes of actualization—during operations such as logging, sawing, and woodworking.[33] In this context, a *tabula rasa*—a condition of original formlessness—is unattainable, and the stipulation of more or less form is never given, objective, or neutral, but re-negotiated by crossing ecological and subecological thresholds. Matter and form only persist as unstable terms—as the poles between which objects simulate oscillations.

[33] It is interesting to note that even Victor Frankenstein consistently refers to the body parts and limbs used to stitch together his creature not by their proper names, but using terms such as "lifeless clay" and "my materials." Mary Wollstonecraft Shelley, *Frankenstein: Or, The Modern Prometheus*, vol. 1, 3 vols (London: Lackington, Hughes, Harding, Mavor & Jones, 1818), 90–91.

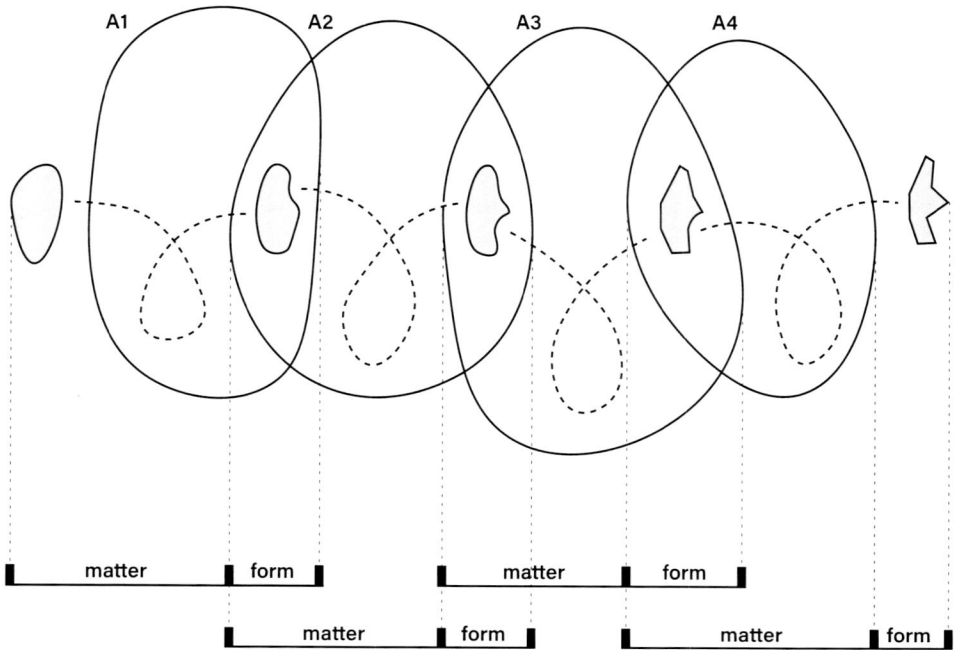

Figure 2.9 The terms *matter* and *form* are not absolute or universally valid, but roles assigned to object (inputs and outputs) in narrow subecological contexts.

2.3 Individuation

While the term *hylomorphism* never appears in Aristotle's writings, it serves as recurrent counterpoint in Gilbert Simondon's discussion of individuation, the first part of which was published in 1964 in *L'individu et sa génèse physico-biologique* (the individual and its physical–biological genesis). Broadly speaking, the question of individuation interrogates the coming-into-being of individual objects—of things that, like flowers, crystals, Socrates, and window sills, are numerically distinct, singular, and differentiated. The French philosopher re-thinks the problem of individuation by questioning the primacy of the individual (Aristotle's substance or *sunolon* as the fundamental reality to be explained), its articulation (an individual as output, an individuation process, and a principle of individuation that sets that process into motion), its orientation (the top-down *in-formation* of matter), and its temporality (a sequential operation that begins with a principle of individuation and ends with an individuated object).[34]

Firstly, Simondon rejects the assumption that *being* strictly corresponds with fixed individual substances or units, noting that the ontological primacy of individuals approaches ontogenesis—the question of how individuals are made—upside-down, seeking to post-rationalize given outputs rather than investigating their individuation

34 Jacques Garelli, "Introduction à la problématique de Gilbert Simondon," in Simondon, *ILFI*, 9–19.

as it unfolds.[35] Furthermore, this leads to a circular argument that accounts for the existence of individuals by presupposing that of more fundamental terms or individuating principles (e.g., atoms, matter, form) that are also, in a sense, already individuated.[36] In the case of hylomorphism in particular, assuming that substances are produced by the encounter of form and matter—that either matter or form suffice as their individuating principles—fails to account for the "real dynamism" and specificity of the operations involved.[37] "The specific being that one can show," writes Simondon, "this brick drying on this plank, does not result from the union of a generic matter with a generic form."[38] He continues:

> If we take fine sand, wet it and place it in a brick mold: after de-molding we will obtain a heap of sand, and not a brick. If we take clay and pass it through a rolling mill or spinneret: we will not obtain a plate or filament, but an accumulation of broken sheets and short cylindrical segments. Clay, conceived as supporting an indefinite plasticity, is an abstract matter. The rectangular parallelepiped, conceived as the form of a brick, is an abstract form. The concrete brick does not result from uniting the clay's plasticity with the parallelepiped. In order to have *a* parallelepipedic brick, an individual that really exists, it is necessary for an effective technical *operation* to establish a mediation between a certain mass of clay and this notion of parallelepiped.[39]

Not only are the abstract clay and parallelepiped of Aristotelian hylomorphism unfit to describe the real-world specificity of each term; neither can their interactions be summarily described by (or resolved in) the molding operation, or in the top-down imposition of a geometric form upon a lump of clay assumed to be brute and indeterminate.[40] As in the case of the tree and printer discussed in the previous chapter, an individuating operation curates the "encounter between two realities belonging to heterogeneous domains," allowing them to communicate.[41] Therefore, the individuation of a brick is understood not only as the encounter between clay and mold (the moment in which the former is pressed into the latter), but as spanning preparatory chains in two directions—from the parallelepiped to the clay and vice versa—that will eventually attain a degree of compatibility in character and scale (a common ground and language).[42] The abstract geometrical form of the parallelepiped must be first translated into a mold, which is designed to be closed and opened without damaging its contents, fabricated out of rigid materials, and lined with powder to prevent the moist clay from sticking to its walls.[43] On the other side, the raw clay must be cleared of impurities (e.g., roots, gravel, sand) and processed (dried, crushed, sifted, wetted, and kneaded) before achieving the homogeneous consistency and paste-like texture required to fill the mold and maintain its shape while drying.[44]

[35] This is what Simondon calls "une ontogénèse *renversée*." Simondon, *ILFI*, 23.

[36] Ibid.

[37] In the original French, "Le dynamisme réel." Ibid., 39.

[38] Ibid., 40. My translation.

[39] Ibid. My translation.

[40] Ibid.

[41] Ibid.

[42] Ibid., 41.

[43] Ibid., 40.

[44] Ibid., 41.

The two half chains (and opposite orientations) that describe the fabrication of a brick mediate between incompatible scales and contexts, preparing each term and establishing protocols for identifying and unlocking the internal potentials in a brick-making ecology. Yet Simondon is keen to demonstrate that these protocols do not follow the overarching directionality of an ecology of inception (the making of a brick), or at least that top-down plans and operations of "embodiment" are inflected by effective structures and orientations at the material and molecular level. In fact, form is not only active in the translation of an abstract parallelepiped, at the scale of the mold, or through the human *in-formation* of a formless material substrate: a successful brick-making operation depends on the colloidal properties of the hydrous aluminum phyllosilicates in the prepared clay, which allow for the molecules in the paste to homogeneously transfer and distribute deformations (the pressing energy of the workman) throughout the mold.[45] The modeled clay is therefore "not only passively deformable" but "actively plastic."[46] It is not subject to arbitrary molecular displacements, but organizes its own plasticity, steering and distributing deformations according to a molecular structure that precedes the encounter with the mold.[47] Not only is the clay actively involved in the brick-making operation (while the mold serves as a mere modulating edge and limit)—it does not depend on it to attain a form.[48]

On one side, Simondon recognizes and vindicates an *implicit* structuring of matter, as well as its role in individuating operations, acknowledging that forms exist at both ends of the technical spectrum, and at various levels and scales.[49] On the other, if matter must be capable of undergoing deformations—if it is "capacity of becoming" as Simondon claims—it must lack a definite (objectual) form, but feature "all forms indefinitely, dynamically."[50] The clay paste must not only be plastic, but able to transfer the pressure exerted by the workman, to propagate it through its mass and fill the mold, thus actualizing the potential energy in the hand–clay–mold system.[51] "The preparation of the raw matter," writes Simondon "has the purpose of rendering the matter homogeneous as a support for a defined potential energy; it is through this potential energy that matter becomes; form becomes not."[52] The homogeneity of the clay paste (its purity) is therefore a condition for its internal communication and "resonance"—for the transmission of forces, not from above or as imposed from the outside, but moved and reverberated across the mass of clay, molecule by molecule.[53] As Jacques Garelli notes, "the good form is no longer a stabilized or fixed form [...] but one rich in energetic potential, charged with transductions to come."[54] Simondon's philosophy will redefine ontogenesis as adhering to the "character of the becoming of being,"[55] and shift the focus of ontology from discrete individual substances to preindividual fields and individuating processes. Yet what interests me here is Simondon's use of the term *hylomorphism*.

As noted above, the philosopher associates hylomorphism with the two individuating terms in Aristotle's philosophy of substance (material

45 Ibid.

46 Ibid.

47 Ibid., 42.

48 Ibid.

49 Ibid., 52.

50 Ibid., 42.

51 Ibid., 43.

52 Ibid., 44. My translation.

53 Ibid.

54 Ibid., 16.

55 In the original French, "Le caractère de devenir de l'être." Ibid., 25. My translation.

cause and formal cause; matter and form) and, more generally, with the supposition that the latter can be imposed from the top-down upon an inert former, and that form only occurs at the level of objects. Acknowledging the "implicit" colloidal structures in the prepared clay neutralizes Aristotle's oppositional understanding of individuation, according to which "a statue (or any other thing that has been shaped) [comes] from shapelessness," and "everything that comes to be or passes away comes from, or passes into, its contrary" or "a product of contraries."[56] Whereas Simondon's account of potential energy and of its expenditure (the fact that it can only be associated with the prepared clay, and not with sand or with the fired brick) refutes a conception of matter as generic and indifferent to specific formal instances and contexts, recognizing the (often irreversible) role played by material transformations at the molecular level, his treatment of physical individuation fails to foreground or reject—as a central feature in Aristotle's hylomorphism—the exclusive association of matter with potentiality and form with actuality. While recognizing that potentials in the clay–mold–hand ecology depend on structures (that is, on actualized forms) at the molecular level—and that matter and form are active across a wide spectrum of scales and not mutually exclusive, and therefore that the distinction between them has little validity—Simondon still maintains a fundamentally hylomorphic view according to which "matter becomes" and "form becomes not."[57] If the preindividual field that necessarily precedes any process of individuation, through preparatory chains in two directions, mediates between an "inter-elementary" and "macro-physical" order that is larger than the individual (the various tools, molds, designs, and workmen in the brick-making ecology), and an "intra-elementary" and "micro-physical" one that is smaller (the aluminum hydro-silicates in the prepared clay) and allows them to communicate, Simondon is chiefly interested in the latter—in the energetic exchanges within the mold.[58]

While the philosopher's stance on biological and psychic individuation will necessitate a more radical approach (the transindividual),[59] his discussion of physical individuation remains predicated on the difference between the preindividual and the individual—one charged with potentials, the other drained of them and unable to change. In other words, whereas the notion of transduction in the living will be characterized by the propagation and preservation of metastability, physical individuation is described alongside a limited trajectory—an actualization involving the progressive exhaustion of potentials towards fixed and stable outputs (the "resolution of a metastable system").[60] In this context, preserving individual end-points (the crystal, the fired brick) automatically implies a degree of hylomorphism—their association with actuality, and an inversely proportional poverty in powers. Furthermore, Simondon's energetic understanding of potentiality recasts matter as "capacity to become";[61] as a vehicle for the translation and mediation of energetic inputs. "Matter is matter because it harbors a positivity that allows it to be modeled," writes Simondon, meaning

56 Aristotle, "Physics," trans. R.P. Hardie and R.K. Gaye, in *The Complete Works of Aristotle*, 10.

57 Simondon, *ILFI*, 44.

58 Ibid., 40.

59 Ibid., 29.

60 Ibid., 26.

61 Ibid., 42.

62 Ibid.

not "undergoing arbitrary displacements, but ordering its own plasticity according to the specific forces that stabilize the deformation."[62] And again:

> For matter to be modeled in its becoming, it must be [...] of a deformable reality, that is to say, a reality that does not have a defined form, but all forms indefinitely, dynamically, because that reality, while possessing inertia and substance, is depositary of force, at least for an instant, and it identifies itself with that force, point by point.[63]

63 Ibid., 42. My translation.

Now, on one side, Simondon's account overcomes an Aristotelian, Platonic, or Pre-Socratic understanding of matter as prime, indefinitely fluid, and indeterminate (what Vilém Flusser aptly describes as "that which is stuffed into forms" and "a filling"),[64] at least insofar as the abstract coupling of matter with potentiality is rendered through a sophisticated understanding of plasticity at the molecular level, and foregrounds the need to consider individuals in association with a specific milieu.[65] On the other side, however, it surrenders to the hylomorphic articulation of potentiality (the ability to change) as directly proportional to a degree of formlessness, or, in other words, to the assumption that the actualization of potentials relies, rather exclusively, on molecular capacities (on pure and homogeneous bodies capable of transferring and translating forces), excluding both objectual capacities and material systems that fail to achieve the requisite degree of (internal) purity; and consigning communication to the ability to speak one or two predetermined languages.

64 Vilém Flusser, *The Shape of Things: A Philosophy of Design* (London: Reaktion, 1999), 22.

65 Simondon, *ILFI*, 24.

Despite his professed dislike of hylomorphism, Simondon preserves the separation between matter (the molecular) and form (the objectual), assigning to matter a privileged role in the ontogenetic process. Tellingly, one finds a similar portrayal in Aristotle's *Physics*:

> when anything has been completely shaped or structured, we do not call it by the name of its material: e.g. we do not call the statue bronze or the candle wax or the bed wood, but we use a paronymous expression and call them brazen, waxen, and wooden respectively. But when a thing has been affected and altered in any way we still call it by the original name: thus we speak of the bronze or the wax being fluid or hard or hot (not only that—we also call the fluid or the hot stuff bronze), giving the matter the same name as the affection.[66]

66 Aristotle, "Physics," 120.

In Aristotle as in Simondon, individuated items are characterized by stasis and inertia, while transformations (being affected or altered; distributing or transferring forces; becoming) naturally pertain to a material domain. Matter is understood as a collection of teleologically charged molecules—a homogeneous and potentialized field rather than an objectual mass or lump. Yet this very distinction, while increasing the material's resolution, is also problematic. To define matter as that which becomes (that which can change) is not only to assume that materials and objects are ontologically different (that there really is a wood separate from the bed, or a bronze detachable from the sculpture, and that bed and sculpture cannot change), but also that *proper* matter is not any matter, but only one kind of matter (a material) that has been prepared for a target ecology or process, purified, and thus potentialized.

Yet, this is not always the case. There is ample evidence of the fact that objects (heterogeneous lumps) do change. The difference between the prepared clay pressed into the mold and a sheet of glass or teapot falling to the ground and shattering into a thousand pieces is not that the force of the pressing hand and that of the impact with the pavement are qualitatively different, or that the two objects are more or less capable of translating energetic encounters. Rather, it depends on whether such operations are technically coded and thus, to a degree, controllable. It is not a question of metastability, but one of obedience.

Following a relational understanding of potentiality, powers can only be set against a specific horizon—they can only be claimed for (or, in accordance with) a given framework, set of relations, or system. There is no doubt that the prepared clay can transfer forces in a way that a sheet of glass cannot, but this is only true in relation to the specific forces and strength exerted by the human hand, or in the context of a brick-making ecology. Both objects, that is, may harbor *other* powers, ones that have nothing to do with energetic exchanges, or with the roles assigned to them in a given ecology.

If EoIs do indeed promote a "mattering" of objects in a Simondonian sense, as a way to install and facilitate translation protocols between disparate items (the tree and the printer, the parallelepiped and mud), this can never mean that such preparations are developed along—or deploy—the only possible communication channels, or that they trigger and unlock altogether new levels of existence. If some channels appear to be more natural, or charged with more potentials, it is only because of the associated eco-socio-technical framings. There is no deep-seated difference between the kicked soccer ball and the pressed clay—objects and molecules, hybrids and homogeneous materials, are equally entitled to powers.

Part II

Hypermaterials

Chapter 3
Purity beyond Nature and Culture: Wildfires, Hypermaterials, and Co-option

3.1 Vitruvian Conflagration

As seen in the previous chapters, a technical *tabula rasa*, by exerting violence upon a pre-existing substrate, unlocks its potentials and funnels them along set trajectories and orientations. As the very notion of *rasura* presupposes a binary system comprising an active term (the biting tooth) and a passive one (the apple), one might be tempted to subsume the actors on the two ends of these cosmetic operations, the agent and the patient, under the broad categories of culture and nature. Indeed, it may be safe to assume that this binary and its many avatars (clean and dirty, organized and disorganized, purposeful and aimless, background and foreground, etc.) are, to some extent, at stake in the technical and poietic systems discussed here.

The treatment of the nature/culture divide by Vitruvius is particularly illuminating. In the *Ten Books on Architecture*, he ascribes the origin of culture and language to deforestation—a wildfire around which men spontaneously gathered and began to socialize.[1] Consistent with the hylomorphic association of potentiality with a lack of form, the ensuing clearing (the absence of trees) opens the forest soil up for a range of possible appropriations, including pasture, agriculture, settlements, and roads. The Vitruvian figure of conflagration establishes potentiality as the ability of culture (the artificial and potentialized glade) to emerge, and as inversely proportional to wilderness (the forest in its uncleared state). Henceforth, the purifying torch of Western society is moved into the realm of proaction, and technologized to either reproduce the interiority of the clearing (cutting implements and fire) or to maintain and protect it (fences, walls, fire pits, traps, etc.) against an unbridled vegetal/animal exterior that threatens to invade and annex it.

Evolved from an animal technology of appropriation (the marking of one's territory)[2] and from localized survival strategies, the labor of staking out, maintaining, and defending social space against centripetal

[1] Vitruvius, *The Ten Books on Architecture*, trans. Morris Hicky Morgan (New York: Dover, 1960).

[2] This insight by Michel Serres will be further discussed in Chapter 6. See Michel Serres, *Malfeasance: Appropriation through Pollution?*, trans. Anne-Marie Feenberg-Dibon (Stanford: Stanford University Press, 2011).

DOI: 10.4324/9781003015444-6

3 Le Corbusier, *Towards a New Architecture*, trans. Frederick Etchells (New York: Dover Publications, 1986), 71.

4 John Locke, *Second Treatise of Government*, ed. and with an introduction by C.B. McPherson (Indianapolis and Cambridge, 1980), sec. 32.

5 Locke, *Second Treatise*, sec. 28. For Locke, it is precisely labor that unlocks ownership: "A man owns whatever land he tills, plants, improves, cultivates, and can use the products of. By his labour he as it were *fences off* the land from all that is held in common." Ibid., sec. 32. However, ownership, once established, requires maintenance. Locke associates the commons (nature, uncultivated land) with a lack of inherent value, and casts the limits of ownership in use value and a continued and diligent *practice*. He writes that "if the grass of his enclosure rotted on the ground, or the fruit of his planting perished without being harvested and stored, this part of the earth was still to be looked on as waste-land that might be owned by anyone else—despite the fact that he had enclosed it." Ibid., sec. 38.

6 Brenna Bhandar writes that, in the context of settler colonialism, for example, "the types of use and possession of land that justified ownership were determined by an ideology of improvement. Those communities who lived as rational, productive economic actors, evidenced by particular forms of cultivation, were deemed to be proper subjects of law and history; those who did not were deemed to be in need of improvement as much as their waste lands were." Brenna Bhandar, *Colonial Lives of Property: Law, Land, and Racial Regimes of Ownership* (Duke University Press, 2018), 8.

7 Le Corbusier, *When the Cathedrals Were White*, trans. Francis E. Hyslop Jr. (New York, Toronto and London: McGraw-Hill Book Company, 1964), 4.

dangers is thus re-articulated negatively, like hollowing out a room (from solid to void) or folding a sock inside-out. From the privileged viewpoint of the clearing, and as seen across the new boundary between inside and outside, the forest can be reduced to a single definition (that which the glade is not) and decoupled from all manner of nuanced experience or animal/mineral/vegetal identity. In fact, differences do not play a significant role in the Vitruvian account—the origin of culture is not sparked by a spontaneous ignition of alterity, or by the differential tension across distant terms, but perpetuated and sustained through the re-enactment of a local mutilation and translation.

While the gradual polarization of these terms into reified (and capitalized) generalities—Nature and Culture—would seem to presuppose two fixed sets of intrinsically different objects, the Vitruvian account shows that their separation is not given and requires a continued and persistent work of differentiation, figures of which persist from the Enlightenment all the way to the Corbusian imposition of "order by means of measurement" upon an untidy forest.[3]

One could perhaps identify three distinct movements in this gradual history, as it is performed in the Western and colonial tradition: the first one enshrines the technical *tabula rasa* with religious virtue, coupling labor (deforestation; the cultivation of land) with a divinely sanctioned right to "subdue the earth," and endowing productivity with the force of a moral mandate.[4]

The second, parallel, movement or *rasura*, the enclosing of land for private ownership, replays the Vitruvian clearing at the level of the individual or family unit, both inventing otherness within the sphere of the social (a kind of human wilderness to be feared and avoided) and intensifying the first movement (property as the domain upon which a proprietor exerts unrestrained control and power). Here, it is still labor that marks "those things off from the rest of the world's contents,"[5] and the imperative to unlock internal potentials—for instance, those pre-approved by patriarchal, Anglo-European or capitalist ecologies—becomes the stick with which humans and nonhumans are measured, and their worth estimated. The bodies perceived to be (and thus made to become) unproductive, or not productive enough, are not only devalued, rejected, or reformed, but also appropriated, enslaved, and destroyed.[6]

Finally, Le Corbusier's defiant attitude towards nature serves as an illustration of how the previous movements (the Aristotelian *tabula rasa*; the Vitruvian clearing; and Locke's unproductive land) are taken up, combined, and normalized. Equating human intervention (or, rather, the actions of *some* humans) with purity and potentiality ("[w]hite, limpid, joyous, clean, clear, and without hesitations")[7] re-configures the Western world to exclude, subjugate, and commodify nonhumans and *other* humans, and redefines agency as qualitatively entangled with the consciousness, projects, and values of the moderns—concealing the persistent and violent *rasurae* required to confirm and canonize such a divide.

Dominique Laporte eloquently elucidates the dynamics at play: "without a master," he writes, "one cannot be cleaned. Purification, whether by fire or by the word, by baptism or by death, requires submission to the law."[8] Similarly, Bruno Latour writes that "[o]rder is extracted not from disorder but from orders."[9] And in this sense, purity is nothing but a corollary of power, and may be wholeheartedly dismissed—the master only claims it for that which he controls, for that which abides by his rules. After all, as Max Liboiron explains, Mary Douglas' "matter out of place" does not only concern the need to remove one's shoes from the dining table, but the very ability to assign dirtiness—and thus, disposability—to a human or nonhuman *other*.[10]

"The category of nature," writes Val Plumwood,

> is a field of multiple exclusion and control, not only of non-humans, but of various groups of humans and aspects of human life which are cast as nature. Thus racism, colonialism and sexism have drawn their conceptual strength from casting sexual, racial and ethnic difference as closer to the animal and the body construed as a sphere of inferiority, as a lesser form of humanity lacking the full measure of rationality or culture.[11]

Yet, whereas purity does not actually flow in the vein of things (it is normatively mapped onto them), powers may. In a psychological framework, for example, one's ability to interact is punctuated and scaffolded by non-neutral encounters with one's environment, scanning it for the ability to be acted upon. This mode of animal interfacing, which involves intentional acts as well as autonomic reactions (what DeLanda refers to as "muscular intelligence"),[12] confirms that potentiality is not within things in the form of independent or intrinsic powers (a man's ability to walk), but unlocked through relations (walking as afforded by the alliance of biological features with a firm ground). It is not truly I who *can* walk or run, but a confederation of muscles, glucose molecules, bones, strands of cartilage, synovial fluids, neural networks, flat pavements, soil compositions, and so on.

De-centering (out-sourcing) potentiality locates it outside a clear-cut animal envelope and within a more fluid network of exchanges, one closely related to James J. Gibson's notion of affordance, and to its overcoming of "the dichotomy of subjective-objective."[13] Therefore, as the potentiality of object A is dependent on another object B, it can only be described as a function of their encounter. And while Gibson was chiefly interested in one-directional exchanges (when an animal meets an environment, what can the environment offer to it?)[14] I am going to endorse a more symmetrical approach: when two objects A and B meet, what can they offer one another? Hereafter, Vitruvius' wildfire will be viewed as potentializing not because it effectuates a *rasura*, burning down the trees, but because it replaces the

8 Dominique Laporte, *History of Shit*, trans. Nadia Benabid and Rodolphe el-Khoury, with an introduction by Rodolphe el-Khoury (Cambridge: MIT Press, 2000), 2.

9 Bruno Latour, *The Pasteurization of France*, trans. Alan Sheridan and John Law (Cambridge and London: Harvard University Press, 1988), 161.

10 Max Liboiron, "Waste Is Not 'Matter out of Place,'" *Discard Studies* (blog), accessed May 23, 2020.

11 Val Plumwood, *Feminism and the Mastery of Nature* (London: Routledge, 2003), 4. This point will be further developed in Chapter 8.

12 Manuel DeLanda, "Homes: Meshwork or Hierarchy?," in *Nomadic Trajectories*, ed. John Sellars (Coventry: Dept. of Philosophy, University of Warwick, 1998), 18.

13 James J. Gibson, *The Ecological Approach to Visual Perception* (New York: Psychology Press, 2011), 129.

14 Gibson, *The Ecological Approach*, 127.

trees with affordances: the ability to warm oneself up by the fire, to scare predators away, and ultimately to repurpose (inhabit/domesticate) the glade.

3.2 Irreductions

My proposed re-booting of potentiality as interactive, as well as the dismissal of built-in purity, owes a great deal to the work of Bruno Latour, master disavower of potency as something innate and inherent. Latour rejects the notion that a human or nonhuman actor could be intrinsically stronger than another—that strength exists in a vacuum. The ground of his ontological cosmology is rather established on the principle that "nothing is, by itself, either reducible or irreducible to anything else"; that there is no strength or weakness, "only trials," only the patient work of actants enlisting one another and building networks from which, collectively and in their relative positions, strength and weakness are performed.[15] To the fundamental injustice and blind teleology of essences and inborn potency, Latour opposes alliances amongst actors that are equally weak, a "democracy extended to things."[16] This does not deny the existence of hierarchies, identities, asymmetries, complex networks, or irreversible transformations, but reveals their formation as ecological (dependent on others) and incrementally wrought.[17] He writes:

> Nothing is by itself ordered or disordered, unique or multiple, homogeneous or heterogeneous, fluid or inert, human or inhuman, useful or useless. Never by itself, always by others. [...] Each weakness distributes a complete range of roles. Depending on what it expects from the others, it distinguishes the stable and the ordered from the shapeless and the moving. But since the others all distribute roles as well, a beautiful tangle ensues. Still, it is comprehensible why entelechies may mistake those they broke down, dismembered, or seduced for shapeless matter.[18]

In other words, there is no such thing as matter without form, or potentiality without actuality; and no such thing as a *tabula rasa*. "No matter how far we go," he continues,

> there are always forms; within each fish there are ponds full of fish. Some believe themselves to be the moulds while others are the raw material, but this is a form of elitism. In order to enroll a force we must conspire with it. It can never be punched out like sheet metal or poured as in a cast.[19]

Matter and form are not categories of reality, but roles reciprocally assigned to one another by networked actants; *equipmental roles*, that is, that can never be allocated in advance of their encounter, nor have

15 Latour, *The Pasteurization of France*, 167–68.

16 Bruno Latour, *We Have Never Been Modern*, trans. Catherine Porter (Cambridge: Harvard University Press, 1993), 12.

17 "No actant is so weak that it cannot enlist another. Then the two join together and become one for a third actant, which they can therefore move more easily. An eddy is formed, and it grows by becoming many others." Latour, *The Pasteurization of France*, 159.

18 Ibid., 161.

19 Ibid.

an ontological grounding of their own. An object cannot *be* matter or form, ordered or disordered, useful or useless, dirty or clean, natural or cultural; it can only *behave* as such in relation to (or as enlisted by) another actant or set of actants. Absolute dualities like nature/culture, matter/form, and human/nonhuman become untenable and are dissipated in favor of subtler and more localized struggles—translations, affinities, associations, and gradients of resistance. The innate powers of the God–King fall to the ground like heavy clothes, replaced by hordes of generals, foot soldiers, and military engineers. And so the boundaries and dividing partitions running across these "strange fabrics"[20] suddenly appear naked, fragile, porous, and movable, starting from our very skin. Is the forest-lung coupling any less human than the functional pairing of kidneys and bone marrow? Is the fish in the pond any more nonhuman than the gut microbiome? Latour's ontology refuses to waste time with such problems, or at least to presume that they could be settled. And while the philosopher does not prohibit the assignment of natural or cultural labels to things, he reminds us that human experience, psychology and habit—and not reality—are the referents of any such labels. This is meant not to signify that pine trees, volcanoes, and tar sands are constructed by conceptual schemes, but that so is their membership in nature—that the term *nature* is coined for affirming or denying purity.

Already in *The Pasteurization of France*, Latour ties purity to the reductionist strength of the modern world,[21] yet it is in *We Have Never Been Modern* that this argument takes center stage, shedding a particularly illuminating light on the problem of the technical *tabula rasa*. While the metaphysics foregrounded in his 1980s texts already proposed the overcoming of pure oppositions and absolute dualisms, effectively demonstrating that nature and society coproduce one another,[22] this later essay aims to uncover the reasons behind their continued success. If there actually aren't, as Harman puts it, "two mutually isolated zones called 'world' and 'human' that need to be bridged by some sort of magical leap,"[23] then why do these zones persist in *our* cultural imagination? And who is responsible for the work that perpetuates and maintains them?

For Latour, the answer rests with modernity (what he calls the "modern constitution"), which establishes and comes to designate two distinct and mutually exclusive sets of practices: on the one hand, the work of translation and mediation (the creation of admixtures, hybrids of nature and culture); on the other, the work of purification, the stacking of all things in two neat ontological piles. And while the success of the moderns relies on both practices, the effectiveness of the latter depends on the clandestinity of the former: it is only by concealing (by not formalizing) the networks that cut across the nature/culture divide, that such a false dichotomy can remain in place and operational. The modern constitution, Latour writes, "*allows for the expanded proliferation of the hybrids whose existence, whose very possibility, it denies.*"[24] It is thus—propelled by an irreducible contradiction—that the moderns become invincible.[25]

20 Ibid., 199.

21 "how did such a rabble of weak, illogical, and vulgar nonbelievers manage to conquer the cohesive and well-policed multitudes? […] They were stronger than the strongest because they arrived *together*. No, better than that. They arrived *separately, each in his place and each with his purity,* like another plague on Egypt." Ibid., 202. "Each group thus lent its strength to the others without admitting it, and therefore claimed to have retained its purity." Ibid., 203.

22 See Bruno Latour, *Science in Action: How to Follow Scientists and Engineers through Society* (Cambridge: Harvard University Press, 1987).

23 Graham Harman, *Prince of Networks: Bruno Latour and Metaphysics* (Melbourne: re.press, 2009), 57.

24 Latour, *We Have Never Been Modern*, 34. Italicized in the original.

25 It is interesting to note that a similar "typically Corbusian self-contradiction" is at play in modern architecture, where, according to Colin Rowe and Fred Koetter, "the pride in objects and the wish to dissimulate pride in this pride, […], is something so extraordinary as to defeat all possibility of compassionate comment." Colin Rowe and Fred Koetter, *Collage City* (Cambridge: MIT Press, 1978), 58.

But how is this paradoxical narrative enforced and embedded within the technical process itself? What mechanisms convince the makers of hybrids, inhabitants of what Latour calls the "Middle Kingdom," that they have access to (and can mobilize) the transcendent poles of Nature and Society? And how do they mistake translating for purifying, and mixing for separating?

My suspicion is that the translation software in the modern operating system does not only steer the natural object towards a cultural *telos* (towards an ecology of inception), but automatically transports it across ontological realms, transcoding a nonhuman format (a tree, a cow) into a human one (timber, beef).[26] This movement, which drains the "raw" object of any natural content and reassigns it fully to culture, is responsible for neutralizing hybridity in the very moment of its production; for rendering it unthinkable. Re-coded and re-appropriated, the tree and the cow become unrecognizable, even to the logger and butcher who fell and slaughtered them.[27] The modern magician is not afraid of revealing the secrets of his trade precisely because his tricks will continue to mesmerize and induce the opaque trance of inexplicability: the spectator's eyes will still be drawn to the flamboyant arm gestures and wand movements. A "magical leap" indeed occurs, which instead of adapting the natural object along a continuous flow of transformations, resulting in what Latour and Serres call a quasi-object,[28] resets it to a new (cultural) beginning, a new entity, rebranded as wholly human.

3.3 Material Hyperobjects

3.3.1

The technical *tabula rasa* is, of course, this modern transcoding apparatus, which attributes purity (cultural homogeneity) where there is none. It is not a *rasura* in the sense of erasure or destruction (of actual formlessness), but of categorization and cosmetic re-appropriation. Nature is not entirely overcome, only redressed. By re-starting the object from scratch, by re-naming it, by shedding its particular qualities and changing it into a generic (albeit quantifiable) lump, and by turning its hylomorphic switch from formal to material, modernity doesn't only replace it with a cultural artifact; it also links it up to a well that feeds directly into Nature—a distant, homogenous, stable, and continuous entity, as far as possible from the trials of the Middle Kingdom. The single tree drowns in the pile of material under the *wood* or *lumber* denomination, losing all singularity, all circumstantial interconnectivity. And even the slab of timber is nothing but the local expression of an extended material stream, a spring surfacing from a network of subterranean rivers. In other words: when the moderns fell a tree, not only do they remove it from a localized sylvan network;[29] they also endow it with a degree of universality—with the gift of ubiquity. It is by cutting down the natural tree while simultaneously universalizing it in Nature, that the moderns can culturalize it without the embarrassment of denying its obviously nonhuman origin.

26 I should note that what interests me here are not names per se—the word "tree" is as reductive as the word "timber"—but the networks of ecological interaction (industrial, artisanal, artistic, et cetera) that these denominations mobilize and unlock.

27 This contributes, for instance, to the invisibility of the violence associated with extraction.

28 A quasi-object resists assimilation into either nature or culture, a humanist or anti-humanist camp, remaining instead grounded in (and integral to) the work of coproduction. See Michel Serres, "Theory of the Quasi-Object," in *The Parasite*, trans. Lawrence R. Schehr (Baltimore: Johns Hopkins University Press, 1982), 224–34. See also Latour, *We Have Never Been Modern*, 51–55.

29 I am referring in particular to the work of Suzanne Simard, who demonstrated that mycorrhizas form subterranean networks through which the trees in a forest communicate and exchange resources. Suzanne Simard, *Finding the Mother Tree* (New York: Alfred A. Knopf, 2021).

Hacking Timothy Morton's felicitous term, one could call these rivers, these universal avatars and placeholders, *material hyperobjects*, in the sense that they maintain object-status (a sort of ideal unity) despite being wildly distributed in time and space (the global materials economy).[30] Their defining feature is not a lack of qualities, as was the case with the Greek *apeiron*, but their generalization and standardization, which averages values into tabulated spreadsheets and engineering manuals—from things to data, from stuff to mathematics. When the architect specifies red cedar, larch, or oak for a project, it is these values and sets of abstract properties and parameters (e.g., color, density, texture, grain, durability, elasticity, compressive strength), which are independent of and precede any particular log or tree, that she mobilizes and invokes. During the harvest, and across future woodworking chains, these abstract qualities are projected back onto the tree, appropriating and culturalizing it by reduction. Yet these lists render the tree with the same accuracy and sophistication with which a passport or clinical chart describes a person—at embarrassingly low resolutions.

30 Timothy Morton, *Hyperobjects: Philosophy and Ecology after the End of the World* (Minneapolis: University of Minnesota Press, 2013).

3.3.2

The principle of verification by reproduction informing State science [...] requires that experimental results be reproduced independent of circumstances; within the parameters set by controlled variables, the same result will always occur, no matter when, where, or by whom the experiments are conducted. The theorematic power of State science is achieved by isolating its experimental operations from any particular conditions "on the ground" at a specific time, thereby making its results appear eternal and universal.
Eugene W. Holland, *Deleuze and Guattari's A Thousand Plateaus*[31]

31 Eugene W. Holland, *Deleuze and Guattari's A Thousand Plateaus: A Reader's Guide* (London and New York: Bloomsbury Academic, 2013), chap. 3, E-book.

Design practice remains largely grounded in the hylomorphic and essentialist rule of hypermaterial purity. The Word still precedes the flesh ("And the Word became flesh and dwelt among us," John 1:14), and matter is still summoned into existence by desire or command—the forceful yet generous "let there be" of Genesis. Materiality is not ignored wholesale—the modern designer does indeed revise and adjust her intents by interrogating material properties and constraints, yet these are rarely punctuated or inflected by positive or situated encounters, or by the particular objects under consideration. In the majority of cases, materials remain relegated to paraphrase and approximation, and knowable from a distance. Only hypermaterials ever come into focus; only the disciplined, nonlocal, unmoored objects certified by the modern constitution and by its industrial emissaries—in the guise of product inventories, price lists, manufacturer's specifications, online catalogues, brochures, downloadable CAD blocks, construction standards, advertisements, performance certifications, and building materials directories. Indeed, as Katie Lloyd Thomas has shown, since the expansion of mass manufacturing during the 1930s, architects have increasingly assumed the role of shoppers.[32]

32 Katie Llyod Thomas, "The Architect as Shopper: Women, Electricity, Building Products and the Interwar 'Proprietary Turn' in the UK," in *Architecture and Feminisms: Ecologies, Economies, Technologies*, eds. Hélène Frichot, Catharina Gabrielsson, and Helen Runting (London and New York: Routledge, 2018), 54–65.

33 Katie Lloyd Thomas, "Building Materials: Conceptualising Materials via the Architectural Specification," PhD diss., (Middlesex University, 2010), 74.

34 Katie Lloyd Thomas, "Specifications: Writing Materials in Architecture and Philosophy," *Architectural Research Quarterly* 8, no. 3–4 (December 2004): 277–83.

35 Lloyd Thomas, "Specifications," 282–83.

36 Lloyd Thomas, "Building Materials," 183.

37 Ibid., 105.

38 In his study of technical evolution, having recognized a certain proximity in the elementary methods and tools used to transform different kinds of materials, André Leroi-Gourhan similarly decides to "abandon matter itself to retain only its properties in a state of processing." André Leroi-Gourhan, *L'homme et la matière: évolution et techniques* (Paris: Éditions Albin Michel, 2013), 161, 320.

Yet, it is Lloyd Thomas' work on the architectural specification (the written, contractual document that describes the products and materials to be used in a project, and the associated workmanship) that is of interest to the present discussion. Lloyd Thomas is concerned with operating a distinction between the generic term *matter* and the specific properties of *materials* as involved in engineering, manufacturing, procurement and construction processes, rejecting the view that the latter is merely a particular instance of the former.[33] Whereas architectural discourse has tended to regard matter as dependent on form (as the hatch between the lines in a drawing), the diverse range of sections, clauses, and definitions in the architectural specification account for the stubborn particularity of materials, for their nongeneric properties, and for the different sets of recipes, fabrication processes, testing regimes, and functional roles they inform and contribute to.[34] By reading the architectural specification—by taking it seriously—Lloyd Thomas finds an "alternative means of defining materiality" in architecture, one that "reveals that the materials of buildings are themselves cultural constructs" steeped in socio-technical and economic histories, and "produced through their place in the building process," rather than "existing prior to it."[35]

Expanding on Simondon's account of technical individuation, and resolving the hylomorphic biases identified in the previous chapter, Lloyd Thomas understands building materials as constituted by the preparatory chains that potentialize raw substrates toward specific processes, interactions, and behaviors.[36] For her, a material—be it Simondon's prepared clay, concrete mixed *in situ*, or the float glass in insulated glazing units—is matter that has been readied, and has therefore attained a degree of metastability. On one side, this makes it hard to conceive of materials in isolation, without the wider systems—physical and extra-physical—that drive their mobilization in the construction of buildings. On the other, however, these very systems are responsible for translating embodied materials into abstract hypermaterials. In fact, the specification formats Lloyd Thomas analyzes—the process-based clause and the performance clause—point precisely towards such translations. In the former, as in Holland's quotation at the beginning of this section, materials are replaced by recipes and step-by-step descriptions (for example, of how to mix or pour concrete on site), and "produced in such a way that a body of knowledge can be built up about them which appears universal, and in such a way that they are suited to mass production."[37] In the latter, materials are instead described on the basis of their projected performance and behaviors (of what they can do; of herding instructions), and are produced—or undergo modifications—in order to address specific problems.[38]

Systems of functional or co-functional reference also extend to a product's installation; to uses that are projectively encoded, scripted, and warrantied. Families of compatible modules and parts are linked through predetermined grammars and syntaxes. [**Figure 3.1**] Graphic

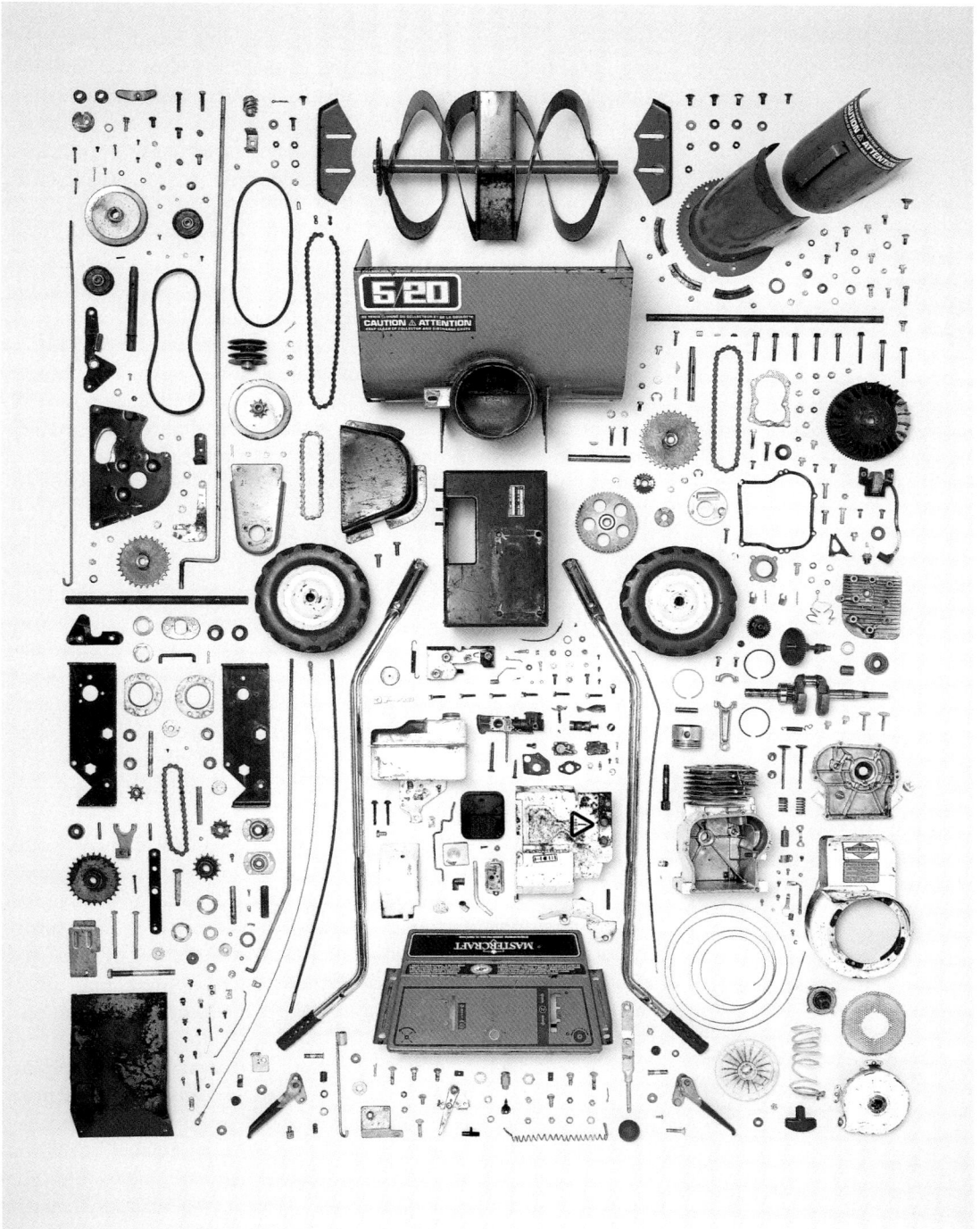

Figure 3.1 Todd McLellan, *Things Come Apart, Disassembled Snow Blower*, 2013.

representations of wall assemblies detail the overlapping of products, the endorsed layering of vapor barriers, insulation boards, waterproofing membranes, flashing strips, and copings. Overlaps and combinations are themselves branded, certified, guaranteed as durable and pure, standardized, and recommended: the spacing between wall studs in a gypsum board drywall; the chemical bond between primer and paint; the rubber gaskets between pressure caps, mullions, and glazing units; the optimal geometry and relative positioning of drip edges, weep holes, and brackets; the intumescent coating sprayed on structural steel; the sloping angles of sills and roofing elements; the depth of air cavities between panes of glass; the increased environmental performance of low emissivity coatings and ceramic fritting; and so on.

Each product and material is supplied within the virtual orbit of a construction system, as part of either a proprietary ecology spread across components and product lines, or sets of predefined standards, metrics, and established practices. A missing natural context (the networks undone by the Vitruvian fire) is thus substituted by an artificial hypercontext, which catalyzes more *rasurae*, and the continued proliferation of products, and extraction of raw materials.

Samples also belong to this rarefied ecology, as limbs excised from a larger, invisible hyperbody—half relics and half laboratory specimens. Used to represent and control the aesthetic qualities of materials like stone, fabric, leather, and glass (or rather, to stand in for all other instances of these objects), they embody a kind of exponential materiality, of which they are at once discrete illustrations and multiplicands. Yet they can only survive in the controlled and pure environments that frame and perpetuate their ideal alliances; once the 5" x 5" marble tile cracks, the aluminum plate gets scratched, and the swatch yellows, access to the hyperuranion and its inhabitants is promptly interdicted.

Hypermaterials don't play by the rules of the physical, living world. Their reality belongs to numbers, averages, and Platonic solids, chemical formulas, templates, recipes, folk stories, Euclidean geometries, social contracts, bank statements, historical archives, and ticked boxes. The clay, stone, and concrete they encode know nothing of adjacency, growth, decay, and symbiosis; of efflorescence, moisture, and rot; of intensive concentrations of sodium chloride and sulfur; of humidity, dryness, and mildew; of structural collapse; of the gradual deposition of dust, soot, and pollution; of solar radiation and sintering; of delamination, peeling paint, and termite infestations; of biofouling, lichens, and mosses. They ignore the breath of stuff—its fragility and tendency to squirm, quiver, degrade, weather, erode, reappropriate, transform, and recombine. Hypermaterials participate in a naive materialism: the assumption that at some (deeper and more fundamental) level, matter is unchangeable; that its transitions are nothing but superficial effects (or, in other words, that materials can exist in the absence of a medium, context, or environment).

Perhaps the continued success of hypermaterials has to do with their ability to fade out of sight. As with most of the invincible tricks of modernity, as soon as a hypermaterial is embodied locally and re-contextualized (as soon as it appears), it immediately disappears, leaving in its place a mere substance or object.

3.4 Nonlocal Approximations

The emergence of material hyperobjects may have philosophical roots in Plato's separation of Ideas (Forms) from the sensible things that *participate* in them—the former being eternal and unchangeable, the latter being transient and mutable. While Anaximander's *apeiron* resolved the problem of decay and degradation by returning objects to a kind of universal compost, Plato proposes a different kind of transcendent solution, one that immortalizes things through their differences and similarities. The tree is no longer just a sensible object in the world (this tree), but an abstract essence shared by all trees, and, importantly, one that can be understood and communicated in the absence of a positive/situated encounter. This rift is then made operational (adoptable) by Aristotle, who describes substances as composite sets of definitions (*logoi*) that reveal and compose their essence.

A number of fixed properties come to identify the make-up of a certain species or object, allowing both for fluctuations in secondary attributes (this is granite regardless of whether it is polished, honed, or flamed) and for internal gradients within set orientations (for instance, a human embryo passing through the different stages of development, from plant-like living thing to animal to individual human being).[39] It is critical to highlight here the term *internal*, because essentialist transformations always occur within a precise spectrum—the natural body of the species—and without crossing what Montgomery Furth usefully designates as "migration barriers."[40] Purity is a necessary ingredient in the essentialist recipe, attained and attended to by limiting and rendering stable the horizon of possible predications allowable under a distinct genus or species. But if the essence of a thing can only be revealed or confirmed within a set and circumscribed range of migrations (jumps across species or classes, such as in the forbidden creatures of *Leviticus*, are prohibited),[41] a measure of care—the tracing of boundaries, as well as a maintenance or enforcement plan—must be introduced; an *essentialist practice*, capable of averting the dangers of disorder and hybridization; capable of, following Mary Douglas' formula, keeping matter in its place.

Essences, in other words, do not have absolute validity in the way that Plato's ideal forms did, as metaphysically deeper than the sensible world. For Aristotle, reality fundamentally rests with primary substances—with beings that cannot be either in other beings or predicated of them; with the stuff of this world.[42] If primary substances (Socrates the man) do indeed belong to universal categories (human beings in general) that

39 Aristotle, *On the Generation of Animals*, trans. Arthur Platt, vol. Book II, accessed 30 May 2020, sec. 3.

40 Montgomery Furth, *Substance, Form, and Psyche: An Aristotelean Metaphysics* (Cambridge and New York: Cambridge University Press, 1988), 121.

41 Douglas writes: "the underlying principle of cleanness in animals is that they shall conform fully to their class. Those species are unclean which are imperfect members of their class, or whose class itself confounds the general scheme of the world. [...] In the firmament two-legged fowls fly with wings. In the water scaly fish swim with fins. On the earth four-legged animals hop, jump or walk. Any class of creatures which is not equipped for the right kind of locomotion in its element is contrary to holiness." Mary Douglas, *Purity and Danger: An Analysis of Concepts of Pollution and Taboo* (London and New York: Routledge, 2002), 69.

42 Aristotle, *Categories*, trans. E.M. Edghill, The Internet Classics Archive, accessed April 14, 2019. See also Paul Studtmann, "Aristotle's Categories," in *The Stanford Encyclopedia of Philosophy*, ed. Edward N. Zalta, accessed December 23, 2020.

are characterized by essential features (rationality), these categories or "secondary substances" must be verified and validated experimentally—human beings must confirm their essential rationality (and, therefore, their humanity) by continuing to act rationally. In view of this essentialist regime, one could perhaps re-articulate the aims of technology as describing not a neutral "extension of man," but rather the preservation of secondary substances, and the retracing of normative maps and networks that perform and reverse-engineer categories, fulfilling their prophesies. It is this tension between primary and secondary substances—between a particular object and the active shadow cast on it by its universal counterparts—that can be seen as grounding modern hypermateriality as a practice that replaces things with lists of attributes and behaviors.

The attribution of purity depends not only on regimes of enforcement and compliance, but on ones of generalization and decreased resolution (on the sharing—and privileging—of common traits). Abstraction (the flight from primary to secondary substances) facilitates the acquisition of characteristics that are assumed to equally describe all members of a given category. The boundaries drawn around secondary substances therefore designate zones of equivalence, transforming particular objects (and their qualitative differences) into eminently exchangeable quantities. Henri Lefebvre writes that abstract space, "bound up as it is with exchange […] depends on consensus more than any space before it."[43] And hypermaterials could indeed be understood as the *consensus-materials* required to lubricate and fuel exchange and mass production at a global scale. In this sense, they serve two functions in a capitalist society: on one side, they build bridges across physical (embodied) materials and their smooth (abstract) avatars, converting situated objects into commodities to be used and exchanged (or, in Karl Marx's terms, translating natural forms into value forms);[44] on the other, they obscure the object's material history, and the source of its value (the labor incorporated within it), blurring all manner of emplaced (social and environmental) relations. "Exchangeable on the market," writes Jane Hutton, "a commodity is equivalent to like-things from elsewhere: wheat is wheat, stone is stone, regardless of vastly different labor conditions or environmental consequences."[45]

Whereas currency merely defines comparable units of exchange, hyperobjectivity permeates the objects themselves, reducing them to generic meshes upon which value points can be easily mapped, from a distance. To each node in the mesh correspond ready-to-plot, average datasets: appearance, properties, and behaviors.

A bag of sand will be measured by weight and described in terms of the average size, shape, and composition of its particles, which determines the appropriate use.[46] To the eyes of the architects designing a concrete frame, or even to those of the workmen mixing aggregates on site, the lands and conditions associated with the mining and dredging of sand (the scarring of riverbeds; the damaging of fisheries, livelihoods, and ecosystems; the working conditions of miners) will have been rendered invisible.[47]

43 Henri Lefebvre, *The Production of Space*, trans. Donald Nicholson-Smith (Malden: Blackwell, 2011), 57.

44 Karl Marx, *Capital: Volume One.*, trans. Samuel Moore and Edward Aveling (Ware: Wordsworth Editions Ltd, 2013), 87.

45 Jane Hutton, *Reciprocal Landscapes: Stories of Material Movements* (Abingdon and New York: Routledge, 2020), 6.

46 Raymond Siever, *Sand*, Scientific American Library Series, no. 24 (New York: Scientific American Library, 1988).

47 See, for example: Fred Pearce, "The Hidden Environmental Toll of Mining the World's Sand," *Yale Environment 360*, February 5, 2019; Vince Beiser, "Why the World Is Running out of Sand," *BBC Future*, November 18, 2019.

Yet, the issue for designers is not only one of visibility—or, following Lloyd Thomas, of understanding materials as complex socio-technical systems, rather than neutral or natural lumps of stuff. Our challenge is not—or at least, not only—to search for "sustainable" or "ethical" concrete aggregates, replacing cement with fly ash or ground plastic. The question is rather: what would doing away with hypermaterials entail? Could architects and designers refuse to sustain the extraction- and growth-dependent material economies of late capitalism? If embodied materials (a *tabula plena*) were foregrounded as the starting point of design potentials, how would our methods, laws, infrastructures, and value forms—and indeed, our material ecologies—change?

3.5 Nomadic Encounters

> The ground-level plane of the Gothic journeyman is opposed to the metric plane of the architect, which is on paper and off site. The plane of consistency or composition is opposed to another plane, that of organization or formation. Stone cutting by squaring is opposed to stone cutting using templates, which implies the erection of a model for reproduction.
>
> Gilles Deleuze and Félix Guattari, *A Thousand Plateaus*[48]

A compilation of designs sampled from prehistoric times up to modernity (from the Neolithic spearhead to the kitchen appliance) would display an increasing disregard of natural objects in favor of cultural motives, and describe a progressive shift towards abstraction and hylomorphism, in the Simondonian sense of a mark impressed from the outside over generic, inert matter (or, as articulated by Deleuze and Guattari, of the full assignment of matter to content and of form to expression).[49] To design before the advent and codification of material hyperobjects—prior to the invention of "raw matter"; to the universalization and standardization of glass, concrete, aluminum, and steel; or to the development of industrial processes for their extraction, manufacturing, and distribution, or of a strict division of labor—would have required a direct exchange and active collaboration with one's material surroundings; a careful surveying of spatially and temporally situated affordances, which would necessarily inform and orient the design and fabrication process. The object's nongeneric qualities would steer the craftsman's aspirations: a pointy rock towards weaponry, a shell towards carrying liquids, a soft wood towards carving, et cetera. The technical know-how of the craftsman would grow alongside opportunistic adaptations to locally gathered resources, ones either found through chance encounters or purposefully sought out in the environment. No design could occur remotely, or be thinkable outside of a precise material context or contingent relational fabric. And while the progressive distance between goods and their site of harvest, fabrication, and consumption—and the corresponding degeneration of forms into averaged and approximated matters—have, in the global economy,

48 Deleuze and Guattari, *A Thousand Plateaus*, 368.

49 Ibid., 369.

increasingly excluded embodied materials from an active design role, this separation is by no means natural, given, or the clear mark of progress.

Anthropologist Tim Ingold postulates two ways of making: co-optive and constructive.[50] In the former—for example, when a flat stone is co-opted to become a hammer and used to knock in a nail—"things can be made without undergoing any actual physical alteration at all."[51] Sara Ahmed explains that when birds nest in a postbox, one learns something about its shape. "We learn about form," she writes,

> when a change in function does not require a change in form. Different uses of the same thing change how we refer to the thing: a *who* change as a *what* change. When the postbox becomes a nest, it ceases to be a postbox. [...] Something is what it provides or enables, which is how what something 'is' can fluctuate without changing anything at the level of physical form.[52]

When surveying embodied materials, one doesn't encounter a raw matter, but the potential of forms—of the uses they could afford, with minimal effort or energy. Seventeenth-century boat-builders surveyed forests in search of ready-made tree shapes suitable for becoming ship knees and frames.[53] [**Figure 3.2**] More recently, a similar approach was adopted by the students and tutors in the Design + Make program at the Architectural Association. The *Wood Chip Barn* at Hooke Park in Dorset, United Kingdom, was developed by surveying the naturally occurring forks in the trees surrounding the site, and, after selecting the most suitable ones, by using them to fabricate trusses. [**Figures 3.3-3.6**] The arching structure of the barn exemplifies a co-optive or exaptive design paradigm. Each beech tree maintains a precise and localized identity, one that cannot be reduced to a generic wood hypermaterial, or to the average orientation of grains and fibers. Rather, the differences between particular trees, tree sections, and crotches are carefully identified and analyzed. Instead of reformatting the tree—of transforming it into abstract and homogeneous timber elements for future bending or joining—the project repurposes the existing tree junctions, taking advantage of their localized shapes, grain patterns, and strength.[54] Martin Self writes that "if the loading condition within a structure matches the forces that a component was subjected to when it was part of a tree, it will have a grain arrangement that is preoptimized as a structural joint."[55]

The project can exploit the irregular geometries of the trees, the anisotropic properties of timber, and the moment-resisting capacities of the beech forks, because its materials are not purified and standardized for the global marketplace, but surveyed *in situ*, and harvested for specific uses and users.[56] Indeed, affordances only emerge as a function of encounters—the chair is not "sit-on-able" without human buttocks, and the postbox only becomes a nest when occupied by birds.

50 Tim Ingold, *The Perception of the Environment: Essays on Livelihood, Dwelling & Skill* (London and New York: Routledge, 2000), 175. I will further elaborate on notions of co-option and exaption in Chapter 7.

51 Ingold, *The Perception of the Environment*, 175. Surprisingly, for Ingold this image exemplifies the mistaken assumption that "the essence of making lies in the self-conscious authorship of design," rather than a blurring of the distinction between design and use (building and dwelling).

52 Sara Ahmed, *What's the Use? On the Uses of Use* (Durham: Duke University Press, 2019), 34–35.

53 Charles Jencks and Nathan Silver, *Adhocism: The Case for Improvisation* (Cambridge: MIT Press, 2013), 16.

54 Duncan Slater and Roland Ennos, "Interlocking Wood Grain Patterns Provide Improved Wood Strength Properties in Forks of Hazel (*Corylus Avellana* L.)," *Arboricultural Journal* 37, no. 1 (2 January 2015): 21–32, quoted in Martin Self, "Hooke Park: Applications for Timber in Its Natural Form," in *Advancing Wood Architecture: A Computational Approach*, ed. Tobias Schwinn and Oliver David Krieg (London and New York: Routledge, 2017), 150.

55 Self, "Hooke Park," 150.

56 Architectural Association, "Design & Make: 2014–15: Wood Chip Barn," *AA 2016* (blog), accessed December 29, 2020. See also: "Wood Chip Barn," Hooke Park, accessed May 31, 2020.

Figure 3.2 Plate 103, *Encyclopédie Méthodique Marine*, 1798. The naturally occurring curvatures in trees are mapped for their potential use in shipbuilding.

In this case, there is no doubt that the logging industry could potentialize the properties shared by all trees, and mobilize them in timber construction—yet only a recognition of the differences between trees, of their irregularities and nonconformities, can fully attend to their structural potential. Besides, the *Wood Chip Barn* demonstrates that a co-opting ethos is not relegated to spontaneous and unthinking hacks (Ingold's rock-as-hammer), nor can it only change items that, like discarded rotor blades, old windows, and obsolete grain silos, have run their equipmental course. Rather, if co-option (exaptive design) is to be taken seriously, it must be understood as capable of investing all manner of objects with a measure of design consideration and intelligence, and of informing and steering all manner of constructive acts.

If one manages to avoid an evolutionist gaze, and resist the urge to belittle co-option as primitive and rudimentary (and, indeed, the *Wood Chip Barn* was developed using sophisticated 3D-scanning technology, evolutionary optimization software, and robotic fabrication)—if one refrains from instinctively ridiculing the naive builders scouting the forest for twigs, or firing bricks on site—one might recognize that their wandering follows a smooth and *nomadic* trajectory, in Deleuze and Guattari's sense of both losing one's bearings (the disorienting and serendipitous effects of deterritorialization)[57] and resisting the top-down

57 See Andrew Ballantyne, *Deleuze and Guattari for Architects* (London and New York: Routledge, 2007), 38.

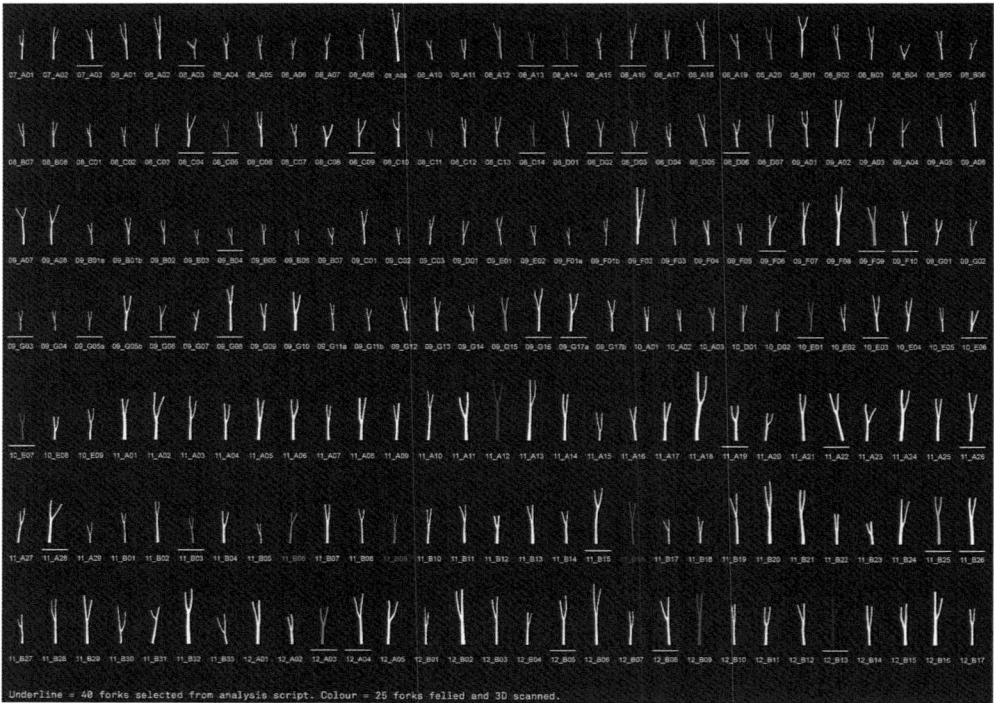

Figure 3.3 Zachary Mollica, Architectural Association, *Wood Chip Barn*, Hooke Park, Dorset, UK, 2016. Survey of forked components.

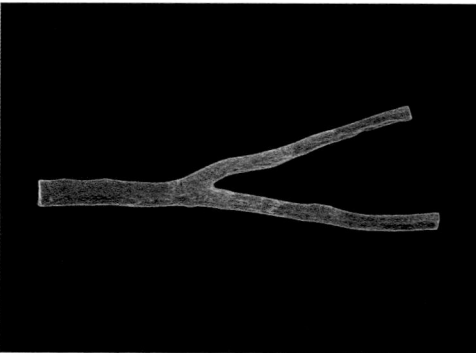

Figure 3.4 Zachary Mollica, Architectural Association, *Wood Chip Barn*, Hooke Park, Dorset, UK, 2016. Scan of a single fork.

impositions of regimes and apparatuses (political, economic, legal, scientific, disciplinary, etc.) that appropriate by limiting and annexing, internalizing and ordering, measuring and stabilizing. As the nomad's milieu is one of exteriority—the "war machine" resists assimilation by (or the installation of) stable powers—so does the nomadic designer push against the protocols of "pure" design practice and hypermateriality, inhibiting the ossification of properties and roles, and replacing the imposition of preconceived forms (the hylomorphic cookie cutter) and of economic orthodoxies with the openness and fluidity of chance encounters and material interactivity. On-site, physical contact becomes not only required and generative (the straight line cannot exist without rectification), but also, crucially, a precondition for design.

These supposedly primitive (preindustrial, precapitalist, prereproductive) methods resist the foreclosure of materials within the bounds of ideas and purity, allowing them to precede (and recede from) meanings, functions, and the adherence to preestablished scripts. The question

Figure 3.5 Valerie Bennett, Architectural Association, *Wood Chip Barn*, Hooke Park, Dorset, UK, 2016. Interior view of primary structure.

is not whether buildings could actually be erected from materials found on site (mud, sand, rocks?), or whether the approaches developed at Hooke Park could be actually scaled up and adopted more widely, but whether materiality could (re)become contextual; whether the very notion of site—as that which is surveyed at the outset of an architectural project—could be expanded to include existing structures and locally available building materials.

It is not by chance that, in the quote at the beginning of this section, Deleuze and Guattari counterpose their nomadic hero, the Gothic journeyman, to the figure of the architect. While the stone cutter abandons Euclidean geometry for "an operative logic of movement" whereby the "cutting line propels the equation,"[58] one that favors corporeality, immanence, and on-site experimentation against hylomorphism, the architect remains faithful to the "primacy of the fixed model of form, mathematical figures, and measurement,"[59] one that can be imposed from a distance. Yet, to issue orders remotely is to unbridle their powers—to admit that on-site conditions are irrelevant, while also foreclosing the ability to effectively respond or adapt to them.

Figure 3.6 Evgenia Spyridonos, Architectural Association, *Wood Chip Barn*, Hooke Park, Dorset, UK, 2016. 6-axis robotic arm transforming fork.

58 Deleuze and Guattari, *A Thousand Plateaus*, 364.

59 Ibid., 365.

75

3.6 Material Context vs. Design Context

When commissioned to design a new building, the architect agrees upon a program, a set of objectives and aspirations, a budget, and a site (often a vacant plot). The site, the only element that—in a typical brief, and in the pragmatic context of the architectural profession—exceeds the terms of the commission, is surveyed and investigated to ground decisions and weave the project, which would otherwise remain on paper, into existing social, environmental, and infrastructural fabrics—building regulations, community benefit clauses, transportation networks, utility lines, topography, climate data, views, drainage, the direction of the sun, and so on. The information thus collected, and its presentation in maps, soil boring tests, zoning diagrams, interview transcripts, utility plans, photographs, and a range of other documents, inform design proposals that address the client's expectations while also delineating the architect's own "creative agenda." The latter—the so-called *architectural intent*—combines conceptual underpinnings and disciplinary ambitions with the architect's *habitus* (her authorial preferences and proclivities).

What transpires from this ordinary—if oversimplified—sequence of events is that architectural intents—the ideas, purposes, and aims associated with the design of a building—precede even the most feeble and preliminary engagement with materiality. Largely absent from a project's groundwork and from site surveying procedures, materials enter the design stage only as a means to translate, declare, or fulfill intents: a wide-spanning overhang might invoke the use of reinforced concrete or steel; a desire to visually connect interior rooms with out-of-doors spaces might call for large glazed surfaces and extruded aluminum mullions; the acoustics in a triple-height atrium might require sound-absorbing materials such as perforated timber panels and upholstered furniture. Materials (or, rather, their projected effects) are selected on the basis of their adherence to the architect's intentions. Their purity is measured in compliance, in the fidelity of their appearance or performance to an architectural or engineering script.

The fact that ambitions precede materiality might seem reasonable—how do you begin to discuss *how* something will be built if you don't know *what* that something is? Yet this apparently uncontroversial position disguises a predilection for novelty, control, and individual authorship: the assumption that *how* and *what* can never coincide, and that the act of designing and that of finding reside at opposite ends of the creative spectrum (or, in other words, that the creativity of a human or nonhuman "other" is not worth considering as such). Furthermore, it assumes that materials are universal and equidistant, mass produced and smoothly exchangeable across the globe—forgetting the diverse and uneven geographical, climatic, social, and political conditions surrounding their production, and that their metastability (in Lloyd Thomas' extended sense) depends, in the best of cases, on local knowledges, skills, and traditions.[60]

60 I am thinking particularly of the exemplary non-Western and Indigenous technologies and tectonic inventions presented in Julia Watson and Wade Davis, *Lo-Tek: Design by Radical Indigenism* (Taschen, 2020) as compared, for example, to the deskilling of labor imposed by the modernist adoption of reinforced concrete, as described in Sérgio Ferro, "Concrete as Weapon," trans. Silke Kapp and Alice Fiuza, and with an introduction by Silke Kapp, Katie Lloyd Thomas, and João Marcos de Almeida Lopes, *Harvard Design Magazine*, Fall/Winter 2018. Skills are, of course, indispensable for reuse. Susan Strasser writes that "[f]ixing and finding uses for worn and broken articles entail a consciousness about materials and objects that is key to the process of making things to begin with. Repair ideas come more easily to people who make things. If you know how to knit or do carpentry, you also understand how to mend a torn sweater or repair a broken chair." Susan Strasser, *Waste and Want: A Social History of Trash* (New York: Owl Books, 2000), 12. Similarly, Steven J. Jackson asks: "Can breakdown, maintenance, and repair confer special epistemic advantage in our thinking about technology? Can the fixer know and see different things—indeed, different worlds—than the better-known figures of 'designer' and 'user'?" Steven J. Jackson, "Rethinking Repair," in *Media Technologies: Essays on Communication, Materiality, and Society*, ed. Tarleton Gillespie, Pablo J. Boczkowski, and Kirsten A. Foot, Inside Technology (Cambridge: The MIT Press, 2014), 229.

Against a materiality that is fully subordinated to the desires and aspirations of a project's stakeholders, and against Leon Battista Alberti's bias towards the "lineaments" of buildings—the idea that lines and angles define a project's form and appearance "without any recourse to the material"[61]—I propose here a different notion of contextuality that is not exhausted by harvesting data towards effective or even thoughtful decision-making, but is, perhaps more crudely, engaged with sourcing a building's very bricks and mortar. The pragmatic privileging of a *design context* predicated on the acquisition of information and on decisions does not preclude the possibility of a *material context* predicated on encounters.

Indeed, the rift between site and material survey, the Albertian architect and the medieval master-builder, designing and making or finding, produces two distinct and qualitatively different conceptions of site-specificity. Both expand the significance of *site* and *context* beyond the mere boundaries of a plot: while the former—the *design context*—includes the constraints, pressures, flows, and networks affecting a site and its development, the latter—the *material context*—corresponds with the stuff out of which the building will be constructed.[62] Again, this is not limited to the mud, rocks, or bricks presumably found on the premises, or even to existing buildings or materials, but encompasses an expansive survey of *localized* and codesigning substrates; of objects that are emplaced (nongeneric, experienceable, physically present on a specific site) and predate the design process, which they help to steer and orientate. Based on this expanded notion of context, one might describe reuse and repurposing as the operations that endow materials with the ability to propose and impose their own lineaments.

Yet, the difference between a design context and a material one cannot be reduced to the neat distinction between a goal-oriented and a means-oriented design approach, or between use and reuse.[63] Rather, it promotes a more nuanced understanding of how the scope of the terms *reuse* and *repurposing* changes in different settings. In a design context, they might refer to interior design or "adaptive reuse" projects that rehabilitate existing buildings by combining them with new material layers and volumes—ones that are not necessarily reused or repurposed.[64] For the sake of a more precise set of labels, I will refer to these cases as instances of *design reuse* or *design repurposing*. One such example is Anne Lacaton & Jean-Philippe Vassal's celebrated transformation of a housing estate in Grand Parc, Bordeaux, where—rather than razing the three existing apartment blocks to build something "better," as others might have shortsightedly suggested—the architects extended the modernist towers by adding a generous 3.8-meter layer of prefabricated concrete balconies and winter gardens; replacing the original façades with floor-to-ceiling windows and sliding doors, and flooding the flats with views and natural light.[65] [**Figures 3.7 + 3.8**] Another example is Heatherwick Studio's *Zeitz MOCAA* in Cape Town, South Africa, where a grain silo complex was carved and extended to become a museum of contemporary art.[66] [**Figure 3.9**]

61 Leon Battista Alberti, *On the Art of Building in Ten Books*, trans. Joseph Rykwert, Neil Leach, and Robert Tavernor, (Cambridge and London: MIT Press, 1997), 7.

62 I am not implying that the distinction between a design context and a material one is universally valid—the opposite is often true, demonstrating that the ability to potentialize objects does not depend on the purifying force of a *tabula rasa*, on hypermateriality, or on the division between intellectual and manual labor. However, I do mean to suggest that this rift in Western architectural practice is fueled by the refusal to tell purity (mastery) apart from potency, and by the dualisms this refusal mobilizes (nature/culture, matter/form, etc.) towards the perpetuation of social, racial, and environmental injustice.

63 For this distinction, see Ed van Hinte, Césare Peeren, and Jan Jongert, *Superuse: Constructing New Architecture by Shortcutting Material Flows* (Rotterdam: 010 Publishers, 2007), 77.

64 Graeme Brooker and Sally Stone write of *intervention* when old and new are intertwined and indivisible; of *insertion* when they remain independent but the new has been formally/dimensionally dictated by the existing; of *installation* when the two remain relatively separate. Graeme Brooker and Sally Stone, *Rereadings: Interior Architecture and the Design Principles of Remodelling Existing Buildings* (London: RIBA Publishing, 2017), 79.

65 See also Frédéric Druot et al., *Plus: Large-Scale Housing Developments, an Exceptional Case*, 2G Books (Barcelona: Ed. Gustavo Gili, 2007).

66 In this case, cutting the original silos also required lining them with new concrete walls.

Figure 3.7 Lacaton & Vassal, Druot, Hutin, *Rehabilitation of 530 dwellings*, Grand Parc, Bordeaux, France, 2017. Building G (before and after). Photographs by Philippe Ruault.

67 Rural Studio is the design–build programme at Auburn University. Founded in 1992 by D. K. Ruth and Samuel Mockbee, it aims to "provide a decent community for all citizens." Andrea Oppenheimer Dean and Timothy Hursley, *Proceed and Be Bold: Rural Studio after Samuel Mockbee* (New York: Princeton Architectural Press, 2005), 8.

68 See also Flores & Prats et al., *44 Doors and 35 Windows for the New Sala Beckett* (15-L FILMS, 2016).

69 van Hinte et al., *Superuse*, 5–17. To put this into perspective: while Jongert suggests that the harvest map could have an indicative diameter of 50 kilometers, the "Regional Materials" credits in the LEED rating system (BD+C: New Construction V3, 2009) could be attained by sourcing materials "extracted, harvested or recovered, as well as manufactured within a 500 mile [800 kilometer] radius of the project site." LEED, "Regional Materials" (USGBC, 2009).

70 Ibid., 18. *Urban mining*, and the main challenges faced in its implementation, are discussed in detail in Michaël Ghyoot et al., *Déconstruction et réemploi: Comment faire circuler les éléments de construction* (Lausanne: Presses Polytechniques et Universitaires Romandes, 2018), 90–95.

In a material context, on the other hand, the additions curated by a project are embodied—they don't rely on hypermaterials—but might involve a more extensive construction program. I will refer to these cases as instances of *material reuse* or *material repurposing*. One such example is the *Lions Park Playscape* designed by Rural Studio in Greensboro, Alabama, where galvanized drums, originally used to store mint oil, are turned into floors, walls, soffits, and light wells; [**Figures 3.10 + 3.11**] another is the studio's *Shiles House* in Hale County, where tires form structural walls, and shipping pallets—cut into shingles—clad the façade.[67] [**Figures 3.12 + 3.13**] It is of course the case that these approaches can be dosed, mixed and combined, as in the *Sala Beckett* by Flores & Prats, where a derelict workers' cooperative in Barcelona is evocatively transformed into a drama center (an instance of design repurposing) and the existing doors and windows are inventoried, reconditioned, repainted, modified, and moved to different locations (an instance of material reuse).[68] [**Figure 3.14 + 3.15**]

In the 2007 book *Superuse: Constructing New Architecture by Short-cutting Material Flows,* Ed van Hinte, Césare Peeren, and Jan Jongert offer a provocative take on material contextuality. Aiming to re-link design with embodied (locally available) materials, and having coined the term *superuse* to extend reuse and repurposing strategies to industrial byproducts and dead stock, the authors suggest that projects should be coupled with a "harvest map"—a map of the area around a building site, where "superuse scouts" might find reusable materials, both diverting waste flows and minimizing the transportation needs of a project.[69] According to Peeren, these local metabolisms would transform buildings into "living organisms, constantly changing, growing and degenerating, absorbing the superfluous that they find in their surroundings and setting free whatever is no longer needed."[70] Accordingly, a design might either be prompted by the availability of local materials or, inversely, a project might establish a "shopping list" according to which available materials will be sought and selected. For the *Wikado Playground* discussed in Chapter 2, for example, Superuse

Figure 3.8 Lacaton & Vassal, Druot, Hutin, *Rehabilitation of 530 dwellings*. View of winter garden. Photograph by Philippe Ruault.

Figure 3.9 Heatherwick Studio, *Zeitz MOCAA*, Cape Town, South Africa, 2011. Photograph by Iwan Baan.

Figures 3.10 + 3.11 Rural Studio, *Lions Park Playscape*, Greensboro, AL, 2010. Photographs by Timothy Hursley.

Figures 3.12 + 3.13 Rural Studio, *Shiles House*, Hale County, AL, 2002. Photographs by Timothy Hursley.

Studios sought to find "volumes" that children could inhabit and walk/play on, and considered a number of options (e.g., grain silos, cars, buses, airplanes) prior to choosing the rotor blades, largely due to their size and strength.[71]

Finally, the local harvesting of materials does, at least in principle, begin to undermine what some economists and political scientists have called "unequal exchange": the asymmetrical concentration of bio-geophysical wealth (of embodied energy) in core "developed" regions, which consigns the extractive regions on the periphery to underdevelopment, resource depletion, environmental overload, pollution, and socio-political atrophy.[72]

3.7 Architectural Bricolage

[A]nimals and plants are not known as a result of their usefulness; they are deemed to be useful or interesting because they are first of all known.

Claude Lévi-Strauss, *The Savage Mind*[73]

A shift towards reuse and repurposing requires methodologies and evaluation criteria that challenge the modern design apparatus and its presumed superiority. *The Savage Mind* by anthropologist Claude Lévi-Strauss offers such an opening, inviting the reader to regard alternative (magical, mythical) knowledge systems—those recorded in premodern and totemic societies—not as primitive or inferior to modern science, but as operating on a different level, that of a *concrete science*.[74] Consequently, usefulness or effectiveness, understood in a narrow positivist sense, are no longer deciding factors. He writes:

The real question is not whether the touch of a woodpecker's beak does in fact cure toothache. It is rather whether there is a point

71 Personal communication with Césare Peeren.

72 For a discussion of unequal exchange as constitutive of architecture, see Kiel Moe, *Unless: The Seagram Building Construction Ecology* (New York: Actar Publishers, 2020), 70–85.

73 Claude Lévi-Strauss, *The Savage Mind (La Pensée Sauvage)* (London: Weidenfeld and Nicolson, 1966), 9.

74 He writes: "It is [...] better, instead of contrasting magic and science, to compare them as two parallel modes of acquiring knowledge." Lévi-Strauss, *The Savage Mind*, 13.

Figure 3.14 Flores & Prats, *Sala Beckett*, Barcelona, Spain, 2016. Photographs by Adrià Goula.

of view from which a woodpecker's beak and a man's tooth can be seen as 'going together' [...], and whether some initial order can be introduced into the universe by means of these groupings. Classifying, as opposed to not classifying, has a value of its own, whatever form the classification may take."[75]

75 Ibid., 9.

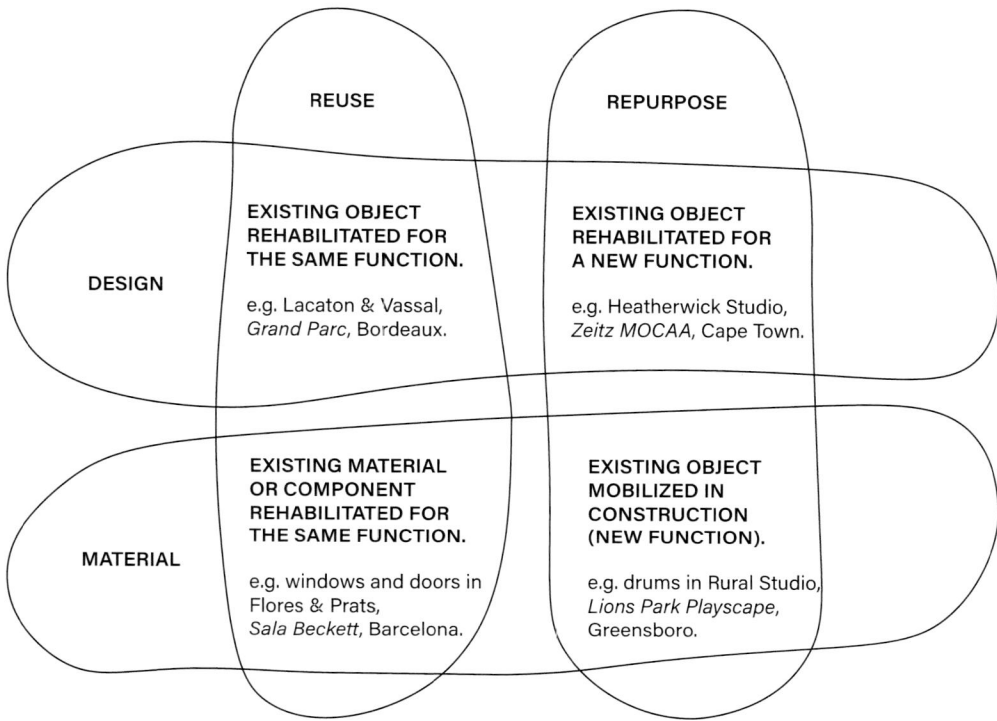

Figure 3.15 The differences between reuse and repurposing in a design or material context.

Encounters—as opposed to actions—are not passive through and through, but prelude an active (and designerly) classification process; the intentional sorting of one's environment, and the ability to negotiate or orchestrate value systems. Again, things "are deemed to be useful or interesting because they are first of all known." Whereas an ecology of inception links objects by assigning (enforcing) equipmental roles—and thus identifies *other* humans, animals, or minerals to be sacrificed and wasted—mythical thought allows for plastic configurations and relative positions that do not depend on fixed ecological enclosures (the hammer's ability to perform hammer-ness) but on reciprocal differences (the hammer's capacities, in the broadest possible sense). As there are no stable grounds for purifications or evictions, objects remain in a state of suspension and "freeplay" (they partake in no stable relations of interiority), and meanings, as well as functions, are allowed to fluctuate and be periodically reconfigured.

Indeed, structuralist thought provides a useful counter-model to the purposive hierarchies and linear orientations of industrial manufacturing, and to the orthodoxy of the market economy.[76] Hacking an imaginary structuralist sentence, one might utter the following words: if ~~meaning~~ value is arbitrary and there is no real-world referent outside of

76 I'm referring to the work of Ferdinand de Saussure as collected by his students in the *Course in General Linguistics*, in particular to the insights regarding the designation of meaning through differential ecologies of signifiers and signifieds.

language things, the differential tension between ~~signifiers~~ forms should be sufficient to keep them in play (out of the garbage bin), the degree or success of their participation in ecologies of inception notwithstanding. That is to say, if one substitutes *signs* (or, following Derrida's more radical stance, *signifiers*) with analogous *things*, one might describe re-use and repurposing as transversal or spectral (barrier-traversing) design languages predicated on a deep ecology of savage (floating) piles of stuff.[77] More importantly still, such an approach could help one *deconstruct* material discards and their presumed lack of value, locally and at the level of actual forms rather than potential lumps of matter.[78] Here, the ability to keep objects in circulation—to keep them suspended—is prioritized over particular aims and ecologies, which are viewed as necessarily partial and arbitrary. And while discarded polyethylene bottles, carpet tiles, and footballs, despite being more durable and stable than the use values associated with them,[79] do not actually amount to mere "floating signifiers"[80]—the industrial processes that "individuated" them also embedded them with specific properties and functional orientations—a structuralist/post-structuralist position may begin to illuminate, if only metaphorically, a different methodological ground. An illustration of what this approach may entail is offered by Lévi-Strauss himself, who, explaining the workings of mythical thought, introduces the figure of the *bricoleur*.

> The "bricoleur" is adept at performing a large number of diverse tasks; but, unlike the engineer, he does not subordinate each of them to the availability of raw materials and tools conceived and procured for the purpose of the project. His universe of instruments is closed and the rules of his game are always to make do with "whatever is at hand", that is to say with a set of tools and materials which is always finite and is also heterogeneous because what it contains bears no relation to the current project, or indeed to any particular project, but is the contingent result of all the occasions there have been to renew or enrich the stock or to maintain it with the remains of previous constructions or destructions.[81]

The bricoleur, as opposed to the engineer or to D&G's architect,[82] skips the first step of modern fabrication (the *tabula rasa*; the orientation of raw hypermaterials, according to designs/signifieds formed *a priori*) and proceeds instead from a material context of contingent (albeit limited) opportunities; from the articulation of a new language based on a collection of heterogeneous and preexisting signs—of floating parts that have forgotten, and precede, wholes.

> His first practical step is retrospective. He has to turn back to an already existent set made up of tools and materials, to consider or reconsider what it contains and, finally and above all, to engage in a sort of dialogue with it and, before choosing between them, to

77 Deep ecology is a philosophical movement that promotes the inherent worth of all living beings. See for instance: George Sessions, ed., *Deep Ecology for the Twenty-First Century* (Boston and New York: Shambhala, 1995).

78 In a system predicated on differences, increased differentiation at multiple scales is more interesting than homogeneity.

79 One of the chief realizations of the current geological period, the Anthropocene, is that the anthropogenic trace will outlast the Anthropos.

80 The term refers to signifiers to which no signifieds or meanings have yet been assigned or attributed.

81 Lévi-Strauss, *The Savage Mind*, 17. It is interesting to note that this is almost the exact opposite of what Simondon calls "concretization" (*concrétude*), understood as the evolutionary trajectory that progressively increases the resolution (the "internal resonance") and functionality (the pluri-functionality of parts) in technical objects. Gilbert Simondon, *On the Mode of Existence of Technical Objects*, trans. Ninian Mellamphy and with a preface by John Hart (University of Western Ontario, 1980), 15, 48.

82 Lévi-Strauss writes: "the engineer works by means of concepts and the bricoleur by means of signs." Lévi-Strauss, *The Savage Mind*, 20.

index possible answers which the whole set can offer to his problem. He interrogates all the heterogeneous objects of which his
treasury is composed to discover what each of them could "signify"
and so contribute to the definition of a set which has yet to mate-
rialize but which will ultimately differ from the instrumental set
only in the internal disposition of its parts.[83]

83 Ibid., 18.

In Lévi-Strauss's account, the stock or treasury accumulated by the bricoleur replaces the obedience of hypermaterials with the stubbornness
of a *savage archive* made up of elements that are "pre-constrained" and
have been "collected or retained on the principle that 'they may come
in handy.'"[84] The anthropologist recognizes that the savage archive, as
I have called it, runs on the ability of the collected items to remain
in a state of suspension; to exist between value systems and roles. He
writes of the collected objects: "They each represent a set of actual and
possible relations; they are 'operators' but they can be used for any operations of the same type."[85] And also: "in the continual reconstruction
from the same materials, it is always earlier ends which are called upon
to play the part of means: the signified changes into the signifying and
vice versa."[86] That is to say: while modernity claims to translate Nature
into culture along a trajectory of progressive purifications, the bricoleur
allows for nature and culture to mix, and for their surrogate roles—
dirty/clean, meaningful/meaningless, matter/form, and the like—to be
periodically renegotiated.

84 Ibid., 18–19.

85 Ibid.

86 Ibid., 21.

The term *bricolage* might conjure images of electric drills and suburban do-it-yourself garden sheds, or of the spontaneous constructions
built by artists Kurt Schwitters (*Merzbau*) and Clarence Schmidt (*House
of Mirrors*). At the scale of the city, one might associate it with informal
settlements, or with the "highly successful and resilient traffic jam of
intentions" that seventeenth century Rome offered, in Colin Rowe and
Fred Koetter's view, as an "alternative to the disastrous urbanism of
social engineering and total design" of the 1930s.[87] Yet, if the modernist *tabula rasa* (for example, the destructive and obtuse violence of Le
Corbusier's *Plan Voisin* of 1925), with its "messianic passion" and "anx-
iety both to end the world and begin it anew,"[88] delivers a hyperbolic
and scaled-up version of the technical *tabula rasa*, I am less inclined to
embrace bricolage as a counterbalancing strategy of spontaneity and
"making do" than to suggest that—quite apart from, or before, any
making—what is most challenging and inspiring in the figure of the
bricoleur is the commitment to establishing and maintaining a stock of
"operators" capable of representing—and thus, potentially also *in*capable of representing—"actual and possible" future relations. Here as with
the hoarders discussed in Chapter 1, the relationship of care and trust
between the bricoleur and her treasury takes precedence over any actual
instance of bricolage, or goal.[89]

87 Rowe and Koetter, *Collage City*, 106–7.

88 Ibid., 13.

89 It should also be noted that the stock or savage archive, as a figure of suspension (of taking time), is fundamentally at odds with the drive of financial capitalism toward low latency, ultra-speedy response times, ever-increasing precision in the prediction of market demand, and the algorithmic (hands-off) optimization of supply chains. See, for instance, Miriam Posner, "Seeing like a Supply Chain" (UCLA, February 11, 2021).

It is in this latter sense that the Brussels-based design firm Rotor offers an exemplary translation of the ethos of the bricoleur in the context

of architecture and construction, establishing a practice that is predicated on the recovery and reuse of existing materials and components, and placing material flows—and not designed outputs—at the center of design services and expertise. The practice's own organizational and economic trajectory may be viewed as an experiment in the implementation of what I have called savage archives—stocks of second-hand parts, materials, and components stored for future use—at the scale of entire buildings, cities, and countries. From an initial interest in the *ad hoc* usage of construction and demolition waste, the collective steadily progressed towards larger networks and scales—and towards increasing pragmatism and economic expediency.

Recognizing that reuse is, as a design paradigm, limited by an informal and disconnected ecology of companies specialized in the collection and sale of salvaged and reclaimed materials, in 2011 Rotor set out to survey and map the supply chains in second-hand and reconditioned materials around Brussels, later expanding the project to include the whole of Belgium, the Netherlands, France, and the United Kingdom. The resulting guide and website—*Opalis*—organizes the compiled information so that it may be searched by component (e.g., windows, doors, staircases, pavers, radiators), by company, and by location.[90]

However, noting that the vast majority of the salvage and reclamation market focuses on narrow sets of components and materials (and often solely on antiques), and wishing to increase the scope of material reuse in Brussels, in 2014 the cooperative launched its own salvage company—Rotor Deconstruction—to "dismantle, condition and sell materials from quality buildings undergoing transformation or demolition,"[91] first using the buildings themselves as showrooms for off-site reclamation (during the limited time preceding the issue of a demolition permit), and later acquiring a warehouse/showroom of their own. [**Figures 3.16 + 3.17**] Yet Rotor DC treats its savage archives not as mere accumulations of materials, but as an inventory undergoing genuine re-potentializing processes (or potentializing reprocessing).[92] Aside from undertaking the classification, measuring, and reconditioning tasks that will reintegrate reclaimed materials in valuing (clean/visible/nameable) ecologies, the practice also aims to guide architects, commissioners, and contractors in navigating—and rewriting—the construction industry's workflows and protocols (tendering processes, specifications, legal and regulatory frameworks, etc.), which are implicitly formulated with first-hand manufactured materials in mind. [**Figures 3.18 + 3.19**]

The group champions a model of materials recovery that resists hippie aesthetics, self-built DIY fads, the fetishization of time-worn surfaces, and the mere circulation of easy-to-reuse modules.[93] Beyond the marginal appeal of these practices and their limited impact on the materials economy (on the vast amounts of waste generated by the construction industry; on the environmental damage and carbon expenditures associated with the extraction, transportation,

90 For Belgium, the Netherlands and France, see Opalis EU, accessed May 31, 2020, https://opalis.eu/fr.

91 Rotor, "Rotor DC: Reuse Made Easy," Rotordb.org, accessed May 31, 2020.

92 As Lasse Kilvær, managing director of the Oslo-based deconstruction firm Resirqel, convincingly argues, in this context "waste is a material without proper documentation." Lasse Kilvær, Personal communication (lecture at ESALA), 22 February 2021.

93 Lionel Devlieger, "Architecture in Reverse," *Volume 51: Augmented Technology*, October 2017, 9–10.

Figure 3.16 Rotor, deconstruction process, 2018–19. © Rotor.

processing, and disposal of building materials), their architectural brand of bricolage aims to replace careless demolition (the destruction powered by tools such as hydraulic jackhammers, bulldozers, and crane-mounted wrecking balls; or by the detonation of explosives in spectacular Pruitt-Igoe fashion) with careful deconstruction and disassembly, seeking to revive a materials recovery tradition that dates back, in the West, to at least Ancient Roman times, and to extend it beyond the colonialist display of *spolia* as indexes of pillaging or as looting trophies—promoting it instead as the narrative continuation of material parts, traces, and memories across buildings, histories, and ecologies.[94] The work of Rotor—and their ability to bring reuse into the architectural limelight through publications and exhibitions—is of obvious practical relevance to this book. Yet, it also offers the opportunity for a more nuanced understanding of how potentials are maintained across ecologies of inception, and how EoIs themselves may be articulated in more complex terms—as more than simple self-contained teleological enclosures.

Figure 3.17 Rotor, deconstruction process, 2018–19. © Rotor.

94 Devlieger, "Architecture in Reverse," 12. For a brief history of how demolition practices rapidly changed in the 20th century, see Ghyoot et al., *Déconstruction et réemploi*, 29–38. See also Jeff Byles, *Rubble: Unearthing the History of Demolition* (New York: Three Rivers Press, 2006).

The objects Rotor tends to salvage are nonstructural elements such as office partitions, lighting fixtures, false ceilings, cladding tiles, sanitary fittings, curtains, and furniture.[95] That is: not every material qualifies. Selection criteria are based on market value and demand, and include consideration of the object's weight and ease of dismantling, as well as of the number of elements available. Lionel Devlieger, one of the founders, writes:

> How do you select appropriate components that can be reused in a new project? The cost of extraction is a decisive factor, as is the state of conservation of the part in question, its solidity, the durability of the materials that compose it, the ease with which it can be integrated into its new state, its functional and symbolic value, … Our job is to take these parameters into consideration when we go through a building to decide what to preserve and what to leave in the hands of the demolishers. A poor judgment can be expensive. Our assessment of the monetary value of the components obviously depends on the market, but the latter can be influenced, stimulated. Where demand does not yet exist, it can be sparked; where supply is lacking, it can be encouraged.[96]

Figure 3.18 Rotor, reclaimed tiles, 2018. © Rotor.

96 Devlieger, "Architecture in Reverse," 12.

And again:

> The criteria outlined above could be rephrased as follows: extracting parts of a building that needs to come down means identifying the entities that, once detached from the set, will have the best chance of individual survival. As with surgery, it is important to know where the dotted line is.[97]

97 Ibid.,13.

As with organs, extending the lifespan of materials—avoiding rejection—requires careful consideration of the (immunological) context into which they will be transplanted. Yet, the ability of parts to survive the demise of the specific EoIs to which they belong, all the while maintaining a consistent functional orientation and identity, necessarily betrays their simultaneous membership in multiple (overlapping) ecologies. In other words: an object's potentiality may not only rely upon an immediate set of ecological associations and emerging properties (the ability to fulfill a particular equipmental role; the unlocking and actualizing of target potentials), but also upon looser and more generic layers of ecological definition or enclosure. If the

Figure 3.19 Rotor, showroom, 2019. © Rotor.

Figure 3.20 Rotor, dismantling tiles in the Institute of Modern Engineering, Liège, 2016. Photograph by Olivier Béart.

ceramic tiles in the abandoned Institute of Modern Engineering in Liège, Belgium, can be dismantled and refitted in a trendy grocery store in Ghent,[98] this is because the "tileness" of these colorful objects survives their "floorness" or distinct parthood (their equipmental affiliation with the Institute's floor). [**Figures 3.20 + 3.21**] Rather than describing clear-cut boundaries and univocal scripts, EoIs would therefore seem to comprise several enclosures—a thickened boundary capable of addressing a range of potential gradients and a wide spectrum of alliances and reciprocal positions.

Like the layers in an onion, EoIs may be peeled back to partially release objects of their ecological chains and facilitate transfers from one set to the next, adjusting the equipmental control knob backwards and forwards. In some cases, these shifts will require physical migrations, and their success will depend on the object's degree or manner of tethering: a chair can be easily moved across buildings, whereas a tile or cladding panel, in order to gain the required agility, might necessitate a certain amount of dismantling effort.[99] Yet, migrations might also suggest movements of a more static or subtle kind: between uses, users, languages, and values.

In any case, the layering I am proposing does not correspond with what Frank Duffy and Stewart Brand call "shearing layers"—the insight that site, load-bearing structure, exterior envelope, services, interior layout, and furnishings change at different rates; and that, in order to be able to adapt, a building "has to allow slippage" and enable these "differently-paced systems" to change independently of one another.[100]

98 See Maarten Gielen, "Lecture at CCA" (Canadian Centre for Architecture, February 4, 2016).

99 The difference between an element's resale value and the costs incurred in the dismantling operations required to "release" it will usually dictate whether its reuse is commercially viable. See Ghyoot et al., *Déconstruction et réemploi*, 98.

100 Stewart Brand, *How Buildings Learn: What Happens after They're Built* (New York: Penguin Books, 1995), 20. Brand further develops the notion of "pace layering" in Stewart Brand, *Clock of the Long Now: Time and Responsibility: The Ideas Behind the World's Slowest Computer* (Basic Books, 2008), 34–39.

Figure 3.21 Rotor, dismantling tiles in the Institute of Modern Engineering, Liège, 2016. Photograph by Olivier Béart.

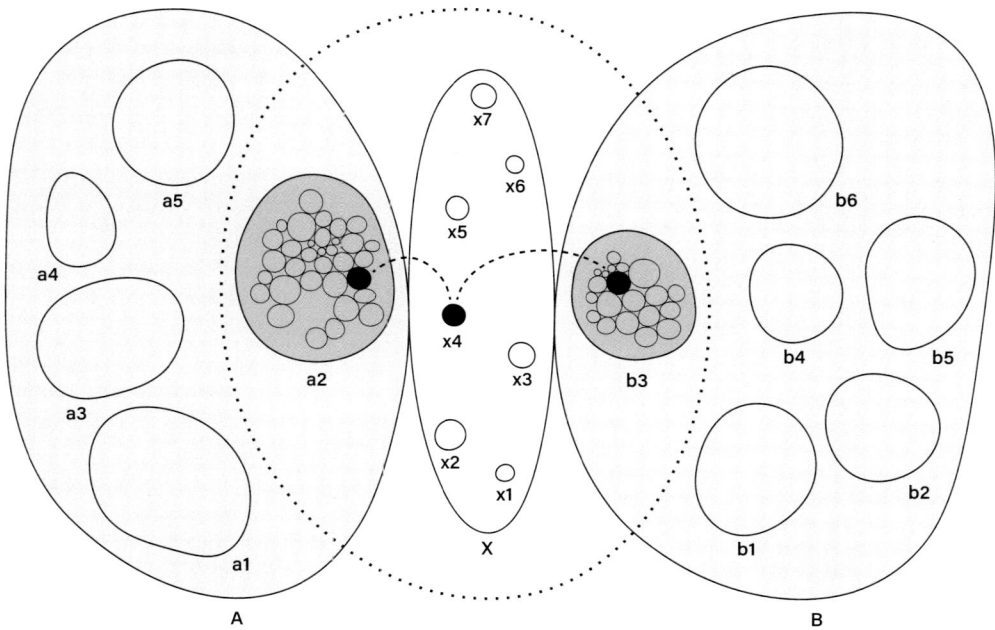

Figure 3.22 With A and B representing two ecologies of inception (e.g., two different buildings), and a2 and b3 representing two subecologies (e.g., interior partitions), the diagram illustrates that an intermediate step—a translation from *part of* to *individual unit*, and vice versa—is required in order for a component (e.g., a brick) to move from A to B. The ecology identified with X (e.g., the salvaging of used bricks; the workshop in which they are reconditioned; or the showroom where they are neatly stacked and labeled) is not entirely foreign to the original subecologies, with which it shares an ecological layer (the dotted line): the persistent brickness of the individual bricks, in spite of ongoing deployments or parthood relations.

If Brand and Duffy are (justifiably) preoccupied with the adaptability of the building as a whole, I am also interested in single components or objects, and in how the loosening and sharing of ecological scripts may negotiate their survival. [**Figure 3.22**]

3.8 Boundary Archives

In many ways, this model of overlapping ecologies resembles what sociologists Susan Leigh Star and James R. Griesemer have called *boundary objects*—"objects that are both plastic enough to adapt to local needs and the constraints of the several parties employing them, yet robust enough to maintain a common identity across sites." They continue: "They are weakly structured in common use, and become strongly structured in individual-site use."[101] Leigh Star and Griesemer refer to objects (in the widest possible sense, including artifacts, documents, etc.) shared by heterogeneous groups (for instance, clinical and basic researchers, or amateur natural history collectors and research scientists—who operate within different time horizons, and with disparate methods, goals,

101 Susan Leigh Star and James R. Griesemer, "Institutional Ecology, 'Translations' and Boundary Objects: Amateurs and Professionals in Berkeley's Museum of Vertebrate Zoology, 1907–39," *Social Studies of Science* 19, no. 3 (1989), 393.

102 Susan Leigh Star, "The Structure of Ill-Structured Solutions: Boundary Objects and Heterogeneous Distributed Problem Solving," in *Distributed Artificial Intelligence*, ed. Les Gasser and Michael N. Huhns, vol. II (Elsevier, 1989).

103 Star and Griesemer, "Institutional Ecology," 393.

104 Ibid., 412.

105 Ibid., 410.

106 Ibid.

107 Ibid.

108 Ibid., 411.

and attention regimes), which however allow for the successful mediation and reconciliation of datasets and approaches, as well as for cooperation.[102] "The creation and management of boundary objects," they write, "is a key process in developing and maintaining coherence across intersecting social worlds."[103] Of particular interest is, however, the fact that coherence never slips into univocal forms of consensus. Rather, boundary objects continue to "contain at every stage the traces of multiple viewpoints, translations and incomplete battles."[104]

Leigh Star and Griesemer identify four types of such objects, albeit admitting that the list may not be exhaustive: (1) repositories like museums and libraries ("ordered piles of objects which are indexed in a standardized fashion" and out of which people can draw on the basis of their own purposes, interests, and views);[105] (2) ideal types (or Platonic objects) like diagrams and descriptions, which are "fairly vague" and abstracted from specific local conditions and contingencies, but adaptable to a variety of local sites because of it (for instance, a generic species versus any specific specimen);[106] (3) coincident boundaries like maps, which "have the same boundaries but different internal contents";[107] and (4) standardized forms and labels, as "methods of common communication across dispersed work groups."[108]

Now, it is not by chance that a practice like Rotor systematically relies on boundary objects such as repositories and labels. Whereas it may be sometimes possible to earmark salvaged materials for reuse in a target EoI—to transfer them directly from an original ecology A to a target ecology B—in many cases, this will not be feasible. The introduction of boundary objects such as the Rotor DC showroom (where visitors—contractors, architects, and the general public—may browse "ordered piles" of reclaimed items and attach values to them according to diverging sets of commitments and priorities) therefore constitutes a highly strategic approach to the recirculation of building parts—one that, while largely maintaining the functional orientation of components (a lamp is still a lamp, a tile is still a tile, and so forth), loosens boundaries and valuing criteria, radically increasing the object's "chance of individual survival." [Figure 3.23]

If the term *savage* in the bricoleur's stock referred to the overcoming of synchronous or reliable modes of equipmental compliance (to the uncertain emergence of future value or utility), here the term acquires a further connotation of openness and porosity, one that allows a measure of bricolage to be taken up by (and distributed across) as many actors and stakeholders as possible.

Not only can one begin to understand hypermaterials as boundary objects of sorts, and the loosening of local constraints as necessary for the horizontal transfer of objects across sets—one can perhaps,

Figure 3.23 Rotor, showroom, 2019. © Rotor.

metaphorically speaking, begin to think of any salvageable material (of any window frame, door handle, and coping stone) as potential boundary objects; not only as items that are or can be entangled in (or intersected by) enough ecologies to retrieve a measure of fitness, but also as entities whose contextual specificity or degree of communicative potential can be continually retuned or dialed down in response to shifting conditions. The loosening of local scripts and dependencies—its very possibility—also implies that rooms, radiators, and hammers always exceed (they are always more-than) their ecological determinations and the corresponding networks and exclusions.

Chapter 4

Circularities: Technical Nutrients, Hyperobjects, and Rooms

4.1 Teleological and Molecular Purity

In the last chapter, I introduced the notion of hypermateriality and claimed that its philosophical roots stem, at least in part, from Aristotelian essentialism, both in the use of definitions that invoke shared features and in the tension between primary and secondary properties—the shadow of the latter requiring an active confirmation in the reality of the former. Having noted the impossibility of intrinsic purity (of the existence of purity in the absence of a context for its designation), I can now identify two main horizons for its attribution in architecture and design.

The first one (*teleological* or *objectual purity*) excuses hybridity by wrapping it in social, cultural, or technical *teloi*, and by placing it in the service of an ecology of inception or equipmental whole. Here, purity does not coincide with homogeneity in a chemical sense—it cannot be tested in the lab—and cleanliness exceeds a mere preference for consistency and self-similarity, or a narrow focus on molecular scales. Instead, it necessarily invests and informs objecthood, steering morphogenetic processes and orienting matter towards strict behaviors, referential networks, value systems, and conventions of use. The vitreous glaze fused to the surface of a ceramic cup, while violating the hypermaterial virginity of the clay paste or terracotta vessel, is endorsed as dignified in its embodiment of a *telos* (the Lockean "improvement"). The end justifies the means, and the decrease in surface porosity allows the cup to become impermeable, thus fulfilling a worthwhile equipmental role (holding liquids).

Admixtures (e.g., the paperboard, aluminum, and polyethylene layers in a milk carton; the mixed colors and canvas in a Hilma af Klint painting; the butter, sugar, and flour in shortbread) are granted a degree of purity and value that is proportional to their powers—to their ability to perform, interact, and be used. The attainment of objectual purity coincides with the object's inclusion within a system or ecology, and while physical properties and molecular composition do play a role in its fitness, the object is evaluated on the basis of the capacities unlocked (those

DOI: 10.4324/9781003015444-7

unlocked *within* the system). High concentrations of hybridity are concealed and disguised using common names (e.g., a cup, a milk carton, a sheet of paper, a carpet tile) and the designation of clear, legible affordances. Readability is paramount because labels and codes of conduct are not imparted synchronously from a pulpit, but programmed to emerge "spontaneously" from cultural/personal memory (knowing what a cup is; recognizing cups amongst other objects) and from the encounter with things, having been imprinted—and implied—in their form (the hollowness of the cup towards containing liquids; the handle towards the ability to hold it without burning one's fingers, and so on). [**Figure 4.1**] Designers of stuff in all fields and at all scales—from pencils to sidewalks, railway stations to living rooms, dishwashers to belts—are vehicles and enablers of both this embodiment of purpose and its enforced clarity.[1]

The second one (*molecular purity*), is instead dependent upon physical composition, but according to two diverging (energetic and hypermaterial) models. *Energetic purity* approaches the definition of matter from a Simondonian perspective (the prepared clay discussed in Chapter 2), as a medium for the effective distribution and exchange of energetic and poietic inputs. While also defined within the narrow confines of an interior ecology—and in relation to a target set of transmissions and translations—the attribution of energetic purity is predicated on a degree of preparation (on the expulsion of unwanted elements) and homogeneity (on the lack of internal difference; on the object's ability to behave consistently across points and dimensions). Instead, *hypermaterial purity* moves the identification of homogeneity beyond specific energetic operations, tools, or conditions, describing objects as universal and averaged distillations (physical or virtual as these may be). The chief requirement is not the ability to contribute to (or modulate the inputs within) a situated milieu or ecology, but to be measured and valued outside (and exchanged/shared across) particular contexts or instances.

Over the course of this chapter, I will use (and revise) these simple definitions of purity—teleological, energetic, and hypermaterial—to interrogate current upcycling paradigms. Terms such as purity, value, and internal potency will often overlap and be used interchangeably—purity being at once a measure of the attribution of value within target systems (of their potentiality) and promoted by increased levels of communicability across constituents.

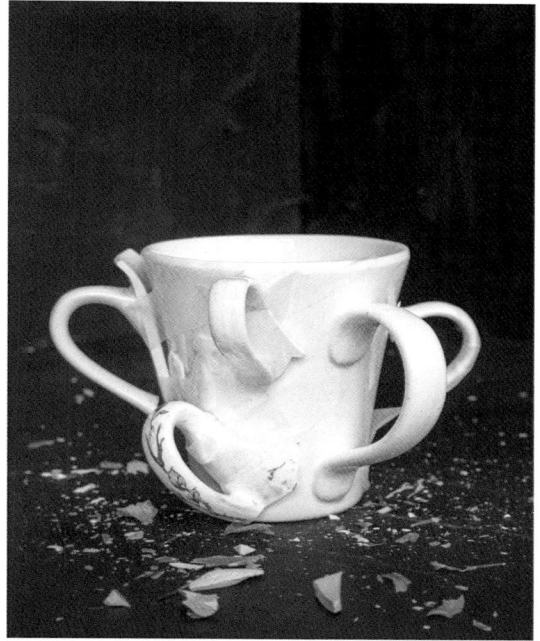

Figure 4.1 James Henkel, *Sharing Cup*, 2017. It is only because one intuitively identifies the cup's handle with the powers it unlocks (the ability to be held), and because we are familiar with the movements associated with holding (and drinking from) a cup, that Henkel's piece gains, in relation to an expected and implied horizon of use, an evocative and somewhat disturbing aura.

1 See for instance Donald A. Norman, *The Design of Everyday Things* (New York: Doubleday, 1990). See also Kevin Lynch, *The Image of the City* (Cambridge: MIT Press, 2005).

4.2. What Is the Upcycle? (The Trouble with Technical Nutrients)

2 William McDonough and Michael Braungart, *Cradle to Cradle: Remaking the Way We Make Things* (New York: North Point Press, 2002).

Architect William McDonough and chemist Michael Braungart, authors of one of the key texts in twenty-first century design sustainability—*Cradle to Cradle: Remaking the Way We Make Things*—propose "upcycling" as a paradigm for recycling materials while also increasing (or not decreasing) their value.[2] [**Figure 4.2**] Inspired by the circulation and transformation of matter in natural systems (from the ingestion of plants to the calories powering the metabolism of animals to manure to fertile soils to new plants, and so on), McDonough and Braungart rethink materials as existing in natural cycles or closed industrial loops, either as "biological nutrients" that, at the end of their lives, can safely return to the environment (to beneficial rotting and composting ecologies), or as "technical nutrients" that can continue to circulate, notionally *ad infinitum*, within industrial manufacturing cycles.[3]

3 McDonough and Braungart, *Cradle to Cradle*, 104.

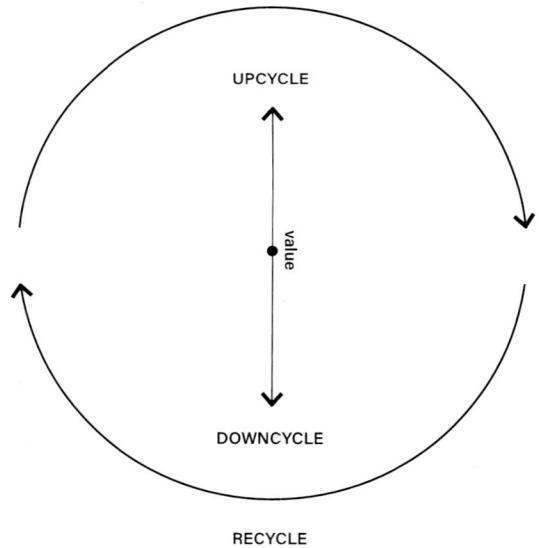

Figure 4.2 Measuring transformations in terms of increasing and decreasing quality or value, as the terms "upcycling" and "downcycling" do, risks presupposing that these terms are objective and neutral, and that they can precede the encounter with specific contexts and things. The term "upcycle," as the subset of a recycling ecology, privileges circulation and exchange. It is therefore not interchangeable with the terms "reuse" and "repurposing," which privilege suspension and use.

Biological and technical cycles depend on purity—on clean loops. Not only must the respective materials be energetically pure in the sense described above (able to biodegrade and transfer their nutrient load back to the soil, or to be melted and reprocessed into technical objects of equal value)—they must also remain separate or separable. Their value and potential (their ability to change) depends on it—not to maintain or achieve higher ontological rankings (the circulation of a capital *A* aluminum, or a capital *C* carbon), but in order to address practical problems like different melting temperatures or the leaching of toxic chemicals into waterways or healthy soils. In other words: if one were to recycle a bike part that has aluminum and plastic components, separating the two materials prior to melting them down would afford a greater level of control and workability, as well as better results—it might even be possible to recycle the resulting objects again in the future. Accordingly, technical nutrients rehearse Simondon's definition of matter as "capacity to become" and are attributed value (potentials) not in general or according to a wide range of contexts and multi-scalar orientations (of which some may be as-yet-unknown), but in compliance with set recycling and remanufacturing ecologies.

In fact, the Cradle to Cradle approach poses a series of problems for the discussion of potentiality in the context of design. The term *biological nutrient* merely identifies the beneficial circulation of carbon and nutrients in natural systems (McDonough and Braungart's "waste equals food";[4] Laporte's "shit to gold";[5] and Whitman's "such sweet things out of such corruptions").[6] In these systems—ones where waste effectively does not exist—the designer must merely watch, learn, and maintain/conserve/protect, avoiding the introduction of pollutants (for instance, the chromated copper arsenate used in the treatment of timber)[7], and substituting toxic and hazardous materials with renewable and biodegradable ones.[8] Indeed, non-Western and Indigenous societies that find value in webs of reciprocity with the natural world—as opposed to those driven by the hubristic purifications and increasing metabolic rifts of modernity—have known and practiced this for a long time. Robin Wall Kimmerer writes of her indigenous ancestors:

> In the settler mind, land was property, real estate, capital, or natural resources. But to our people, it was everything: identity, the connection to our ancestors, the home of our nonhuman kin-folk, our pharmacy, our library, the source of all that sustained us. Our lands were where our responsibility to the world was enacted, sacred ground.[9]

Technical nutrients are more problematic. Firstly, their monolithic definition disagrees with the many guises that "waste"—or, inversely,

4 Ibid., 92–117.

5 Laporte, *History of Shit*, chap. 2, E-book.

6 Walt Whitman, "This Compost," in *Leaves of Grass*, ed. Jim Manis, The Electronic Classics Series (PSU-Hazleton, Hazleton PA), accessed June 5, 2020.

7 Anna Augustsson et al., "Persistent Hazardous Waste and the Quest Toward a Circular Economy: The Example of Arsenic in Chromated Copper Arsenate-Treated Wood: Arsenic Flows with CCA-Treated Wood, Sweden," *Journal of Industrial Ecology* 21, no. 3 (June 2017): 689–99.

8 It should be noted that, when applied to plastics, the term "biodegradable" is often not sufficient to guarantee compostability. As explained by Samantha MacBride, the sourcing of materials from plants and animals does not guarantee their biodegradability, and both traditional (fossil fuel-based) and bio-based plastics can be manufactured to either be fully compostable or not compostable at all. Samantha MacBride, "The Fungibility of Carbon Waste: Plastics, Organics & Thermal/Biological Treatments" (Jean Thomas Lambert Environmental Lecture, Discarded: Unmasking & Understanding the Waste Stream, Lear-Conant Symposium, Connecticut College, March 6, 2021). See also Rebecca Altman, "The Myth of Historical Bio-Based Plastics," *Science* 373, no. 6550 (July 2, 2021): 47–49.

9 Robin Wall Kimmerer, *Braiding Sweetgrass: Indigenous Wisdom, Scientific Knowledge and the Teachings of Plants* (Minneapolis: Milkweed Editions, 2013), 17.

10 Vincent Moreau et al., "Coming Full Circle: Why Social and Institutional Dimensions Matter for the Circular Economy," *Journal of Industrial Ecology* 21, no. 3 (June 2017): 497–506.

11 See for instance Benjamin Franta, "Shell and Exxon's Secret 1980s Climate Change Warnings," *The Guardian*, September 19, 2018, Online edition.

12 Andreas Malm, *How to Blow up a Pipeline: Learning to Fight in a World on Fire* (Brooklyn: Verso Books, 2020), 62.

13 Michael Braungart, William McDonough, and with a foreword by President Bill Clinton, *The Upcycle: Beyond Sustainability – Designing for Abundance* (New York: Farrar, Straus & Giroux, 2014), Introduction, E-book.

14 They write that "ultimately a regulation is a signal of design failure. In fact, it is what we call a *license to harm*: a permit issued by a government to an industry so that it may dispense sickness, destruction, and death at an 'acceptable' rate." McDonough and Braungart, *Cradle to Cradle*, 61. Aside from the irony of this being precisely, as we will see, how their certification system also works, there is no reason why regulations couldn't forbid *any and all* pollution, rather than establish "acceptable" thresholds of toxicity (which are often acceptable, of course, because foisted on someone else/elsewhere).

15 Slavoj Žižek, "First as Tragedy, Then as Farce" (online lecture, the RSA, London), accessed February 18, 2020. See also Oscar Wilde, "The Soul of Man under Socialism," in *The Soul of Man under Socialism and Selected Critical Prose*, ed. and with an introduction by Linda C. Dowling (London and New York: Penguin Books, 2001), 125–62.

value—can take in socio-technical systems, preferring a one-size-fits-all solution driven by capitalist orthodoxy to more diverse and locally considered economic alternatives and approaches. By foregrounding economic viability (the ability to effectively flow in the global market economy) as the key criterion for success, it trivializes efforts driven by *other* values (biodiversity, wellbeing, equity, etc.), at least insofar as these are not coextensive with economic profitability, cost effectiveness, and growth.[10] The assumption that the two can perfectly align (that industrial systems can be optimized to harness the abundance and positivity of natural systems for all people, all the while maximizing profits) is as inspiring as it is improbable, ignoring ample and persistent historical evidence to the contrary (for instance, the criminal behavior of fossil fuel executives, who, over the past 40 years, aggressively lobbied for climate change denial while factoring climate change in their calculations, and continuing to knowingly cause irreparable environmental damage to *common* planetary systems).[11] Indeed, as Andreas Malm puts it, "the historical victory of capital and the ruination of the planet are one and the same thing."[12]

McDonough and Braungart's dislike of regulatory frameworks (in their view, regulations are mere temporary fixes indexing "something to be redesigned")[13] and their reliance on the generosity of sympathetic/enlightened CEOs is anything but objective or politically neutral.[14] In wishing to optimize current industrial systems, Cradle to Cradle runs the risk of preserving capitalism-as-is (albeit in a greener guise), effectively stalling more radical societal transformations, and leaving broader questions relating to uneven exchanges and systems of governance unanswered. Indeed, philosopher Slavoj Žižek warns against the dangers of cultural (green) capitalism and its insidious numbing effects—against the convergence of ethics and consumption. With Oscar Wilde, he asks: is it moral for private property to alleviate the evils that result from the institution of private property?[15]

Secondly, technical nutrients are activated by material exclusions—by the very same scripts that originate waste in the first place. Not only do technical nutrients (mostly polymers and metals) perpetuate a hylomorphic bias—the preference for molecular determinations of purity and potentiality, and the belief that only materials (not objects) are capable of (or worth) changing—they also reject an exceedingly large amount of noncompliant items. Designing waste away, as Cradle to Cradle claims to do, also establishes the wasteness of the majority of the objects (toxic, hybrid, and monstrous as they may be) currently flowing in the materials economy. Indeed, the notion of technical nutrient conflates potentiality (the ability to change; to become, and to regain a measure of value) with molecular purity (a material's obedience and reliability), hypermaterial purity (its exchangeability in the global market economy), and circularity (the liquefaction of preexisting forms, which are returned to an "original" and "raw"—and thus eminently deformable—state).

If technical nutrients are conceptualized in time, as steady flows of synthetic matter (and this is, of course, one of McDonough and Braungart's most persuasive ideas: replacing a linear "cradle-to-grave" material paradigm with one characterized by cyclical regeneration), they continue to rely on a technical *tabula rasa*—to understand the design and manufacturing of products, and the recirculation of materials, as necessarily dependent on an intermediate state of formlessness. If materials are allowed to have structure, this is merely at the *implicit* level of molecules within larger—homogeneous, plastic, shapeless—lumps. In fact, the term upcycling is so attached to the circulation of technical nutrients that using it to refer to repurposed objects that have gained or retained value (for example, the polyethylene terephthalate bottles in the *PET Tree* by Superuse Studios; or the rotor blades in their *Wikado Playground*) would be incorrect.[16] [**Figures 4.3–4.5**]

Revealingly, if *Cradle to Cradle* (as a book, method, and set of aspirations) caters to an audience of designers, its practical implementation largely evades the architect's office, preferring the board rooms and R&D departments of corporations.[17] It is here that the

16 Braungart and McDonough are explicit about this. When upcycling is mentioned in *Cradle to Cradle*, it is in reference to a nutrient cycle. Speaking about the book itself, they write that "it has the potential to be upcycled: dissolved and remade as polymer of high quality and usefulness." And again later: "to be upcycled rather than recycled—to retain high quality in a closed-loop industrial cycle." McDonough and Braungart, *Cradle to Cradle*, 72, 110.

17 This shift is also evident in McDonough and Braungart's following book, *The Upcycle: Beyond Sustainability – Designing for Abundance*.

Figure 4.3 Superuse Studios, *PET Tree*, Almere, 2013. Photograph by (©) Denis Guzzo.

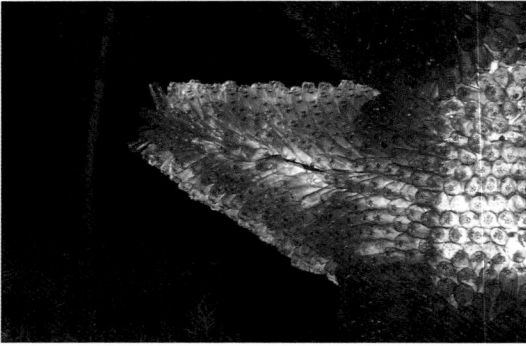

Figure 4.4 Superuse Studios, *PET Tree*, Almere, 2013. Photograph by (©) Denis Guzzo.

manufacturing recipes and assemblies yielding the materials that architects routinely specify (fabrics and curtain wall systems, insulation boards and roofing membranes, paints and office chairs, concrete pavers and ceiling panels, etc.) are designed, and that their supply chains are routed and optimized. And it is this audience—with the enlightened executive at its helm—that the "Cradle to Cradle Certified Product Standard" addresses. Started in 2010, the certification program assesses the sustainability of products, including materials and subassemblies, across five categories (Material Health, Material Reutilization, Renewable Energy and Carbon Management, Water Stewardship, and Social Fairness) and awards five progressive levels of achievement for each category.[18] For the purpose of the present discussion, I will briefly examine the first two categories, Material Health and Material Reutilization, which, together, probe the purity of materials as a function of their "green chemistry" (the absence of harmful ingredients) and circularity (their nutrient potential and actualization).[19]

In the Material Health category, manufacturers conduct an inventory of generic materials and supply chains. The "homogeneous materials" included in their product, defined as "materials of uniform composition throughout that cannot be mechanically disjointed, in principle, into different materials"[20] are listed, characterized, and rated *a*/*b* for optimal, *c* for moderately problematic, *x* for highly problematic, and *grey* for unassessed. Different levels of certification are awarded based on these categories' contribution to the overall weight of the product. Complying with a list of banned chemicals (arsenic, mercury, polyvinyl chloride, etc.), assessing at least 75% of materials, and developing a phase-out strategy for *x*-rated materials yields a bronze-level certification;[21] increasing the percentage of assessed materials to 95 and avoiding carcinogens, mutagens, or reproductive toxins unlocks a silver-level certification; and finally, a full assessment (100% of the product by weight) and the replacement or phasing out of all *x*-assessed chemicals in the product and in the production processes are rewarded with gold and platinum respectively.[22]

In the Material Reutilization category, products are evaluated based on the percentage of recyclable and/or compostable nutrients, and on the role manufacturers play in their recovery.[23] Firstly, each material must be assigned to a biological or technical cycle. Secondly, the percentage of recyclable, biodegradable, compostable, recycled, and rapidly renewable (homogeneous) materials in a product is determined, and the corresponding "reutilization score" calculated.[24]

18 See "What Is Cradle to Cradle Certified™?," Cradle to Cradle Products Innovation Institute, accessed February 18, 2020.

19 McDonough Braungart Design Chemistry (MBDC), "Cradle to Cradle Certified™: Product Standard, Version 3.1" (Cradle to Cradle Products Innovation Institute, 2016).

20 MBDC, "Cradle to Cradle Certified," 19.

21 (100% of biological nutrients to be released directly into the biosphere as a part of their intended use). Ibid., 18.

22 "Material Health Certificate: The Cradle to Cradle Certified™ Products Program" (Cradle to Cradle Products Innovation Institute), accessed February 18, 2020.

23 MBDC, "Cradle to Cradle Certified," 9.

24 According to the document, "a recyclable material is a material that can be recycled *at least once* after its initial use *somewhere in the world*." Ibid., 49. My emphasis.

The highest levels of accreditation also require manufacturers to develop a "nutrient management strategy" for the recycling or recovery of materials (gold), and the implementation of—or adherence to—specific collection programs (platinum).

At this level of granularity, it is difficult to imagine how the standards imposed by Cradle to Cradle (for instance, the requisite absence of carcinogenic materials, or low VOC emissivity) could be more effective in a voluntary certification program, or spearheaded by visionary clients and architects, than as imposed by sweeping regulatory frameworks. What is gained from—and *who* is advantaged by—a rhetoric that emphasizes design and free choice over policies and regulation, or that assumes that the two cannot coincide? Could it be that, as Rotor suggests in a study on the circularity of gypsum board, what the program's "zero impact" claims establish is the guilt-free and uninhibited perpetuation of present levels of production and consumption?[25] And isn't the voluntary submission to moderate levels of optimization or toxicity (to polluting less) an environmental form of charity, in the sense condemned by Oscar Wilde?[26] In other words, is it moral for polluters to alleviate the evils that result from pollution?[27] Is this really the best "sustainability" a society on the verge of climate collapse can aspire to? Or must a sustainable future necessarily begin by accepting the fundamental irreconcilability of the imperatives of capitalism (e.g., GDP, economic growth, the maximization of shareholders' dividends, the exploitation of labor and of natural resources) with the well-being of an entangled human and nonhuman "world community"?

Again, according to Wall Kimmerer, "all flourishing is mutual."[28] In her work, a surge in value—an upcycle—is not about formlessness, the flow of technical nutrients, or poietic control, but about the way "gifts" move and gain value by changing hands. "The more something is shared," she writes,

> the greater its value becomes. This is hard to grasp for societies steeped in notions of private property, where others are, by definition, excluded from sharing. [...] The essence of the gift is that it creates a set of relationships. The currency of a gift economy is, at its root, reciprocity. In Western thinking, private land is

Figure 4.5 Superuse Studios, *PET Tree*, Almere, 2013. Photograph by (©) Denis Guzzo.

25 Lionel Billiet, Michaël Ghyoot, and Maarten Gielen, "Le Cerisier et La Plaque de Plâtre," *Criticat* 9 (March 2012), 110.

26 In principle, Braungart and McDonough reject this "eco-efficient" paradigm in favor of an "eco-effective" one. McDonough and Braungart, *Cradle to Cradle*, 62.

27 See, for example, Francisco Valenzuela and Steffen Böhm, "Against Wasted Politics: A Critique of the Circular Economy," *Ephemera: Theory & Politics in Organization* 17, no. 1 (2017): 23–60.

28 Wall Kimmerer, *Braiding Sweetgrass*, 21.

29 Ibid., 27–28.

understood to be a "bundle of rights," whereas in a gift economy property has a "bundle of responsibilities" attached.[29]

4.3 Designing Hyperobjects

In recent years, a wave of new materialist philosophies and environmental discourses, along with the increasing pressures exerted by the climate emergency, have prompted a reconsideration of the materiality of buildings. On one side, feminist and political theories of agency and knowledge (e.g., Karen Barad's "agential realism";[30] Donna Haraway's "situated knowledges";[31] Jane Bennett's "distributed agency")[32] have emphasized the entanglement between humans and nonhumans, doing and being, epistemology and ontology—rejecting the centrality of the *anthropos* and denouncing the violence of objective or universal positions (what Haraway calls the "god trick of seeing everything from nowhere").[33] These approaches invite a re-situating of objects, buildings, and landscapes that accounts for (and makes accountable) their embodied energy and material ecologies, as well as their enabling or impairing of bodies.

30 Karen Michelle Barad, *Meeting the Universe Halfway: Quantum Physics and the Entanglement of Matter and Meaning* (Durham: Duke University Press, 2007).

31 Donna Haraway, "Situated Knowledges: The Science Question in Feminism and the Privilege of Partial Perspective," *Feminist Studies* 14, no. 3 (1988): 575–599.

32 Jane Bennett, *Vibrant Matter: A Political Ecology of Things* (Durham: Duke University Press, 2010).

33 Haraway, "Situated Knowledges," 581.

34 See, for example, Ravi Srinivasan and Kiel Moe, *The Hierarchy of Energy in Architecture: Energy Analysis* (London: Routledge, 2015), 85–108.

On the other side, the tendency to conflate sustainability with a reduction in the energy required for buildings to operate (and with heat in particular), or with notions of efficiency, has been supplemented by growing evidence pointing to the large role played by building materials (by their extraction, transportation, processing, installation, maintenance, demolition, and disposal) in the dissipations of energy associated with the built environment, not to mention the harm inflicted on lives and ecosystems.[34] From this perspective, and straddling production studies, thermodynamics, and environmental design, a novel *archeological* understanding of buildings and landscapes has emerged—one that suspends the shallow claims and regurgitated press releases of "green architecture" and subjects them to the reality of an output's energetic histories and material geographies. The contributions of two scholars—Jane Hutton and Kiel Moe—are of particular relevance to the present discussion.

35 Jane Hutton, *Reciprocal Landscapes: Stories of Material Movements* (Abingdon and New York: Routledge, 2020).

In *Reciprocal Landscapes: Stories of Material Movements*, Jane Hutton sets out to trace the flows of five materials (guano from Peru, granite from Maine, steel from Pittsburgh, trees from Rikers Island, and ipe hardwood from Brazil) that feature in prominent New York City landscapes (Central Park, Broadway, Riverside Park, Seventh Avenue, and the High Line).[35] In so doing, she establishes a tension—a reciprocity—between the sites at each end of these flows, implicating them in each other's story. Understanding materials as "fragments of other landscapes; as the livelihoods and habitats of people who live near them" and "as connections between the most tactile aspects of a design and the global circulation of matter driven by capitalism," Hutton reads sites of subtraction and construction, production and consumption—and the unequal exchanges between them—as continuous and necessarily entangled.[36] In the complex histories she uncovers and makes visible, the trees lining Seventh Avenue are the product of forced prison labor, and the guano used as fertilizer in Central Park cannot be separated from the exploitation and enslavement of Chinese laborers on the Chincha Islands, or from the rapid depletion of millennia-old guano deposits. In Hutton's stories, that is, materials do not occupy an abstract marketplace, nor do they exist in a socio-political and environmental vacuum (a *tabula rasa*). They cannot be described by listing properties or quantities, or (only) according to the recipes and outputs of a design project, individuation process, or equipmental script. As a consequence, not only doesn't the history of a landscape, object, or building coincide with an account of its commissions and authors, but the intents and aspirations associated with the projects that mobilize materials can no longer be meaningful without—and may be neutralized or contradicted by—the longer (and often violent) trajectories described by their progressive embodiment.

In *Empire, State & Building*, Kiel Moe investigates the development of a plot of land in New York City—the parcel onto which the Empire State Building will be eventually erected. From common land to the Thompson Farm (1799–1825), from undeveloped land (1825–1854) to the mansions of the Astor family (1856–1887), from the Waldorf and Waldorf-Astoria Hotels (1893/1897–1930) to the Empire State Building (1931–),[37] Moe tracks the incoming and outgoing flows of materials associated with the vertiginous waves of building and un-building on the site, recording how each new cumulative and dissipative cycle is met by exponential growth in material throughput and by supply chains with an increasingly global reach. For example, if the wood, stone, and glass required to build the farm and its many alterations and additions would have been predominantly sourced locally, and the building's total mass amounted to under 7,000 kilograms, the materials used in the construction of the Empire State Building came from as far as Guyana, Germany, Italy, and Malaysia, and reached almost 61 million kilograms in architectural terracotta alone.[38] Yet, if the embodied energy (in Odum's sense of energy–memory, or e*mergy*)[39] of each output can be calculated by considering the energy expenditures associated with the extraction, processing, transportation, installation, maintenance, demolition, and end-of-life disposal of each material or component—by the amount of energy captured over time—Moe argues that such values are not meaningful in isolation, or even on a building basis, but only in relation to the exergy (the amount of available energy) afforded, and to a longer process of urbanization. "Regarding the ecological efficacy of any plot of land," he writes, "high or low emergy constructions do not reveal much about the ecology of built environments. Rather, it is the work (available energy and affordances) provided by that emergy that must be considered from an ecological and thermodynamic point of view. The long view of emergy/exergy ratios in shifting pulses of

36 Hutton, *Reciprocal Landscapes*, 5.

37 Kiel Moe, *Empire, State & Building* (New York: Actar, 2017), 44–125.

38 Moe, *Empire, State & Building*, 128–78.

39 Howard T. Odum, *Environmental Accounting: EMERGY and Environmental Decision Making* (New York: Wiley, 1996).

construction, deconstruction, use, and dispersion provides a succinct, cogent perspective, never considered in architecture, on the general urban ecological efficacy of parcels."[40]

In other words: whereas the embodied energy alone increases in direct proportion to the scale of the developments on the plot and to the expansion in the scope of their material geography (farm < mansions < hotel < tower), calculating the ecological efficacy of each development through emergy/exergy ratios (for instance, considering the amount of people served by each development) and comparing them to one another with the plot as system boundary, yields very different results. In fact, the Empire State Building achieves, despite having the highest embodied energy, the lowest ratio (the highest level of ecological efficacy), followed, not unexpectedly, by the farm.[41] Moe's research doesn't only connect buildings with their material history and with technical processes of formation. By tying their meaning to successive waves of construction and deconstruction, it demands that architects refrain from reducing buildings to objects (to their appearance), and rather consider them as "open thermodynamic and ecological system[s]" and "fundamental processes of urbanization."[42]

The archeological approaches discussed above trouble the presumed coextension of designed outputs—of objects, landscapes, and buildings—with the boundaries of the system one must consider to describe and assess them. This also prompts a reformulation of EoIs, or the need to reconsider (or better consider) their boundaries. As discussed in previous chapters, an ecology of inception unlocks and curates potentials in both space (between objects that are either contiguous or distant) and time (as powers that are either withheld or actualized). Therefore, EoIs exceed a simple description of physical outputs in the here and now. Like Heidegger's equipment or Hutton's landscapes, they cannot denote or describe a single object in isolation ("one equipment") without implicating (or, rather, comprising) a wider set of actors and relations. Yet, if Heidegger's notion of equipment suspended tools in synchronous networks linked by their ability to communicate with one another (their sympathies, and strivings for common goals), EoIs are less preoccupied with communication per se than with how communication is wrought and maintained; less with constellations of coordinated tools than with the diachronic extrusion of the materials, distributed as these may be, that are mobilized towards their fabrication and continued use.

Timothy Morton uses the term "hyperobject" to describe "products such as Styrofoam and plutonium that exist on almost unthinkable timescales."[43] Amongst these pervasive materials are plastic bags outliving biological life on the planet;[44] radioactive materials like strontium-90 penetrating living tissue from a distance;[45] the endocrine disruptors in pesticides like Roundup;[46] oil and mercury spills; and global warming—real and yet only detectable through passing local manifestations (a tsunami, a blade of sunlight, a drop of rainwater).[47]

40 Moe, *Empire, State & Building*, 216.

41 Ibid.

42 Ibid., 242–49.

43 Timothy Morton, *The Ecological Thought* (Cambridge: Harvard University Press, 2012), 19.

44 "If I could meet my maker," says the plastic bag in Ramin Bahrani's movie, "I would tell her just one thing: I wish that she had created me so that I could die." Ramin Bahrani, *Plastic Bag* (Noruz Films and Gigantic Pictures, 2009). See also Timothy Morton, *Hyperobjects: Philosophy and Ecology after the End of the World* (Minneapolis: University of Minnesota Press, 2013), 60.

45 Morton, *Hyperobjects*, 33–34.

46 Ibid., 38.

47 Ibid., 70.

Hyperobjects are viscous (global warming "never stops sticking to you, no matter where you move on Earth");[48] they are nonlocal ("massively distributed in time and space");[49] they come and go, occupying a "higher-dimensional phase space" of which one can only experience "somewhat constrained slices";[50] and they are interobjective ("enmeshed into a relationship with other objects in the mesh").[51]

What interests me here is that, if one were to reduce them in scope, one could find traces of hyperobjectivity in the outermost layers of the ecologies that produce mobile phones and glazing panels, concrete walls, pork chops, apple pie, and plywood furniture. Whereas ecologies of inception, by claiming high levels of control within clear-cut boundaries, might at first appear to antagonize hyperobjects, one might use Morton's term to soften their perimeter and cut them open, combining individual organs into monstrous assemblages—into bodies that can be somehow recognized despite their spatiotemporal distribution and opacity.

An ecology of eating pork chops—pork-chop-eating as a kind of hyperobject—does not (only) call into play a choreography of mouths, forks, blood, and barbecue sauce; or a specific recipe, grill, and set of ingredients. It also involves at least a farm, a farmer, and one specific pig: its life (the conditions it was reared in, its feed, excrement, etc.) and its death in the slaughterhouse. The farming/butchering of pigs and the cooking of pork chops (or of other cuts) are dependent upon—and would not exist without—one another. In other words: pigs would not be farmed (at least not industrially) if nobody ate bacon and pork. And nobody would eat pork if none were produced. The two activities, physically and logistically separate as they may be (the farmer and the chef may never meet or coordinate their efforts), coproduce one another—one provides the context within which the other's potentials can be unlocked. And this (rather obvious) point could also be made of, for example, sand mining in Lake Poyang in relation to the industrial production of glass and concrete for buildings in Shanghai;[52] of the extraction of lithium in Chilean salt flats or of cobalt in Congolese mines vis-à-vis the manufacturing of rechargeable batteries for electric vehicles in San Francisco;[53] or of the felling of old-growth trees in the Amazonian rainforest in relation to the specification of tropical hardwood decking for luxury condominiums in London.

An ecology of inception is, in this sense, what emerges out of the reciprocal coproduction of its subecologies, or between the linked technical chains it oversees. That is: while a teleological orientation—a project, a script, a protocol—must drive specific subecologies (an ecology of farming, an ecology of butchering, an ecology of packaging and distributing, and ecology of mixing concrete, etc.), larger ecological enclosures also come into being on account of the potentials activated between them, both negotiating transitions between subecologies (from form to matter) and redirecting them towards novel objectives (larger enclosures). If EoIs can be usually associated with a design (a *telos* or

48 Ibid., 48.

49 Ibid.

50 Ibid., 74.

51 Ibid., 83.

52 See for instance, Vince Beiser, "Sand Mining: The Global Environmental Crisis You've Probably Never Heard Of," *The Guardian*, 27 February 2017.

53 See for example Thea Riofrancos, "What Green Costs," *Logic Magazine*, 7 December 2019; Annie Kelly, "Apple and Google Named in US Lawsuit over Congolese Child Cobalt Mining Deaths," *The Guardian*, December 16, 2019.

project), they need not exist within its confines, or within the regimes of control and coordination they curate (for instance, as supply chains in the manufacturing of a single product). Instead, they can emerge as properties of the unscripted or remote/implicit exchanges between ecologies that, like the farming of pigs and the frying of bacon, or the dredging of sand and the pouring of concrete, have no formal or local connections (share no scripts), but nonetheless feed and coproduce one another in the context of the global market economy. Like distributed or noncontiguous organs that are nonetheless capable of performing bodily functions (e.g., the coupling of lung and tree), ecologies of inception metabolize materials and move them across territories, often without touching them at all. [**Figure 4.6**]

As with Hutton's reciprocal landscapes and Moe's thermodynamic conception of buildings, the layering of ecologies of inception (or what, paraphrasing Harman, one might call "ecologies wrapped in ecologies wrapped in ecologies")[54] invites designers to broaden the scope of their practice—the "parochial purview" that blinds them to the "designed and specified but 'unintended' degradation" they cause[55]—and to reappraise the presumed centrality of their intentions, projects, and outputs. Yet, naming these sticky systems—identifying their emergent/diachronic ecologies as hyperobjects (rather than as unrelated processes or strings of individual outputs)—also calls into question the presumed proportionality (1:1 ratio) between responsibility (as a distributed, futural, and planetary-scale pursuit) and any specific action.

[54] Graham Harman, *Guerrilla Metaphysics: Phenomenology and the Carpentry of Things* (Chicago: Open Court, 2005), 85.

[55] Kiel Moe, *Unless: The Seagram Building Construction Ecology* (New York: Actar Publishers, 2020), 91.

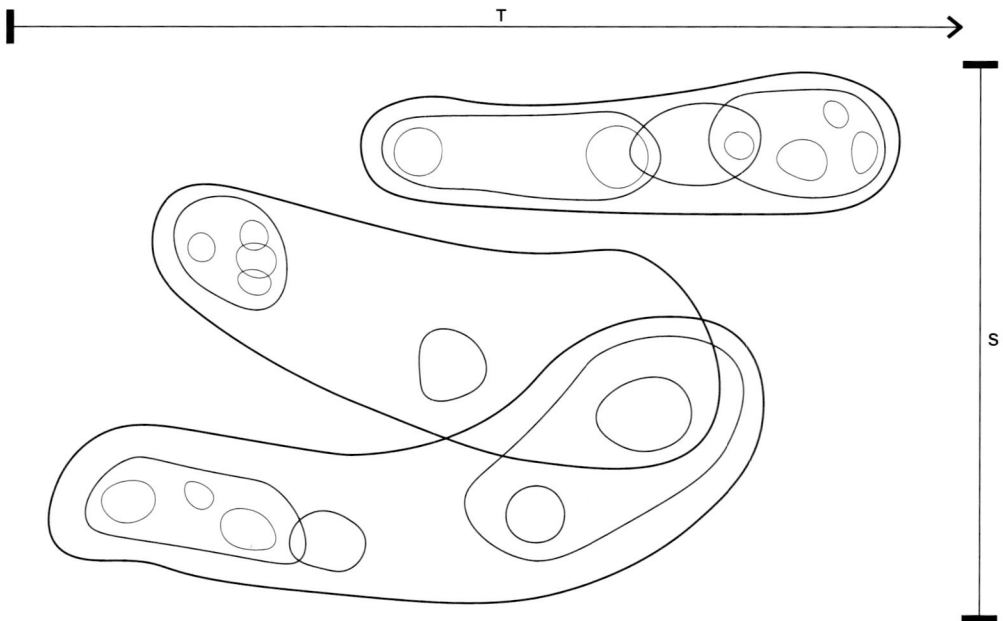

Figure 4.6 Mapping ecologies and subecologies along two axes (T for time, S for space).

To recognize hyperobjects, and not just objects, as the *actual* outputs of design (be they pen sharpeners, schools, garments, door frames, parks, or hammers) might force designers to both admit that their responsibilities spill past the system boundaries considered at any given time (those framed by commissions, projects, and ecological scripts) and that their outputs, and the powers they unlock, are as significant as they are intrinsically partial, tentative, and incomplete. "It is extremely healthy," writes Morton, "to know not only that there are monstrous beings, but that there are beings that are not purely thinkable, whose being is not directly correlated with whatever thinking is."[56] Perhaps understanding EoIs coincides with the realization that one can never just design bicycles, museums, sofas, and skyscrapers; we are always (also) designing monsters.

4.4 Circularity (the Wrong Metaphor)

The circular economy, of which *Cradle to Cradle* represents one of the most popular instances, has a complex history at the intersection of economy, environment, and design—from Rachel Carson's *Silent Spring* (1962)[57] to the "blue marble" photographed by the Apollo 17 crew in 1972, which starkly revealed, for the first time, the fragility of the Earth and the finitude of its resources;[58] from Nicholas Georgescu-Roegen's coupling of the flows in economic and biophysical systems—and the distinction between (renewable) funds and (nonrenewable) stocks[59]—to Robert Ayres and Allen Kneese's rethinking of externalities in the interactions between economic processes and the environment;[60] from Walter Stahel and Geneviève Reday-Mulvey's 1976 report "The Potential for Substituting Manpower for Energy," which already imagined an economy in loops,[61] to Stahel's later *Performance Economy*, which further articulated the need to replace owned goods with services, and to link taxation and undesirability (nonrenewables);[62] from John Tillman Lyle's promotion of regenerative design methods,[63] or Janine M. Benyus's work on biomimicry,[64] to Sim Van der Ryn and Stuart Cowan's coinage of the phrase *ecological design*.[65]

The list could continue, yet my aim here is not to provide a comprehensive account or definitive history of the circular economy, or to contextualize it within broader developments in sustainable design, but to recognize the heterogeneity of the approaches that in recent years have, often under the aegis of the Ellen MacArthur Foundation, cohered around the term.[66] In this sense, a circular approach to the materials economy, as exemplified by the so-called "butterfly diagram," might be understood to include a wide range of disparate concerns and strategies (e.g., reduce, reuse, repair, remanufacture, repurpose, recycle)—some of which are, as I will argue, at odds with one another. Yet, at the center of the circular economy remains the pursuit of the enhanced and continued circulation of nutrients, and their separation into pure technical and biological flows. [**Figure 4.7**]

56 Morton, *Hyperobjects*, 64.

57 Rachel Carson, *Silent Spring* (Boston: Houghton Mifflin, 1962).

58 "Blue Marble – Image of the Earth from Apollo 17," NASA, November 30, 2007.

59 Nicholas Georgescu-Roegen, *Analytical Economics: Issues and Problems* (Cambridge: Harvard University Press, 1967).

60 Robert U. Ayres and Allen V. Kneese, "Production, Consumption, and Externalities," *American Economic Review* 59, no. 3 (1969): 282–97.

61 Geneviève Reday-Mulvey, Walter R. Stahel, and Commission of the European Communities, "The Potential for Substituting Manpower for Energy: Final Report 30 July 1977," Study (Battelle Geneva), 1977, published as: Walter R. Stahel and Geneviève Reday-Mulvey, *Jobs for Tomorrow: The Potential for Substituting Manpower for Energy* (New York: Vantage Press, 1981).

62 Walter R. Stahel, *The Performance Economy* (Houndsmille and New York: Palgrave Macmillan, 2010).

63 John Tillman Lyle, *Regenerative Design for Sustainable Development* (New York: Wiley, 1994).

64 Janine M. Benyus, *Biomimicry: Innovation Inspired by Nature* (New York: Morrow, 1997).

65 Sim Van der Ryn and Stuart Cowan, *Ecological Design* (Washington: Island Press, 1996). For a succinct history of ecological design, see Lydia Kallipoliti, "History of Ecological Design," in *Oxford Research Encyclopedia of Environmental Science* (Oxford University Press, 2018).

66 "Homepage," Ellen MacArthur Foundation, accessed June 7, 2020.

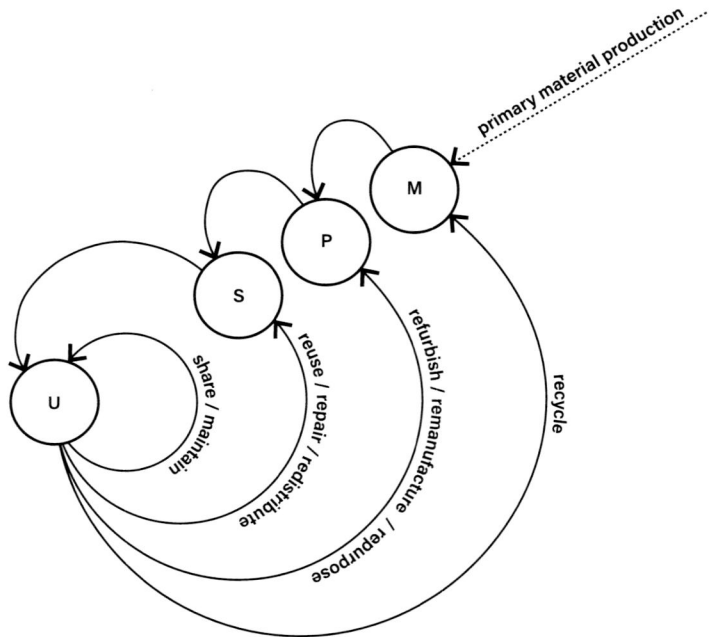

67 See for example: Nicholas Georgescu-Roegen, *The Entropy Law and the Economic Process* (Cambridge: Harvard University Press, 1971); Markus Reuter, Antoinette Schaik, and Miquel Ballester, "Limits of the Circular Economy: Fairphone Modular Design Pushing the Limits," *World of Metallurgy - ERZMETALL* 71 (March 19, 2018): 68–79; Samantha MacBride, *Recycling Reconsidered: The Present Failure and Future Promise of Environmental Action in the United States* (Cambridge: MIT Press, 2013); Trevor Zink and Roland Geyer, "Circular Economy Rebound," *Journal of Industrial Ecology* 21, no. 3 (June 2017): 593–602; Trevor Zink and Roland Geyer, "Material Recycling and the Myth of Landfill Diversion," *Journal of Industrial Ecology* 23, no. 3 (June 2019): 541–48.

68 See for example: Vincent Moreau et al., "Coming Full Circle"; Jordon Lazell, Solon Magrizos, and Marylyn Carrigan, "Over-Claiming the Circular Economy: The Missing Dimensions," *Social Business* 8, no. 1 (May 31, 2018): 103–14; Jouni Korhonen, Antero Honkasalo, and Jyri Seppälä, "Circular Economy: The Concept and Its Limitations," *Ecological Economics* 143, no. C (2018): 37–46; Jonathan M. Cullen, "Circular Economy: Theoretical Benchmark or Perpetual Motion Machine?," *Journal of Industrial Ecology* 21, no. 3 (June 2017): 483–86. SCP/RAC, "Plastic's Toxic Additives and the Circular Economy," September 2020.

Figure 4.7 The management of material stocks in a circular economy, describing the flows between a user U, a service provider S, a part or product manufacturer P, and a producer of materials M. Based on (and adapted from) the Ellen MacArthur Foundation's *Circular Economy System Diagram* (February 2019). I should also note that the terms *refurbish* and *remanufacture* are defined as "restor[ing] an old product and bring[ing] it up to date" and as "us[ing] parts of [a] discarded product in a new product with the same function" respectively (Potting et al., 2017). In this book, I have preferred the more general—but precise—term *reuse* to indicate the ecological reintegration of discarded objects (or parts of objects) that maintain their formal integrity and functional orientation.

Painted in broad strokes, this aim easily resonates with designers, clients, and the public. Who wouldn't prefer being surrounded by non-harmful materials that may one day be safely re-absorbed into the biosphere, or favor the eternal recirculation of materials over their wasteful disposal and dispersal? Yet, evidence-based analyses in fields such as discard studies, industrial ecology, and ecological economics have started to carefully unpick the circular economy and test its claims—exposing the dissipative and entropic dimensions of recycling processes, as well as their inefficiencies and historical failures (their inability to reduce resource extraction and material throughput, or to displace primary production);[67] pointing to difficulties in defining a system's spatiotemporal boundaries vis-à-vis social and environmental impacts, and addressing the need to account for all materials and inputs (including fossil fuels and hazardous chemicals) when calculating circularity;[68]

identifying the fundamental misalignment between sustainability and economic growth (between a circular economy and growing consumption rates);[69] et cetera.[70] While these on-going discussions primarily examine whether material loops can be actually closed, however, my intention is to reconsider, from the point of view of potentiality, the viability of the circle as a figure of sustainability.

In many technical systems, the circulation of materials follows a linear trajectory (take/make/consume/dispose) that, over the life of a product, dissipates its embodied energy, moving it from ecologies of use and value to landfills, pollution, and waste-to-energy facilities (incinerators). Traditional recycling programs bend this linear path, aiming to retain and retrieve the material value of objects, albeit in lower-grade form due to progressive contaminations and hybridization (downcycling).[71] Therefore, if recycling slows an object's march towards entropy, the processes associated with it draw the figure of a vertical spiral or corkscrew, rather than a circle.[72] Only when a more suitable substance (a technical nutrient) is recycled, or a better collection, sorting, and processing ecology is put in place, the loop does, at least in principle, and with the addition of external energy, close (upcycling). Here, the determination of circularity is both quantitative (the ratio between inputs and outputs) and qualitative (their chemical equivalence, which measures the molecular purity of the upcycled material).

What is remarkable about this technical loop, the practicability of which is, as seen above, highly contested, is that its most basic premise—the horizon of its ambitions—already perpetuates a hylomorphic and object-erasing bias, and this bias is, I would argue, the keystone of the circular economy, and gives it its name. In other words: what upcycling forgets and erases (the price it willingly pays for the recirculation of materials) are the resources, labor, and lands associated with the manufacturing of the discarded object—its hyperobjective memory. The ability to recycle the entirety of an aluminum window frame (to remelt it into a billet and extrude it into new forms), admirable as it may seem,[73] still dissipates the 54 kilograms of minerals, 5 kilograms of chemicals, 70 kilograms of water, and 39 kilograms of fossil fuels required to manufacture it;[74] it still nullifies and makes vain the labor expended and damage (environmental and otherwise) caused in bringing the original object into existence. And furthermore, it sanctions the "sustainability" and desirability of the comparatively "moderate" damage inflicted by the secondary processing of scrap aluminum.

In the book *Aluminum Upcycled: Sustainable Design in Historical Perspective*, Carl A. Zimring describes the numerous recorded diseases and health hazards associated with secondary aluminum production, and their polluting effects on land, air, and water.[75] He writes:

> [S]econdary aluminum producers acknowledged releases of ammonia, sulfuric acid, hydrochloric acid, chromium compounds,

69 Johann Fellner et al., "Present Potentials and Limitations of a Circular Economy with Respect to Primary Raw Material Demand," *Journal of Industrial Ecology* 21, no. 3 (June 2017): 494–96.

70 Useful summaries of key topics are provided in: Hervé Corvellec et al., "Introduction to the Special Issue on the Contested Realities of the Circular Economy," *Culture and Organization* 26, no. 2 (March 3, 2020): 97–102; Kris De Decker, "How Circular Is the Circular Economy?: Why This Proposed Solution Is Little More than a Magic Trick," *Uneven Earth* (blog), November 27, 2018; John Mulrow and Victoria Santos, "Moving the Circular Economy beyond Alchemy," *Discard Studies* (blog), November 13, 2017.

71 McDonough and Braungart, *Cradle to Cradle*, 56–58.

72 Antonio Valero and Alicia Valero, "Thermodynamic Rarity and Recyclability of Raw Materials in the Energy Transition: The Need for an In-Spiral Economy," *Entropy* 21, no. 9 (September 8, 2019): 873.

73 The primary production (mining and smelting) of aluminum is a "spectacularly destructive activity" that causes deforestation, pollutes ground water, damages the habitats and health of both humans and nonhumans, and displaces local communities. Carl A. Zimring, *Aluminum Upcycled: Sustainable Design in Historical Perspective* (Baltimore: Johns Hopkins University Press, 2017), 32.

74 Marian R. Chertow, "Waste, Reuse, and Symbiosis: Closing Material Loops" (Discarded: Unmasking & Understanding the Waste Stream, Lear-Conant Symposium, Connecticut College, March 6, 2021).

75 Zimring, *Aluminum Upcycled*, 75–76.

76 Data from Right to Know Network, Toxics Release Inventory database. Search term "331314: Secondary Smelting and Alloying of Aluminum"; search conducted May 4, 2015. Quoted in Zimring, *Aluminum Upcycled*, 76.

77 Ibid.

ethylbenzene, hydrogen fluoride, and lead, among other toxins.[76] The closed loop of recycling does result in energy savings and extensions of the life of materials. Producing those technical nutrients, however, releases toxins that could poison workers, neighbouring residents, and ecosystems.[77]

Again, one might ask: should the charitable benevolence of "toxicity in moderation"—or, the strategic (colonial, racist, classist) sacrificing of *some* workers, neighborhoods, and ecosystems—really be hailed as the apex of sustainability? And does the difference between recycling and upcycling in this context (whether the new object will be sold for more or less than the original object) actually matter? As Jennifer Gabrys asks,

> Does the intractability of remainders signal the exhaustion of materials, or does it suggest that exhaustion extends as much to the economic and material processes that cast objects through strange loops of materialities imagined to be free of environmental or political consequence?[78]

78 Jennifer Gabrys, "Salvage," in *Depletion Design: A Glossary of Network Ecologies*, ed. Carolin Wiedemann and Soenke Zehle (Amsterdam: Institute of Network Cultures, 2012), 138.

Zimring's historical analysis of aluminum upcycling—of its success, and of the dramatic increase in primary aluminum production that nonetheless accompanies it—further troubles the figure of the circle (of a closed loop of eternally recirculating resources).

> While a Norman Foster chair made entirely from recycled aluminum will have a life-cycle assessment of a closed materials loop, it helps build a market for more aluminum furniture. As designers create attractive goods from aluminum, bauxite mines across the planet intensify their extraction of ore at lasting cost to the people, plants, animals, air, land, and water of the local areas. *Upcycling absent a cap on primary material extraction does not close industrial loops so much as it fuels environmental exploitation.* Despite aluminum's high recycling rate, the appropriate schematic for aluminum use looks less like a closed loop than it resembles an upward spiral or funnel cloud drawing more primary material into the cycle of production as material demand increases.[79]

79 Ibid., 163. Italics in the original.

The circle has (again) become a spiral. Now, strangely enough, another set of (very different) loops are promoted by the same literature: the shorter trajectories describing cycles of repair, reuse, refurbishment and, eventually, remanufacturing. If upcycling sought molecular stability and availability across states, what persists here are forms of use. Or, more accurately: if loops of technical nutrients followed the whereabouts of materials from the exclusive perspective of molecular purity, these shorter routes are driven by teleological purity, and follow the adventures of a variety of characters in space and time: objects, users, and ecologies of use. Therefore, they cannot be reduced to the simple figure of the loop—they draw rather more complex sets of shapes.

It is hard to overstate how fundamentally antagonistic these two approaches (what the Ellen MacArthur Foundation might casually refer to as "long" and "short" loops) are. On one side, technical loops that claim to "design waste out" are predicated on the designation or sanctioning of waste in the first place—on a form of *objectual down-cycling*—whereas reuse ecologies begin precisely by contesting the merits of that designation. For example, if a bike is discarded, a "long loop" approach, taking the bike's lack of use value as a given, will separate its homogeneous materials and attempt to recycle/upcycle the resulting scrap metal. This forecloses possible *other* uses (or uses *by others*) and consigns the bike's value and powers (its metastability) to the circulation of its materials—to recycling ecologies, exchange values, and economic orthodoxy. Instead, a reuse or repurposing strategy will presume that the bike (as an object with specific properties, histories, and sets of components; as embodied labor and energy; as a hyperobject) indeed *has* powers, and will begin to move it across ecologies—and to peel off ecological layers— in order to find the contexts (users, equipment, etc.) that will activate and unlock them. In this sense, the circular economy does not eliminate rubbish as much as changes the parameters for its designation.

Instead, to actually do away with waste would demand a renunciation of fixed classification (ordering, purifying) systems—not by abandoning ecologies of inception or their cosmetic biases as valuing/potentializing apparatuses, but by proclaiming and defending their impermanence and relativity, and by avoiding their coalescing into monolithic or totalizing—and therefore unchangeable—enclosures (such as, for instance, the global market economy). Reuse and repurposing, as forms of political and social activism, reclaim the precedence of use over exchange, of situation over circulation—keeping value and powers at arm's length.

When Edinburgh-based artist/musician Tim Vincent-Smith hired a moving company to transport his piano to a new flat, he discovered that the company was often asked to remove discarded (nontunable) pianos from people's homes, and ended up paying a third party to burn them, retrieving only the leftover scrap metal.[80] Soon after, the company started to leave the pianos with Vincent-Smith instead, who stored them first in the basement of St. Margaret's House, where he rented a studio, and later on the premises of The Forge, a community center and maker space in the Fountainbridge area of Edinburgh. Vincent-Smith began to take the pianos apart and to use the components as building materials, and eventually resolved to build an amphitheater out of defunct pianos—a *Pianodrome*. [**Figure 4.8**] While Vincent-Smith and community members experimented with disassembling/reassembling pianos and developed protocols and prototypes, one of the cofounders of The Forge, Matt (Leon) Wright,

80 Personal communication with Vincent-Smith.

Figure 4.8 *Pianodrome*, cast iron harps, 2018. Photograph by Olivier Bardina.

took on the role of producer, applying for grants and securing the funds necessary to rent a warehouse to store (and work on) the 50-odd pianos collected. [**Figure 4.9**] Finally, over the course of two months, Vincent-Smith, Wright, and a group of professionals and volunteers (artists, musicians, carpenters, builders, students, prop makers, etc.) came together to build the five "wedges" of the amphitheater, which were installed as a public performance space at the Royal Botanic Garden during the Fringe Festival (2018, with a geodesic dome), and later inside the Leith Theatre (2019). [**Figure 4.10**] In each one of the three sections in a seating wedge, an upside-down piano is cantilevered from an upright piano using timber brackets and two cast-iron harps—all repurposed from discarded piano frames. [**Figure 4.11**] This primary structure is then fitted with other piano parts turned seats, steps, and balustrades. In one of the three sections of each wedge, the bottom piano can be played, transforming the amphitheater into a large and spatially distributed instrument, and eroding some of the barriers between stage and seats, performers and audience.

Figure 4.9 *Pianodrome* (under construction), 2018. Photograph by Chris Scott.

Figure 4.10 *Pianodrome*, Hebrides Ensemble performance, Leith Theatre, 2019. Photograph by Chris Scott.

It is unlikely that the *Pianodrome* displaced, in any literal sense, the production of primary materials (those typically used to build amphi-theaters, or pianos). Yet, even as the project preserves the energetic memory and integrity of piano components that would have otherwise been recycled, incinerated, or landfilled, its story exemplifies—beyond the measuring of carbon or the calculating of economic expediency—the ecological reclaiming of value; the design of sys-tems for its local re-designation and re-situation. Here as in the gift economy described by Wall Kimmerer, objects increase in value by changing hands—by moving across ecologies. To accept the discarded pianos is to become responsible for their storage; to obtain a warehouse or apply for funding is committing to completing an am-phitheater made entirely of piano components; to contribute to the build is to spend one's time

Figure 4.11 *Pianodrome*, hoisting and fastening the up-per piano into position, 2018. Photograph by Olivier Bardina.

and sweat towards a common project, which the public will be able to enjoy. The value of *Pianodrome* is not measurable in terms of ex-change or equivalence (how much), but of the reciprocal networks (of care, trust, collaboration, assistance, maintenance, etc.) woven during

81 Stefano Harney and Fred Moten, *All Incomplete,* with a foreword by Denise Ferreira da Silva, photos and an afterword by Zun Lee (New York: Minor Compositions, 2021), 14.

its conception, fabrication, and continued use. If, as Stefano Harney and Fred Moten claim, "[a]ll property is loss because all property is the loss of sharing," could reuse and repurposing make objects, once again, "vulnerable to sharing"?[81]

In any case, while molecular purity establishes its loop-closing criteria and system boundaries in advance (for instance, the recipe for a specific aluminum alloy), teleological purity can be measured on the go, and according to parameters that respond and adapt to changing opportunities, inputs, and preoccupations.

Using the lens of hylomorphism to compare the linear and circular modes of production discussed above with the *nodal* approach proposed in Chapter 2 can shed further light on this distinction. [**Figure 4.12**] A linear system of production transforms a matter-input into a form-output, and eventually releases it as waste (matter/form/waste). A circular mode of production links the first and last steps, matter and waste, and thus turns the latter into the input for a new productive cycle or ecology (matter/form/waste/matter/et cetera). In both cases, the potentials—the metastability—required to fuel an individuating

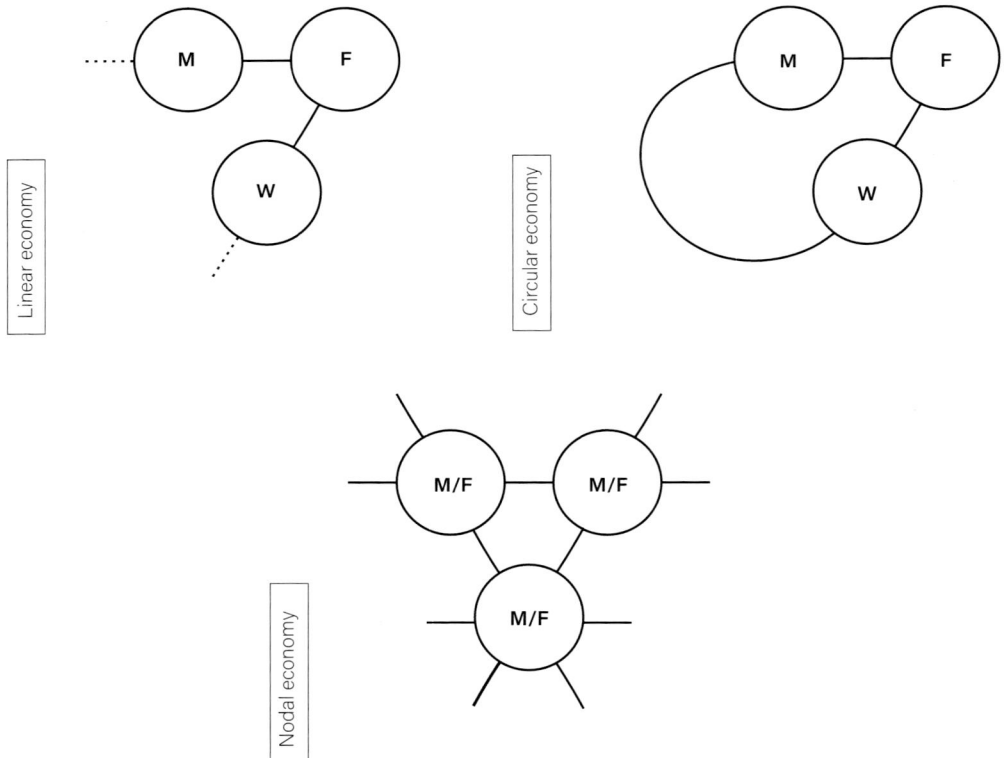

Figure 4.12 Comparing linear (Matter–Form–Waste), circular (Matter–Form–Waste–Matter), and nodal (Matter *or* Form) ecologies.

operation rely on the potentializing force of a matter-input, and assume both matter and form to be objective things in the world (timber and a table, clay and a brick). Instead, a nodal approach does not follow Aristotle in coupling matter with potentiality and form with actuality, but understands matter and form to be roles that any object can, in principle, perform—switches that can be relationally and contextually turned on or off. Yet, if matter and form are scripts defined by an ecological interior, so is waste, which exists only as expelled by that same interior (the inability to comply never precedes the design of compliance parameters). Hence, the question is no longer how to transform waste into a resource, or turn it back into a potentialized material, but how to find or draw new role-shuffling ecologies. Waste was never "objectively" there anyhow.[82]

I have presented the difficulties one encounters in applying the figure of the loop (the *ouroboros*) to the broad church of the circular economy (to anything other than recycling). The problem is not only that, as I have repeatedly claimed, recycling perpetuates the same hylomorphic bias that generates waste in the first place. Assuming that reuse and recycling are part of the same family of solutions (that one may "reuse if possible, recycle otherwise") disincentivizes an earnest and systemic uptake of reuse and repurposing—one that, alongside other growth-limiting and pollution-curbing measures, is urgently needed in order to displace primary materials and reduce extraction.[83]

Furthermore, one can detect between the lines, in the Ellen MacArthur Foundation's definition of the circular economy—"restorative and regenerative *by design*," and aiming to "keep products, components, and materials at their highest utility and value *at all times*"[84]—a further danger. The insistence on the agency of the designer (on her ability to find solutions, "by design") and on the extended temporal viability of those solutions ("at all times") reveals, alongside a high-modern panache, another requisite feature of circularity: control. Closing the loop requires an exasperated level (and spatiotemporal distribution) of control. Not only must the flow of products and materials be meticulously orchestrated in advance, across supply chains and geographies; it must also account for a virtually perpetual succession of cycles, which extrude materials, protocols, and uses far into the future, presuming a measure of intergenerational compliance.

Yet, is this the future *we* wish for—one that preserves the arrogance and hubris of modernity and extends it in space and time, in the name of sustainability? One that believes in top-down optimization and improvement as a valid (and politically neutral) program? One that ignores the shortsightedness of human systems (of our designs, organizations, desires, history) in relation to the timespans of the geophysical world? One that forgets our humanity—the vital importance of play, misuse, imprecision, improvisation, failure, surprises, and suspension?

[82] To be sure, this does not imply a lack of toxicity. While much waste is indeed toxic, toxicity is not accrued upon being discarded, but designed into commodities from the start. What might differ in discarded items is that toxins and toxicants, once detached from the ecologies and thresholds associated with the object's primary use, might increase in power or availability.

[83] Would a marital agreement to "be faithful if possible, and cheat otherwise" incentivize faithfulness? Likely not. In addition, behavioral studies have shown that recycling could increase consumption. See Monic Sun and Remi Trudel, "The Effect of Recycling versus Trashing on Consumption: Theory and Experimental Evidence," *Journal of Marketing Research* 54, no. 2 (April 2017): 293–305.

[84] Ellen MacArthur Foundation, "Towards a Circular Economy: Business Rationale for an Accelerated Transition" (Ellen MacArthur Foundation, November 2015). My emphasis.

85 Timothy Morton, *Being Ecological* (UK: Pelican, 2018), 50.

After all, isn't ecological awareness, as Timothy Morton puts it, "awareness of unintended consequences"?[85]

Indeed, many of the ideas under the circular economy umbrella have the potential to catalyze positive, real change. However, it might be time to abandon the loop as a figure of sustainability. In its absence—without its sweet reassurance that *we* can keep consuming with the same careless joy of times past, and that consumption and sustainability can blissfully hold hands—with reuse and humility as keystones of a novel materials economy, *we* might be forced to re-learn how to manufacture, consume, design, and coexist.

4.5 Bridges and Rooms

The circular economy proposes to do away with waste by building expansive ecologies of inception that loop together processes of extraction, production, distribution, consumption, and disposal, absorbing them into a single, coordinated enclosure. Within this envelope, objects would acquire and retain a degree of equipmental value that is proportional to their ability to perform a scripted role, and to circulate in perpetuity. However, such an ecology (the enforcement of a boundary and the associated re-zoning of value) would still generate wastes—either by exclusion (leaving *other* objects out), by expulsion (rejecting components that fail to perform or comply), or by design (releasing the ecology's byproducts). It soon becomes clear that wastelessness cannot be achieved by increasing the size of a system (by exerting more control; by building larger and more efficient enclosures; or by progressive annexations), but by linking ecologies to one another. Resilience has little to do with the hubristic design of a solution-machine, or with the assumption that such a machine won't eventually break, leak, degrade and—in time—be forgotten. Rather, it can be sought on the outer surface of EoIs, stitching one machine (one project or generation) to the next. Value, that is, cannot be merely designed into EoIs, which are always also de-valuing apparatuses—it must be sought in the gaps between them.

Two types of transition are able to maintain or increase value across (sub-)ecologies: "form–matter nodes" and "form–form nodes." In form–matter nodes, typical of the links in a supply chain or between steps in a recipe, the formal output of a subecology becomes the material input for the following one. This form–matter transition can be scripted in advance (the MDF boards manufactured by one IKEA subcontractor are transported to the next one, who will feed them to their assembly line to produce BILLY bookcases) or be delayed (the MDF boards are displayed on the shelves of DIY stores and sold as materials). In form–form nodes, on the other hand, the output of the preceding subecology coincides with the end product (a door, a toilet bowl, a bookcase), and is therefore already slated for a target ecology. In order to reach it, however, it must often undergo a period of suspension. In shipping containers, warehouses, online inventories, and showrooms, the product waits to join an active ecology of use.

One might identify two key features in the productive transfers between ecologies of inception: bridges (direct links between an ecology A and an ecology B) and rooms (spaces within which the output of ecology A may remain suspended until a connection with other ecologies is established—until a suitable door B, C, D, etc., is found). [**Figure 4.13**] While bridges transfer objects across subecologies following

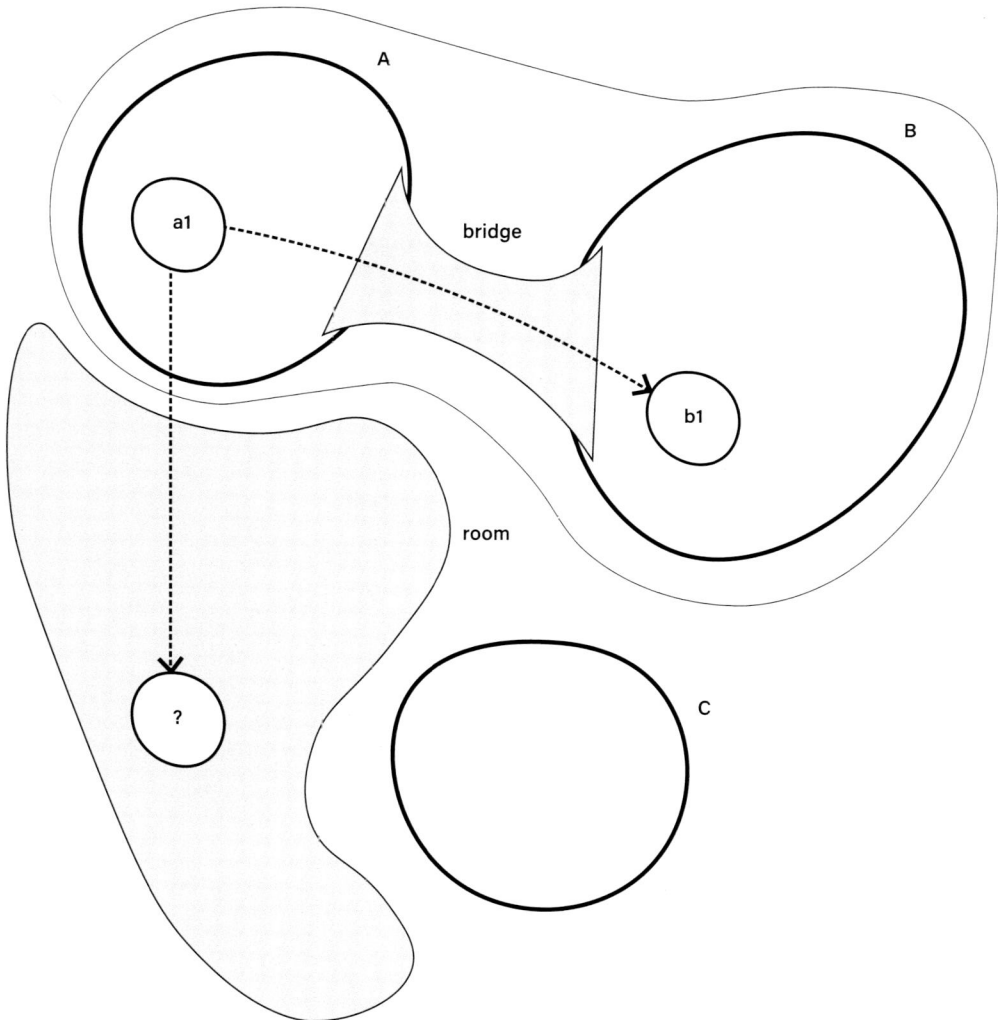

Figure 4.13 While bridges link two subecologies A and B, curating the direct transfer of outputs and components from one to the other, rooms hold them in a state of suspension, according to which they remain underdetermined (and possibly capable, in the future, of passing into an ecology C, or into as-yet-unknown ecologies D, E, and so on).

predetermined corridors (a larger EoI mediates between them), rooms do not impose fixed roles or translation protocols. Even as they normally function to lubricate the distribution of commodities (of ecologically valuable outputs), rooms remain, by definition, spaces within which ecological affiliations are loosened and partially suspended. Not only can anything, in principle, enter a room—anything can leave it; previously unseen doors might suddenly appear.

Once the discarded lampshade is cleaned and displayed in the salvage yard or antiques store, value-generating encounters can ensue—visitors might fall in love with its shape and color, purchase it, and install it in their home. And so might an architect finding three-hundred identical doors online decide to reuse them in a building, or a community with access to discarded pianos work together to combine them into a public amphitheater and performance space. The encounters within rooms (of which advertisements are, of course, one example) can activate unscripted potentials. It is therefore clear that, if one wants to understand how potentials are unlocked in space and time, one mustn't pay attention to the sole teleology of EoIs, but walk the wandering paths and breathe the potentializing air within rooms—within what I will call *ecologies of suspension*.

Part III
Authorship

Chapter 5

Rasura Tabulae:
From Formats to Media

5.1 *Rasura Tabulae*

5.1.1

Formats enforce, and operate within, normative relational ecologies and precise functional orientations. Whereas "form" can, in Aristotelian terms, be understood in isolation—as mere actualized matter—"format" (from the Latin *formatus*, shaped) is, in the wider connotation used here, the result of an active chain of operations that *in-form* matter towards a specific set of relationships and contexts of use. In other words: whereas form designates individual substances, a *format* describes them in relation to one another. In this sense, standardization consists in the selection and technical deployment of preferred—often more efficient or effective—communication channels between substances (objects and people). For example, the A4 sheet of paper is defined by the standard ISO/DIN proportions (aspect ratio of the square root of two) that afford it productive interactions (e.g., the physical correspondence between printer tray and sheet of paper as the basic requisite for printing). Similarly, the shape and size of a Styrofoam packing box follows that of the item it contains and insulates; a queen-sized bed affords the lying of two human bodies next to one another, while also determining the dimensions of mattresses, duvets, pillows, and sheets; a chair is designed for sitting on; the external thread of a metal bolt matches the internal thread of a nut; et cetera.

Formats across scales unlock relational affordances while simultaneously forcing objects into obligatory, often instrumental, interactions. Form(at) follows function, and the resulting monocultures reject, conceal, and foreclose all manner of *other*—nonteleological, bottom-up, spontaneous, queer—encounter. This should not be taken as a naïve denial of the fact that such encounters occur and have value—that, as Reyner Banham points out, a chair is sometimes used as a door stop, step ladder, work bench, stand, clothes hanger, and even as bongo drums;[1] and indeed some objects may be designed to be more

1 Reyner Banham, "Chairs as Art," *New Society*, April 20, 1967. Quoted in Nigel Whiteley, *Reyner Banham: Historian of the Immediate Future* (Cambridge: MIT Press, 2002), 354.

DOI: 10.4324/9781003015444-9

susceptible than others to unscripted uses—but as a reminder that the material economy of chairs (manufacture, marketing, acquisition, disposal) inevitably hinges upon their primary function: being objects for sitting on. Effectively, the violation of primary functional scripts (in the sense of the broken hammer famously described by Martin Heidegger, but also in a wider spectrum of valuing and devaluing industrial and cultural orthodoxies) often results in rejection and eviction—in the production of waste.

The devaluation of objects—their obsolescence—is not unlocked in a theater of generic and universal worth, or in the playful context of secondary uses, but in response to deficiencies within a primary functional ecology, in the same way that the definition of dirt, for Mary Douglas, is always interwoven with (and coproduced by) a specific context.[2] When the chair breaks and coffee is spilled on the sheet of paper, they are discarded regardless of the secondary uses that might have been previously supported or tolerated, which either no longer apply or fail to claim sufficient relevance. In this sense, the functional value of an object is not necessarily determined by its intrinsic properties (rigidity, porosity, weight, texture, etc.), but by the object's equipmental fitness—by how well it adheres to and augments an ecology of interconnected tools. While formatting enables objects to productively talk to one another (to form alliances), it also installs the principles whereby they will be muted, and become obsolete. The single-use polyethylene bottle is a case in point: once it exhausts the capacity to transport mineral water from the factory to the consumer, and can no longer perform a "proper" (formatted, designed) role, it is discarded—regardless of whether it has undergone any actual physical change.

Media, in the McLuhanian sense of the term, promote looser and more plastic sets of possibilities, beyond the design and naming of perfectly fitting and predictable machine cogs. Rather than referring to a mere communication channel or extension of human faculties, I will use the term "medium" to denote the distance that, in complex ecologies, intervenes between equipmental scripts (the ability of parts to communicate) and the potentials they unlock. The light bulb, for instance, facilitates the environment within which a wide range of nocturnal activities and interactions become possible.[3] And so does a musical instrument activate, on the horizon of its playability, all manner of sounds, from the "Happy Birthday" song to Chopin's *Nocturnes* to Annea Lockwood's *RCSC*.[4]

What sets the primary uses of a piano-medium apart from those of a chair-format is therefore a difference in latitude—*to play* is to actualize a broad spectrum of potentials, whereas *to sit* is to actualize one (with minor postural differences).[5] While a medium always depends on localized infrastructures—implicit or explicit, simple or complex, designed or spontaneous as these may be—it also invites liquid and unscripted encounters: the development and unfolding of unexpected and transitory *teloi*. Guided by McLuhan's celebrated formula "the medium is the

2 Mary Douglas, *Purity and Danger: An Analysis of Concepts of Pollution and Taboo* (London and New York: Routledge, 2002), 44.

3 Marshall McLuhan, *Understanding Media: The Extensions of Man* (Cambridge: MIT Press, 1994), 8–9.

4 Ricardo Descalzo, *Annea Lockwood - RCSC* (Alicante: NEUMA Records & Publications, 2014).

5 André Leroi-Gourhan writes that "a chair can never achieve perfection in terms of strict functionality, for to do so, it would have to be designed for just one individual sitting in just one position. A degree of functional plasticity will always be present." André Leroi-Gourhan, *Gesture and Speech* (Cambridge: MIT Press, 1993), 301. Sara Ahmed adds: "Functional plasticity means more can fit because the relation between form and function is made less precise. […] each person fitting less well means more can fit." Sara Ahmed, *What's the Use? On the Uses of Use* (Durham: Duke University Press, 2019), 44.

message," one might ascribe the difference between formats and media to the presence or lack of associated messages, or to their interpretability. And while the two terms can be imbricated and even coextensive (is a light bulb, or a sheet of paper, not both?) a format potentializes by exclusion and a medium by inclusion/annexation. This different approach reflects two possible interpretations of the *tabula rasa* as a figure of potentiality.

5.1.2

Giorgio Agamben traces the philosophical origin of the *tabula rasa* back to Aristotle's *De Anima,* in which the intellect (*nous*) is likened to a writing tablet (*grammateion*) "on which nothing is actually written."[6] The passage into actuality (*energeia*) of potentiality (*dynamis*) is represented by the act of writing, by engraving text (content, form) on the blank (contentless, formless) surface of the *grammateion*. Yet how can a rigid implement such as a tablet represent, even metaphorically, the indeterminacy of potential thought? Agamben seemingly condones this contradiction: "The difficulty that Aristotle seeks to avoid through the image of the writing tablet is that of the pure potentiality of thought and how it is possible to conceive of its passage to actuality. For, if thought in itself had a determinate form, if it were always already something (as a writing tablet is a thing), it would necessarily appear in the intelligible object and thus hinder intellection."[7]

In other words, Aristotle employs the image of a "determinate form" (a format: the tablet) to illustrate an indeterminate being (a medium: the intellect) that is, by definition, formless. Both the *tabula rasa* and the *tabula scripta* are however already actual, and exist as things. Agamben excuses this disjunction because the philosopher "takes care to specify that *nous* 'has no other nature than that of being potential, and before thinking it is absolutely nothing.'"[8] After all, the tablet–thing is for Aristotle merely a vehicle for blankness. It is the nakedness of the tablet, the fact that nothing is written on it, that allows it to mirror the nothingness of mind. However, precisely in the fracture that seems to expose the incompatibility of potentiality (nothing) with actualized form (something), one might find a key to undermine the trope of "creation from scratch" and to redefine and repurpose the *tabula rasa*.

My starting point is an observation by Alexander of Aphrodisias, who suggested that Aristotle should have spoken of *epitedeiotes*, the thin layer of wax covering a writing tablet, rather than of *grammateion*, the tablet itself.[9] This apparently modest shift in focus, from a *tabula rasa* to a *rasura tabulae*, resolves the contradiction by replacing the rigidity of the wood with the suppleness of the wax, which, like mind, is malleable and can't therefore be fixed into definitive, stable forms. But more importantly, it substitutes the blankness of the tablet with the plasticity of the writing surface, a formatted lack of content with a medium. It no longer matters whether the tablet is uninscribed, whether the wax

6   Giorgio Agamben, *Potentialities: Collected Essays in Philosophy*, trans. Daniel Heller-Roazen (Stanford: Stanford University Press, 1999), 244.

7   Agamben, *Potentialities*, 245.

8   Ibid.

9   Ibid.

has been recently melted and smoothed clean or engraved with words. The wax is shapeless insofar as its shape can change: plasticity—not blankness—is the figure of pure potentiality. The shift from a *tabula rasa* to a *rasura tabulae* suggests that formats can be re-oriented towards previously unforeseen functions, becoming *de facto* media. Indeed, misusing a chair (a thing to sit on) turns it into a mutable (playable) instrument—a step ladder, dance prop, shelf, foot rest, bongo drum, building block, et cetera.

5.2 Chairs as Media (1)

One way to identify a medium is to ask: "is it playable?" If the answer is "yes," chances are we are dealing with one. But I should clarify what the term "play" entails here. To play a piano, or the playability of a piano, presupposes the possibility that a key, once pressed, will return to an unpressed (and potentially pressable) state. It is by retrieving a previous position—and by moving between potential and impotential states—that the musical instrument becomes playable, as opposed to just played. A piano *can* be played because it can continue to be both played and not played, to produce sounds and to remain silent. If Heidegger attributes this quality to the reliability of tools (and the peasant woman can forget about the shoes she is wearing),[10] I suggest ascribing it to their plasticity (the malleability of the wax on the writing tablet). What does it mean, then, to *play a chair*? It presupposes the chair's ability to fluctuate between primary and secondary functions, backwards and forwards.[11] It presumes a diversion (e.g., from chair to step ladder) that, like the pressed key in a piano, can be undone, and return the object to an original state of rest (a primary function; a seat). [**Figure 5.1**]

In both cases, the object-as-medium is one that oscillates between uses and states. In order to be playable, both piano and chair require a degree of flexibility. However, if the playability of the former is inscribed within an equipmental script (an ecology of piano playing), the latter becomes playable by transgressing one (by moving the object beyond an ecology of sitting). This prompts a reconsideration of the difference, proposed in Chapter 2, between external impotentiality (a generic lack of communicability) and internal impotentiality (the temporary suspension of a designed communication channel), neither of which quite describes the chair-as-medium. Even as the primary function of a chair anchors its secondary uses, an intermediate kind of potentiality is needed, or the admission that *other* functional scripts can coexist with—or be attached to—the chair as seat. The word "internal" would then include any nonprimary function associated with the chair. That is, an object's "internal potentiality" would not coincide with the potentials unlocked by a primary design ecology, but with those unlocked by any ecology enlisting the given object (including, of course, the primary one, for which it was made).

10 Martin Heidegger, "The Origin of the Work of Art," in *Basic Writings: From Being and Time (1927) to The Task of Thinking (1964)*, ed. David Farrell Krell (San Francisco: HarperSanFrancisco, 1993), 87.

11 I don't mean to invoke Umberto Eco's distinction between primary (denotative) and secondary (connotative) functions, but a simpler registering of intended (designed for) vs. unintended ones. Umberto Eco, "Function and Sign: The Semiotics of Architecture," in *Rethinking Architecture: A Reader in Cultural Theory*, ed. Neil Leach (New York: Routledge, 2005), 173–86.

Figure 5.1 The chair as medium.

This approach is consistent with a co-optive design sensibility, of which *adhocism* represents one of the most celebrated articulations. In the book *Adhocism: The Case for Improvisation*, first published in 1972, Charles Jencks and Nathan Silver name—and map across various fields and disciplines—a "principle of action" that "involves using an available system in a new way to solve a problem quickly and efficiently."[12] Doing something *ad hoc* ("for this purpose") addresses a goal or need by diverting functional ecologies (materials at hand) or combining previously unrelated ones. [**Figure 5.2**] In this sense, adhocism and co-option may denote the transitory steps ("eureka flashes") or supplementary stages in traditional design and manufacturing chains, contributing to the establishment and strengthening of ecologies of inception. However, the authors privilege creative collisions, hybridity, and improvisation—and their readability as a "style"—as strategies for undermining, diverting, and customizing mass-produced commodities.[13] When objects cross the threshold of their "proper" uses and meanings (of the ecologies that sanctioned them), the full spectrum of their internal powers clicks into gear.[14]

Furthermore, these diversions can be exercised from the bottom up, and used to challenge purity (as a generic reality) and purification (as a potential form of violence). Dismissing "the recurrent dream of starting over again from scratch, or the equally powerful desire to construct a unified utopia based on ultimate values such as equality and freedom," Jencks regards adhocism as "a transitional philosophy based on the premise that the future goal of man, a single destiny for the species, cannot be specified in advance."[15] Rejecting and muddying universal and normative projects, well-intentioned as they may be (see my discussion of the circular economy in the previous chapter), adhocism reclaims the need for *all* potentials to be determined—and to remain determinable/retunable—locally, and from a multitude of viewpoints. The refusal to comply or to go along is the rupture or tear needed for changes to take place, and for new ecologies to come into view.

If at the end of the eighteenth century, "with the development of expert knowledge and modern institutions," writes anthropologist Arturo Escobar, "social norms were sundered from the life-world and defined heteronomously through

12 Charles Jencks, "The Style of Eureka," in Charles Jencks and Nathan Silver, *Adhocism: The Case for Improvisation* (Cambridge: MIT Press, 2013), vii.

13 Ibid., viii.

14 Jencks coins the term "multivise" or "restricted potentiality" to describe an object's "complementary qualities—the 'multi'-potentiality of any form as well as its inherent vise-like restrictedness." Jencks and Silver, *Adhocism*, 44–46.

15 Ibid., 35.

Figure 5.2 Lucas Muñoz, *Banfai Temple Stool*, Isaan region, Thailand, 2017. Leftovers from the Bun Banfai rocket festival are combined into a stool, using no tools, glue, screws, or nails.

16 Arturo Escobar, *Designs for the Pluriverse: Radical Interdependence, Autonomy, and the Making of Worlds* (Durham: Duke University Press, 2018), 32.

expert-driven processes,"[16] adhocism, and adhocist practices more generally, challenge modernity by privileging embodied materials, situated encounters, and local knowledges over hypermaterials, average users, and expert- or market-driven ecologies. Limited in scope as the *ad hoc* interventions may sometimes be, they represent a rejection of official or "appropriate" functions and tastes, moving design towards heterogeneity and pluralism (of interests, uses, ends, and values).

The adhocist pluriverse might even invoke or prefigure a different ontology. As sociologist John Law explains in his dismissal of a "one-world world" view:

> [D]ifferences are *not* simply matters of belief. They are also a *matter of reals*. What the world *is*, is also at stake. Our orderings (for instance our propensity to distinguish between nature or the natural on the one hand, and culture or the social on the other) do not carry to other places.[17]

17 John Law, "What's Wrong with a One-World World?," *Distinktion: Journal of Social Theory* 16, no. 1 (January 2, 2015): 127.

Law uses the example of the Australian Aboriginal people, according to whom land is continually performed through life, work, and rituals, and does not exist in the Western model of a reified and independent container—a "space" that can be owned or parceled up.[18] Different cultures cannot be ascribed to (or contained within) a single underlying reality without implying that such a reality (*the* world) coincides with *our* reality (the Western world as predicated, in this case, on the independent existence of a "large space–time box").[19] The only way out of this oppressive circle is to acknowledge the existence of (and, as Arturo Escobar suggests, to design for) many worlds—a pluriverse.[20]

18 Ibid., 126.

19 Ibid., 127.

20 Escobar, *Designs for the Pluriverse*.

5.3 Pedagogical Experiments

Before returning to adhocism and media, a few student projects will help illustrate how an adhocist practice might be put to work in a teaching context. Since 2018, I have led a third-year studio option in the undergraduate architecture program at the Edinburgh School of Architecture and Landscape Architecture (ESALA), the University of Edinburgh. Taught with Asad Khan, the *Radical Coauthorship* unit is a laboratory for the repurposing and revaluing of materials, and for a pedagogy that privileges encounters and physical prototyping over authors and concepts. The unit brief aims to "propose an alternative model for architectural practice, one where materials precede ideas, ecologies are given priority over intents, and creativity is understood as partial, distributed, and collaborative."[21]

21 Simone Ferracina, "Unit 2: Radical Coauthorship" (MA Hons. & BA Architecture Programs, ESALA, September 17, 2018).

The first exercise usually involves the surveying and mapping of materials, movements and events that would be otherwise excluded from "proper" architectural undertakings, or assumed to have no relevance. Students can investigate anything they like: the deposition of dust in a room; the baking of apple pie; the airflow through a space; the objects in a flat; the piles in a metal scrapyard; et cetera. At the outset, diffidence prevails. Yet, by the time students begin to prepare and reconfigure the tools needed to pay due attention to their selected objects and environments, it becomes clear that the significance of the drawing has shifted—from a tool used to illustrate ideas (to convey information) to one capable of establishing forms of communication, conversation, and conviviality (to give a voice). Furthermore, students quickly discover that drawing conventions—the language architects use to describe the world—cut reality into narrow slices that fail to represent its diversity, complexity, and vibrancy. How does one draw the humidity condensing onto a window pane, the smell of wild garlic, or the kneading of dough? How does one draw regimes of maintenance and care, or the slow decay of matter? How are networks of equipmental interdependence depicted? Or how might one represent the memories associated with an old photograph, or the toxicity of a discarded toy? By devising the tools and notational systems capable of registering and representing the selected ecologies and events, students make them worthy of study and attention, turning the drawing into a tool for caring, taking seriously, and making visible—for empowering worlds. [**Figure 5.3**]

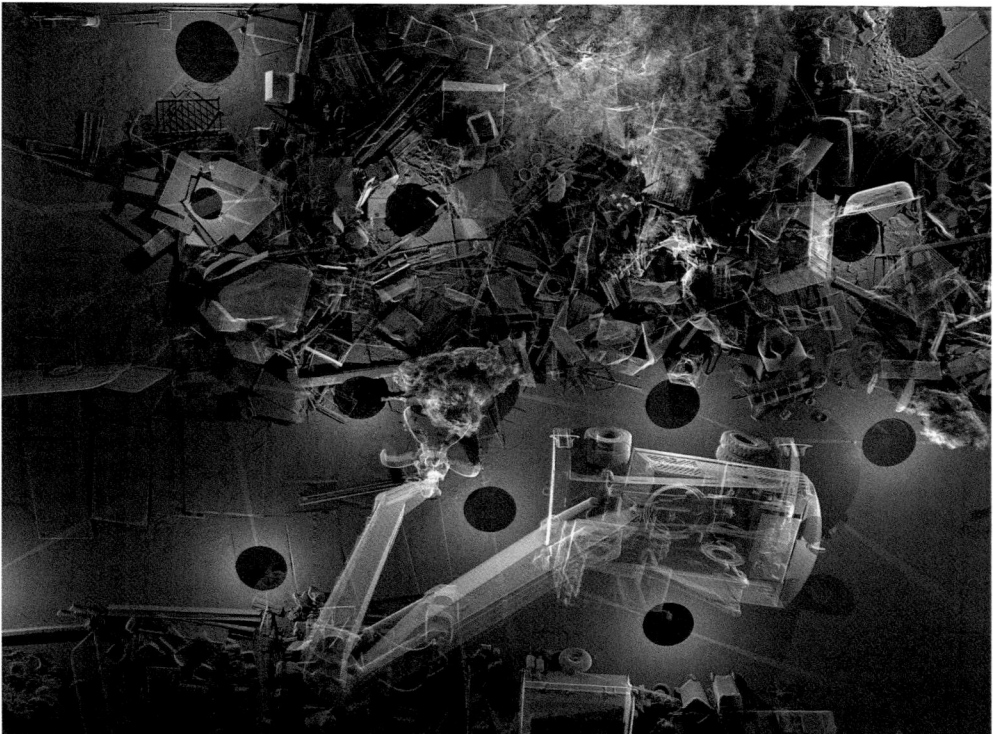

Figure 5.3 Cameron Angus, Jamie Begg, and Hannah Davis, *LIDAR Scan of Scrapyard and Crane*, AD3 Unit 2 Radical Coauthorship, Edinburgh School of Architecture and Landscape Architecture (ESALA), 2018–19.

The second exercise takes a more pragmatic approach to revaluing, asking students to identify and divert local waste flows, transforming discards of their choice (tires, glass bottles, rags, avocado peels, coffee grounds, rusty bike chains, etc.) into architectural materials and units of construction. Students begin by sourcing, classifying, and experimenting with discarded objects, testing affordances and prototyping three-dimensional assemblies.[22] In the course, and as discussed in Chapter 3, the term "material" is never assumed to designate natural or objective substrates—the *hyper*-glass, concrete, steel, stone, and timber of contemporary building construction. Materiality is not assigned in advance, in a vacuum, or from a distance, but patiently and responsively wrought into being, and woven into relational ecologies—knowledges, capacities, affordances, and functional sympathies. Finally, during the last phase of the 11-week course, students deploy the physical prototypes developed during the previous exercises to design a full-scale architectural intervention, thus introducing the goals and constraints (e.g., bodies, performances, environments) that will inform another round of experimentation and decision-making.

It is perhaps easy to dismiss these exercises as another instance of "garbage architecture."[23] However, I'd like to claim that their pedagogical value is independent of whether the proposed assemblages and solutions could (or should) be scaled up and adopted more widely. In the context of teaching, that is, the point is not to claim that such projects could reduce material throughput or even make lasting changes, but to test a different methodological and ethical ground for design. The adhocist paradigm of starting a project from materials at hand, for example, introduces students to a distributed and participatory understanding of creativity (the sharing of herding roles discussed in Chapter 2), in sharp contrast with the discipline's hubristic tendency to attribute architectural value to concepts or authorial intents. For example, when one group of students harvested nettles to make string, and used it to tie PET bottles together, the tectonic layering of the resulting islands, and particularly of the vertical structures cantilevering from the floating platform, was not dictated by formal or conceptual considerations, but tested in the water—in order for the cantilevers not to cause the island to tip over, appropriate "footings" were designed to attain a suitable ratio of buoyancy to weight (the relative positioning of empty and filled bottles). [**Figure 5.4**]

The protocols designed and knowledges acquired by students during the prototyping phases of their projects are relevant in more than one way. Firstly, they are foregrounded as necessary ingredients in any material recipe, reminding students that without them, the material would not exist—that there is more to materials (or to metastability) than mere matter, and that materials *are*, indeed, designed. Secondly, the specific expertise developed by students over the weeks (for instance, the most suitable recipe for making avocado-pit-based bioplastic sheets, and the casting/drying procedures needed to attain different textures or

22 Similar studio work, developed around the same time, is published in Caroline O'Donnell and Dillon Pranger, eds., *The Architecture of Waste: Design for a Circular Economy* (New York: Routledge, 2021).

23 I am referring to the movement led by Martin Pawley in the 1970s, which promoted, through research and teaching, the diversion of consumer by-products towards the construction of affordable housing. See, for example, Martin Pawley, *Garbage Housing* (London: Architectural Press, 1975). See also Curt Gambetta, "Throwaway Houses: Garbage Housing and the Politics of Ownership," in *The Culture of Nature in the History of Design*, ed. Kjetil Fallan (London and New York: Routledge, 2019), 221–36.

Figure 5.4 Elida Harjo Hansen, Esther Fletcher, and Skye Brownlow, *Floating Ecologies: Building a Post-natural Island*, AD3 Unit 2 Radical Coauthorship, Edinburgh School of Architecture and Landscape Architecture (ESALA), 2020–21.

levels of opacity; or the most appropriate configuration and temperature required to slump clusters of glass bottles in a kiln; etc.) perturbs a hierarchical model of teaching according to which tutors have all the answers at the outset, promoting a probabilistic and open-ended (as well as more collaborative and interdisciplinary) studio culture. Similarly, we (tutors) remain suspicious of final outputs, viewing them not as goals, but as instances in a longer trajectory of discovery and knowledge creation. Accordingly, mistakes, setbacks, and failures are not erased and concealed, but recorded and celebrated as learning opportunities.

Thirdly, the hands-on approach of the unit causes prototyping and design—full-scale construction and decision-making—to cohere, and to become unthinkable without one another, or alongside customary spatiotemporal divisions between "intellectual" and "manual" labor. This re-embodiment of design is observable—and surprisingly moving—in the sourcing and preparation of discards, for which students are solely responsible. One group, for example, began by collecting soy milk cartons from friends and family, but soon realized that larger quantities would be required. While also developing the technical know-how needed to repurpose and recombine the cartons, and beginning to turn them inside-out to

Figures 5.5 + 5.6 Alannah Marie Cumming, Andrew Stuart Wyness, and Kaja Isobel Hellman-Hayes, *TetraHak/TetraPa(r)k*, AD3 Unit 2 Radical Coauthorship, Edinburgh School of Architecture and Landscape Architecture (ESALA), 2019–20.

expose the intermediate layer of aluminum foil, they developed a weekly collection routine, involving several local coffee shops and prompt washing (to avoid bad smells). Their final project, of which a section was built in the studio, proposed to occupy the Dyers Close in Edinburgh with inhabitable tree-like structures made entirely of cartons, also used for storing rainwater. [**Figures 5.5 + 5.6**] Similarly, another group, after surveying, classifying, and quantifying the waste produced daily in a nightclub, set out to repurpose the discarded synthetic corks and cocktail stirrers, which are not recyclable. After weeks of collection and cleaning, and having developed flexible construction blocks by using the stirrers as dowels, the students envisioned their continued accretion as adaptable urban structures (vaults, benches, rooms, ramps) and constructed full-scale prototypes of furniture pieces. [**Figure 5.7**]

Perhaps the lengthiest cleaning and conditioning procedures were those put in place by the group that diverted cast-off clothes. In the first place, the malodorous contents of large bales were washed, sanitized, and classified. Then, in contrast with common landfilling or recycling practices, the students decided to preserve and use the garments—which are intrinsically human-scaled—as units of construction and spatial choreography. Rather than filling them with

Figure 5.7 Ryan Liu, Ivy Yan, and Tenny Zhang, *Corktecture*, AD3 Unit 2 Radical Coauthorship, Edinburgh School of Architecture and Landscape Architecture (ESALA), 2020–21.

24 Nader Khalili and Iliona Outram, *Emergency Sandbag Shelter and Eco-Village: Manual—How to Build Your Own with Superadobe* (Hesperia: Cal-Earth Press, 2008).

sand, in a manner reminiscent of architect Nader Khalili's shelters,[24] they began to collect spent coffee grounds from the bars around the university, and to dry them in long strips along the perimeter of the studio floor, next to the heating grilles. Once devoid of moisture, the coffee grounds were poured into trousers that had been stitched together to form partitions, seats, shelves, and openings, taking shape and volume as if worn by novel (tentacular) bodies. [**Figures 5.8 + 5.9**] In all these cases, the availability of materials depended on weekly increments, and on "alliances" with local businesses—on the staff working at pubs, coffee shops, restaurants, and hair salons going out of their way to set discards aside for students. I have grown

Figure 5.8 Myrto Efthymiadi, Sarah Kemali, and Rana Tabatabaie, *The Nomadic [Wear]House*, AD3 Unit 2 Radical Coauthorship, Edinburgh School of Architecture and Landscape Architecture (ESALA), 2019–20. Photographs of 1:50 model.

Figure 5.9 Myrto Efthymiadi, Saran Kemali, and Rana Tabatabaie, *The Nomadic [Wear]House*, Edinburgh School of Architecture and Landscape Architecture (ESALA), 2019–20. Full-scale prototype.

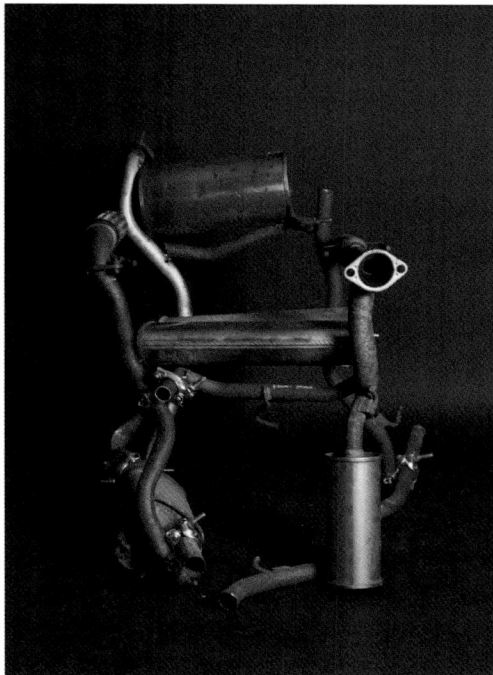

Figure 5.10 Cameron Angus, Jamie Begg and Hannah Davis, *Exhaust Chair*, AD3 Unit 2 Radical Coauthorship, Edinburgh School of Architecture and Landscape Architecture (ESALA), 2018–19.

Figure 5.11 Mimi Hattori, Cindy Chananithitham, and Rachel Leong, *AnthropoFELT*, AD3 Unit 2 Radical Coauthorship, Edinburgh School of Architecture and Landscape Architecture (ESALA), 2019–20. Prototypes of human-hair felt and dog-hair quilt for architectural envelopes.

to recognize in these unglamorous acts of preparation and collaborative sourcing, as well as in the washing and reconditioning efforts that accompany them—in the inclusion of these activities in the design canon, as what designers do and care about—one of the most significant lessons of the studio.[25] At the same time, the projects developed in the unit, including a chair made out of discarded car exhausts and a series of architectural envelopes fabricated by felting human hair, begin to trouble the expectations of purity, order, and propriety implicit in (and uncontested by) most contemporary construction materials. [**Figures 5.10 + 5.11**]

5.4 Chairs as Media (2)

> What are the unintended consequences of the artifact's design, and how does one smoke them out and allow them to reveal their potential? How can new options be inserted into the seemingly closed systems in which these objects function? How can these systems be rendered sites of potential and unexpected plasticity?[26]
>
> Gean Moreno and Ernesto Oroza, "Generic Objects"

How can objects be turned into "sites of potential and unexpected plasticity," and become media? Of the ingenuous copes (e.g., "how to make X out of an old pair of Y") described in *Popular Mechanics* or in *Heloise's Housekeeping Hints,* Nathan Silver writes: "A suspicion arises that the suggestions offered there are not meant to be carried out, but merely intended to tingle the reader with appreciative delight."[27] A similar suspicion accompanies the many instances of "upcycling" (often a misnomer) and "repurposing" featured in contemporary design magazines and blogs, where the magic of the turned object—the colander used as lampshade—obscures more interesting or genuine considerations of materials and reuse. Indeed, the student projects described above, and much of the work presented in this book, don't aim to find quick fixes to problems in orthodox adhocist fashion, but to turn the lessons of bricolage and adhocism—their engagement with embodied materials—towards a radical re-situating of design. If, in a capitalist economy, adhocism remains a "minority style"[28] and a "mostly supplementary approach"[29] to design, this book imagines reuse and repurposing, or what in Chapter 7 I will call *exaptive design,* as primary modes of material- and value-making in a post-extractivist and pluriversal future.

An adhocist ethos can however be imagined at scale. Two examples illustrate the possibility of its widespread adoption. In a paper entitled "Technological Disobedience," Ernesto Oroza recounts his childhood in Cuba, where Fidel Castro's policies and the United States' embargo—and the ensuing lack of material resources—prompted a way of life based on self-sufficiency, repair, and repurposing.[30] [**Figures 5.12–5.14**] "From the endless, ongoing restoration of the iconic 1950s Buicks to the creation

25 This is consistent with Steven J. Jackson's invitation to think not only about the "congealed forms of human labor, power and interests that are built into objects at their moment of production," but also about "the ongoing forms of labor, power, and interest—neither dead nor congealed—that underpin the ongoing survival of things as objects in the world." Steven J. Jackson, "Rethinking Repair," in *Media Technologies: Essays on Communication, Materiality, and Society*, ed. Tarleton Gillespie, Pablo J. Boczkowski, and Kirsten A. Foot (Cambridge: The MIT Press, 2014), 230.

26 Gean Moreno and Ernesto Oroza, "Generic Objects," *E-Flux Journal*, no. 18 (September 2010).

27 Jencks and Silver, *Adhocism*, 125.

28 Jencks, "The Style of Eureka," viii.

29 Ibid., xv.

30 Ernesto Oroza, "Technological Disobedience," *MKSHFT.ORG* (blog), July 7, 2020.

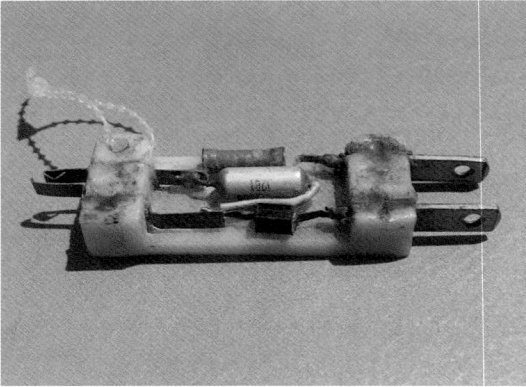

Figure 5.12 Battery charger for non-rechargeable battery. Produced by Enildo Peréz, Havana. *Technological Disobedience* Archive. Photograph by Ernesto Oroza, 2005.

Figure 5.13 Hand-cut Coca Cola bottles and bottle-top stems injected in plastic with a home-made machine, Havana. *Technological Disobedience* Archive. Photograph by Ernesto Oroza, 2004.

Figure 5.14 *Rikimbili*. Bicycle propelled by a fumigation machine engine, Havana. *Technological Disobedience* Archive. Photograph by Ernesto Oroza, 2005.

of baby toys made from milk cans and dried beans," he writes, "fabricating goods not officially available on the island became an essential skill."[31] Oroza describes a culture that, during the 1970s, develops in the workplace but soon permeates domestic life, where "[t]he same engineer would, during his day shift, repair the engine of a Soviet MIG15 jet fighter and, in the evening—faced with a country-wide shortage of matches—build an electrical lighter out of a pen and light bulb."[32] The uncertainty surrounding resource availability during this time transformed Cuban homes into repositories for all kinds of objects. Quoting Oroza at length:

> Accumulation [...] separated the object from the Western intent and lifecycle it was destined for. This is technological disobedience. When people held onto things, they also kept the technical principles and an idea of how they fit together. In any critical moment, they would scratch their heads to conjure the exact piece that could solve the problem. When the power went out, the fan broke, or the chair snapped, the family kept an ear out for technological whispers from the patios, under the beds, or from obscure corners of rooms guarding piles of old things—either parts or in their entirety.
>
> Seemingly insignificant things were assigned new, useful tasks. The tops of penicillin vials have become the best solution for valves on pressure cookers. Deodorant canisters proved excellent electrical switches [...]. Defective fluorescent tubes now make up 3D picture frames. An old 33-rpm vinyl, cut properly, would serve as a fan blade—and its creators could reproduce copies of it.[33]

The standardized and generic nature of the accumulated goods—the fact that they were identical—meant that hacks and re-inventions (e.g., a school metal tray turned TV antenna) could be shared, spread across households, and adopted widely. Here, an adhocist paradigm begins to unravel the object as consumer product, as well as its primary functions and the associated rates of obsolescence.

Speaking about the economic crisis that struck the island in the 1990s, Oroza writes that Cubans had finally become "desensitized to designed objects."[34] He continues:

> They stopped seeing the original purpose of the object; instead it became a sample of parts. This is the first Cuban expression of disobedience in their relationship with objects—a growing disrespect for an object's identity and for the truth and authority it embodies.[35]

In fact, as Steven J. Jackson explains, "innovation rarely if ever inheres in moments of origination, passing unproblematically into the bodies of the objects and practices such work informs. For this reason," he continues, "the *efficacy* of innovation in the world is limited—until extended, sustained, and completed in repair."[36]

31 Oroza, "Technological Disobedience."

32 Ibid.

33 Ibid.

34 Ibid.

35 Ibid.

36 Steven J. Jackson, "Rethinking Repair," 227.

Alfred Sohn-Rethel's portrayal of technology in Naples—what he jokingly calls "philosophy of the broken"—resembles the one described by Oroza. According to the German economist and philosopher, who briefly lived in the Italian city during the 1920s, "the essence of [Neapolitan] technology lies in making what is broken work."[37] While most technical devices in the city do indeed appear to be broken,

> [it is] not, however, that they are broken because they do not work: for the Neapolitan it is only when things are broken that they begin to work. Even when the wind is up, he will take to sea in the kind of motorboat which we would hardly dare to set foot in. And although things never go as might be expected, somehow they always go well. As if it were the most natural thing in the world, he manages, for example, although just three meters from the cliffs upon which the surge of the waves threaten[s] to smash him, to remove the petrol canister into which water has penetrated and refill it without the motor cutting out. If necessary, he could even, at the same time, rustle up some coffee for his passengers on the motor. Or, in a display of matchless mastery, he succeeds in restarting his broken-down car by, in some impossible manner, attaching a small piece of wood which just happened to be lying in the street—only, that is, until it soon, and this much is certain, once again breaks down.[38]

In Sohn-Rethel's account, the Neapolitan abhors the idea that repairs could last. Rejecting the "misanthropic magic of intact mechanical functions," he "makes use of his veto against the closed and hostile automatism of machines and plunges himself into the world. And when he does, he proves to be leaps and bounds ahead of technical laws. For he does not take control of the machines by studying the manuals and learning how to use them, but by discovering his own body inside the machine."[39] "The broken," writes Sara Ahmed, "can be queer kin. To offer a queer way of working is not to start anew, with the light, the bright, the white, the upright; it is to start with the weighty, the heavy, the weary, and the worn."[40] In the refusal to use properly—to use in accordance with predefined scripts—the body of the Neapolitan is reaffirmed as the measure and arbiter of all powers.

Whereas Jencks endorses a minor and peripheral role for adhocism in order to safeguard the balance between exceptions and rules—"to make the uncanny normal," he writes, "is to rob it of its strength"[41]—the socio-technical paradigms introduced above are able to increase in both scope and power because the co-optive *exception* is no longer predicated on bounded ecologies (on the difference and spatial separation between normality and abnormality, usefulness and uselessness, background and foreground, and so on), but on their precariousness and temporal instability. It is in this sense that the Cuban and Neapolitan objects mentioned above are, or at least can be, media.

37 Alfred Sohn-Rethel, "The Ideal of the Broken Down: On the Neapolitan Approach to Things Technical," *Hard Crackers: Chronicles of Everyday Life* (blog), February 15, 2018.

38 Sohn-Rethel, "The Ideal of the Broken Down."

39 Ibid.

40 Ahmed, *What's The Use?*, 227.

41 Jencks, "The Style of Eureka," xv.

5.5 Ecological Enclosures

The plasticity of *epitedeiotes* (vs. its wooden support) introduces an alternative potentializing paradigm to the *tabula rasa*, one according to which *dynamis*, rather than pointing to the object's ability to undergo changes, unlocks platforms for the production of variable contents. In other words: uses and effects can emerge not only in relation to a local script, either positively (formatting towards and maintaining a specific operation) or negatively (obsolescing and de-formatting), but by broadening the scope of design to allow scripts to be overwritten and fluctuate.

In the previous section, I have suggested that objects may—like musical instruments—become playable, and noted that while the playability of a violin is already programmed within its ecological horizon, the playability of a chair, or of the motorbike engine used in a Neapolitan *latteria* to whip cream, relies on the loosening of ecological boundaries, and challenges their authority. Yet, if turning objects into media entails transpassing, thickening, or stretching ecological enclosures, it should be clear that these are dismantling acts—EoIs hold together precisely by occluding other (nonecological, external) evaluation criteria, and by only registering (and responding to) interior inputs and metrics. An ecology of packaging, for example, selects its ideal material—expanded polystyrene foam (EPS)—based on the capacity to store and transport appliances (e.g., durability; resistance to photo-oxidation; shock absorption; impermeability; weight; cost; ease of fabrication). The environmental price of manufacturing and distributing EPS (what economists would aptly call an "externality") is, from the crude perspective of the EoI, invisible, and therefore irrelevant. That is: every ecology or project is born out of a deliberate shortening of sight; the establishment of protocols that partition what it can see. It is perhaps for this reason that philosopher Vilém Flusser can provocatively write:

> Whoever decides to become a designer has decided against the pure good. […] They may disguise this as much as they wish (for example, by refusing to design rockets and limiting themselves to designing doves of peace). They remain, by their very involvement, trapped within the ambit of functional good. If they in fact begin to inquire into the pure good of their activity (for example, by asking themselves what their design for a dove of peace might be good for in the end), they are forced not just to design the dove of peace badly, but not to design it at all.[42]

The myopia imposed by the "functional good"—by any teleological horizon—is not necessarily confined to or entirely reabsorbed within the ecology, but off-gasses associated messages, codes, and narratives. These, in the form of reports, press releases, ads, policies, and manifestos, are at once broadcasted to wider audiences and validated within the limited confines (and according to the sole criteria) of the EoI, treading a sweet line along which claims can be at once true and false. One might

42 Vilém Flusser, *The Shape of Things: A Philosophy of Design* (London: Reaktion, 1999), 33.

43 See Julija Nėjė, "Coca-Cola Invents 16 Bottle Caps to Give Second Lives to Empty Bottles," *BoredPanda* (blog), accessed April 14, 2019.

44 OgilvyAsia Admin, "2nd Lives," Ogilvy's Asia, May 7, 2015.

45 For a recent summary, see Elizabeth Claire Alberts, "'Our Life Is Plasticized': New Research Shows Microplastics in Our Food, Water, Air," *Mongabay*, July 15, 2020.

46 It is worth remembering that Coca-Cola did originally sell their product in reusable glass bottles, with a return rate of 96 percent in 1948, and an average reuse rate of twenty-two times per Coke bottle. Elmore Bartow J., *Citizen Coke: The Making of Coca-Cola Capitalism* (New York: W. W. Norton & Co., 2014), 225. Quoted in Finn Arne Jørgensen, *Recycling* (Cambridge: The MIT Press, 2019), 71–72.

47 Samantha MacBride, *Recycling Reconsidered: The Present Failure and Future Promise of Environmental Action in the United States* (Cambridge: MIT Press, 2013). See also Samantha MacBride, "Does Recycling Actually Conserve or Preserve Things?," *Discard Studies* (blog), February 11, 2019.

48 MacBride, *Recycling Reconsidered*, 23-85. See also Heather Rogers, *Gone Tomorrow: The Hidden Life of Garbage* (New York and York: New Press , 2006), chap. 6, Ebook.

consider, for instance, Coca-Cola's *2ndlives* campaign, which promoted the repurposing of plastic bottles by manufacturing a suite of additional plastic caps, some larger than the bottles themselves.[43] Developed in collaboration with the ad-agency Ogilvy & Mather China, the campaign advertised 16 screw-on caps that would activate Coca-Cola bottles towards a range of secondary uses, turning them into implements such as soap dispensers, paintbrushes, dumbbells, spray bottles, bubble makers, and pencil sharpeners. Launched in Vietnam in 2014, the campaign gave one cap away with each purchase of a Coke bottle, for a total of 40,000 caps.[44] The proposal was ingenious, well designed, and seemingly trying to address problems—solid waste; plastic pollution—the company contributes to on a large scale. Yet, at the same time, it made very little sense. How many bubble makers or whistles does a regular Cola-Cola consumer need? And how does manufacturing more polyethylene terephthalate (PET) and polypropylene (PP) help alleviate a problem caused by the overabundance, toxicity, and near-ubiquity of these materials?[45]

An honest engagement with these problems would have prompted a re-thinking of packaging materials, disposability, and modes of delivery; and the replacement of single-use plastic bottles with refillable glass ones, or with compostable containers.[46] What is necessary to a profitable and productive ecology of soft-drink manufacturing and distribution, however, is not a resolution or mitigation of the solid waste problem, or of rampant plastic pollution and microplastic contamination, but the ability to carry on with business as usual, distracting the public on one side while continuing to pollute on the other. Nonetheless, if ecological boundaries, sharing two opposite orientations, can facilitate the faulty or misleading translation of inward-facing objectives into outward-facing messages, one cannot impute the failure of the campaign entirely to the company's rhetoric or bad faith. The distance between what one *could* do and what one *actually* does also matters, perhaps more than anything else.

Let's consider the wider context of the recycling movement. In the previous chapter, I have argued that, despite being heralded as a noble civic and environmental duty, and proposed as the first step towards circularity and a waste-less society, recycling perpetuates the same hylomorphic bias that generates waste in the first place. In her comprehensive study of recycling in the United States, sociologist and waste management expert Samantha MacBride further problematizes the rift between recycling's internal protocols and its real-world effects and achievements.[47] On one side, she and others have shown that, around its inception in the United States in the 1970s, the recycling movement was heavily subsidized by the very industries it targeted, which wished to oppose or preempt bottle-bill legislation that would either ban/cap "one-way" containers or require the beverage industry to impose deposits on them.[48] In New York City, for instance, the Environmental Action Coalition (EAC)—one of the groups that campaigned for the establishment of curb-side recycling at the municipal level—was funded and supported by "aluminum, steel, glass, paper and plastic trade associations; bottlers; container manufacturers; retailers and retail associations; beverage producers; beer distributors; and newspapers."[49] On the other side, the focus on recycling and its empowerment of individual do-gooders was designed to shift the public's opinion, deflecting moral and fiscal responsibility away from the source of the pollution (the producers of waste-generating commodities) and towards consumers and their behavior.

The figure of the litterer, exemplarily portrayed in the popular "Crying Indian" ad by a man flinging discards out of a speeding car, came to neatly embody the reckless polluter, holding the public accountable ("people start pollution, people can stop it"), and allowing the actual culprits to recede into the background.[50] Yet MacBride's research also underscores the fundamental difference between an internal and external understanding of recycling ecologies. While in the former a progressive increase in processed discards, measured in percentages and tonnage; or the generation of revenue; or the avoidance of regulatory roadblocks; or the ability to feel better about one's environmental footprint are all sufficient to deem municipal recycling successful and worth pursuing, in the latter—from an extra-ecological or systemic point of view—recycling and its environmental and fiscal outcomes can only be validated by a decrease in the demand for (and actual extraction and production of) raw materials.

MacBride determines that municipal solid waste recycling, particularly in the case of glass and plastics, has currently no such impact or effect, and it does "only slightly ameliorate the sited burdens associated with transfer stations, truck routes, landfills and incinerators."[51] But the interior of recycling ecologies in the US performs yet another trick: the very definition of recycling that is framed by curb-side collections and the homonymous movement excludes the "nonhazardous" heterogeneous wastes that arise from the manufacture of products like "glass, plastic, metal, paper, textiles, processed food, chemicals, electronics," and other "machines."[52] These might include, in a 2001 sampling by the Pennsylvania Department of Environmental Protection:

> linoleum, detergents and cleaners, filters, rubber, contaminated soil, fertilizers, glass, ceramics, pesticides, gypsum board, leather, pharmaceutical waste, pumps, textiles, photographic film and paper, piping, industrial equipment, asbestos-, oil-, and PCB-bearing wastes, storage tanks, electronics, metal-bearing wastes (e.g., foundry sands, slags, grindings, and shavings), residues such as sludge (from the treatment of public water supplies, emission control, lime-stabilized pickle liquor, paints, electroplating, and waste from the manufacture of lime and cement).[53]

MacBride shows that so-called "nonhazardous" industrial wastes, despite being neither safe nor inert, and being more abundant than those generated domestically or in offices,[54] have remained, in the

49 MacBride, *Recycling Reconsidered*, 59.

50 Heather Rogers writes about the nonprofit Keep America Beautiful (KAB), which commissioned the ad: "The center-piece of the organization's strategy was its cultural invention: *litter*. This category of debris existed before, but KAB masterfully transformed its political and cultural meaning to shift the terms of the garbage debate. KAB wanted to turn any stirrings of environmental awareness away from industry's massive and supertoxic destruction of the natural world, telescoping ecological disaster down to the eyesore of litter and singling out the real villain: the notorious 'litterbug.'" Rogers, *Gone Tomorrow*, chap. 6, Ebook.

51 MacBride, *Recycling Reconsidered*, 234.

52 Ibid., 89.

53 PA DEP (Pennsylvania Department of Environmental Protection), 'Background Paper on Residual Waste' (Philadelphia: PA DEP, 2001). Quoted in MacBride, *Recycling Reconsidered*, 91–92.

54 MacBride compares the only official figure on annual U.S. manufacturing waste available at the time of her writing (7.6 billion tons of solid waste, according to the EPA's 1999 *Guide for Industrial Waste Management*) to the annual U.S. municipal solid waste reported in 2008 (250 million tons, according to the EPA's *Municipal Solid Waste Generation, Recycling, and Disposal in the United States: Fact and Figures for 2008*). Ibid., 87. She also points out that, based on a later study (Matthew J. Eckelman and Marian R. Chertow, "Quantifying Life Cycle Environmental Benefits from the Reuse of Industrial Materials in Pennsylvania," *Environmental Science & Technology* 43, no. 7 (April 1, 2009): 2550–56) the gap between the two appears to be narrowing. MacBride, *Recycling Reconsidered*, 91.

55 Ibid., 87–123. It is also worth noting that the EPA classifies wastes as "hazardous" on the sole basis of ignitability, corrosivity, reactivity, or toxicity. Ibid., 90.

United States, largely unmonitored, unreported, and virtually unresearched.[55]

Following the examples discussed in this section, it is clear that ecologies of inception assign roles by narrowly defining the problems they address. They both generate contents and are themselves messages. Therefore, to repurpose is not only to modify an object or to change the way it is used (or who can use it), but also to challenge the partial truths it produces and upholds.

5.6. Design Medium

5.6.1

Until this point, I sought to register the plasticity of the *rasura tabulae* in individual objects, following their fluctuations across (and persistence beyond) particular instances of use, reuse, and repurposing. I suggested that chairs, metal trays, and motors can be played like musical instruments, without necessarily coinciding or cohering with a definitive player, setting, or tune. However, if potentials depend on the reciprocal roles and mutually reinforcing positions assigned to objects within and across ecologies—if communication relies not only on a user-centered equipmental fabric, but on the material and immaterial nodes within the networks that maintain and sustain it—one might identify, in these larger constellations, another kind of medium. My use of the term "medium" here is not limited to specific users, technologies, or devices but encompasses assemblages and frameworks (technical, economic, social, environmental, political) that are capable of guiding, either directly or indirectly, the generation and exchange of contents. In this sense, a medium always lurks behind a message or use, intersecting EoIs at different scales. Indeed, McLuhan's preference for media (as opposed to contents or uses) hinges on the lucid realization that they structure behavior and effect changes on a large scale, in ways that are both more profound than messages and dangerously subliminal. This would suggest a shift in focus, from an object (a building, chair, or garment) to the infrastructures, platforms, and apparatuses that organize and steer its design, fabrication, and usage; from what appears on the surface to what recedes into the background.

56 Keller Easterling, *Medium Design* (Moscow: Strelka Press, 2018), chap. 1, E-book. Easterling's privileging of field over object is reminiscent of Stan Allen's celebrated 1985 essay "Field Conditions." Stan Allen, "Field Conditions," in *Constructing a New Agenda: Architectural Theory 1993–2009*, ed. Krista Sykes (New York: Princeton Architectural Press, 2010). However, while Allen is interested in a quintessentially spatial problem (the reorganization of figure and ground, as well as of parts and wholes, in relation to the horizontal distribution of the American city), Easterling addresses a more diverse network (in the Latourian sense) that is characterized by the triggering and unfolding of spatial effect over time.

Architect and theorist Keller Easterling proposes the term "medium design" to describe the inclusion, in the architect's purview, not only of "buildings with shapes and outlines," but also of "the matrix of activities that inflects them."[56] Just like committing to the efficient or "proper" operation of specific EoIs may cause a myopic or distorted view of the outer world (the dilemma invoked by Flusser's "functional good"), Easterling sees the modern preference for closed loops—for enclosing and naming individual ecologies, and for defending them against contradiction—as leading to self-righteousness and complacency, and to unavoidable conflicts and impasses. Medium design emerges as a counter-strategy capable of undermining or eluding blunt assumptions and simple binaries. She writes:

> Rather than only declarations, right answers, objects and determinations, you can detect and manipulate the medium or matrix in which they are suspended and in which they change over time. Just as this *medium thinking* inverts the typical focus on object over field, maybe *medium design* can invert some habitual approaches to problem solving, aesthetics and politics.[57]

"Medium thinking" casts a wide theoretical net that connects McLuhan's famous reversal (from content to content-delivery platforms) and Gilbert Ryle's accounts of disposition as latent agency (of "knowing how" rather than "knowing that"),[58] with the notion of *dispositif* or apparatus in the philosophies of Michel Foucault and Giorgio Agamben—as the networks established between discourses, institutions, laws, buildings, and objects;[59] or as the largely invisible partitions within which most living beings find themselves captive.[60] At the same time, her adoption, following the work of John Durham Peters,[61] of a broadened understanding of media (as inclusive of not only communication devices, but also atmospheric elements such as water, air, earth, and fire),[62] allows Easterling to see the "lumpy, heavy material of space itself as an information system" and as an "inclusive mixing chamber" for the activation, actualization and maintenance of social, political, and technical contents.[63]

In local interactions with formatted objects, ecology-sanctioned roles and behaviors can be either abided by or disrupted. Instead, by intervening at the level of the medium, one might hope to overcome the binary logic of loops and boundaries (e.g., inside vs. outside; right vs. wrong), and to engage the repeatable formulas, standards, and protocols upon which formatting systems rely. This extra-ecological medium, what Easterling calls "infrastructure space," is the operating system responsible— the architect's hubris notwithstanding—for organizing, shaping, and reproducing much of our cities, buildings, and material goods.[64]

Infrastructure space and medium design offer a new perspective to my discussion of EoIs, media, and powers. As mentioned above, Easterling attends to McLuhan's realization that media are more significant on a planetary scale than contents, shifting the focus from the design of singular messages and fixed "object-forms" or masterplans, to the detection and steering of what she calls "active forms"—the spatial recipes and dispositional parameters that guide the development and operation of populations of objects over time. Importantly, Easterling also recognizes that, as discussed in the previous section, there is a gap or "blind spot" between what an organization says (its outputs and messages) and what it actually does. In *Medium Design: Knowing How to Work on the World*, she writes:

> Medium design works on the histories of things that do not happen. [...] Organizations have inherent capacities to include,

57 Easterling, *Medium Design*, chap.1, E-book.

58 Keller Easterling, *Extrastatecraft: The Power of Infrastructure Space* (London and New York: Verso, 2014), chap. 2, E-book. See also Gilbert Ryle, *The Concept of Mind* (London and New York: Routledge, 2009), 16–20.

59 Michel Foucault, *Power/Knowledge: Selected Interviews and Other Writings, 1972–1977*, ed. Colin Gordon (New York: Pantheon Books, 1980), 194.

60 Giorgio Agamben, *"What Is an Apparatus?" And Other Essays*, trans. David Kishik and Stefan Pedatella (Stanford: Stanford University Press, 2009), 13.

61 John Durham Peters, *The Marvelous Clouds: Toward a Philosophy of Elemental Media* (Chicago and London: University of Chicago Press, 2015).

62 "Media," he writes, "are vessels and environments, containers of possibility that anchor our existence and make what we are doing possible." Peters, *The Marvelous Clouds*, 2.

63 Easterling, *Medium Design*, chap. 1, E-book. A summary of the thinkers and concepts discussed in this paragraph is also provided in Keller Easterling, *Medium Design: Knowing How to Build the World* (London: Verso, 2021), 25–40.

64 Easterling, *Extrastatecraft*, Introduction, E-book.

65 Easterling, *Medium Design: Knowing How to Build the World*, 119.

66 See the discussion of Rotor's work in Chapter 3. See also: Easterling, *Medium Design: Knowing How to Build the World*, 106; Keller Easterling, *Subtraction*, ed. Nikolaus Hirsch and Markus Miessen (Berlin: Sternberg Press, 2014).

67 Robert A. Frosch and Nicholas E. Gallopoulos, "Strategies for Manufacturing," *Scientific American* 261, no. 3 (September 1989), 144. The poster child for this brand of industrial symbiosis is the municipality of Kalundborg, Denmark, where flows of material (water, steam, gypsum, fly ash, sludge, sulphur, etc.) link activities as diverse as municipal district heating, oil refining, power generation, water treatment, fish farming, enzyme and insulin production, and cement and gypsum plasterboard manufacturing.

68 As Moreno and Oroza poetically write: "every object is an elastic surface: if it receives a blow, it channels it to the entire system." Moreno and Oroza, "Generic Objects."

69 Susan Strasser, *Waste and Want: A Social History of Trash* (New York: Owl Books, 2000), 222–26.

70 Martin Pawley, *Garbage Housing* (London: Architectural Press, 1975), 24.

exclude, nurture, or harm, even in the absence of an event or declaration. This violence does not happen, because it is ever-present as a latent property or an ongoing series of actions.[65]

Now, having defined ecologies of inception as the enclosures that potentialize objects towards one another, it is impossible to operate a neat distinction between the resulting outputs and their ability to communicate, or even between overt declarations and latent dispositions (as discussed in Chapter 2, EoIs can be described as sets of temporarily suspended relations). Furthermore, while ecologies of inception might already command the kinds of "interplay" Easterling is interested in (e.g., growth protocols, governors, time-released instructions, multipliers, switches, repetitive formulas, inversions), these tend to be subordinated to a given *telos*, recipe, or form of use. However, if one were to loosen the envelopes that bind EoIs, or to disregard their definitions and declared objectives, new spatial variables, links, and opportunities would come into view—a fabric that may be read transversally and manipulated without necessarily complying with original scripts or partitions. In this sense, infrastructure space re-articulates EoIs (and not only their outputs) as plastic and susceptible to inflection and deflection.

Deconstruction, for example, implements a subtractive design protocol potentially capable of disrupting ecologies of real-estate development; of steering construction methods (towards disassembly); of generating skilled jobs; of reframing notions of heritage; and of allowing buildings to move or adapt in response to shifting economic and environmental conditions.[66] Similarly, the design of links, switches, and proximity between traditionally separate industrial activities promotes symbiotic relationships and the formation of "industrial ecosystems" wherein "the consumption of energy and materials is optimized, waste generation is minimized and the effluents of one process [...] serve as the raw material for another process."[67] Finally, one might hack EoIs by tweaking single nodes in a referential (herding) network,[68] or by introducing parasitical instructions that insinuate the requirements of secondary functions, other users, or future ecologies into current ones, turning their industrial scales of reproduction into multipliers for reuse and repurposing.

One such attempt was the manufacturing of "dual-use" packages marketed by American companies during the 1930s, such as the sugar and flour sacks designed, with cotton fabrics and washable labels, specifically to be turned into garments.[69] Another was the WOBO (World Bottle) system, designed in 1963 by Dutch architect John Habraken. [**Figure 5.15**] Conceived and commissioned by Alfred Heineken, head of the eponymous brewing corporation, the WOBO system redesigned beer bottles so that, once empty, self-builders around the world might collect them and use them as bricks. "In this enterprise," writes Martin Pawley in *Garbage Housing*, "the orthodox economics of bottle production and distribution would merely serve as a *carrier* for a secondary use article whose life would only begin when its primary use as a container was over."[70] Unfortunately, Habraken's brilliantly squared and interlocking bottles were never

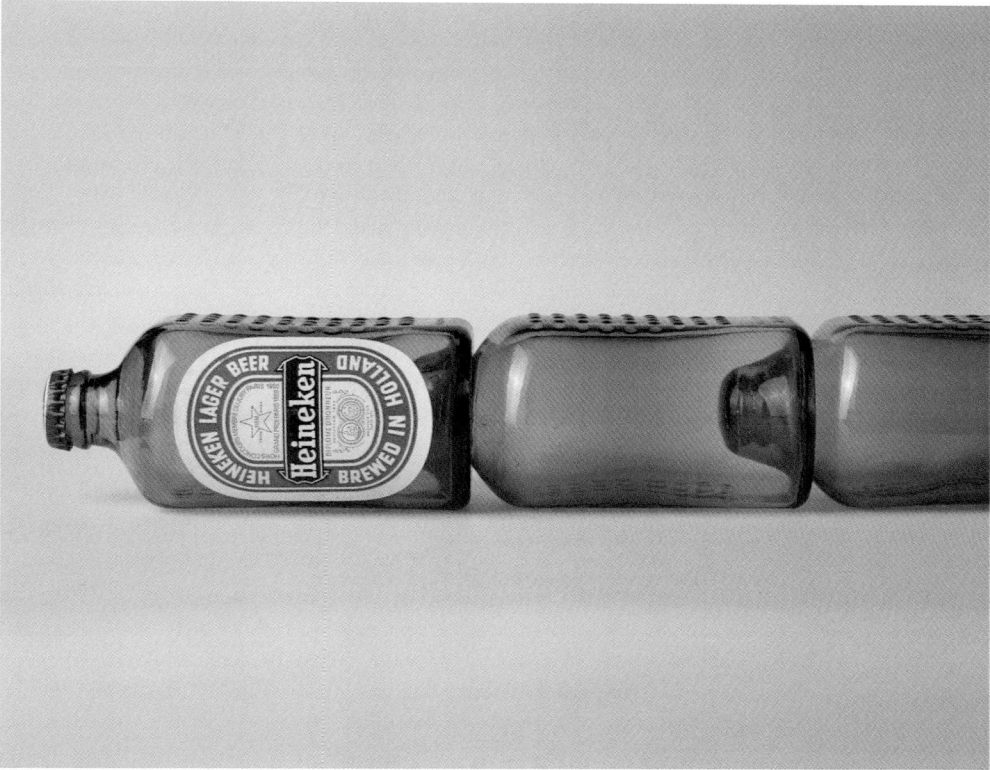

Figure 5.15 John Habraken, *The WOBO (World Bottle)*, 1964. Courtesy of the Heineken Collection Foundation.

espoused by the Heineken marketing team, or implemented at scale, and the only 1:1 prototype in existence was built in 1965 as a proof-of-concept summer house in the grounds of Heineken's Noordwijk villa.[71] However, the WOBO's most provocative lesson—that objects can be designed as carriers of secondary functions, or as time capsules—remains exceptionally relevant. In the twenty-first century, shouldn't most objects and buildings be designed as temporary collections of materials and components stored for future generations and uses? And wouldn't such practices turn notions of ownership, care, and value upside-down?

Perhaps this is what the shift from a *tabula rasa* to a *rasura tabulae* entails, exemplified by how the terms ecology of inception and infrastructure space diverge in their articulation of potency: as relational in the former (the ball rolling down the incline or kicked; the ball defined as that which rolls), as dispositional in the latter (the ball being capable of—but not reducible to—rolling, and only in relation to the incline or foot).[72] Both ecologies of inception and infrastructure space describe spatial and material potentials over time, pointing to the medium or matrix within which object-forms become active or interactive.

[71] Pawley, *Garbage Housing*, 33.

[72] François Jullien, *The Propensity of Things: Toward a History of Efficacy in China* (New York: Zone Books, 1999). Quoted in Easterling, *Extrastatecraft*, chap. 2, E-book.

However, if EoIs curate goal-oriented *projects* characterized by closed operating and maintenance protocols, Easterling's infrastructure space is at ease within looser networks of control and purpose, deploying not comprehensive designs, fixed templates, or one-time solutions, but contingent and responsive strategies for change. "It is not about fixing positions," she writes, "but, rather, releasing relational potentials. The outcome is indeterminate and unfolding."[73]

Whereas EoIs organize matter by redefining the parameters according to which something can be deemed right, effective, or valuable—and they must continually enforce and defend these limits—active forms may either work or not work, be right or wrong, and are therefore more agile and capable of adaptation. "Harvesting failures of any kind," writes Easterling, "mines a planetary geography of value different from the mineral values that have driven human industry and capital. [...] A world brimming with problems is brimming with potential. Constantly renewed, it presents a raw and limitless field of value."[74]

Learning from medium design, reuse and repurposing might graduate from the singular ad-hoc concoction or PR stunt to diversions that are contagious, invasive, and capable of distributed effects—durable but also responsive and unstable.

That said, to imagine reuse and repurposing at scale—as a nonextractivist and anti-colonial ethos for the twenty-first century—is to imagine them active on a transformed planet. In other words: reuse and repurposing are not, by themselves, enough. Not only will these practices *not* meaningfully reduce material throughput without a cap on primary production; they are also not intrinsically positive or insubordinate, and may act as unwitting multipliers of a system's violence and injustices, fueling production and disposability (colonial land relations),[75] spreading toxicants, and inflicting harm on human and nonhuman beings.[76] Reuse and repurposing are not design solutions for changing the world as much as maintenance regimes—and testing grounds—for one that has already changed.

73 Keller Easterling, *Medium Design: Knowing How to Build the World*, 81.

74 Easterling, *Medium Design: Knowing How to Build the World*, 109.

75 In the introduction to the book *Pollution is Colonialism*, Max Liboiron links a "threshold theory of pollution" (the widespread notion that "a body can handle a certain amount of contaminant before scientifically detectable harm occurs") with the "accompanying entitlement to Land to assimilate that pollution." They write about plastics, for example: "The structures that allow plastics' global distribution and full integration into ecosystems and everyday human lives are based on colonial land relations, the assumed access by settler and colonial projects to Indigenous lands for settler and colonial goals." Max Liboiron, *Pollution Is Colonialism* (Durham: Duke University Press, 2021), 5–7.

76 See for example the reuse of toxic mine tailings and quarry waste in the construction of low-cost housing. Hannah le Roux and Gabrielle Hecht, "Bad Earth," *E-Flux Architecture*, Accumulation, August 21, 2020.

Chapter 6

Ecologies of Suspension: Potentiality without Intentions/ Relations

6.1 On Drawing Silence

6.1.1

How would one draw silence? An aporia is implicit in the desire to do so—one that likens it to such impossible tasks as time travel or walking on water; or to the legendary love between sun and moon. Indeed, the terms *drawing* and *silence* belong to opposite sides of the ontological spectrum, at least in the hylomorphic tradition according to which matter (the lump of clay) and form (the fired clay figurine) are associated with potentiality and actuality respectively.

In this philosophical context, a *tabula rasa* represents silence—a figure of potentiality, of the deferral of actualizing impulses, and a precondition to the hearing of sounds—while a *tabula scripta* represents drawing—the implementation of actualizing drives towards precise graphical outputs (from *graphein*, to make a mark). The mark (the sound) neutralizes and undoes blankness (silence); the stylus scratches away the tablet's wax; the emergence of one is privation of the other. To draw silence therefore suggests a bizarre circular performance: making marks so that they may be erased; or, drawing backwards in time. A static opposition of empty and full, presence and absence, is replaced by the dynamic staging of existence and nonexistence, appearance and disappearance—by fluctuations, ebbs, and eddies.

6.1.2

Thomas Zummer's contribution to the *Text Messaging* exhibition at the Islip Art Museum in 2008, a work entitled "Essay on Potatoes,"[1] invokes and problematizes the temporality of the authorial mark. [**Figure 6.1**] Beyond the "unavoidable physical pun" activated by the title's ambiguous use of the preposition *on*, referring both to the essay's content (its

1   While this is the title featured in the museum catalogue, the full title of the work is *On 'potatos' as a Philosophical Exemplar in the Works of Immanuel Kant, G. W. F. Hegel, Friedrich Nietzsche, Martin Heidegger, Meyer Shapiro, and Jacques Derrida*. Personal communication with the author, August 26, 2020.

DOI: 10.4324/9781003015444-10

Figure 6.1 Thomas Zummer, *On 'potatos' as a Philosophical Exemplar in the Works of Immanuel Kant, G.W.F. Hegel, Friedrich Nietzsche, Martin Heidegger, Meyer Shapiro, and Jacques Derrida.* Archival ink on 36 potatoes, 2008.

subject matter) and its medium (the essay being actually written on the skin of 36 potatoes), the work stages a play on the precariousness of the work of art—and of the value ascribed to it.[2] Rather than being performed or interpreted, however, the text—an academic essay that Zummer has not otherwise published or made available—is consigned to the unstable surface of the tubers.

According to the exhibition catalogue, the essay analyzes the metaphorical use of potatoes in philosophical texts, beginning with G. W. F. Hegel bemoaning the war-imposed dormancy of Ludwig van Beethoven's musical scores ("lying about in a cellar like sacks of potatoes").[3] In this anecdote, perhaps the potato substitutes the writing tablet as a figure of potentiality, not as the empty canvas upon which new scripts may be written, but as a medium preserving the playability of existing ones (Beethoven's musical scores). Silence is no longer just absence of sound, but its temporary suspension—Beethoven's music not being played, but having been played before, and remaining playable in the future. The literal coupling of text and potatoes in the gallery further complicates this relationship, foregrounding the cultural and contextual mediations involved in the designation and preservation of value (what Zummer calls

2 Thomas Zummer, "Essay on Potatoes," in *Text Messaging: September 17 - November 16, 2008*, ed. Karen Shaw (Islip Art Museum, 2008).

3 Zummer, "Essay on Potatoes."

"the stability—and destability—of the work of art at every moment").[4] Indeed, "the potatoes," writes Zummer, "whose skin bears the text of this essay are, for a moment—as long as they are in this museum—art; still, they are just potatoes, and very soon they will return to their low, thingly nature, and be just potatoes after all."[5]

Delivering a philosophical text to potatoes, rather than writing it on a sheet of paper, or on other (more durable) substrates, consigns it to the life of their tuberous bodies; to peels that will dry up, crease, and decay; to cycles of decomposition and rot. It stipulates an expiration date—planned obsolescence as the progressive muffling and deliberate silencing of authorship; as an ethical stance against the prolonged imposition of one's voice. Following Plato's admonition against the written word, perhaps Zummer extinguishes his own marks to prevent them from becoming dangerously decontextualized, misunderstood, or permanent.

6.1.3

The undoing of Zummer's artwork is reminiscent of what Georges Bataille describes as the formless (*informe*). He writes: "A dictionary begins when it no longer gives the meaning of words, but their tasks. Thus, formless is not only an adjective having a given meaning, but a term that serves to bring things down in the world."[6] On one side, formlessness denotes a generic absence of form. On the other, it points to an operation; it is a call to bring down (*déclasser*) and de-form. If the absence of form in the first case invites hylomorphic processes of formation (the standard formulation of potentiality as ability to act, produce, order, and make a mark); it is the preexistence of form—its being there in the first place, in a specific place—that enables acts of de-formation (potentiality as the ability to undo and unravel): "a term that serves to bring things down in the world, generally requiring that each thing have its form."[7]

The shift from constructive (additive) to destructive (subtractive) potentiality would seem to displace the *tabula rasa*, locating it not at the beginning of a new project—the blank canvas or slate; the silence preceding utterances—but at the end of a previous one. Furthermore, the formless does not describe a complete dissolution of form, or its utter absence. Rather, it instigates a different kind of mark, that of a squashed spider or earthworm.[8] Bataille writes: "affirming that the universe resembles nothing and is only formless amounts to saying that the universe is something like a spider or spit."[9]

If one considers, as suggested by Alexander of Aphrodisias and discussed in the previous chapter, not the writing tablet (*grammateion*) but the thin layer of wax covering its surface (*epitedeiotes*), the notion of *tabula rasa* drifts towards a *rasura tabulae*—from the blankness of the tablet to the act of scraping it clean. Instead, while also describing the transition from a noun to a verb, Bataille's formless does not yield

4 Ibid.

5 Ibid.

6 Georges Bataille, "Formless," in Yve-Alain Bois and Rosalind E. Krauss, *Formless: A User's Guide* (New York and Cambridge: Zone Books, 1997), 5. See also Georges Bataille, *Œuvres Complètes* (Paris: Gallimard, 1970), 217.

7 Bataille, "Formless," 5.

8 Ibid.

9 Ibid.

an idealized or conceptual cleanliness or absence of form, but a *destructive formation* that resists and counters the impetus to purify, name, and enclose. In this sense, de-formation undermines form not only by squashing it or by tearing it apart, but by de-programming it, leaving it open to as-yet-unknown interpretations, capacities, values, and use(r)s. "[S]omething like a spider or spit." Spitting challenges the polite orthodoxy of eating, drinking, and speaking scripts, diverting the mouth towards emissions that replace proper language (the grammatical and syntactical organization of words) with the base dialect of saliva. Reprogramming words also includes, in this sense, preventing them from being uttered—not only potentiality to do or to undo, but potentiality to not do; the ability to not speak, to remain silent.

6.1.4

"I would prefer not to," declares repeatedly Bartleby, the copyist in a law office and the protagonist of Herman Melville's eponymous story, progressively refusing to proofread, to reread copies, to go on errands, to walk into the next room, to write, to leave, to move, to speak, and even to eat.[10] From doing "an extraordinary quantity of writing,"[11] Bartleby gradually decelerates, slowing down until the attorney eventually discovers him lifeless.

As the short story develops, the phrase *I would prefer not to* at first shocks and dumbfounds ("for a few moments I turned into a pillar of salt," "I was thunderstruck").[12] Then, it takes root and proliferates, gaining force, lingering, and spreading ("of late I had got into the way of involuntarily using this word 'prefer' upon all sorts of not exactly suitable occasions," "I must get rid of a demented man, who already has in some degree turned the tongues, if not the heads, of myself and clerks").[13] Just as Bataille's *informe* "brings things down in the world" so does Bartleby's formula unravel, unfold, and infect, pulling the scrivener towards increased equilibrium (silence, stillness, death), and those around him into a stupefying sense of vertigo.[14] Bartleby's silence is not, however, a simple refusal to speak. As Deleuze remarks, it is "as if he had said everything and exhausted language at the same time."[15] The French philosopher writes:

> The formula is devastating because it eliminates the preferable just as mercilessly as any nonpreferred. It not only abolishes the term it refers to, and that it rejects, but also abolishes the other term it seemed to preserve, and that becomes impossible. In fact, it renders them indistinct: it hollows out an ever-expanding zone of indiscernibility or indetermination between some nonpreferred activities and a preferable activity."[16]

The suspension of discernibility described by Deleuze atrophies hylomorphism, making it impossible to distinguish between background

10 Herman Melville, "Bartleby," in *The Piazza Tales* (New York: Dix & Edwards, 1856), 31–107.

11 Melville, "Bartleby," 46.

12 Ibid., 51, 81.

13 Ibid., 72–74.

14 Gilles Deleuze, "Bartleby; or, The Formula," in *Essays Critical and Clinical*, trans. Daniel W. Smith and Michael A. Greco (London and New York: Verso, 1998), 68–90.

15 Deleuze, "Bartleby," 70.

16 Ibid., 71.

and foreground, canvas and paint, substrate and drawing, matter and form. If the tension between a *tabula rasa* and a *tabula scripta* relied on the ability to tell them apart—on contrast; on the intentionality, originality, and legibility of the authorial mark (black ink on white paper)—and, inversely, Bataille's *informe* depended on the preexistence of the forms one might tear down (a destructive or subtractive mark); Bartleby's formula gradually neutralizes oppositions, abolishing boundaries by refusing to endorse the privilege afforded by the ecologies they enclose.

Whereas, as Michel Serres convincingly argues,[17] the animal marking of a territory and its cultural renditions (e.g., lines, buildings, signatures, pollution) enclose and appropriate space, claiming ownership over ideas, land, animals, people, and environments, Bartleby remains resolutely "without references, without possessions, without properties, without qualities, [...] too smooth for anyone to be able to hang any particularity on him."[18] He is not absorbed or immersed into his context in either a mimetic or equipmental sense, but rather performs, through the formula *I would prefer not to*, smoothness as a function of ecological slipperiness, as an active refusal to take part, to be complicit. The individual is no longer seeking to appropriate and enclose, nor is he gathering strength through ecological alliances. He is active in the world not in a *normal* (animal, productive) capacity, but to "reveal its emptiness."[19] He is "not subject to the influence of his milieu; on the contrary," writes Deleuze, "he throws a livid white light on his surroundings, much like the light that 'accompanies the beginning of things in Genesis.'"[20] This image brings one back to a kind of *rasura*, but not in a purifying, decontextualizing, or subtractive sense. To make figure and ground indistinct does not lead to their actual dissolution (a lack of contents; the impossibility to read). Rather, it suggests a state of "extreme proximity" and "absolute contiguity" with the *other*—not through "a natural filiation, but an unnatural alliance."[21]

By highlighting the passage from family lineage (genetics, filiation, consanguinity, titles, property) to nonlinear alliances undertaken by the protagonists of Melville's novels (what he calls the "originals"), Deleuze introduces a new iteration of the formless, one that de-forms the paternal function (and closed referential loops in general) towards a novel community—a *community of celibates*: "All referents are lost, and the formation of man gives way to a new, unknown element, to the mystery of a formless, nonhuman life, a *Squid*."[22] The mark as territorial, genetic, and reproductive technology; the drawing of clear boundaries that can be communicated, translated, enforced, and protected; the delineation of an active and productive identity or contexture—are converted by the originals into a form of hybridity; a closeness that does not enclose. This is reminiscent of the stickiness of hyperobjects, or of Morton's understanding of abjection as "the basic feeling of ecological awareness."[23] They write: "I find myself surrounded and penetrated by other beings that seem to be glued to me, or which are so deeply embedded in me that to get rid of them would be to kill me."[24]

17 Michel Serres, *Malfeasance: Appropriation through Pollution?*, trans. Anne-Marie Feenberg-Dibon (Stanford: Stanford University Press, 2011). See also Michel Serres, *Le Mal Propre: Polluer Pour s'approprier?* (Paris: Pommier, 2008).

18 Deleuze, "Bartleby," 74.

19 Ibid., 83.

20 Ibid.

21 Ibid., 78.

22 Ibid., 77.

23 Timothy Morton, "Frankenstein and Ecocriticism," in *The Cambridge Companion to Frankenstein*, ed. Andrew Smith (Cambridge: Cambridge University Press, 2016), 155.

24 Morton, "Frankenstein and Ecocriticism," 155.

6.1.5

Returning to Aristotle's blank tablet as a figure of the pure potentiality of thought (*nous*), Agamben reads Melville's scrivener against the cabalistic tradition according to which divine creation is conceived as an act of writing.[25] Here, Avicenna addresses the technical difficulties in accounting for the potentiality of thought and its passage into actuality by describing creation as a reflexive act (a divine intelligence thinking itself) and by recasting potentiality as patiently unlocked through learning: a *material potency* at the stage of a child's inability (but projected ability) to write; a *possible potency* during the time in which she is beginning to write letters, and familiarizing herself with ink and paper; and a *perfect potency* when the scrivener has mastered the art of writing (but is not actually doing so).[26] The degree of potentiality (or rather, its expressibility) increases in passing from one stage to the next.[27]

There is a distinct similarity between this progression and the movement of raw materials across the technical chains that potentialize them towards specific contexts and ecologies of use (from tree to log to 2x4). This process is not however lossless; while placing potentiality along a spectrum of perfectibility may seem useful or even accurate (the playing ability of the violinist exceeds that of the untrained fiddler); it also funnels it through teleological pipelines, binding powers to increasingly precise functions and routines. For one thing, the violinist's ability to play is not attained once and for all, but confirmed and maintained through hours of daily practice. Becoming a violinist (achieving perfect potency in playing the violin) will typically limit or rule out other interactions or powers. In addition, the titles of *violinist* and *scrivener*, much as the common designations of *chair*, *bicycle,* or *hammer*, establish the implicit criteria that will be used to measure one's capacities. In other words: to assess whether something tastes good or is baked well, it is useful to know if it's supposed to be pizza, toast, or sugar pie.

A broad field of possibility is inversely proportional to the "perfect" achievement of one discrete potential, or of a few; perfection and specialization reduce a system's capacity for extra-ecological communication, both disabling it and making it seem irrelevant. It is perhaps in the tension and modulations between ecological and extra-ecological potentials—between a drive to enclose and specialize, and an opposite impetus towards openness and generality—that design can negotiate an ethical dimension. Bartleby's formula may be read in this light—as triggering a redistribution of powers. His refusals neutralize a paraphrastic understanding of objects, one according to which they coincide with—and are reducible to—their functions (the chair as object to sit on; the scrivener as writing man). The formula rescinds the promise of productivity, compliance, and reliability, and, by replacing necessity with preference, it suspends ecology-driven binaries (e.g., on and off; sound and silence; writing and not writing).

25 Giorgio Agamben, "Bartleby o della contingenza," in Gilles Deleuze and Giorgio Agamben, *Bartleby: La Formula della Creazione* (Macerata: Quodlibet, 2012), 53.

26 Agamben, "Bartleby o della contingenza," 53–54.

27 Ibid., 55.

Bartleby is at first described as an efficient appliance for writing and copying ("did an extraordinary amount of writing. As if long famishing for something to copy, he seemed to gorge himself on my documents," "he is useful to me"),[28] yet the scrivener-machine progressively deteriorates and breaks down, turning, in the eyes of the attorney, into furniture and still life ("he remained as ever, a fixture in my chamber," "useless as a necklace," "like the last column of some ruined temple, he remained standing mute and solitary in the middle of the otherwise deserted room")[29] and almost disappearing ("a ghost;" "you are harmless and noiseless as any of these old chairs; in short, I never feel so private as when I know you are here").[30] If, as sociologist and philosopher Zygmunt Bauman maintains, employment and productivity are the litmus tests for a positive contribution to modern society,[31] Bartleby's refusals upset any direct or natural correlation between the two, both crossing the "migration barriers"[32] that separate humans from nonhumans, living beings from inert stuff, and neutralizing agency (speaking, copying, writing, following orders, moving) as an indicator of humanity, or as a way to confirm and maintain hierarchies, roles, and essences.

Whether, as Bauman explains, "[t]he modern way of being consists in compulsive, obsessive change: in the refutation of what 'merely is' in the name of what could, and by the same token ought, to be put in its place,"[33] Bartleby's formula forestalls and delays change, staying with (and preserving) what already is. His withdrawal from the tasks and conventions of the law office is not, however, just a symptom of brokenness and inertia, or a vanishing act. Like Heidegger's broken hammer, Bartleby re-emerges as "present-at-hand," as more than a mere scrivener, or writing tool. Rather than representing a call to passivity, the formula *I would prefer not to* claims a new way of being—the possibility of an existence beyond essences and effects.

6.1.6

Agamben compares Bartleby to a *tabula rasa*: "The scrivener," he writes, "has become the writing tablet; he is now nothing other than his white sheet."[34] For him, Melville's character is the figure of a potentiality that is pure and absolute—not constrained by will or necessity. That is why, according to the philosopher, Bartleby "dwells so obstinately in the abyss of potentiality and does not seem to have the slightest intention of leaving it."[35]

By using the formula *I would prefer not to* rather than *I do not want to*, Melville refuses to reduce potentiality—or to entrust its passing into actuality—to decisions and goals.[36] Here, the openness and ambiguity of potency (as both potentiality and impotentiality) cannot be resolved, controlled, or organized on the basis of what one *wants* or *must* do (what Agamben refers to as "the perpetual illusion of morality").[37] Instead, the formula reclaims the priority of a state of suspension. "It is not that [Bartleby] does not *want* to copy or that he does

28 Melville, "Bartleby," 46–47, 56.

29 Ibid., 76–78.

30 Ibid., 59, 87.

31 Zygmunt Bauman, *Wasted Lives: Modernity and Its Outcasts* (Cambridge: Polity, 2011), 11.

32 Montgomery Furth, *Substance, Form, and Psyche: An Aristotelean Metaphysics* (Cambridge and New York: Cambridge University Press, 1988), 121.

33 Bauman, *Wasted Lives*, 23.

34 Giorgio Agamben, "Bartleby, or On Contingency," in *Potentialities: Collected Essays in Philosophy*, trans. Daniel Heller-Roazen (Stanford: Stanford University Press, 1999), 254. It is also worth noting the following passage in Melville's story: "The scrivener's pale form appeared to me laid out, among uncaring strangers, in its shivering winding sheet." Melville, "Bartleby," 66.

35 Agamben, "Bartleby, or On Contingency," 254.

36 Agamben, "Bartleby o della contingenza," 64–65.

37 Ibid.

38 Agamben, "Bartleby, or On Contingency," 255.

not *want* to leave the office," writes Agamben, "he simply would prefer not to. The formula that he so obstinately repeats destroys all possibility of constructing a relation between being able and willing."[38]

Bartleby is no longer on the outside looking in—the writer has become the very surface on which he writes; pen and paper have merged. He writes not on the skin of potatoes, but on his own—wherever that may be. Legibility and authorship have lost all relevance, replaced by an immersive and probing ethos (*praeferre*, to carry in front), and by life itself.

6.2 Thresholds (Superecologies)

According to Heidegger, withdrawal is a precondition for utility and functionality: for a tool to become active (for us), it must first fuse with an equipmental totality—a wider network of reference and co-orientation. EoIs generalize this predicament, showing that it is not exclusive to the use or usability of completed tools, but a step that necessarily recurs in the socio-technical chains alongside which tools are made. Furthermore, while the Heideggerian tool only contributes to equipmental effects in relation to declared functions (the hammer *qua* hammer), EoIs can account for misuses, and for diachronic processes and provisional stages and states (the progressive unlocking of material potentials towards an ecology of hammering; the unfinished handle or hammer head as pre-equipmental objects; et cetera). Indeed, as Zoë Sofia remarks, "Heidegger's discussion of causality in the relation to the chalice leaves out the question of where the silver for making it came from."[39]

39 She continues: "the appearance of materials within the smithy's workshop—the ore, the coal for heating and smelting it, the apparatus and tools used for refining and working it—is only possible through a prior set of techniques and technologies for extracting, moving, and storing resources, for securing or coercing human labor power (for example, the slave miners of antiquity), and for tunneling, digging, gathering, carrying, storing, trading, shipping, and delivering. Heidegger's elision of this activity of extraction, transport, and provisioning in respect to an artisanal mode of production allows it to be more dramatically contrasted with modern intensities of macro-containment and mega-supply." Zoë Sofia, "Container Technologies," *Hypatia* 15, no. 2 (2000): 197.

In this sense, EoIs articulate an ecology of moving equipmental targets, one that reduces Heidegger's "totality of equipment" to the partial network enlisted for specific translations and communication protocols at any given time. Through the lens of EoIs, that is, an equipmental whole is not a neutral collection of interconnected parts (a world), or what emerges from their alliance. Rather, it participates in the selective and reductive annexing of its parts and, as such, is able to conceal and discard the aspects of reality that do not suit it and, vice versa, to empower those that fit. EoIs, by describing the evolutionary trajectory of technical objects (the instability of figures and grounds; the dimming of some objects or aspects over others), reveal that backgrounds and foregrounds are not simply and innocently given, or dependent on regimes of attention and inattention, but designed and enforced. If one operative term of equipmental absorption—*assignment*—already presumes the possibility that a project or ecological enclosure may be violent, the other—*reference*—can be subtler (undeclared), and its violence more insidious and diffuse.

Indeed, the challenge faced by a relational and referential understanding of potentiality is a reactionary tendency to perpetuate and reinforce (positively or negatively) the status quo. This is also the limit of dispositional (Easterling) or networked (Latour) accounts of action—ones that Bartleby's formula so uncompromisingly and completely overcomes.

In a narrow sense, *reference* has to do with the effective communication within ecologies, as curated by herding commands. Yet, more broadly, it describes the larger areas or zones within which ecologies are allowed to emerge. [**Figure 6.2**] The transformation of a cow–individual into a beef–material, for example, has as much to do with ecologies of farming and butchering as with the social acceptability of beef consumption. That is, the collective ability to view some animals (and not others) as *meat* makes their slaughter possible in the first place. In this sense, the cow recedes into beef prior to being actually slaughtered. Withdrawals anticipate transformations, activating them *in potentia*.

Now, refusing to attribute the cow's butcherability to its essential "cowness," one must recognize, in its invention and presumed banality,

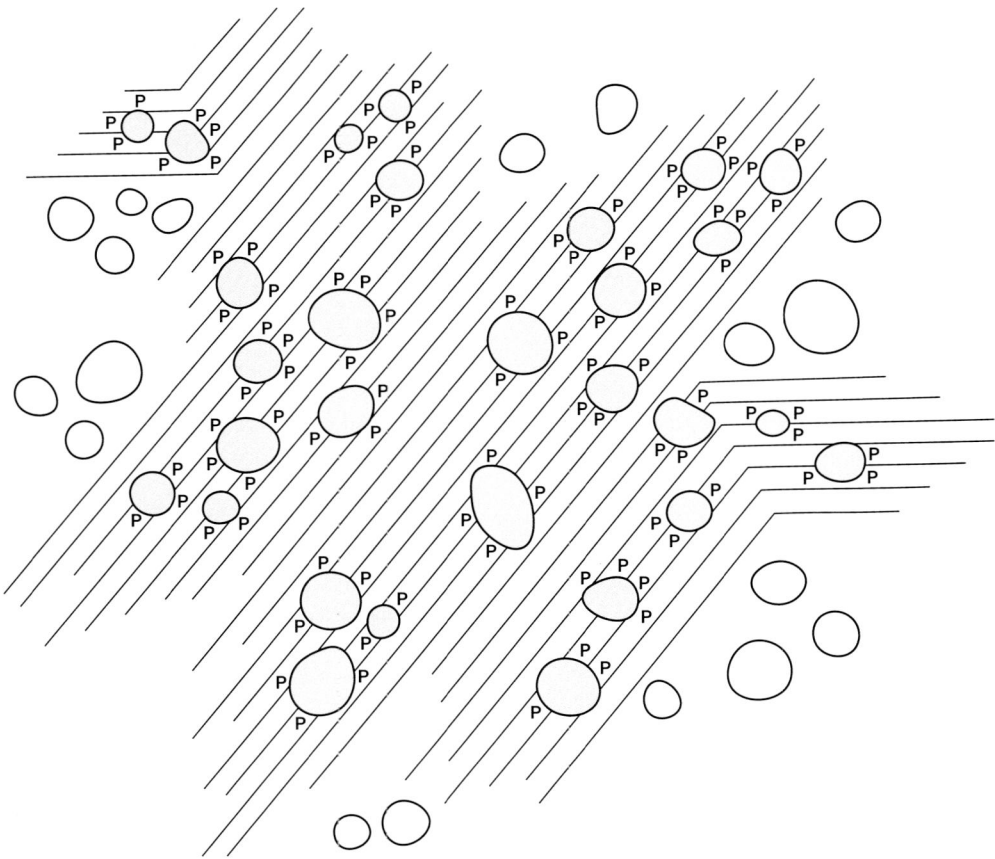

Figure 6.2 A threshold or superecology identifies a zone within which ecologies (and their powers) are allowed to emerge.

40 Jakob von Uexküll, *A Foray into the Worlds of Animals and Humans: With A Theory of Meaning*, trans. Joseph D. O'Neil, with an introduction by Dorion Sagan and an afterword by Geoffrey Winthrop-Young (Minneapolis: University of Minnesota Press, 2010).

41 Sara Ahmed, "Declarations of Whiteness: The Non-Performativity of Anti-Racism," *Borderlands E-Journal* 3, no. 2 (2004).

42 Ahmed, "Declarations of Whiteness."

43 Saidiya Hartman, "The End of White Supremacy, An American Romance," *Bomb*, June 5, 2020.

44 Keller Easterling, *Extrastatecraft: The Power of Infrastructure Space* (London and New York: Verso, 2014), Introduction, E-book.

an intermediate step—the zone across which poietic transitions (between form and matter, figure and ground) must be first negotiated and agreed. This is what I would call a *threshold* or *superecology*. It is not an ecology of inception, or a constellation of communicating objects—it has no obvious scripts to defend. And yet, it is able to draw the contours alongside which ecologies can (or cannot) be extruded. These outlines or worlds—which are indeed traced or designed—are not natural *Umwelten*,[40] or objective spatiotemporal coordinates, and only potentialize certain projects, bodies, or objects. Superecologies are fields—understood, following Sara Ahmed, "as the forgetting of gestures that are repeated over time."[41] One might see them as coextensive with the systemic inequities and inequalities that afflict our societies, and with the specters of patriarchy, homophobia, transphobia, racism, and white supremacy. "Seeing whiteness," writes Ahmed, "is about living its effects, as effects that allow white bodies to extend into spaces that have already taken their shape, spaces in which black bodies stand out, stand apart."[42] As Saidiya Hartman writes of a black messenger in New York:

> The distance between the landing and the sidewalk isn't great, yet he inhabits one world and the white men in their suits and ties, advancing and walking briskly through the streets, exist in another. No, it is more like they are in the world and he has been cast out.[43]

6.3 Surface Medium

6.3.1

The last section of this chapter will add yet another dimension to my exploration of media. As discussed in the previous chapter, Easterling's *active forms* must be sought below the surface of the water—in the spatial software (the circular movement of water molecules, the river's flow and currents) of which ripples and waves are mere indexes and effects. She writes: "For each technology in infrastructure space, to distinguish between what the organization is saying and what it is doing—the pretty landscape versus the fluid dynamics of the river—is to read the difference between a declared intent and an underlying disposition."[44]

Similarly, one could contend that cars, brushes, smart phones, and buildings are only partial snapshots or superficial protrusions within the extensive and receding spatiotemporal body of EoIs, which is often invisible (unaccountable) and difficult to grasp. Yet, media don't always simmer in abysmal and inscrutable depths. Graham Harman's object-oriented philosophy (OOP) proposes quite the opposite: that they exist on the surface of things. Chapter 8 will examine Harman's metaphysics in more detail, interrogating its (somewhat troubling) relationship with architectural design and authorship. For now, it will suffice to provide a general overview of object-oriented philosophy, and to link it to the present discussion.

The key insight of OOP stems from Harman's reading of Heidegger's *Being and Time*, where the German philosopher discovers—contra the phenomenological tradition preceding him—that objects are not always ripe for apprehension, but largely recede into equipmental networks. Using a tool (or being able to view it as usable) cloaks it with a measure of invisibility. The hammer—its shape, material qualities, et cetera—will heave back into view only when broken or otherwise unable to perform (or comply with) functional scripts. Similarly, a computer hard drive will come to one's attention when failing, and the inner tube of a tire will become noticeable when pierced—and deflated—by a shard of glass.

Yet, for Harman the gap between *vorhanden* (the broken "present-at-hand" tool) and *zuhanden* (the functioning "ready-to-hand" one) uncovered by Heidegger does not only describe attention regimes (experience; our access to the world; knowledge), but reality—an ontology of objects withdrawn from relations. This should not be taken to mean that the broken hammer is somehow more real that its functioning counterpart, or that present-at-hand vacuum cleaners are deeper than ready-to-hand ones. Rather, precisely the ability of the hammer and vacuum cleaner to flicker between states demonstrates that the encounters with things are necessarily partial—that experience can never access or exhaust the full reality of either object. Or, in Harman's words, "the opposition is not really between tools on one side and broken tools on the other, but between the withdrawn tool-being of things on one side and both broken and non-broken tools on the other."[45]

Object-oriented philosophy does not merely combine Heidegger's *tool-being* with moves and positions from Aristotelian essentialism (an ontology of substances), German idealism (Kant's Copernican revolution; the existence of a noumenal realm beyond reach), and phenomenology (the rift between adumbrations, intentional objects, and *eidos* in Husserl), but radically reformulates their insights into a novel metaphysical landscape: expanding the definition of *object* beyond physical substances; vindicating a reality outside of human access/epistemology (and demanding a role for nonhumans in philosophical enquiry); and describing human–object relations as instances, special as these may be, of causality in general—of the relations (or nonrelations) between all objects.

While an adequate engagement with these traditions and ideas is beyond the scope of the present summary, an introduction to OOP should probably start with the definition of *object*. With the term, Harman seeks both to account for the relatively stable entities one encounters in their day-to-day experience (e.g., a person beyond their changing moods, haircuts, and ages), and to offer an alternative to scientific naturalism, or to supplement its monopoly on reality (e.g., a person beyond clusters of atoms, biochemistries, and organs). OOP's objects do not depend on materiality (on what bodies or instruments might be able to detect or interact with them on a physical plane), and can

45 Graham Harman, *The Quadruple Object* (Winchester and Washington: Zero Books, 2011), 54.

therefore include historical figures, fictional characters, poems, and organizations, as much as atoms, sheep, oceans, water molecules, human beings, bicycles, umbrellas, cities, and volcanoes. To be classified as such, an object must simply resist undermining (being reduced to its basic components or subsumed under a cohesive substrate or flux), overmining (being reduced to bundles of qualities or to effects), or duomining (being simultaneously undermined and overmined).

Two features of this definition interest me here: the articulation of a flat metaphysical topography that denies an ontological basis for privileging humans over giraffes, Easter eggs, and plutonium (or some humans over others); and the admission that a lack of effects does not immediately trigger a shortage in reality. While the former point suggests a reframing of philosophical investigations beyond anthropocentric perspectives and human–world correlates—and the potential for a radical rethinking of design, as I will explore in Chapter 8—the latter one returns to the discussion, in Chapter 3, of mythical science and the bricoleur: recognizing objects as both autonomous (independent of who perceives or is affected by them) and capable of existing in a state of suspension, detached from equipmental networks, ecological lenses, and relations. Harman calls the most extreme of these cases *dormant objects*. He writes that "the sleep of a dormant object would […] be a state of perfect sleep, in which an entity would be real without entering into further relations at all," and that "some objects might remain dormant forever. They might be perfectly real without ever being discovered, caressed or capitalized upon in such a way as to enter into a higher object, like drops of water forever at the surface of the ocean."[46] The stability of objects in OOP does therefore not correspond with the strict essentialist checklists of Aristotelian philosophy, but with a subtler and more mysterious core, one that is simultaneously differentiated and bubbling with possibility.

There is also a significant shift in the way OOP understands potentiality. Harman, like Latour, rejects potency as an intrinsic or predefined trajectory of development. For him, the acorn is an object in its own right, and not the preindividual path that will eventually lead to an oak–tree individual. Yet more importantly, he views potentiality as a "disingenuous way of equating the actual with the relational."[47] Gilbert Ryle, mentioned in the last chapter in the context of Keller Easterling's work, already recognized that the brittleness of glass precedes the encounter with a shattering object, and enlisted brittleness as a "dispositional property," differentiating between being in a certain state, or undergoing specific changes, and being "bound or liable to" be in that state or undergo those changes.[48] Instead, Harman views brittleness as already fully inscribed in the actuality of the withdrawn window pane. He writes:

> the lethal character of the plutonium is never triggered, yet this deadliness remains a part of its actuality. The plutonium's act

46 Harman, *The Quadruple Object*, 123.

47 Graham Harman, *Circus Philosophicus* (Winchester: Zero Books, 2010), 10.

48 Gilbert Ryle, *The Concept of Mind* (London and New York: Routledge, 2009), 31.

of killing will surely exist only in relation to a living thing, but this misses the point. For I speak here not of the killing (which is obviously a relation) but of that lethal portion of the plutonium's reality that is never manifest in cases where nothing is killed.[49]

Furthermore, while actuality cannot be confused with an object's outer effects or with how its existence is verified or recorded,[50] it is also more than a mere collection of "properties not currently expressed" (and necessarily expressed in the future).[51] Rather, withdrawal means that "it remains a mystery where and what the actuality of the plutonium really is."[52]

6.3.2

Not a wrinkle of agitation rippled him.

Herman Melville, *Bartleby*[53]

Contra Harman, there might be an unexpected complicity between potentiality and the withdrawal of objects, as if the latter had at some point violently feasted on the former in order to gain its strength. Redefining actuality as partially hidden and withheld, as OOP does, means that potentiality can be folded and collapsed inside it—replaced by the interior of objects. Now, if this argument produces a sense of *déjà vu* in the reader, it is because it resonates with the discussion of impotentiality in Chapter 2. Following Agamben, I had argued that potentiality and actuality are not mutually exclusive, as is generally maintained; that potentiality does not fully pass into actuality, but is preserved within it. When the trunk of a tree is carved into the shape of a chair, surely the trunk's potential to be that chair is actualized, yet the potentiality to not be that chair (to become something else) survives at the heart of the object. Therefore, impotentiality (the ability to forgo relations) guarantees not only the persistence of powers—avoiding their immediate actualization or continuous deployment—but also ensures that actualized forms can continue to change; that they can hold in reserve a supply of alternate futures.

Having introduced one of the key tenets of object-oriented philosophy—the withdrawal of objects, and their existence independent of human knowledge and perception—I should now turn to how these nonrelational units actually manage to affect one another. In order to do so, I must take a few steps backwards and outline another crucial principle in Harman's metaphysics: the four ontological poles within objects—sensual qualities, sensual objects, real qualities, and real objects—and the tensions between them.[54] [**Figure 6.3**] Firstly, Harman draws a distinction between *real objects* (the withdrawn and nonrelational entities considered thus far) and *sensual objects* (their

49 Harman, *Circus Philosophicus*, 10–11.

50 Graham Harman, *Guerrilla Metaphysics: Phenomenology and the Carpentry of Things* (Chicago: Open Court, 2005), 232.

51 Harman, *Circus Philosophicus*, 11.

52 Ibid.

53 Melville, "Bartleby," 49.

54 It is worth noting that, strictly speaking, the term *tension* for Harman always "involve[s] an object-pole and a quality-pole." Harman, *The Quadruple Object*, 108.

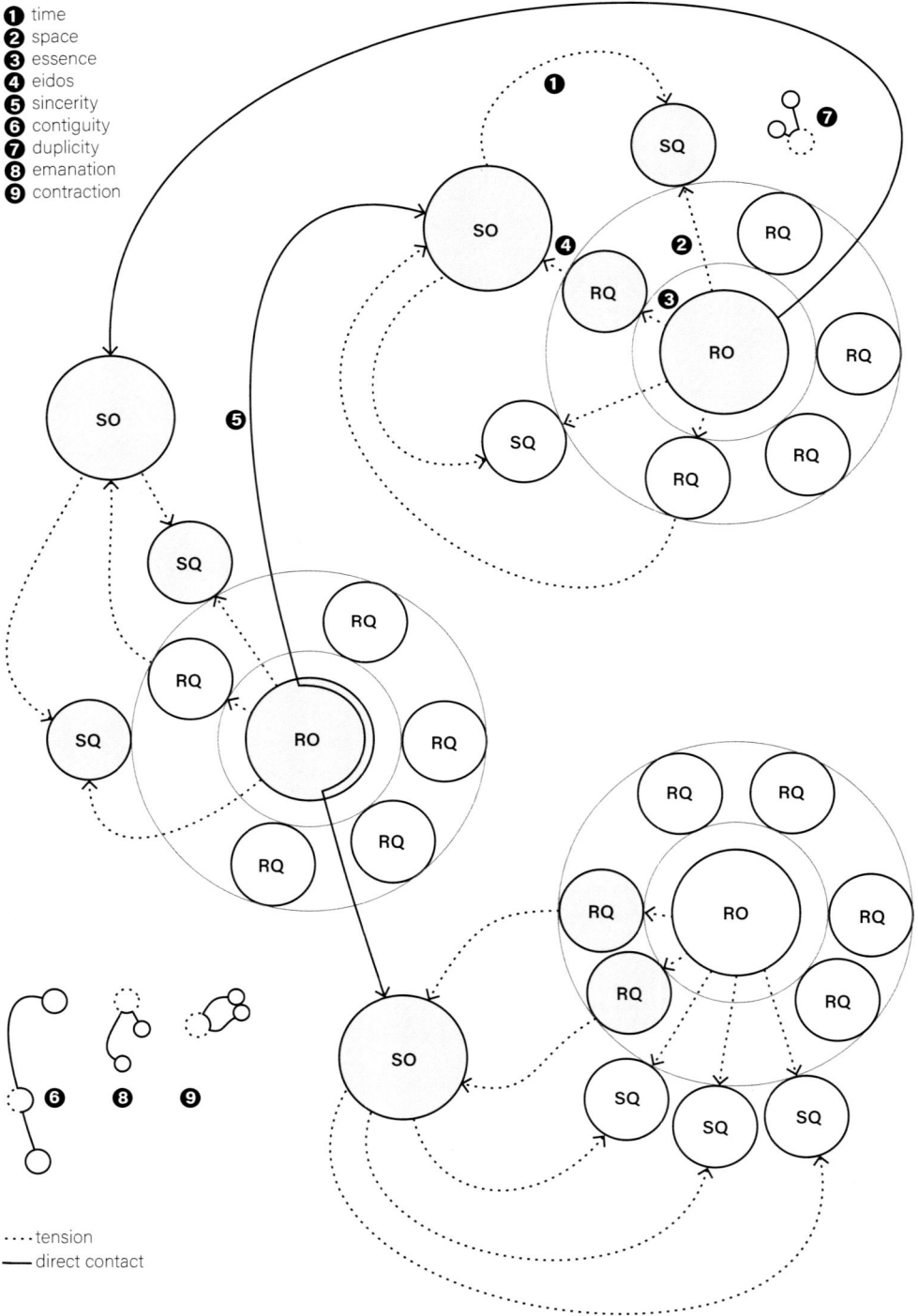

Figure 6.3 The encounters between real objects (RO), sensual objects (SO), real qualities (RQ), and sensual qualities (SQ) according to object-oriented philosophy.

partial translations as experienced through relations). In the phenomenal realm, Harman follows Husserl in recognizing a rift between unified sensual objects and the ever-shifting qualities encrusted on their surfaces (the same basic house vs. the way it looks and feels across different emotions, times, temperatures, states of repair, paint colors, and levels of illumination). Here, the sensual object and its sensual qualities are thoroughly immanent, and the former plays both the role of connecting medium and substrate, disproving the empiricist claim that qualities are portable (that they can be experienced in isolation). This first tension between sensual objects and sensual qualities is what Harman calls *time*.

In the noumenal realm, on the other side, Heidegger's tool–being is viewed as proof that real objects withdraw beyond all contact, and are impervious to other real objects. While the latter do possess real qualities, without which they would not differ from one another (they would lack content), the two do not naturally cohere, but can only be fused together by means of a third mediating term.[55] In the example often used by Harman to explain vicarious causation, fire causes one real quality of the cotton ball (its flammability) to fuse with the real cotton ball and eventually reduce it to ashes, while its other qualities (whiteness, softness, etc.) remain, in relation both to the fire and to the cotton ball, disengaged. This second tension between real objects and their real qualities is what Harman calls *essence*. He writes: "A real object is real and has a definite character, but its essence is first produced from the outside through causal interactions."[56]

Moving to the "exotic mixture"[57] of the real and sensual poles, the third tension is characterized by "the interplay of relation and nonrelation" between a real object and its sensual qualities, which Harman calls *space*.[58] As in the case between real objects and real qualities, the original terms are not conjoined by birth, but must be fused together by a third (real) object, given that it is only for such an object (the perceiver) that sensual qualities exist in the first place. However, whereas a real object could enter into direct contact with a sensual one, sensual qualities can only gesture towards a withdrawn/sleeping object from a distance, by allure. The fourth and final tension is the one between the sensual object and its real and hidden qualities, which Harman calls, following Husserl, *eidos*. Here, the two terms are "always fused in advance," and can only be split into their components through theory.[59]

One finally begins to glimpse an inversion of the standard McLuhanian view of message and medium, with secret messages sinking into the illegible depths of real objects and media floating along their sensual surface, where all causation begins.[60] Object-oriented philosophy does not, however, promote a stable cartography of surface media and subterranean autonomous tunnels, one that can be reliably associated with specific scales, physical features, dimensions, edges, backgrounds, and foregrounds. Instead, for Harman "the sensual is what exists only

55 Ibid., 105.

56 Ibid., 107.

57 Ibid., 105.

58 Ibid., 100.

59 Ibid., 104.

60 Ibid., 75.

61 Ibid., 110.

in relation to the perceiver, and the real is whatever withdraws from that relation."[61] Provided that OOP invests all objects with equal (albeit different) powers of perception—sponges as well as math teachers, cotton balls, chemical compounds, Paris, and moths—surfaces and underground chambers are constantly redefined and discovered across levels, magnitudes, instruments, perceptual apparatuses, and modes of interaction, along an "infinite regress" of objects and constituent pieces.

6.3.3

Whereas Marshall McLuhan recognizes that areas of attention and inattention (figures and grounds) switch places with one another as one focuses on the different environmental stimuli in their lives, he also admits that *ground* prevents, by definition, any attempt to attain sharper resolutions—consigned, as it is, to a blurry and nomadic periphery.[62]

62 Marshall McLuhan and Eric McLuhan, *Laws of Media: The New Science*, (Toronto: University of Toronto Press, 1988), 5. Quoted in Graham Harman, *Bells and Whistles: More Speculative Realism* (Winchester: Zero Books, 2013), 183.

Following McLuhan, there cannot be actual exchanges between figures and grounds insofar as they remain divided, and segregated into separate realms. Messages rise and media sink; the former hypnotizing us while the latter recede into the background. And if contact occurs between figure–messages and ground–media, it involves an invisible process of extrusion: pushing materials through a die that lies in a chasm, well beyond one's reach.

Indeed, Keller Easterling's *Medium Design* invites one to read figures as the effects of their grounds' dispositions and internal tendencies, and to find the potential for horizontal action and change in the hinges, nodes, and repetitive formulas that articulate and propel them.

As the last section already suggested, Graham Harman upturns this reading of McLuhan's medium, challenging standard accounts of the media theorist's famous motto. In a 2012 lecture entitled "McLuhan as Philosopher," Harman writes that

> the medium is by no means that which functions as a hidden background; rather, it is the explicit mediator of contact between two other things. In fact, here it is the very opposite of ground—it is a figure that enables the communication between two grounds that would otherwise not be able to communicate.[63]

63 Harman, *Bells and Whistles: More Speculative Realism*, 182.

Inverting the usual understanding of "the medium is the message," and disputing a strict separation of figure–messages on one side and ground–media on the other, or the suspension of the former within the latter, Harman allows for the two realms to interweave, introducing two hybrid admixtures: figure–media and ground–messages. The ability to act thus rests with the interplay between them; it relies on the malleability of the figure—on the ability of the superficial layer of wax deposited on the writing tablet to negotiate exchanges between real objects: the writer, the reader, the stylus, and the tablet itself. Harman's move does not entail or suggest the eradication of the figure/ground binary. Quite the opposite: it broadens its scope as pertaining not only to environmental psychology (to regimes of attention and inattention), but to ontology—to the very fabric of existence. A medium, following the etymology of the Latin word *medius* (middle), is an intermediary between grounds. He writes that "[t]he figure/ground interplay has nothing to do with the difference between conscious and unconscious and everything to do with how things are distorted and simplified by any relation whatsoever, whether with human or nonhuman things."[64]

In this sense plasticity, as discussed in the last and present chapters, points both to the pure and inexhaustible sleep of ground–messages (to their fundamental inability to be paraphrased, and become figures) and to the ability of figure–media to serve as sites for their partial interaction and translation. I will return to these problems in Chapter 8. For now, and in the last section of this chapter, I will briefly introduce a concept that will prove useful, and steer the discussion, in the pages that follow.

[64] Ibid., 185.

6.4 What Is an Ecology of Suspension (EoS)?

Ecologies of inception guide the transformation of materials along predefined socio-technical trajectories, unlocking their powers. They develop the languages through which disparate objects become able to communicate. In this sense, EoIs fit the counter-definition of media proposed by Harman, as interfaces facilitating the communication between previously incompatible or mute (silent) objects. Note that here potentiality exists chiefly as the objects' ability to relate (to be formatted towards one another). However, following object-oriented philosophy, one must also acknowledge that the alliances installed by EoIs are destined to drip along the surface of the objects they enroll, never able to penetrate or seep into them entirely. Like the distorting mirrors in a carnival, they can only reveal certain qualities or traits, and reflect according to the curvature and glossiness of their own surface.

If the relations installed within EoIs would seem to activate regimes of attention that separate figures from grounds (or rather, that assign them as roles), object-oriented philosophy understands grounds (residues, surpluses) to be more than the negative flip side of relation. Rather, nonrelationality is what exceeds the interplay of spot lights and peripheries. If the discussion of EoIs thus far has focused on relations, with two types of potentiality (intrinsic and extrinsic) predicated upon gradients of communication and upon levels of reciprocal attention and compliance, I must now introduce a nonrelational pole or supplement, which I will tentatively label *ecology of suspension*

(EoS). EoSs articulate and reclaim a role for nonrelationality in the life of designed objects. Firstly, the phrase addresses the superficiality of functional scripts and nomenclatures vis-à-vis the reality of objects. Secondly, it delivers impotentiality and suspension to the center of design explorations. And thirdly, it defies the orthodox coupling of value with relations and intentions. The next chapter will elucidate and challenge this association with regard to architectural authorship.

Chapter 7

Exaptive Design: Radical Coauthorship as Method

7.1 Folk Art Museum

> In love with the tabula rasa, architects have played the role of the perfect modernist—the perfect believer in the obsolescence of successively immanent ideas. [...] The architect's dramatic murder of building is often associated with a desire for an impossible purity, and given the chance, architects usually elect to demolish another architect's work.
>
> Keller Easterling, *Subtraction*[1]

At a press conference in Manhattan on January 28, 2014, Glenn Lowry, director of the Museum of Modern Art (MoMA), finally issued a death sentence: the Folk Art Museum—a 13-year-old building celebrated for its sculptural façade and tightly knit interiors—would be demolished.[2] Three years after acquiring the property, and having endured a protracted clash with hordes of outraged museum-goers, preservationists, and architectural critics, the time had come for MoMA to draw the controversy to a close and to move forward with the projected museum expansion, designed by Diller Scofidio + Renfro (DS+R).

In this chapter, I shall argue that the bulldozing of the Folk Art Museum—the razing of a recently built and critically acclaimed $18.4 million structure[3]—does more than compel indignation towards MoMA (shouldn't it preserve culturally significant buildings, rather than tear them down?), demanding a thorough reassessment of architectural methods and values, especially as these are sieved through the figure of the architect/designer. But let's start from the beginning.

On December 11, 2001, the American Folk Art Museum (AFAM) inaugurated a remarkable new home for its collection. Designed by New York architects Tod Williams and Billie Tsien (TWBTA), the eight-story building, erected on a 40-foot-wide plot on West 53rd Street in Manhattan, next to MoMA, packed an ambitious program (galleries as well as ancillary facilities such as a café, a museum shop,

1 Keller Easterling, *Subtraction*, ed. Nikolaus Hirsch and Markus Miessen (Berlin: Sternberg Press, 2014), 5–6.

2 Robin Pogrebin, "Ambitious Redesign of MoMA Doesn't Spare a Notable Neighbor," *The New York Times*, January 8, 2014, Online edition. See the parallels with the Gillender building, also demolished (in 1910) after only 13 years. Jeff Byles, *Rubble: Unearthing the History of Demolition* (New York: Three Rivers Press, 2006), 45.

3 Jennifer Maloney, "MoMa Rethinks Plan to Raze Former Home of Folk Art Museum," *The Wall Street Journal*, May 9, 2013.

DOI: 10.4324/9781003015444-11

4 Joseph Giovannini, "American Folk Art Museum," *New York Magazine*, December 24, 2001.

5 Giovannini writes: "The gentle revolution here is the shift from universal to particular space, where works of art prosper in individuated environments." Giovannini, "American Folk Art Museum."

6 "The challenge," explained Tsien during an interview about the design of the building, "was to establish a direct relationship between what you see and how it was made, so you make a connection between the hand and the finished object." See C. A. Pearson, "Material Affairs," *Architectural Record*, March 2001, 68–72. The architects also suggested that the composition of the façade was an abstracted representation of a hand, a recurring theme in Le Corbusier's architecture as a symbol of the human mastery over tools.

7 Giovannini, "American Folk Art Museum."

8 Herbert Muschamp, "Fireside Intimacy for American Folk Art Museum," *The New York Times*, December 14, 2001.

9 Adelyn Perez, "American Folk Art Museum/Tod Williams + Billie Tsien," *ArchDaily* (blog), accessed October 19, 2018.

10 A comprehensive list is available on the architects' website: TWBTA, "American Folk Art Museum," Tod Williams Billie Tsien Architects Partners, accessed 18 October 2018.

an auditorium, offices, classrooms, and a library) into a narrow plot, finding spaciousness in vertical cuts, interior setbacks, and zenithal lighting. [**Figure 7.1**] "Williams and Tsien, like miniaturists," wrote Joseph Giovannini for *New York Magazine*, "expand space by creating an interior world."[4] Such a world was introverted, quirky, and suggestive of a different, slower tempo.

Admittedly idiosyncratic, the little building blatantly contravened the rules of orthodox museum design, replacing the neutral white box of contemporary art galleries with bush-hammered concrete planes, translucent corrugated plastic, and cherrywood; challenging the modernist separation of circulation and exhibition spaces; and combining structure and artworks—permanent container and changeable contents—into built-ins and fixed juxtapositions.[5] To the richly atmospheric and densely curated interiors, reminiscent of Carlo Scarpa and Sir John Soane, corresponded, on the outside, a luminous white alloyed bronze skin with panels folding inwards, as if pulled towards the gravitational center of the lot, drawing visitors inside. The panels' lush textural irregularities ("volcanic accidents," as Giovannini calls them) were caused by gases escaping from the molten material during the pouring process, and, in the eyes of the architects, indexed the involvement of the human hand in their fabrication.[6] [**Figures 7.2 + 7.3**]

Yet, beyond a visceral celebration of craft, at the urban scale the building's façade affirmed the identity of the Folk Art Museum (and the value of art by people who are not trained as artists) and its unapologetic cultural independence. "MoMA, the vatican of modernism," wrote Giovannini,

> was supposed to cut the architectural edge with its new building on 53rd Street, but instead, the blandissimo design now rising will, ironically, wrap around the new American Folk Art Museum like a neutral backdrop, setting off the brilliant, just-completed boutique museum as though it were the biggest architectural model in the MoMA collection."[7] [**Figure 7.4**]

The building was met with critical acclaim—the *New York Times* critic Herbert Muschamp hailed its façade as "a Midtown icon,"[8] the *New Yorker*'s Paul Goldberger suggested that it was "as sensual a building as New York has seen in a very long time,"[9] and so on—leading to a string of national and international awards, including the Brendan Gill Prize, the 2003 AIA Institute Honor Award for Architecture, the 2002 World Magazine's Best Public Cultural Building in the World and Best New Building in the World Awards, and the 2001 MAS New York City Masterwork Award, just to name a few.[10]

Financially, however, the venture was less successful. Betting on the proximity with MoMA did not pan out (the Museum of Modern Art remained closed for renovations from 2002 to 2004), a financial crisis erupted, a museum chairman and patron was sentenced to six years in prison for fraud, and both visitor numbers and donations

Figure 7.1 Tod Williams Billie Tsien Architects, *American Folk Art Museum*, New York, 2001. Photograph by Richard Anderson.

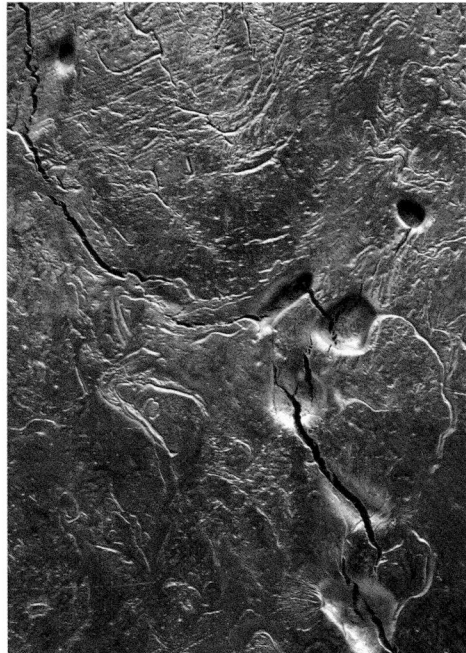

Figures 7.2 + 7.3 Tod Williams Billie Tsien Architects, *American Folk Art Museum,* New York, 2001. Photographs by Scott Norsworthy.

11 Robin Pogrebin, "Options Dim for Museum of Folk Art," *The New York Times*, August 24, 2011, Online edition.

12 Roberta Smith, "Downsizing in a Burst of Glory," *The New York Times*, May 12, 2011, Online edition; Kate Taylor, "Folk Art Museum Considers Closing," *The New York Times*, August 19, 2011, Online edition.

13 Ned Cramer, "The Day MoMA Died," *Architect Magazine*, May 1, 2013. Barry Schwabsky, "MoMA's Demolition Derby," *The Nation*, May 1, 2013.

14 Michael Kimmelman, "Defending a Scrap of Soul against MoMA," *The New York Times*, May 13, 2013, Online edition.

15 Christopher Hawthorne, "Elizabeth Diller Defends MoMA Plan to Demolish Folk Art Building," *Los Angeles Times*, January 16, 2014, Online edition.

16 Hawthorne, "Elizabeth Diller Defends MoMA."

consistently yielded insufficient funding.[11] Having borrowed $32 million by issuing bonds through New York City's Trust for Cultural Resources, in 2009 the museum defaulted on its debt, and in 2011 the trustees voted to sell the building to the adjacent MoMA.[12] Two years later, and in the midst of planning its own eager expansion into a proper corporate *campus*, MoMA revealed the intention to demolish the former Folk Art Museum building, blaming aesthetic differences and the misalignment of floors.[13] Faced with a wave of public outrage, however, the museum quickly back-pedaled and announced that DS+R would be commissioned to design the MoMA campus, and would take up the question of the Folk Art building's future.[14]

After a six-month period, the architects indicated that a convincing reuse strategy could not be found, and that the American Folk Art Museum building would be demolished (and replaced by their own scheme). "We tried very hard to make it work," asserted Elizabeth Diller in conversation with architecture critic Christopher Hawthorne, "to use the [Folk Art] space, to make the circulation work, to make the logistics work. And when that became so difficult—when it passed the threshold of losing its identity—we proposed a different approach."[15] And again:

> We try to make buildings last long and be resilient, but also be not so idiosyncratic that they can't change. I think the reason this [Folk Art] building was very difficult to transform into something else was its degree of idiosyncrasy. If we were to eliminate a lot of those idiosyncrasies, we could use it. But at a certain point it takes on another identity. The very people who are so emotional about the loss would be seeing a very, very compromised building, just to make it work.[16]

Diller is, of course, right—AFAM defenders would have tolerated few modifications, and expected a high degree of integrity; they would have wanted to recognize the Folk Art building, to maintain its celebrated façade intact and to preserve the meticulously detailed quirkiness of its interior spaces. Mere traces or mutilated fragments would not have made the cut. It was therefore in order to preserve the integrity and identity of the Folk Art building (its "impossible purity," in the quotation at the beginning of this section) that, paradoxically, the Folk Art building was demolished. This aporia in no way justifies the resulting environmental waste (labor, energy, materials), the obliteration of a work of architectural merit, or the fact that an institution such as MoMA would have prioritized branding, real-estate development, and problem-solving (the overcrowding of galleries) over the preservation of an architectural masterpiece, reminding us that cultural archives are not universal supra-economic repositories, but commodities whose value can, at any point in time, be renegotiated by their proprietors.

Yet, the absurd destiny of the Folk Art building—preservation by demolition—exposes a deeper, more fundamental flaw in the way notions of identity and authorial integrity channel value into architectural objects, as frameworks that separate them from the coherence and reality of actual physical (matter/form) and relational (human/nonhuman) fabrics.

7.2 Elusive Boundaries

What does *identity* refer to when speaking of buildings? A phenomenological perspective might steer one towards the overlapping sets of memories, expectations, and affordances buildings evoke, relay, and set into motion. The prison guard and the detainee, the child and the school teacher, the stray cat, the raindrop, and the lichen—all have markedly different ways of inhabiting and/or articulating experiences and interactions with(in) the physical body of the prison, school, or residential home, none of which can be subsumed under a monolithic understanding, register, or banner.

Not only does the perceptual apparatus or biochemical disposition of each inhabitant foreclose certain scales and levels of interaction (the raindrop only relates to the inclination or impermeability of a slate roof tile; the movements of a toddler reach out to objects within a meter from the ground) but so do

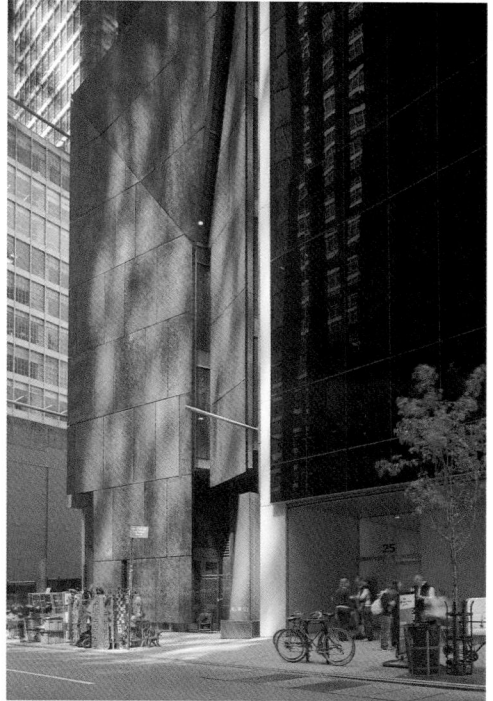

Figure 7.4 Tod Williams Billie Tsien Architects, *American Folk Art Museum*, New York, 2001. Photograph by Richard Anderson.

the temporal, spatial, and socio-economic coordinates within which they operate (the detainee only comes into contact with the cell and common spaces of the correctional facility; the child typically sits in the classroom during school hours, etc.). While such encounters can endure or be repeated, they can never claim to register or distill the entirety of a building because they are inevitably immersed in a life-world, particular and partial, while the very question of identity points towards a self-sameness and discernibility that allows a whole to last beyond specific situations, cases, and interactions.

Similarly, whereas the combination of building parts (bricks, doors, windows, air ducts, pillars, electrical cables, foot mats, etc.) precipitates novel behaviors and properties, it would be difficult to argue that emergence (the whole as different from its parts) delivers fixed identities, or that it always falls within the boundaries of specific buildings, without spilling into the surrounding pavements, utility trenches, topographies, signposts, roadways, Internet cables, parapet walls, trees, and bus stops. Dispositions do not discriminate between interiors and exteriors, or even between proximity and distance. Even if one limited their investigation to spatial features in relative thermodynamic equilibrium (mortar and bricks), they would stumble upon ambiguous and indeterminate configurations, like the walls of two houses adjacent to one another that can be equally understood as bounding each residence or the alleyway between them, suggesting that the attribution of wholeness (to the house or to the alley) is not ontological, but dependent on one's framing of the question, on the effects and properties under consideration in their enquiry, and on their bias. In the same way, the white bronze façade of the Folk Art Museum could have been said to belong to the architecture of 53rd Street as much as to that of the museum; [**Figure 7.5**] and things get only more complicated if, instead of confiding in the clear-cut edges of Euclidean geometry or on the primacy of human experience, one were to represent buildings according to bacterial micro-ontologies,[17] smells, weather fronts, electromagnetic waves, wind patterns, structural loads, or biodiversity, to name a few options.

Whether one focuses on inert structures or infrastructural/environmental exchanges, active human and nonhuman relations reconfigure the life of buildings, stretching them past fixed envelopes, programs, zoning plans, and property boundaries. Such exchanges are thoroughly hybrid, complex, and situated, and cannot be separated into neat compartments (flows on one side, inert structures and materials on the other), in the same way that the global Internet cannot exist without an

17 Myra J. Hird, *The Origins of Sociable Life: Evolution after Science Studies* (Basingstoke: Palgrave Macmillan, 2009).

Figure 7.5 Tod Williams Billie Tsien Architects, *American Folk Art Museum,* New York, 2001. Photograph by Scott Norsworthy.

infrastructure of data centers and undersea fiber optic cables,[18] or photosynthesis does not occur without sunlight and phototrophic (micro) organisms. And if parts fluctuate, change meaning, and jump across scales and sets according to local dispositions, wholes become increasingly difficult to pin down—at least with any stability or authority. The more one looks at a building from the innumerable sets of active contexts it engages, the more *identity* and the hierarchical recognition of *parts* and *wholes* appear to be functions of the lens through which one observes them. This is not intended to mean that hierarchies do not exist, but that they are not intrinsic (Latour's principle of irreduction)[19] and that they exist *alongside*, *inside*, and *across* other hierarchies, without being any less real.

Perhaps the Anthropocene—the realization that anthropogenic changes have reached geological timescales and proportions—corresponds with admitting that emergence does not operate according to language, or within discrete aims, categories, and objects, but is performed across the board, whether one wants it (or is able to name it) or not. There is therefore a fundamental disagreement between the way in which buildings come into being and are apprehended and discussed (as designed and culturally significant wholes) and their situated, post-anthropocenic ontologies (as re-emergent, distributed, and nonexclusive sets of actants performing ad hoc "part" and "whole" scripts). It is in the lack of communication between these two opposite views that the demolition of the Folk Art Museum becomes a viable, albeit obscene, option.

Yet, what identity is DS+R referring to? Until now, I have dwelt on the fact that diachronic (enduring) *identities* can be experienced and interacted with in partial and local ways that privilege embodied relations over the geometrical purity and unity of architectural enclosures. It is, however, evident that when we speak of a certain building, we share conventions (the name Folk Art Museum, or the building's signage) and representations (photographs, maps, logos) that seem to point to a unified notion of what that building is.

The commonsensical referent of any such signs is hardly the actual, physical building taken in its entirety, but rather another signifier, or at most a signified—a concept. This substitution is reminiscent of what Lacan describes as the mirror stage, a "crystallization of images" that renders a child's messy and multidirectional feelings and impulses into a coherent, albeit imaginary, surface identity.[20] At first, it would seem that postulating a gap between images/signs on one side and buildings on the other, or between abstract objects and real-world ecologies, does not help to determine where the identity invoked by DS+R is located, or what it is predicated upon. Yet, if the AFAM "whole" endures through project descriptions, website entries, newspaper clippings, construction sets, models, archived material samples, and photographs—and in the absence of a physical building—there might be a reason. Is the kind of identity I seek so ingrained in the actual building that violating it would, quite literally, wreck it? Or is

18 Andrew Blum, *Tubes: Behind the Scenes at the Internet* (London: Viking, 2012).

19 Bruno Latour, *The Pasteurization of France*, trans. Alan Sheridan and John Law (Cambridge and London: Harvard University Press, 1988), 153–238.

20 Bruce Fink, *The Lacanian Subject: Between Language and Jouissance* (Princeton: Princeton University Press, 1995), 36–37.

it possible that DS+R understands identity as residing outside (and as independent of) the actual building? And if so, where exactly should it be located? To answer this question, I must take another step back and reconsider identity from a philosophical perspective.

7.3 The Project Function

John Locke is often considered to be the philosophical forefather of questions regarding identity and the self. In *An Essay Concerning Human Understanding*, the twenty-seventh chapter posits early on that detecting identity consists in recognizing that a thing in a specific place and at a certain time is "that very thing" and not something else existing elsewhere at the same time.[21] If this seems obvious, so does its corollary: the impossibility of two things occupying the same place at the same time. This articulation allows Locke to define numerical identity in terms of origins: as two things cannot have one beginning, and one thing cannot have two beginnings, then necessarily "what had one beginning is the same thing."[22]

Locke goes on to choose physical integrity as a criterion for identity in simple substances (a lump of matter), claiming that while the arrangement of particles can change, if a single atom is removed or added, the lump is no longer numerically identical. While this solution is not entirely satisfactory (I tend to think of a pre- and post-bite apple as the same apple), one can attribute its stringency to Locke's avoidance of the so-called sorites paradox. According to the latter, one can reliably state that a single grain of sand does not amount to a heap, and that adding a second grain of sand to the previous one will still not cause it to constitute a heap. Yet, if one repeats this operation iteratively, at some point they will end up either claiming that adding another grain of sand makes a heap (which is problematic), or denying that a heap has emerged at all (while it clearly has). A similar problem is at the core of the current investigation, at least according to DS+R. "You pass a tipping point," Diller is reported to have said, "where there's not enough of the original structure to actually maintain its identity."[23]

Yet how many modifications can a building undergo before losing itself? When is a tipping point reached? Upon removing how many bricks or bronze panels exactly? Locke comes to my aid. His strict treatment of a generic lump of matter cannot be repurposed for living things, whose very existence is dependent on metabolic exchanges, periodic transformations, and growth. Therefore, the flag of identity is carried here not by unchanging particles, but by a continued life of which elements partake in virtue of their reciprocal organization. Machines ("a construction of parts organized to a certain end") are similarly held together by the thread of their fitness:

> If we suppose this machine to be one continued body whose parts were repaired, added to, or subtracted from, by a constant addition or separation of imperceptible parts, with one common life,

21 John Locke, *An Essay Concerning Human Understanding*, ed. Jonathan Bennett, vol. Book II: Ideas, 2004, 112.

22 Locke, *An Essay*, 112.

23 Pogrebin, "Ambitious Redesign of MoMA Doesn't Spare a Notable Neighbor."

it would be very much like the body of an animal; with the difference that in an animal the fitness of the organization and the motion wherein life consists begin together, because the motion comes from within; but in a machine the force can be seen to come from outside [...].**24**

24 Locke, *An Essay*, 114.

In order to work out how identity is administered to buildings, one would have to assign them to either collections of inert lumps of matter or to machine–animals (Le Corbusier's *machine-à-habiter*). The former approach highlights inertia, and while consigning identity to thermodynamic equilibrium and changelessness, it also elicits forays beyond strict teleological or functional horizons. In other words: within this identity framework, which I will call *archival*, a building (or any other object, for that matter) can be allowed to endure without performing associated functions as long as it retains a high degree of material integrity (for instance, Elsa von Freytag-Loringhoven's urinal under glass in a museum).

The other approach, which I will call *functional*, insists on the machine-like features of buildings, and views their identity as inextricable from the organization of parts towards specific, coordinated ends. Both the archival and functional approaches underscore the reliance of identity on dedicated maintenance regimes that frame value through conservation (the building as fixed and immutable; the object as value) or use (the building as active and metabolic; operation as value) respectively. Yet how are these criteria installed and enforced? In the case of archival identity, conservation efforts depend on the establishment of a baseline, on a survey that stipulates and labels that which will be conserved (Locke's single beginning). Similarly, in the case of functional identity, the continued effectiveness of the building–machine relies on clear scripts that precede and name its operation, and that can be continuously performed to animate parts towards common goals, despite changes in the building's material constitution. In both cases, and unlike in living organisms, identity is not a given but has to be normatively scored (the beginning, the project) and obediently administered (building maintenance and operation, care).

Perhaps I am getting closer to uncovering what the term *identity* denotes in Diller's interview. For DS+R, the identity of a building—its baseline and script—might correspond with the intentions of its architects. Variations, deletions, and accretions—even improvisation—are certainly possible, but only within a given infrastructural, programmatic, and aesthetic framework; only in accordance with the coherent organization of parts mobilized and perpetuated by the architectural project.**25**

Reading the following passages from Michel Foucault's "What Is an Author?" while recounting the outrageous demolition of the Folk Art Museum (or rather, the obstinate preservation of its identity, which are one and the same), evokes an uncanny sense of *déjà vu*:

We are accustomed [...] to saying that the author is the genial creator of a work in which he deposits, with infinite wealth and generosity, an inexhaustible world of significations. [...] The truth

25 Alois Riegl also separates "a shapeless pile of stones" from a ruin deserving of our attention by identifying "at least a distinct trace of the original form, of the former work of man." Alois Riegl, "The Modern Cult of Monuments: Its Essence and Its Development," in Nicholas Stanley-Price, Mansfield Kirby Talley, and Alessandra Melucco Vaccaro, eds., *Historical and Philosophical Issues in the Conservation of Cultural Heritage* (Los Angeles: Getty Conservation Institute, 1996), 74. See also Gastón Gordillo, *Rubble: The Afterlife of Destruction* (Durham: Duke University Press, 2014), 10.

is quite the contrary: the author is not an indefinite source of significations which fill a work; the author does not precede the works; he is a certain functional principle by which, in our culture, one limits, excludes, and chooses; in short, by which one impedes the free circulation, the free manipulation, the free composition, decomposition, and recomposition of fiction. [...] The author is therefore the ideological figure by which one marks the manner in which we fear the proliferation of meaning.[26]

26 Michel Foucault, "What Is an Author?," in *The Foucault Reader*, ed. Paul Rabinow (New York: Pantheon Books, 1984), 118–19.

If one replaced "fiction" with "buildings," thus reading "a principle [...] by which one impedes [...] the free manipulation, the free composition, decomposition, and recomposition of buildings," it is evident that what Foucault describes in the context of discourse is also relevant in architectural design, and to the case at hand in particular. But what does Western culture fear the proliferation and circulation of? Of parts? Of materials? Of bronze panels, air ducts, and concrete pavers? Of stone friezes, steel anchors, and ceramic urinals? As one might surmise from the razing of the AFAM building, what is circulated, transformed, or destroyed is of little consequence or interest. What is feared is not remixing or an increase of access *per se*, but the emergence of alternative and transversal/promiscuous design methods and modes of valorization.

7.4 Towards a Metabolic Architecture

Flipping through a construction set, architects are well aware of the work that orthographic plans and construction details entail—of the repeated drafts; of long debates amongst designers; of red marks; of coordination with consultants, engineers, and manufacturers; of discussions with clients; of negotiations with city officials; of setbacks and adjustments. Bruno Latour has famously warned against the *salto mortale* that a one-step conversion from real-world objects to abstract representations imagines, forgetting that what seems like a vertiginous jump is rather the wrought unfolding of widely distributed "cascades of transformations" that involve measuring, reformatting, mapping, proportioning, relating, tracing, and translating routines.[27] His warning equally applies to the architectural drawing, which projects an abstracted future that depends on a variety of exchanges between stakeholders, trades, methods, materials, and techniques. And the ANT-inspired turn towards an ethnographic grounding of architectural theory (Yaneva, Cuff, and others),[28] further evidences that architectural authorship is anything but a simple line stretched between one's intentions and the embodiment of those intentions, or the single melodious voice of an architectural genius. While recognizing the "countless voices"[29] involved in architectural endeavors, one must, however, admit that what drives the profession on a day-to-day basis is a call to synthesize, adjust, and re-package.

27 Bruno Latour and Emilie Hermant, *Paris Ville Invisible* (Paris: Les Empêcheurs de Penser en Rond & La Découverte, 1998). Text available in English as: Bruno Latour and Emilie Hermant, "Paris: Invisible City," trans. Liz Carey-Libbrecht, Bruno-Latour.fr, accessed October 19, 2018.

28 Albena Yaneva, *The Making of a Building: A Pragmatist Approach to Architecture* (Oxford and New York: Peter Lang, 2009); Dana Cuff, *Architecture: The Story of Practice* (Cambridge: MIT Press, 1991).

29 Cuff, *Architecture*, 62.

Whereas the design of buildings cannot be ascribed to a single actor (the architect) or group of actors (the architectural firm), it is, however, predicated on absorbing and metabolizing dissonant voices—within and without the office, on the drawing board and on the job site—into a unitary and coherent output. Buildings rarely coincide with the designers' exact aims and aspirations, or with those of the firm's chairman or principal—changes, value engineering, and compromises punctuate and continually divert the process—yet the directorial role played by architects guarantees the orchestration of opposing interests and directions (programmatic, financial, technological, aesthetic, operational, environmental, etc.) into a unified whole. In this sense, a building's identity corresponds with the synthetic seal of the architect, and with the delivery of their project. Furthermore, as Diller's words demonstrate, it is around the construction of such an identity or *project function* that value accretes and deposits, so much so that maintaining the former automatically preserves the latter and, conversely, a loss in identity precipitates a commensurate decrease in value.

The mechanisms described above are consistent with those at work in the broader set of design-related operations I have called ecologies of inception (EoI). EoIs are the connective tissue between processes of individuation and the potentials they unlock, generally describing a path that couples increased specificity with incremental value. They encompass both designed relations and capacities (for instance, a writing ecology as the active encounter of paper and pencil) and the corresponding chains of technical transformations (the progressive orientation of raw materials—trees and graphite ore—towards that encounter). In this sense, they approach what Heidegger called *equipment* or *equipmentality* (the relational networks that coproduce the functionality of tools) from the dynamic point of view of design and extraction/manufacturing processes.

The successful interaction of a pen with a sheet of paper—for instance, the fact that writing, rather than blotching, ensues—is never serendipitous (a mere occurrence, here and now), but the rehearsal of teleological fabrics spun well in advance of the encounter. The paper, a mixture of cellulose fibers, cotton, and additives such as starches, chalks, clays, pigments, and other chemicals, will have been formulated to achieve the perfect ratio of absorbance and impermeability in view of its interaction with ink. Similarly, ink will have been manufactured from pigments and dyes in view of its deposition on paper, to avoid smearing and to optimize drying times. An EoI is therefore not a mere collection of linked objects existing at a particular time and in a particular place, held together by common goals and by shared or complementary operations and meanings, but a *durational set*—a hyperobject, to use Timothy Morton's felicitous term[30]—that, at any stage of its existence, combines actual components (physical or extraphysical as these may be) with virtual ones.

[30] Timothy Morton, *Hyperobjects: Philosophy and Ecology after the End of the World* (Minneapolis: University of Minnesota Press, 2013).

An EoI is never fully actualized or deployed: something is always held in reserve. Matter is recursively switched on and off, illuminated by partial ecologies and then further extruded along derivative trajectories—from tree to log; from log to wood chip; from wood chip to pulp; from pulp to paper; from paper to envelope; and so on. The dance between matter and form, and the arborescent distribution and mixing of materials and aims in space and time, characterize EoIs as much as the horizontal "totality of equipment"[31] activating precise instances within them. A problem therefore arises concerning the assignment of functional identity. If one slices across EoIs horizontally, the resulting section will expose synchronous objects in coherent operational assemblages (ecologies of writing, of potato peeling, of museum going, et cetera). Each item will perform a specific role or script relative to the set, in much the same way that different organs contribute to the collective metabolism of an animal body, or cogs to the automatic mechanism of a watch. Membership in the set is tested periodically: when a component begins to malfunction and fails to accomplish its allotted tasks (when Heidegger's hammer breaks), it is stripped of the associated identity and value, discarded, and replaced. Now, if instead of slicing across EoIs, one were to dissect them longitudinally (through both space *and* time), they would discover not organized constellations of parts, but successive chains of transformations, jumps, deviations, and transitions—of partial *teloi,* phase changes, and temporary designs.

Here, compliance is no longer clear-cut or even detectable; functional identity can no longer depend on the faithful rehearsal of a physiological, mechanical, or operational recipe, but on fostering and sustaining a deeper life that is active beyond and across individual projects and sets. Transferring identity from *projects* (the Folk Art Museum, as designed by TWBTA) to cultural and material *metabolisms* (the Folk Art Museum as provisional and plastic assemblage, amongst others with which it is inevitably entangled) distributes it in excess of fixed intentions, norms, and ambitions, loosening the stronghold of authorship and design on value. Following a deep-ecological ethos, this approach to material assemblages allows for values and meaning to be assigned across and beyond fixed boundaries and objects, eluding paraphrase and avoiding narrow conceptual abstractions.

Within this framework, architectural practice is not denied intentionality or a constitutive measure of control, nor is the validity and necessity of design inputs, concurrent scripts, or projects ever questioned. What is at stake is not a natural and naive accretion of value and meaning, or the spontaneous emergence of affordances (a mere dilution of design inputs), but a critical reassessment of and appreciation for the relativity of each project and its associated intents—as partial individuating instances rather than fully formed individuals.[32] Longitudinal sections that cut EoIs across both space and time reveal materiality as continuous and metamorphic, transforming synchronous designed

31 Martin Heidegger, *Being and Time*, trans. John Macquarrie and Edward Robinson (Oxford: Basil Blackwell, 1962), 97.

32 Following Gilbert Simondon, one could aspire to a state of "permanent metastability" between objects (or populations of objects) and their milieu. Gilbert Simondon, *L'individuation à la lumière des notions de forme et d'information* (Grenoble: Millon, 2005), 237.

objects into diachronic (*living*) hyperobjects, and promoting a metabolic rethinking of value—towards resilience, survival, and reuse. On one side, this approach neutralizes the archive as an apparatus and set of protocols for freezing design outputs, denying both its presumed stability and its association with value (as precondition and/or causal effect); on the other, it trivializes discussions of flexibility and adaptability in architectural design. The latter is particularly relevant in the case at hand, with both DS+R and TWBTA pointing to the idiosyncrasies of the Folk Art Museum building as partially responsible for its downfall.[33]

I have analyzed DS+R's claim that adapting the building to new programs and requirements would have been untenable without compromising the integrity of TWBTA's project. Similarly, disciplinary discussions about the flexibility and adaptability of buildings have tended to focus on the scope and constraints of singular architectural projects, making it virtually impossible to find solutions that look beyond the intentions and aspirations of a generation.[34] Let's consider the following examples: Le Corbusier's free plan separated a building's structure from its interior partitions, thus allowing the latter to change. Kisho Kurokawa and Kiyonori Kikutake's capsule architectures promoted the ability of buildings to be modified and grow by separating systems and components by rates of obsolescence.[35] [**Figure 7.6**] To design buildings capable of changing over time, Kevin Lynch suggested providing additional space for eventual extensions, and separating systems (structural, mechanical, plumbing, etc.) so that each could be maintained and/or upgraded independently.[36] Aiming for a more pragmatic and less costly solution, and rehearsing André Leroi-Gourhan's promotion of a degree of "functional plasticity,"[37] Denise Scott Brown identified the Italian palazzos of the Renaissance as exemplars of forms capable of accommodating, over the course of 400 years, a diverse range of purposes and functions (residences, hotels, museums, universities, etc.)—proposing that buildings should not be designed in adherence to specific programs (the glove, which is graded by size), but as generic sheds (the mitten, which fits a variety of hand sizes).[38] Reyner Banham similarly relaxed the adherence of form to function, accounting for the secondary uses that buildings and objects—in this case, chairs—support:

> Not only are they bought to be looked at as cult-objects, they are also used for propping doors open or (in French farce) shut. They are used by cats, dogs and small children for sleeping in; by adults

Figure 7.6 Kisho Kurokawa, *Nagakin Capsule Tower*, Tokyo, Japan, 1972. Photograph by Koh Noguchi, August 2021.

33 Tod Williams conceded that the building "was certainly a challenging place to hang art." Pogrebin, "Options Dim for Museum of Folk Art."

34 For an account of approaches to flexibility in architecture, see Jonathan Hill, *Actions of Architecture: Architects and Creative Users* (London and New York: Routledge, 2003), 30–62.

35 Kishō Kurokawa, *Metabolism in Architecture* (London: Studio Vista, 1977).

36 Kevin Lynch, "Environmental Adaptability," *Journal of the American Institute of Planners* 24, no. 1 (March 31, 1958): 16–24.

37 André Leroi-Gourhan, *Gesture and Speech* (Cambridge: MIT Press, 1993), 301.

38 Denise Scott Brown, "The Redefinition of Functionalism," in Robert Venturi and Denise Scott Brown, *Architecture as Signs*

and Systems: For a Mannerist Time* (Cambridge and London: Harvard University Press, 2004), 142–74.

as shoe-rests for polishing or lace-tying. They are used as stands for Karrikots and baby baths; as saw horses; as work benches for domestic trades as diverse as pea-shelling and wool winding; and as clothes hangers. If upholstered and sprung, they can be used for trampoline practice; if hard, as bongo drums. They are persistently employed as stepladders for fruit-picking, hedge-clipping, changing lamp bulbs and dusting cornices. And, above all, they are used as storage shelves for the masses of illustrated print that decorate our lives. [...] And the more a chair is anatomically well-designed for sitting in, the less use it is the other 95 per cent of the time.[39]

39 Reyner Banham, "Chairs as Art," *New Society*, April 20, 1967. Quoted in Nigel Whiteley, *Reyner Banham: Historian of the Immediate Future* (Cambridge: MIT Press, 2002), 354.

These approaches loosen the grip of function on form, attesting to the validity of the latter in excess of the former, and legitimizing a proliferation of uses that bypass and divert design intents. The formulation of the ambitions of practices such as Venturi and Scott Brown (the decorated shed) and the Japanese Metabolists (artificial land/plug-in pods), or even of cybernetic systems such as Cedric Price's celebrated *Generator*, despite aiming for flexibility and adaptability, do, however, remain myopically preoccupied with the future (with what happens *after their project*), missing a more radical opportunity to rethink architectural materials and configurations as a continuum that both follows and *precedes* a project, informing and steering its design.

7.5 Exaptations

Secondary functions flourish in designed artifacts, extending well beyond authorial scripts. Still, their emergence or persistence often relies and depends on primary operations: when the chair breaks (when it stops being sit-on-able), it can no longer be used as a step ladder or shoe rest either, and it ends up in the garbage bin or heap. EoIs (for instance, an ecology of sitting), when assessed through synchronous cross-cuts, draw boundaries that demarcate either a functional and productive interior (an active and valuable part), or a broken and dysfunctional exterior (a nonpart; passive and discardable). While sensible in the here and now, such a system appears gratuitously reductive as soon as longer time spans (or larger wholes) are taken into consideration. Indeed, had natural forms evolved according to the same blind intransigence, life as we know it would not exist.[40]

40 As Timothy Morton puts it: "the monstrous is the minimal unit of evolution. [...] Monstrosity is *functional*." Timothy Morton, "Frankenstein and Ecocriticism," in *The Cambridge Companion to Frankenstein*, ed. Andrew Smith (Cambridge: Cambridge University Press, 2016), 152–53.

In the natural world, a permanent or stable adherence of forms to functions is not necessarily given, and the two can exist at some distance. A word borrowed from evolutionary morphology—exaptation—effectively illustrates how a lack or suspension of productivity can, rather than prefigure failure and devaluation, promote the emergence of new features and horizons of use. The term was coined in a 1982 paper by Stephen Jay Gould and Elisabeth S. Vrba entitled "Exaptation—a missing term in the science of form." In the article, the authors argue that the use of the term "adaptation" in evolutionary biology has tended to conflate historical genesis (features built by natural selection for the specific role they perform) with present utility (features enhancing current fitness), assuming or implying that the two coincide.[41]

Already, Darwin had remarked that certain features defied a linear adaptive trajectory. Writing about the unfused sutures in the skulls of young mammals, Darwin remarks that, while this feature might indeed be indispensable for parturition, it can be also observed in the skulls of oviparous animals such as birds and reptiles, and is therefore not, strictly speaking, an adaptation.[42] Similarly, Gould and Vrba point to the evolution of birds (the development of feathers for thermoregulation, rather than flight), of internal supporting skeletons (the storing of calcium phosphates for metabolic purposes, rather than for developing bones) and to repetitive DNA (as useless genetic material) to illustrate evolutionary processes that cannot be reduced to adaptive mechanisms or the corresponding *teloi*.[43]

The authors propose the use of *aptation* as a generic term describing the acquisition of fitness (the development of forms that facilitate specific functions), *adaptation* as a feature built by natural selection for its current role (*ad + aptus*, towards a fit), and *exaptation* as a feature built for another purpose, or for no function at all, and later co-opted by reason of its form (*ex + aptus*).[44] When applied to architectural design and its modes of investigation and invention, Gould and Vrba's text can have paradigm-shifting effects.[45] Firstly, and in line with earlier work on individuation by the French philosopher Gilbert Simondon, the text complicates abstract universal categories (phenotype and fitness), demanding a renewed focus on genetic processes and undermining the assumption that form and function are always coextensive. This new conceptual framework allows the authors to articulate situated and nonlinear processes of aptation, and morphological features that emerge with no specific purpose or goal (without, however, precluding future ones).

The term *exaptation* thus introduces the possibility that forms be not only valued according to what I have called *archival identities* or *project functions*, or as tethered to synchronous and productive EoIs, but in a state of suspension that ignores and defers designs and evaluation criteria. This implies not only that meaning and value can arise independently of intentions and the corresponding industrial chains—a blow to the ego of the architect—but also that all manner of lowly objects and discarded materials (broken dolls, polyethylene bags, white bronze panels, vacant silos, old car shells, insulation boards, rubber duckies, etc.) are granted, *in potentia*, a measure of architectural utility.[46] [**Figures 7.7–7.9**] "We must move past our disgust, to work with the dirt," writes Hélène Frichot. "This is an imperative for coping with our dusty, dirty, defiled world. To think with it, not against it."[47]

41 Stephen Jay Gould and Elisabeth S. Vrba, "Exaptation-A Missing Term in the Science of Form," *Paleobiology* 8, no. 1 (1982): 4–6.

42 Charles Darwin, *On the Origin of Species* (London: J. Murray, 1859). Quoted in Gould and Vrba, "Exaptation," 5–6.

43 Gould and Vrba, "Exaptation," 7–11.

44 Ibid., 6.

45 An early formulation of this claim is presented in Simone Ferracina, "Exaptive Architectures," in *Unconventional Computing: Design Methods for Adaptive Architecture*, eds. Rachel Armstrong and Simone Ferracina (Toronto: Riverside Architectural Press, 2013), 62–65.

46 David Gissen's term *subnature* already claims a role for denigrated forms of nature in matters of architectural concern. See David Gissen, *Subnature: Architecture's Other Environments* (New York: Princeton Architectural Press, 2009). See also Katherine Shonfield, "Two Architectural Projects about Purity," in *Architecture: The Subject Is Matter*, ed. Jonathan Hill (London and New York: Routledge, 2001), 29–43. Similarly, experimental preservation, as articulated by Jorge Otero-Pailos, embraces objects that would be otherwise "considered ugly or unsavory, or unworthy of preservation." Jorge Otero-Pailos, "Experimental Preservation," *Places Journal* (September 2016). An exaptive approach radicalizes these views, trading the freedom to preserve unconventional objects for the presumption that all objects are worth preserving—the architect or preservationist notwithstanding.

47 Hélène Frichot, *Dirty Theory: Troubling Architecture*, (Baunach, Germany: Spurbuchverlag, 2019), 5.

Figure 7.7 Raumlabor, *Rush Hour Rest Stop,* Durban, South Africa, 2014. © Roger Jardin.

The material palette available to design and building construction is thus radically expanded, urging a reassessment of architectural parts that moves beyond professional standards and conventions (beyond the block, plank, and sheet of "raw" material as fundamental units of construction), and recasting architecture as post-disciplinary and omnivorous. [**Figures 7.10 + 7.11**] The role of the architect thus shifts from one of imposing and translating intents (from ideas to their embodiment) to one of surveying, experimenting with, and activating dormant potentials.

Secondly, Gould and Vrba warn that "the evolutionary history of any complex feature will probably include a sequential mixture of adaptations, primary exaptations and secondary adaptations,"[48] emphasizing how teleological/linear and random/nonlinear processes, considered together and over appropriate time spans, yield results that would be unthinkable within a single generation or project.

The understanding of flexibility prompted by these observations sharply disagrees with what architects typically consider, as discussed above; Gould and Vrba ascribe flexibility to the "pool of features available for cooptation (either as adaptations to something else that has ceased to be important

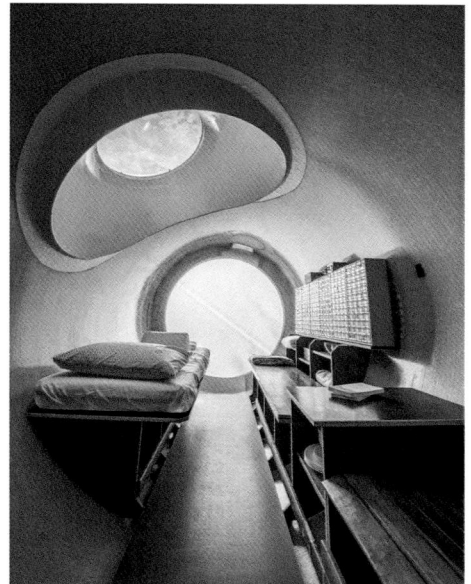

Figure 7.8 Refunc in cooperation with Rose de Beer and Sjaak Langenberg, *Hortus Hermitage*, Haren, Groningen, 2017.

48 Gould and Vrba, "Exaptation," 11–12.

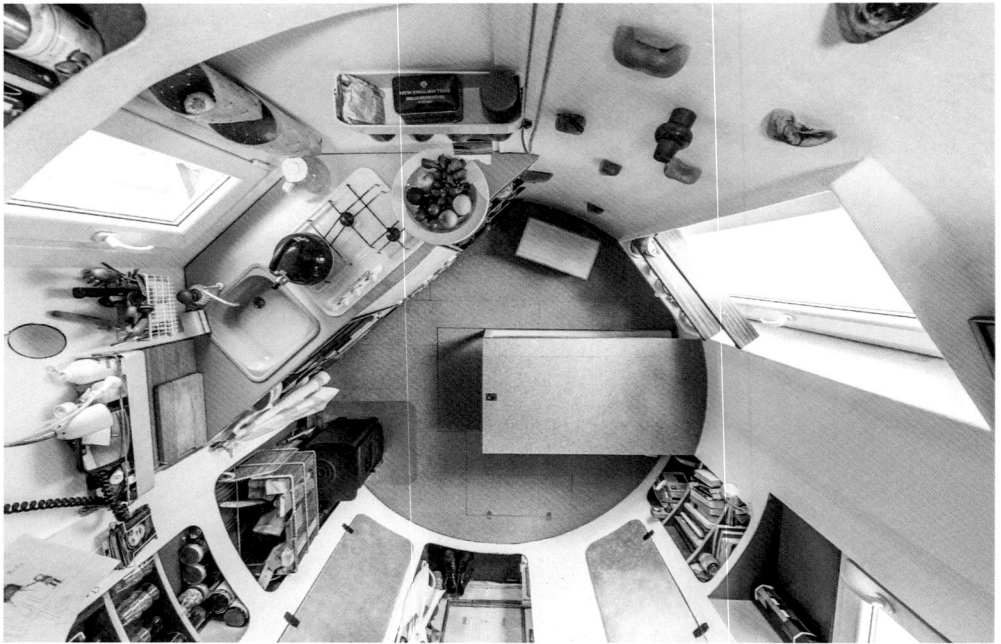

Figure 7.9 Refunc (Jan Körbes and Denis Oudendijk), *Silo City,* Berlin, Germany, 2013. Interior view. Photograph by Ishka Michocka.

49 Ibid., 13.

in new selective regimes, as adaptations whose original function continues but which may be coopted for an additional role, or as nonaptations always potentially available)."[49]

The unsettling beauty of this definition, strikingly alien and out of place in a world dominated by economic and instrumental orthodoxies, invokes not only a broadening of the material scope of architecture, but also a new form of radical coauthorship and distributed identity, one wherein a "common life" does not denote the sacrifice of parts towards the continued operation of a definitive whole, as in the machines of Locke and Descartes or in the presumed integrity of Theseus' ship, but an experiment in designing *with parts, across wholes,* and from a weakened position—by listening, caring, steering, tuning, sharing, and relinquishing a measure of control.

Suspension requires pausing a previously active state; it implies and implicates a negative relationship with—an absence and lack of, an expulsion from—a productive ecology of use. One might think of the ready-made as an exemplar in negating functional identity: *Fountain* continues to index the standard use of a urinal, but the new

Figure 7.10 BakerBrown Studio, *Waste House,* University of Brighton, 2014.

setting (the museum gallery; lack of privacy; being unplumbed) precludes the coming to fruition
of the original purpose. The functional identity of
the urinal is therefore substituted by its archival
counterpart, and its instrumentality by numerical
preservation.[50] Yet, could the notion of suspension
be extended beyond a mere loss or interdiction of
use, and even serve to usher in entirely new uses?
The problem of the glorious body, as examined by
Giorgio Agamben in the homonymous essay, suggests as much.

Agamben retraces the theological discourses
surrounding the status of the resurrected body in
Paradise (age, material identity in relation to the
earth-dwelling body, ability to sense, etc.), and
finds that it is accorded corporeality and—being
"perfectly submissive to the glorified soul"—a special set of superpowers: impassibility (enhanced
sensing), subtlety (the ability to not be palpable),
agility (almost instant and effortless movement),
and clarity (the emanation of a golden and luminous halo).[51]

A more perplexing set of questions, however,
concerns the physiology of the resurrected body: if
the latter comprises all the original organs, including those affiliated with sexual reproduction and
nutrition (penises, vaginas, stomachs, intestines,
etc.), and yet does not need to reproduce or eat,
what is the status of these unused and apparently
redundant parts?[52] Admitting that they are superfluous would imply worthlessness and undermine
the perfection of the glorious body. Thus, to resolve this apparent
contradiction, Thomas Aquinas separates the glorious organ from its
physiological function: "The organ or instrument that [...] remains,
so to speak, in a state of suspension, acquires, precisely for this reason, an ostensive function; it exhibits the virtue corresponding to the
suspended operation."[53]

For Agamben, what is critical in this move is the invention of the inoperative organ of the blessed, a potentialized space that bridges physiological functions with novel uses. He writes,

> It is not potentiality that is deactivated in inoperativity but
> only the aims and modalities into which its exercise had
> been inscribed and separated. And it is this potentiality that
> can now become the organ of a new possible use, the organ
> of a body whose organicity has been suspended and rendered
> inoperative.[54]

Figure 7.11 BakerBrown Studio, *Waste House*, University of Brighton, 2014. In this experimental
building, carpet tiles become a cladding
material, waste vinyl exhibition banners
become vapor control membranes, and
discarded floppy disks, videotapes, tooth-
brushes, DVD cases, and denim offcuts
are turned into insulation.

50 For the sake of this argument,
I will not question whether being
exhibited in a museum also
constitutes a function and assume
that, at least as far as architectural/
design artifacts are concerned, the
archive prevents use.

51 Giorgio Agamben, *Nudities*,
trans. David Kishik and Stefan
Pedatella (Stanford: Stanford
University Press, 2010), 91–96.

52 Agamben, *Nudities*, 97–98.

53 Ibid.

54 Ibid., 102.

That is, the dissociation between form and function does not presuppose a loss or devaluation (uselessness that prompts the discarding of the organ or the tearing down of a building), or even the unavailability of the archive (the urinal protected behind the museum vitrine), but the unlocking of possible inversions and diversions towards a new common use. "In this way, the mouth truly becomes a mouth only as it is about to be kissed," writes Agamben, "the most intimate and private parts become a place for shared use and pleasure; habitual gestures become the illegible writing whose hidden meaning the dancer deciphers for all."[55]

Anthropologist and paleontologist André Leroi-Gourhan describes similar processes of *liberation* ("the freeing of the brain and […] the loosening of certain zoological bonds") in the biological and technical evolution of anthropoids.[56] In his account, the assumption of an erect posture freed the human hands, and the resulting manual expertise (the ability to procure and gather food) released the facial organs from feeding scripts, making them available for speech.[57] He writes:

> Throughout our evolution, […] the human appears as the inheritor of creatures that escaped anatomical specialization. Neither human teeth nor hand, neither human foot nor, when all is said and done, brain has attained the perfection of the mammoth's teeth, the horse's hand and foot, or the brain of certain birds—with the result that humans have remained capable of just about every possible action, can eat practically anything, can run and climb, and can use the unbelievably archaic part of their skeleton, that is, their hands, to perform operations directed by a brain superspecialized in the skill of generalizing.[58]

7.6 Authorial Legibility

A definition of flexibility guided by the notions of aptation, adaptation, and exaptation has the merit of highlighting the role of forms (as opposed to materials or genetic blocks) in the evolution of complex organisms. Gould and Vrba write: "The flexibility of evolution lies in the range of raw material presented to processes of selection. We all recognize this in discussing the conventional sources of genetic variation—mutation, recombination, and so forth—presented to natural selection from the genetic level below. But we have not adequately appreciated that features of the phenotype themselves (with their usually complex genetic bases) can also act as variants to enhance and restrict future evolutionary change."[59]

In other words, the potential for unlocking novel affordances (for instance, the increased ability of birds to fly, from *Archaeopteryx* onwards) might variably depend on genes and on contingent features (*Archaeopteryx*'s large contour-type feathers). In the context of architectural design, this perspective might help articulate a broader approach towards *détournement* and material reuse; it contradicts the classical philosophical understanding of matter and form as associated with potentiality

[55] Ibid.

[56] Leroi-Gourhan, *Gesture and Speech*, 117.

[57] Ibid., 35.

[58] Ibid., 118.

[59] Gould and Vrba, "Exaptation," 13.

and actuality respectively—one whereby, according to Aristotle, matter (the lump of clay) can change and be molded into a variety of shapes, and form (the fired clay figurine) has been frozen into a fixed and stable configuration, and is therefore unchangeable. In line with Gould and Vrba, I have developed a critique of this still predominant hylomorphic bias, and shown that potentiality (the ability to change) is not intrinsic to objects but activated through relations, and that the ability to communicate is more important than any given term, be they raw materials or actualized artifacts.

What is worth reconsidering, however, particularly in view of the present investigation on architectural authorship, is the fact that one finds these associations translated in the Aristotelian figure of the *tabula rasa*, a wax tablet on which nothing is written—a representation of the pure potentiality of thought. Indeed, authorship (or the drawing of authorial marks) might necessitate a *tabula rasa* (blankness, but also the clearing of previous traces) as a precondition for effective implementation. If outputs are to be legible and unambiguous, if the author is to be heard and seen with the highest degree of clarity and resolution, then the most appropriate substrates will be white sheets of paper, blank canvases, silence, and vacant (or vacated) lots. If buildings are to be constructed according to abstract sets of drawings and ideas, the most suitable components will be dull blocks, sheets, and planks that disappear into walls, ceiling, and floors, or lumps of material that can be carved or poured into whatever forms their makers desire. Namely, there is a direct proportionality between the weight and value one attributes to authorial intents (ideas, self-expression, creativity, visibility) and the insatiable need for raw, shapeless, and uniform materials—between the presumption of dominion over matter and the appetite for tearing down buildings and devolving objects into obedient pools of goo.[60]

John Locke, rejecting Aristotle's sophisticated account of the wax tablet (*grammateion*) as a metaphor for the potentiality of thought and a site for its passage into actuality, returns the figure of the *tabula rasa* ("white paper") to mere blankness—a support for writing.[61] In this way, the plasticity of thinking is reduced to an empty container, which only experience can fill. Indeed, according to Locke, the mind of a newborn child corresponds to a blank slate, devoid of innate ideas and progressively developed only through sensations (perceptions of things in the outside world) and reflections (perceptions of operations internal to the mind).[62] The debate around nature and nurture sparked by Locke's essay is not of particular interest to the present discussion, yet his empiricist position links human agency (and the possibility thereof) to the absence of preexisting contents, in a manner that resembles standard modes of design authorship. In other words, the emergence of meaning and ideas is, in Locke as in Alberti or Le Corbusier, inevitably mediated by man/the architect, and never natural or given. This bias towards human creativity and its ability to accrete value becomes ever more explicit in Locke's treatment of property.

60 I am referring to recycling practices as rejections of pre-formed material substrates and, consequently, as the paradoxical perpetuation of the logic that causes waste and obsolescence in the first place; but also to the extractivist destruction of the environment continuously fueled by designs that refuse to start from (and to be steered by) embodied materials and pre-existing objects.

61 Locke, *An Essay*, 18.

62 Ibid., 18–19.

63 John Locke, *Second Treatise of Government*, ed. C.B. McPherson (Indianapolis and Cambridge: Hackett Publishing Company, 1980), sec. 43.

64 Locke, *Second Treatise*, sec.38. I should note here that this very point will become entrenched in colonial regimes of improvement, according to which "land that was not being cultivated according to European models of agriculture was waste, and capable of being legitimately expropriated." Brenna Bhandar, *Colonial Lives of Property: Law, Land, and Racial Regimes of Ownership* (Durham: Duke University Press, 2018), 120. Quoted in Malini Ranganathan, "Property, Pipes, and Improvement," *Power (Buell Center for the Study of American Architecture)*, 16 July 2019.

65 This affinity is of course evident in the history of copyright and intellectual property law. See, for example, Molly Nesbit, "What Was an Author?," *Yale French Studies*, no. 73 (1987): 229–57. It is also worth noting the peculiar transition from the renaissance inscription ("FECIT") with which patrons marked their ownership of a building to the semantic structure ("I built") with which architects declare their authorial paternity/maternity. Tim Anstey, Katja Grillner, and Rolf Hughes, eds., *Architecture and Authorship* (London: Black Dog Publishing, 2007), 7.

66 Michel Serres, *Le Mal propre: Polluer pour s'approprier?* (Paris: Pommier, 2008), 7. Note the play between the two meanings of the French word *propre*, denoting both *property* (one's own) and *propriety* (cleanliness).

67 Serres, *Le Mal Propre*, 7.

68 Ibid.

In the *Second Treatise of Government*, the distinction between *waste* and *good land* hinges entirely upon human cultivation. "It is labour," writes Locke, "[…] that puts the greatest part of value upon land, without which it would scarcely be worth anything."[63] Utility and productivity—as purposefully established and patiently enforced—become the only reliable criteria for adjudicating merit. Furthermore, Locke entangles the beneficial effects of human labor with the appropriation of land (the building of fences, the establishment of property), so much so that

> if the grass of his enclosure rotted to the ground, or the fruit of his planting perished without being harvested and stored, this part of the earth was still to be looked on as waste-land that might be owned by anyone else—despite the fact that he had enclosed it.[64]

This *tabula rasa* coincides not only with a willful exercise of control (for instance, an agricultural or architectural project) or with the ability to subdue, and endow meaning upon, brute preexisting substrates, but also with the deployment of maintenance regimes aimed at preserving outputs (a cultivated piece of land, a suburban front lawn, the Folk Art Museum) and at sustaining their identity (in the sense of the term suggested above). Revealingly, here *identity* facilitates exchanges in two directions: on one side, the project guarantees the continued operation and horticultural/spatial integrity of a piece of land or building; on the other, the resulting effects protect and substantiate claims of authorship and ownership (and violent acts of expropriation and dispossession). Combining Locke's empiricist *tabula rasa* and his philosophy of property reveals a striking affinity between authorship and ownership, one that further corroborates Foucault's treatment of the former as a function for enclosing, fixing, and excluding.[65] Another French philosopher, Michel Serres, definitively links the two through the figure of the animal trace.

In *Malfeasance: Appropriation Through Pollution?* Serres develops a genealogy of appropriation—of property—that originates with the animal body urinating to mark *its* territory and gradually evolves into technology-mediated excretions (*déjections*) such as signatures, logos, and pollution. His convincing argument is that property begins and is maintained by imprinting one's mark, by soiling, by making dirty ("*le propre s'acquiert et se conserve par le sale*").[66] If someone spits in the soup, he writes, no one else will touch it; the soup has been set aside, claimed, appropriated.[67] Some readers may remember verifying the reliability of this technique as children, during a fight with a sibling over the last slice of pizza or cake. The opposite is also true: to be welcoming and accessible (that is, appropriable), a hotel room must be clean; it must have been emptied of the previous guest's stuff and purified of her traces.[68] The overabundant ecology of signifiers employed by hotel staff around the world affirms and advertises cleanliness and purity, as if the room had been scraped back to a virginal and untouched state:

chocolate and flowers on the bed; seals of hygiene; single-use packets of soap and shampoo; courtesy folds; and a distinctly fresh smell.

In this interpretation *à la Serres, tabula rasa* is the cleanness that allows defiling, it is the availability (*disponibilité*) that necessarily precedes and admits all appropriation. The compulsion to purify—that is, the drive to pollute, to stake out boundaries, to brand, to invade, and occupy— can only be overcome through a "process of hominization"—by progressively renouncing a measure of animality, as well as the Cartesian presumption of mastery over (and possession of) the natural world.[69]

7.7 Monstering

An important value for us is drawing together all of the various elements of architecture—materials, space, form, light, color—and producing a unified whole. We're not at all interested in producing a collage.

Tod Williams, "Material Affairs"[70]

The creature's narrative shows us all kinds of non-humans interacting without a human in sight to give them meaning and graciously bestow reality on them. It all happens in a forest, a thickly non-human environment in which trees and mammals and birds and insects (and, we now know, bacteria and fungi) exchange more or less explicit communications without reference to humans at all. This lack of reference is noted by the creature himself as an opacity, ingeniously rendered not as total nothing, but rather as a *meaningfulness not for him*.

Timothy Morton, "*Frankenstein* and Ecocriticism"[71]

At this stage, it might be useful to summarize the arguments presented in this chapter thus far. Through the paradoxical example of the Folk Art Museum, designed by TWBTA and torn down by MoMA only 13 years after its completion in midtown Manhattan, I have identified a fundamental flaw in the way architectural authorship (or a project-sanctioned "identity") regulates the life of a building, from its outer image and operations to the range of changes it can acceptably undergo; even to the point of overwriting common environmental and socio-cultural sense. I have shown that modes of valorization (critical praise, awards, publications, public appreciation) strictly hinge upon the organizational ecologies and part-to-whole relationships curated by the architectural project, so much so that disturbing these scripts or their legibility (in the way that, for instance, Gordon Matta-Clark might split or puncture an existing structure, or that the Folk Art Museum's white bronze façade might have been deconstructed and reused elsewhere)[72] would result in an irreparable loss of value.

The project (or what I have called, following Foucault, the *project function*) prohibits and occludes modes of valorization that elude or contravene its laws, prioritizing architectural compliance (Tod Williams' "unified whole" in the quotation at the beginning of this section) over its myriad material components (a collage of parts). The

69 Ibid., 86.

70 Tod Williams, speaking during an interview published in *Architectural Record* during the final months of construction of the Folk Art Museum. Pearson, "Material Affairs." Another article following the controversy with MoMA reported that "Mr. Williams said he appreciated recent proposals to reuse the most publicly recognizable portion of the building, though he and Ms. Tsien have always maintained that the façade and the building were 'a whole.'" Robin Pogrebin, "Architects Mourn Former Folk Art Museum Building," *The New York Times*, April 15, 2014, Online edition.

71 Morton, "*Frankenstein* and Ecocriticism," 152.

72 Ana María León and Quilian Riano curated the *FolkMoMA* Tumblr website, with the following invitation: "Instead of demolishing the American Folk Art Museum building, we propose it should be incorporated into MoMA's plans for the site. Using an image* of the building, quickly draw/sketch/ photoshop/collage into it offering up possibilities for expansion over/ under/across that incorporate the building. Let's use our collective design abilities to tell MoMA what an incredible opportunity they are wasting." Ana María León and Quilian Riano, "About #FolkMoMA," *FolkMoMA*, accessed October 18, 2018. This resulted largely in renderings and collages testing the relocation of the building's façade to different contexts.

introduction of an exaptive and metabolic approach to architectural design defies the rule of the project function by reclaiming the potential value and autonomy of parts (rooms, staircases, handles, parapets, light switches, etc.). Firstly, as *deep parts*, the temporality of objects might be stretched to geological or anthropocenic scales that ridicule current concerns and equipmental networks, granting parts a measure of intergenerational worth or power. Secondly, as *aptive* or *glorious parts*, components might be allowed to exist in a potentialized state of suspension (without a larger whole to account for them) that preludes the seeding of new functions, uses, and meanings. Finally, as *fundamental parts*, all objects, inside and outside "proper" architecture, and at various scales and levels of interaction, might contradict the orthodoxy of the *tabula rasa* and begin to be taken seriously as potential units for the choreography of space.

I will conclude this chapter by presenting an ongoing work entitled *The Memory of Parts* (MoP). Far from addressing the systemic ambitions (in terms of repurposing and reuse) suggested by the modes of coauthorship proposed above, but in line with many of the concerns expressed in this text, the project sets out to invent new frameworks and protocols for the capture and cultural processing of buildings, beyond authors, programs, and projects. The first installment of MoP, which I will focus on here, was developed under the title "A Spark of Being into the Lifeless Thing" and installed at Carliol House in Newcastle upon Tyne, UK, in November 2017.[73] The title's reference to Mary Shelley's *Frankenstein: or, The Modern Prometheus* was inspired by the circumstances surrounding the event. On one side, the venue for the installation was the art-deco foyer of a vacant building, Carliol House, which in its heyday (1927–48) served as the headquarters for the North Eastern Electric Supply Company (NESCo), responsible for the electrification of large swathes of North East England. On the other, the 2017 *Being Human* festival, to which the exhibition contributed, curated events around the theme "lost and found," suggesting—particularly in the setting of a vacant, unlit, and unconditioned building—an opportunity to engage with and consider new modes of regeneration, reanimation, and reactivation. Frankenstein's creature—a body stitched together from dead limbs and pieces of meat coming from disparate sources—was thus used as a metaphor and lens through which to develop a new methodology for reading and archiving buildings; a *monstering* of Carliol House.

A critical appraisal of Victor Frankenstein's project betrays the presence of normative strategies that resemble those discussed in the context of project functions. On the one hand, the vitalist assumption that matter and flow are separate, and that an electrical charge is required to reanimate the hybrid body of the creature (an otherwise mere collection of inert lumps of flesh), ignores local processes of decomposition and putrefaction, choosing not animation over inertia, but centrally controlled wholes over parts and lower composting ecologies.[74] On the other, the

73 The project was part of the event "Sparks of Life: Frankenstein & Regeneration at Carliol House" organized by Katie Lloyd Thomas and the Architecture Research Collaborative (ARC) at the School of Architecture, Planning and Landscape, Newcastle University, and part of "Being Human: A Festival of the Humanities." "A Spark of Being into the Lifeless Thing" was realized and developed by myself in collaboration with Pierangelo Scravaglieri.

74 Indeed, Victor Frankenstein admits: "a church-yard was to me merely the receptacle of bodies deprived of life, which, from being the seat of beauty and strength, had become food for the worm." Mary Wollstonecraft Shelley, *Frankenstein: Or, The Modern Prometheus*, vol. 1 (London: Lackington, Hughes, Harding, Mavor & Jones, 1818), 83.

creature is assembled according to a rigidly functionalist template (in the image of his creator) that demands, if not beauty ("Why did you form a monster so hideous that even you turned from me in disgust?")[75] at least compliance with preset roles and *modi operandi* (the hand functioning as a hand, the foot operating as a foot, the neck connecting head and shoulders, et cetera). Nonetheless, beyond the creature-as-project, an emergent creature-as-monster also arises, invoking an extra-human spatiotemporal dimension (between inert and alive, dead and living, culture and nature) and an uncanny and unscripted materiality (the yellow glaze in the creature's eyes, its pale complexion, its unexpected actions). The MoP aimed to display and confront this precise monstrosity—and to undermine the prevalent modes with which *we* apprehend, communicate, and valorize buildings. How could one experience Carliol House in its bare materiality, not as a unified machine but as a collage of physical objects and effects? How could one encounter the building on its own terms, before attempting to understand or paraphrase it? And, could I allow knee and eye and foot—stone tread, door frame, and bronze handrail—to wander past their instrumental roles and definitions, towards new assemblages and juxtapositions? I understood early on that to speak of a building effectively—that is, with the degree of abstraction suitable for sharing—leads to conversations about the corresponding project (program, plans, scale models, renderings, photographs, structural calculations, history, intentions) or about macro-features and components (reception desk, chandelier, entrance hall, staircase, cladding panels, revolving door) that guide and signpost a normative use of the space.

As a result, the installation aimed to challenge effective communication and to question the habitual bias towards approximations and wholes, seeking ways to experience and record a monstrous and evasive side of Carliol House—Morton's "meaningfulness not for him" in the quotation at the beginning of this section; the unsung fragments that programs, projects, and authors ignore and efface. We (myself and Pierangelo Scravaglieri) set out to press a white air-drying clay against parts of the building (friezes, stone parapets, wall cracks, steel posts, brass handles, moldings, corners, and so on) with the intention of capturing what seemed unimportant and futile; of problematizing and democratizing the archive; and of expanding it beyond cultural and economic interests. Working with clay unlocked an unusually intimate and tactile register, which did not merely result in a three-dimensional version of Max Ernst's *frottage* (the rubbing of graphite against differently textured surfaces to produce strange and inverted impressions). Rather, Carliol House demanded to be met halfway, each part requiring us to learn a new choreography of movements, a new set of rotations, extrusions, and pressure points; each object involving different amounts of clay, bodily positions, and times of engagement.

Over the course of two weeks, our child-like encounters with the building gained focus and rigor, and we became increasingly proficient in (and fond of) the peculiar language we shared with its inanimate

75 Shelley, *Frankenstein*, vol. 2, 106.

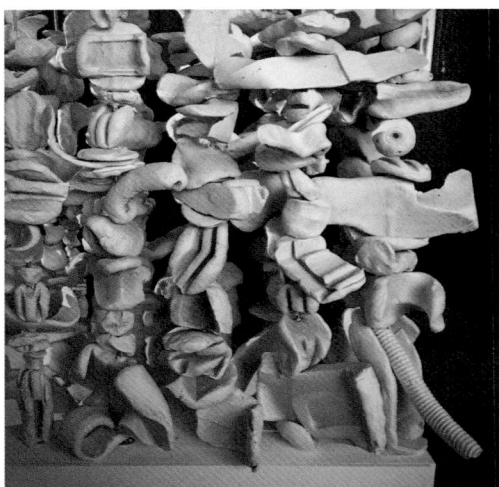

Figures 7.12 + 7.13 Simone Ferracina with Pierangelo Scravaglieri, *The Memory of Parts (A Spark of Being into the Lifeless Thing)*, Newcastle upon Tyne, 2017.

and worthless parts. We could read in each piece the memory of the objects and operations involved, and developed criteria for evaluating the generative potential of each component—a new scale of values designed around the exaptive productivity of our tools. A growing collection of inverted clay pieces lay on the foyer's reception desk, drying like so many bones. They bore the mark of shelves, doormats, levers, and commemorative inscriptions, suggesting not only a new reading of Carliol House, but a new, collaborative way to read.

On the day of the opening, the pieces were drilled and strung together along threaded zinc bars, like chunks of meat on skewers or alien endoskeletons. [**Figures 7.12 + 7.13**] The resulting totemic structures, some reaching two meters in height, staged close encounters with dust depositions and unremarkable building fragments, drawing nonsensical upside-down maps of the foyer and turning corners into jaws, window frames into knuckles, and hinges into ribs. Behind the totems, two videos played on a loop, expanding and contracting a collaged rendering of Carliol House. [**Figure 7.14**]

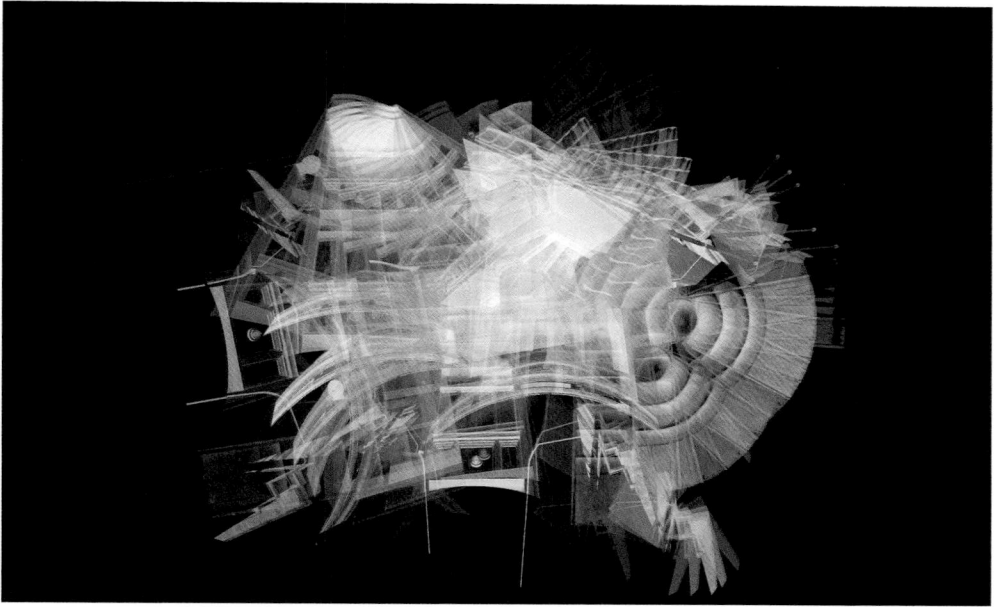

Figure 7.14 Simone Ferracina, *The Memory of Parts (A Spark of Being into the Lifeless Thing)*, Newcastle upon Tyne, 2017. Video still.

The instalment of the MoP project at Carliol House aimed to establish a different (or anti-) archive, prompting architects to *not only* design objects and buildings, but also the social, cultural, and technical platforms and ecologies through which objects and buildings may regain or unlock value, uses, and meanings. In the process, we discovered that a lump of clay could activate inert rooms and invite them to speak.

Chapter 8

Authorship vs. Withdrawal: OOO and Architecture

1 See, for example: *Tarp Architecture Manual*, Spring 2012; Tom Wiscombe, "Discreteness, or Towards a Flat Ontology of Architecture," *Project: A Journal for Architecture*, no. 3 (Spring 2014): 34–43; *Log*, no. 33 (2015); Michael Benedikt and Kory Bieg, eds., *The Secret Life of Buildings* (Austin: Center for American Architecture and Design at the School of Architecture, University of Texas at Austin, 2018); Mark Foster Gage, ed., *Aesthetics Equals Politics: New Discourses across Art, Architecture, and Philosophy* (Cambridge: The MIT Press, 2019); Joseph Bedford, ed., *Is There an Object Oriented Architecture?: Engaging Graham Harman* (London and New York: Bloomsbury Academic, 2020).

2 Coined in 2009 by philosopher Levi Bryant, the term object-oriented ontology (OOO) establishes a common ground for the diverging philosophical positions of Harman, Bryant, Ian Bogost and, from 2010 onwards, Timothy Morton. In this chapter, I will use both terms (OOP and OOO) interchangeably. However, unless otherwise specified, I will be referring to Harman's metaphysics.

3 See Graham Harman, "The Real Problem Is Taxonomy, Not Anthropocentrism," *Object-Oriented Philosophy* (blog), May 22, 2019.

8.1 Design vs. Suspension

The summary of object-oriented philosophy presented in Chapter 6 introduced a nonrelational pole to my investigation of design potentials and ecologies of inception. Yet this move is not entirely new: since at least 2013, Harman's philosophy has been widely debated in artistic and architectural circles across Europe and North America.[1] Before explaining my own reasons for applying OOP (OOO)[2] to architectural design—and to the development of ecologies of suspension—I will therefore survey, in very broad strokes, how this collision has been articulated and pursued thus far. Firstly, I will seek to identify the themes that have gained traction in the field, and begin to sketch out alternative routes, attempting a preliminary resolution of the tensions between a relational bias (ecologies of inception) and a nonrelational one (ecologies of suspension). Secondly, I will challenge the conventional definition of architectural *object,* showing that a narrow interpretation of the term stifles broader disciplinary and professional re-assessments. Thirdly, I will continue to investigate *project functions* and authorship in the context of architectural practice, and come to terms with OOP's nonanthropocentrism (or, more accurately, with its rejection of onto-taxonomy)[3] and its potentially wide-ranging effects on authorial roles and intents.

I should admit at the outset that I am not interested in either embracing or refuting Harman's ontology, but in exploring how an object-oriented approach to architecture might provide some ammunition against the uncontested rule of EoIs. Put differently: while EoIs may be viewed as forms of applied knowledge (in the sense of practical implementation, but also of forcible paraphrase), I will follow OOO in treating knowledge with circumspection—as always partial, reductive, and potentially violent.

In my analysis, I will prioritize the arguments of early adopters, who are usually more earnest in their desire to engage with (and make sense of) how Harman's ontology might affect their field and practice,

DOI: 10.4324/9781003015444-12

and whose words have (for better or worse) set the tone of the exchange. I will focus in particular on the work of American architect David Ruy, who ushered object-oriented philosophy into the limelight of architectural theory with a 2012 text entitled "Returning to (Strange) Objects."[4] The essay delivers a vigorous attack on the relational frameworks that have dominated architectural discourse since the mid-nineties, privileging fields, networks, and systems over discrete objects. He writes: "Even those architects that are primarily interested in form and aesthetics have had a peculiar tendency to search for external parameters and constraints to couch the legitimacy of the architectural object in relationship to a projected external milieu."[5] Presenting Harman's ontology as evidence of an improved philosophical ground for architectural theory and praxis, Ruy proposes a "return" to autonomy, opacity, and strangeness, and the re-empowerment of architectural authors. Lamenting the dependence of design decisions on external criteria and contextual parameters (e.g., environmental, political, technical, professional, ecological), and deploring the "ill-conceived ontological foundation" of preceding paradigms, Ruy sees OOO as capable of inspiring a new brand of architecture *qua* architecture, and of restoring it as a "practice of embodiment" rather than one of "coordination."[6]

Broadly speaking, Ruy's essay attempts to re-model architectural practice and theory after Harman's metaphysics, replacing contingency and relations with autonomy and withdrawal. He writes: "A renewed focus on the architectural object itself should […] be a recognition of what is withdrawn and strange in the architectural object's interaction with other objects."[7] Similarly, architect Tom Wiscombe writes, in a 2014 essay entitled "Discreteness, or Towards a Flat Ontology of Architecture," that "[r]ather than wholes with constituent parts, buildings become objects, wrapped in objects, wrapped in objects," and therefore "architecture becomes an act of *staging* and *characterizing* the spaces of these deferrals," and of articulating objecthood at each level and scale. [8] Accordingly, Wiscombe explicitly converts ontological features into sets of conceptual operations and tectonic strategies (the "figure in a sack," the "implied outer shell," the "supercomponent," the "ground object," the "chunk," et cetera).[9] **[Figures 8.1–8.4]** And in the forthcoming *Architecture and Objects*, Harman also argues that the loose relationship between objects and their qualities "can be accentuated by various aesthetic techniques."[10] Any literal translation from philosophy to design is, however, fraught with difficulties. In the first place, the way things are does not correspond with how they are *designed*. As Bryan E. Norwood writes in *Log*:

> the ontological evaluation that all objects withdraw is not yet a design theory, nor is it even a tool with which we can pass post hoc judgment on built work. Nonrelationality is not yet a normative guide to what sort of architecture the architect should or

4   David Ruy, "Returning to (Strange) Objects," *Tarp Architecture Manual*, Spring 2012. In the pages that follow, I will however use the expanded version of the article available on Ruy's website.

5   Ruy, "Returning to (Strange) Objects," 1.

6   Ibid., 2.

7   Ibid., 6.

8   Wiscombe, "Discreteness," 35–37. My emphasis.

9   Ibid., 39. See also Tom Wiscombe, "A Specific Theory of Models: The Posthuman Beauty of Weird Scales, Snowglobes and Supercomponents," *Architectural Design* 89, no. 5 (September 2019): 80–89.

10   Graham Harman, "Architecture and Objects" (unpublished manuscript, June 9, 2021), 176.

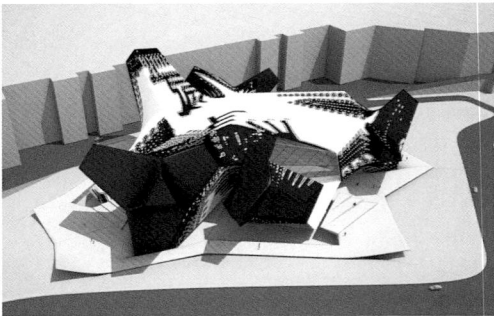

Figure 8.1 Tom Wiscombe Architecture (TWA), *National Center for Contemporary Arts*, Moscow, Russia, 2013.

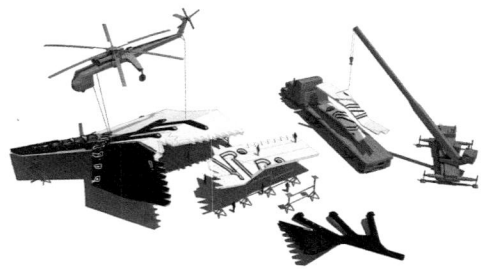

Figure 8.2 Tom Wiscombe Architecture (TWA), *National Center for Contemporary Arts*, Moscow, Russia, 2013. Transportation and assembly of super-components and inlaid/embossed tattoos.

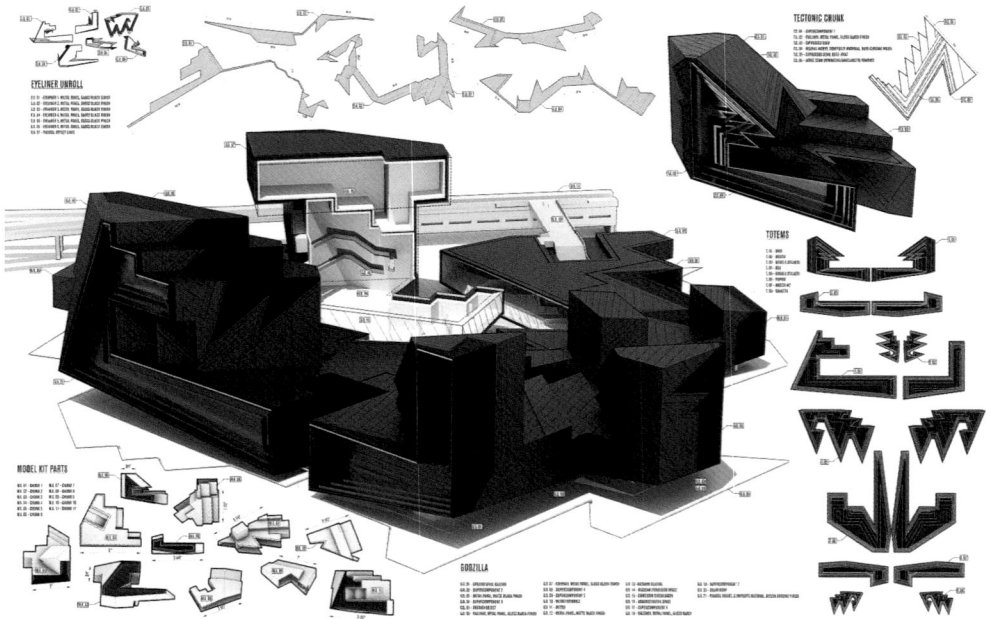

Figure 8.3 Tom Wiscombe Architecture (TWA), *Shenzhen Science Museum*, Shenzhen, China, 2019. Assembly drawing.

could produce. If it is a real object, it will withdraw, and if it is a sensual object, it will be relational. This is not a design proposition; it is a proposition about the way things are. To think that this (or any exploration of ontology) is prima facie going to help us decide whether, for example, interior and exterior should be related or disconnected—to somehow believe that in a Deleuzian world exteriors should flow into interiors, whereas in a Harmanian

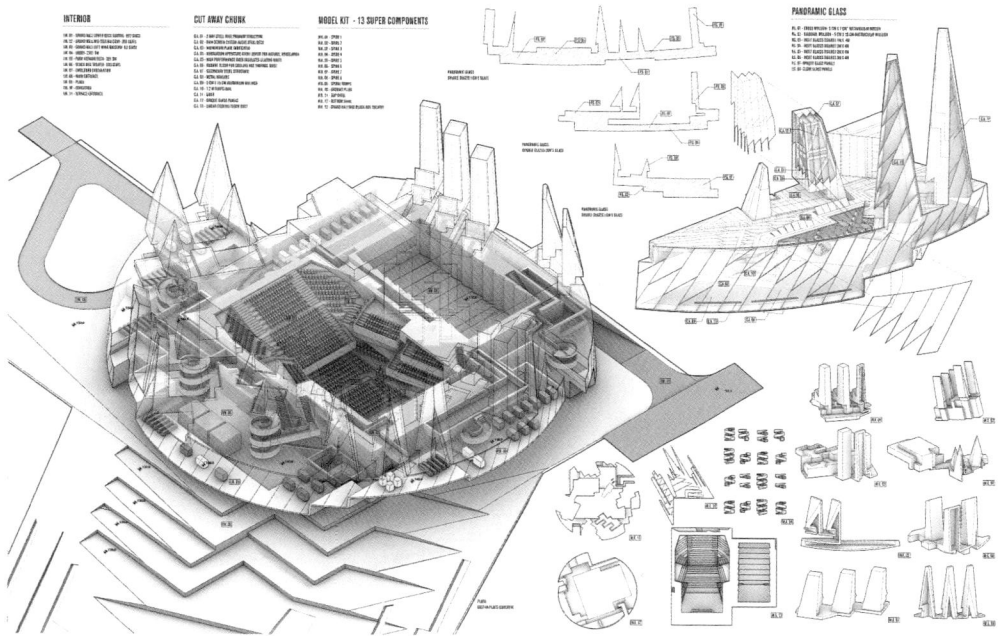

Figure 8.4 Tom Wiscombe Architecture (TWA), *Vilnius Concert Hall*, Vilnius, Lithuania, 2019. Assembly drawing.

world the nonrelationality of objects means interiors and exteriors should be disconnected—is a hackneyed application of philosophy at best. There must be more steps in the move from ontology's evaluation of the nature of existence to a normative guide for design, or even for theoretical or historical evaluation.[11]

11 Bryan E. Norwood, "Metaphors for Nothing," *Log*, no. 33 (2015), 115.

Indeed, if all real objects withdraw, they do so regardless of shape, color, tectonic articulation, or context—their withdrawal does not depend on (nor is it affected by) design decisions. To be sure, one could easily dismiss or bracket this problem by pointing out, with Harman, that architecture's engagement with OOO is primarily metaphorical.[12] Yet, even so, and in light of the discussion of project functions in Chapter 7, it is worth noting a further difficulty: if Ruy's "real object" is ostensibly the output of architectural design (for instance, a building), what he attributes autonomy to are in fact the architect, the architectural project, and the architectural discipline. The autonomy of the real building itself—and in particular its existence in excess of the architect's ambitions and intentions—is largely neglected. It is precisely this conflation of project and output that allows Ruy to vilify all nonauthorial or nondisciplinary relations (ecological, contextual, etc.) as impure and inessential when, in fact, their very existence, and the partiality of authorial claims more generally, neatly exemplify Harman's ontology.

12 Graham Harman, "Non-Relationality for Philosophers and Architects," in *Bells and Whistles: More Speculative Realism* (Winchester: Zero Books, 2013), 198–217.

13 Graham Harman, *Dante's Broken Hammer: The Ethics, Aesthetics and Metaphysics of Love* (London: Repeater Books, 2016), 244.

14 Ruy, "Returning to (Strange) Objects," 5.

In fact, and contrary to popular opinion, OOO does not forbid relations or deny that they occur, and it cannot be reduced to a catch-all anti-relational stance; it merely claims that something is always left in reserve; that relations never fully access, deploy, or exhaust the corresponding relata.[13] But it is not for this reason that one cannot "throw the being of any relational model into doubt," as Ruy advocates.[14] Doing so is simply impossible. Design is relational through and through and, as the development of EoIs in this book has hopefully confirmed, predicated precisely on the orientation of objects *towards* one another.

Design transforms pre-existing substrates in a concerted manner: towards habitation, perception, aesthetic enjoyment, knowledge, tectonic expression, meaning, functionality, interaction, and equipmental cooperation. No design decision can be made in a vacuum, without addressing, either positively or negatively, a wider relational context or milieu. Whether designers respond to a site (its climate, residents, topography, etc.), to the human body (its measurements, capacities, and perceptual apparatuses), or to ecologies of parts formatted towards one another (door jambs, hinges, closers, window sills, faucets, and air ducts; but also living rooms, museums, surfaces, volumes, et cetera) hundreds of overlapping EoIs take center stage, steering design towards interaction and teleology. [15]

15 By *telos* I don't necessarily mean the fulfilment of a functional role, but the fulfilment of a design intention, in the widest possible sense.

The question can therefore not be one of replacing a relational paradigm with a nonrelational one—a position that would effectively ban design in all its forms—but of coming to terms with how practices that are fundamentally relational might address or invoke instances of nonrelationality. The history of autonomy in architectural design and theory—in the Kantian sense of an excision of external influences, values, and criteria—further betrays a relational (albeit negative and antagonistic) origin, confirming that the term has very different meanings in the contexts of metaphysics and design. In the former, as deployed in Harman's ontology, autonomy can refer to a pure withdrawal that is blind and lacks reference and orientation (the "perfect sleep" of a dormant object, as discussed in Chapter 6).[16] Conversely, in the latter, autonomy curates precise deletions, prescribing a limited range of "pure" alliances and sets of practices that closely align with (or adhere to) a disciplinary or authorial interior.

16 Graham Harman, *The Quadruple Object* (Winchester and Washington: Zero Books, 2011), 123.

From Emil Kaufmann to Peter Eisenman and Aldo Rossi, autonomy corresponds with a rejection of external laws and narratives, and with the enclosing of an ecology.[17] Therefore, autonomous design neither rejects relations *in toto* nor is it particularly meaningful without considering the exact context (and socio-political refusals) within which it operates. Yet, perhaps more importantly, autonomy does not rethink how architectural objects are legitimized or ascribed meaning to in general, but simply restricts justification/valorization protocols and parameters to a confined (and easily controllable) internal milieu. Internalizing its own modes of practice and evaluation criteria, it dismisses everything else, including the life of its constructed outputs (the corresponding buildings).

17 See for example Anthony Vidler, "The Ledoux Effect: Emil Kaufmann and the Claims of Kantian Autonomy," *Perspecta* 33 (January 1, 2002): 16–29; Peter Eisenman, "The End of the Classical: The End of the Beginning, the End of the End," *Perspecta* 21 (1984): 154–73; Peter Eisenman, *The Formal Basis of Modern Architecture*, (Zürich: Lars Müller Publishers, 2018).

In this sense, autonomy is not a provocative or countercultural proposition, but the status quo of design—it exemplifies how the architectural discipline functions as an ecology of inception. As shown in the previous chapter, the grotesque demolition of the American Folk Art Museum building was sanctioned precisely by the relevance and value ascribed to project functions in excess of the building's actual existence as a material, ecological, and social assemblage. Here, broadening the scope of autonomy in architecture would not increase disciplinary freedom or professional relevance, as Ruy suggests, but the architect's exponential inability to account for and understand her own outputs, insofar as they exist in a world that is not reducible to intentions and disciplinary values. In the following sections, I will argue for a fundamentally different approach.[18]

8.2 Dynamic Withdrawal

In Harman's philosophy, the ontological gap between sensual qualities and real objects[19] harbors the tensions (metaphor and allure) that can bring "objects directly into play by invoking them as dark agents beneath"—and by separating them from—their surface qualities.[20] Similarly, as discussed in Chapter 6, the real qualities of an object can only be fused to the corresponding real object by means of a mediating term. In this respect, the tension between an object and its qualities, or between what in Chapter 6 I called "ground–messages" and "figure–media," cannot be resolved in advance, and the former must continue to exceed (and recede from) the latter. That is: even though withdrawal runs deeper than any interaction, what exactly will rise to the sensual surface of the object—the very question of what constitutes a surface—cannot be set in advance or affirmed in absolute geometrical terms, but will change with each specific milieu and interaction.

A *metaphysical surface* does not correspond with specific features, properties, or even capacities (e.g., the dispositional brittleness of glass, as discussed in Chapter 6), but with the internal oscillations that foster them—with secret drawers, unstable pressure points, hinges, thresholds, and revolving walls. Accordingly, the plasticity of superficial media invokes a new role for design within the framework of OOO—one that, exploiting the rift between real objects and their (sensual and real) qualities, develops not only forms of poetic allusion or tectonic rendition, but also tools that might facilitate the emergence of new sensual objects out of their real (withdrawn) counterparts.

Without resorting to the figure of the *tabula rasa*, pure potentiality can now be described as a wandering metaphysical surface, which no longer depends on encounters (the relational bias criticized by Harman); on the complicity of figures and grounds towards legibility; or on stable identities and relative positions (the skin as bodily surface), but on the object's internal fluctuations—on the object's ability to reallocate surfaces. Whereas design unlocks and activates potentials through

18 I should note that my take on OOO and architecture is at odds with the one Harman himself articulates in the forthcoming (at the time of writing) *Architecture and Objects*. And while there is no scope here for a more serious engagement with that book and its claims, I should briefly note a few key points of disagreement. For example, Harman maintains that "[b]uildings must serve functional and social needs, must be constructible given the current state of the art, and will often have foreseen and unforeseen political effects." He continues: "[b]ut all this is *merely the precondition for architecture*. When architecture foreswears aesthetics, it becomes engineering or some other discipline." Harman, "Architecture and Objects," 176. Yet the view I take in this book is that aesthetic scripts are just one particular kind of functional script (just another precondition, in Harman's words), and undeserving of the special status they have been attributed (always, of course, by those in a position to do so) in the Western architectural canon. If anything, this book avoids the heroic narratives and self-important claims of avant-guard architects and critics, aiming to propose a different grounding for the appraisal (and construction) of architectural value. Harman also writes that "[s]ocio-political critiques of formalism in architecture bear only on its preconditions: on the social or infrastructural duties it ought to perform. Formalism itself is not politically suspect, any more than poems are for not attempting to save the world." Ibid., 177. Yet, of course, choosing to write a poem while the apartment next door burns to the ground might very well be a sign of negligence, and the writing of poems—unlike the extraction of building materials, or the design of structures that maximize carbon emissions—does not cause widespread environmental degradation. In this book, I reject the idea that aesthetic objects can

be experienced in a socio-political vacuum, and rather contend that, as hyperobjects, they are inevitably fused with the carbon, energy, and violence they embody.

19 Harman, *The Quadruple Object*, 106.

20 Graham Harman, *Guerrilla Metaphysics: Phenomenology and the Carpentry of Things* (Chicago: Open Court, 2005), 150.

relations, *pure* potentiality exists in a regime of suspension, preceding—and withdrawing from—any such encounters. In this sense, ecologies of suspension are still relational (that is, translational) frameworks, but rather than acting upon surfaces that are given (the sensible as broadcasted by EoIs), they exert pressures upon the object's inner core, causing its surfaces to redistribute.

I have reached the end of an arc or trajectory that, from the beginning of Chapter 5, interrogated potentiality through the notion of plasticity, replacing the figure of the blank canvas or contentless tablet with that of the malleable wax deposited on its surface. Accordingly, potentiality no longer hinges upon relations, requiring forms of external activation and validation, but is sustained from within—the suppleness of the wax does not begin with the stylus, nor is it invented by its incisions. I can now discriminate between two kinds of powers: on one side, *simple potentiality* refers to potentials insofar as they can be unlocked (the stylus triggering the wax's inscribability); on the other, *pure potentiality* describes the object's intrinsic potency (the very plasticity of the wax).

The phrase *dynamic withdrawal* applies this understanding of pure potentiality to the withdrawn objects of OOO. Instead of identifying specific properties, or of ascribing more authenticity or reality to some of them over others, it turns the object's withdrawal—the fact that it can never be exhaustively known—into an engine for the production of sensible qualities (of sensual objects). Whereas potentiality remains associated with the intentional and external activation of specific capacities or affordances, *pure potentiality* attends to the silent engine at the heart of things.

The notion of dynamic withdrawal thus re-articulates potentiality—and change—without resorting to either hylomorphism (reducing the object to a formless matter) or relationality (reducing the object to its interactions and effects). Despite residing at the core of things, dynamic withdrawal also avoids Latour's critique of intrinsic potency: it cannot name specific powers, lacking all sense of direction, purpose, and orientation.

8.3 Tempering Autonomy

Two faces of architectural autonomy have flickered before the reader's eyes in the previous sections. The first one, which one might call "disciplinary" or "authorial," relies on refusals, exclusions, and the curation of large ecologies of inception that internalize value, cutting off associated networks and outward-facing modes of justification and decision-making. The second one, which develops out of an understanding of potentiality as a form of intrinsic plasticity, is thoroughly nonrelational, and fueled by the object's own ability to undergo surface/ground permutations. In the latter, a dynamic understanding of withdrawal—of the shifting tensions between objects and their qualities—delivers, contra Harman, the possibility of a pure object-oriented potency, one that combines nonrelationality with the object's ability to oscillate, reallocate, and squirm. In the former, on the other hand, ascribing autonomy to architectural authors and, by extension, to their discipline, confuses a ground (that which withdraws and is excluded from design interactions; what Harman calls the "inwardness of each thing"),[21] with the very sensual media (the active surfaces, so to speak) that compose and guide them. For example, Ruy writes that "in the interaction between the architect, as object, and other objects (be it a place, a material, a piece of software, or a preexisting theory) an architectural object sometimes comes into existence," claiming that "[w]hat exactly happened in this interaction will be occluded."[22]

The account of this occlusion dangerously diminishes the architect's responsibility and accountability, but also preempts, rather disingenuously, design as a rigorous practice involving the articulation of knowledge and the exertion of control. While Ruy is correct in identifying knowledge as a defining theme in object-oriented ontology, and as a question that is central to any serious engagement with Harman's philosophy, our approaches are diametrically opposed. Whereas for Ruy, in line with both predominant modes of architectural production/consumption and historical precedent, autonomy privileges authorial or disciplinary forms of knowledge and evaluation (what, discussing the case of the Folk Art Museum, I called *project functions*), what I learn from OOO is the converse lesson: the existence of objects in excess of the qualities and relations ascribed to them by designers—beyond authorial intentions, disciplinary knowledge, and ecologies of inception.

In my reading, an object-oriented architecture must both admit that design broadcasts and translates deliberate decisions, often with violent consequences (a view that is unhelpfully hindered by the impenetrable figure of the architect-as-object), and recognize that the ensuing ecologies and modes of evaluation are always partial and unstable. In fact, rather than sheltering architecture from extra-disciplinary pressures, OOO demands, in my view, that its knowledge be persistently challenged as ontologically deficient. What is at stake is how design frames its problems and evaluates the corresponding solutions; who defines those agendas; and how forms of knowledge are invented, ratified, and multiplied. Put in OOP terms, perhaps the question is not whether the architectural object (be it the architect, the discipline, the drawing, the building, etc.) is granted sufficient autonomy, but how one defines *object* in the first place, and which *objects* one is willing to acknowledge and address in their designs. Before moving to these considerations in detail, it is helpful to review Harman's approach to autonomy in aesthetics and ethics, particularly as it is tempered by his critique of Kant's formalism in *Dante's Broken Hammer*.

In principle, object-oriented philosophy espouses a Kantian formulation of autonomy, affirming that art's "inherent values" cannot be "subordinated to ulterior aims, including socio-political ones."[23] This is consistent with an ontology of discrete elements that cannot be replaced by knowledge, nor "bleed holistically into everything else."[24] Yet, it also implies that art and architecture—the purveyors and curators of the respective archives and traditions—should be considered

21 Ibid., 188.

22 Ruy, "Returning to (Strange) Objects," 6.

23 Graham Harman, "Object-Oriented Ontology (OOO)," in *Oxford Research Encyclopedia of Literature*, by Graham Harman (Oxford University Press, 2019), 7.

24 Harman, *Dante's Broken Hammer*, 172.

as "objects" in their own right, despite the fact that OOP affirms an object's existence in excess of the ways in which one can know it.

In any case, against Kant's formalism—which privileges universal and monolithic laws and nonsubjective *formal* principles over contextual and *material* modes of judgment or decision-making—object-oriented philosophy both recognizes (and protects) disciplinary boundaries and affirms the plurality and contingency (the materiality) of their contents as they come into partial view. This is evident in Harman's treatment of Kant's ethics, according to which a behavior's intrinsic ethicality is independent of how that behavior actually fares in the world.[25] Here too, Harman supports a dose of autonomy (Kant's avoidance of an ethics of success), but balances the German philosopher's categorical imperative (the notion that actions are ethical if, articulated as maxims, they can be elevated to universal laws) with Max Scheler's *ordo amoris*, substituting the human thinking or willing Kantian subject with a compound unit (a relational object composed of lover and beloved, artwork and spectator, etc.) that is irreducible to its individual terms.[26]

Whereas Kant's appeal to universal human structures absolves "aesthetic judgment of any contact with the world beyond its walls," denying "any aesthetic role for the object itself" and, conversely, exempting nonscientists from any engagement with nonhumans,[27] Harman views aesthetics as a form of first philosophy, and as a "primary means of access to reality, through indirect detection of the gap between an object and its own qualities—a gap effaced equally in both practical life and mathematico-scientific understanding."[28] Denouncing Kant's formalist autonomy insofar as it enshrines special human features (for example, our ability to think) in ontological structures and promotes the dualisms of subject/object and mind/matter (what Harman calls "taxonomic fallacy" or "onto-taxonomy"), the philosopher re-articulates object-oriented ontology as a machine of "detaxonomization."[29] He writes: "the whole point of the object-oriented approach is to expand the subject-object correlate from its usual confinement to humans and spread it out into all corners of the world, so that even the fire-cotton relation becomes just another correlation."[30]

At this point, it should be clear that OOO can no longer be used to justify a retreat into business-as-usual forms of architectural authorship and disciplinarity that continue to privilege human subjects (and *some* more than others) above all else. In the remainder of this chapter, I will try to come to terms with the destabilizing potential of detaxonomization, and to account for a brand of aesthetics that is not easily reduced to—or particularly interested in—novel styles, shapes, and sensibilities. In order to do so, I will follow Val Plumwood in understanding nature as a "*political* rather than a descriptive category."[31] Plumwood notes that its separation from reason (from a universal human master) demands a form of "radical exclusion"—an "unbridgeable separation" that minimizes the evidence of continuity and dependency in order to justify subordination and to naturalize domination.[32] "[T]he master

25 Ibid., 238. Of course, this is only true of behaviors that are at least successful *in potentia* (despite my best intentions, I must be trained as a surgeon before attempting to perform a life-saving open-heart surgery), and does therefore not release architects of their responsibility.

26 Ibid., 215.

27 Ibid., 227.

28 Ibid., 11.

29 Ibid., 234.

30 Ibid., 240.

31 Val Plumwood, *Feminism and the Mastery of Nature* (London: Routledge, 2003), 3, emphasis in original.

32 Plumwood, *Feminism and the Mastery of Nature*, 51.

defines himself by exclusion, against the other. For the master, formation of identity [...] leads to a need to maintain hierarchies to define identity. There must always be a class below," she writes, "whose inferiorisation confers selfhood."[33] The discussion of onto-taxonomy that follows will take the undoing of such an identity—the expression of otherness through hierarchies, or by dehumanizing and making disposable—as its main goal.

It is worth mentioning here, and remembering on the following pages, that the terms anthropocentrism and onto-taxonomy are not interchangeable. As Harman writes:

> the problem is not that humans [...] have been given too much attention and that we therefore need to shift the balance back towards a world without humans. Instead, the problem is that humans and "world" [...] are taken as the two terms in the first place.[34]

Following Harman's careful distinction, my objective will not be to demote humans or to undermine the primacy of their experience, which is evidently central to everything architects and designers do and care about, but to expand—aided by long-standing indigenous and feminist scholarly traditions—the scope of design theory and practice to include (and pay attention to) *other* humans and nonhumans, rejecting modes of valorization and validation that presuppose and strengthen a taxonomical divide.

8.4 Many Architectural Objects

How might one begin to undermine onto-taxonomy in architectural practice and theory? I will start with two different but related questions. The first one addresses the very definition of *architectural object* and its implications for design practice. The second one considers whether the binaries that fuel architectural design (e.g., designer vs. designed; inside vs. outside; matter vs. form) re-enact and perpetuate the rift between humans and nonhumans, contributing to—or rather, enforcing—the latter's poverty in (or lack of) world.

Let's first contemplate the attribution of architectural objecthood. The vast majority of the architects and critics who have written about (or, in some measure, adhered to) Harman's philosophy presupposes that the architectural (withdrawn) object of OOO coincides with the end product of a design process—with a building.[35] Yet, Harman's definition of object ("anything that is more than its components and less than its effects")[36] and his refusal of a priori taxonomical divisions could instead promote a forceful expansion and proliferation of the *objects* entitled to architectural care and attention, not only in an ethnographic or historical capacity, but also towards the activation and articulation of new design protocols and methods. In the following subsections, I will sketch out four such scenarios.

[33] Ibid. See also the meditation on waste, and on Calvino's "La Poubelle Agréée" in particular, in Chapter 1.

[34] Harman, "The Real Problem Is Taxonomy."

[35] Mark Foster Gage recognizes that this need not be the case, but postpones further inquiries. He writes: "For architecture, one basic but fruitful translation of OOO is the unbearably literal equation of *object* with *building*. This should be considered only a starting point, not an endpoint, in the exchange between the abstract philosophy of OOO and the material practice of architecture." Mark Foster Gage, "Killing Simplicity: Object-Oriented Philosophy in Architecture," *Log*, no. 33 (2015): 98.

[36] Harman, *Dante's Broken Hammer*, 218.

8.4.1 Scenario One: Object as Land (Metaphorical Ethics)

Architects are prone to associating the withdrawn objects of OOO with either themselves or with the outputs of their designs—eager to gaze into the tenebrous and expansive depths of their own creativity. Once the mists of architectural vanity have dissipated, however, the obvious pretender to the role of *architectural object* (with the understanding, of course, that this is not a form of ontological precedence, but one concerning disciplinary narratives, methods, and attention regimes) is the site of a project—its context—starting from the building plot and any preexisting structures.

The articulation of a real (withdrawn) *object–site* invites architects to survey the many material and immaterial layers that compose it (social, cultural, climatic, historical, political, geological, infrastructural, legal, et cetera) without the modern presumption of mastery, or the associated desire to order, reduce, and improve. Here, encountering a site is to recognize one's inability to paraphrase it, and to honor that which already exists—buildings and materials, but also knowledges, communities, ecosystems, and so on. The goal is not to extract information and recompile it into colorful diagrams, PowerPoint presentations, or lists of problems to be solved. Rather, it is being mindful of its existence precisely to the extent that it cannot be captured in diagrams, surveyed, or effectively optimized, fixed, instrumentalized, or consumed.

Whereas Harman's notion of allure (of the transversal signals between sensual qualities and real objects) has been mostly considered in stylistic terms (towards the illustration of ontological withdrawal; or to justify a literal aesthetics of nested objects, strangeness, and ambiguity), upon assigning *real* objecthood to the building site, new real–sensual composites emerge that no longer require the embroidered veneer of an enigmatic style.

If one presumes, with Harman, that "the world is made up of chains of real and sensual objects" and that "the basic unit of ethics, aesthetics and metaphysics is neither subject nor object, but a composite in which the 'subject' term need not be human"[37] (a hybrid unit that can negotiate exchanges with reality by linking it to a sensual carapace), then one might consider the coupling of building and site to be one such basic unit, wherein the two terms both correlate and exceed their correlation; conversing at times, whispering secret messages at others. Considering, as the output of architectural design, not a mere building but the entanglements and tensions between two real objects (that is, between their surface qualities and withdrawn reality) and, in this case, between the building and the context within which it is placed, the question of allure can no longer be attended to by architectural styles (which privilege the relation to a human perceiver or to an abstract art-historical baseline), but by the myriad ways in which the inner reality of objects may boil over and spill.

37 Ibid., 247.

In this sense, an ecology of suspension can be thought of as the supplement, in the design of objects, that aims to heat or puncture a site, causing its inner reality to gush out or leak. EoSs are never oriented—as ecologies of inception are—towards straightforward goals and programs; they cannot directly verify or quantify success in the way that, for instance, EoIs readily obsolesce noncompliant objects. Within ecologies of suspension, system boundaries remain tentative and porous, and compliance is unimportant. They operate obliquely and uncertainly—in the domain of hope, doubt, blurred lines, and partial encounters.

The suggestion that a new building or architectural device might cause a preexisting site to reveal something of itself that was previously unseen or concealed is not particularly original, or new. One certainly finds it, for example, in Heidegger's "Building Dwelling Thinking," and particularly in the famous passage describing a bridge, which is worth quoting at length:

> The bridge swings over the stream "with ease and power." It does not just connect banks that are already there. The banks emerge as banks only as the bridge crosses the stream. The bridge designedly causes them to lie across from each other. One side is set off against the other by the bridge. Nor do the banks stretch along the stream as indifferent border strips of the dry land. With the banks, the bridge brings to the stream the one and the other expanse of the landscape lying behind them. It brings stream and bank and land into each other's neighborhood. The bridge *gathers* the earth as landscape around the stream.[38]

38 Martin Heidegger, "Building Dwelling Thinking," in *Poetry, Language, Thought*, trans. Albert Hofstadter (New York: Perennial Classics, 2001), 150.

The construction of the bridge does not merely allow for the stream to be crossed, but facilitates a "presencing" and "gathering" of the site, renegotiating and reorienting the relationship between mortals, earth, sky, and gods. Now, while Heidegger's fourfold and the wider context of this passage does not interest me here, one extraordinary line—"[t]he banks emerge as banks only as the bridge crosses the stream"—can perhaps provide an inkling of how a building–object might bring forth the dormant features of a site–object, and vice versa.

I can now formulate this approach in more precise terms: whereas ecologies of inception format sensual objects towards the productive equipmental communication with other sensual objects (the construction of the bridge as a tool for crossing the river), ecologies of suspension act upon a real object's ability, through dynamic withdrawal, to produce—or receive—other sensual qualities (the emergence of the banks). Whereas ecologies of inception are forms of applied knowledge (and in this sense, they welcome paraphrase as an effective mode of communication), ecologies of suspension are impervious to both knowledge and paraphrase, and their value or worth cannot be

Figure 8.5 Teresa Moller Landscape Studio, *Punta Pite*, Papudo, Chile, 2005. Photograph by Lia Aliaga.

conclusively proven or quantified. In this sense, ecologies of suspension operate on a metaphorical plane, in the plastic interplay of ground and surfaces or, to use Harman's terminology, in the gap between real objects and sensual qualities.

One should remember that the failure of paraphrase—the untranslatability of the object—is what attests to its objecthood, and affirms it in excess of specific recipes and ecological functions (of fixed sensual interfaces). It is for this reason that the aesthetic presentation of an object can interfere with its equipmental compliance, and the bridge is more than a stream-crossing piece of infrastructure. A concrete example, albeit one that is better appreciated through images than articulated with words, is landscape architect Teresa Moller's intervention in Punta Pite, along the coast of central Chile. [**Figure 8.5**]

Commissioned to design a footpath linking the coastline with new residential developments between the towns of Zapallar and Papudo, Moller curated an ecology of fragments that "embrace the character of the site," leaving its sculptural granite cliffs largely untouched, and stitching steep and uneven surfaces

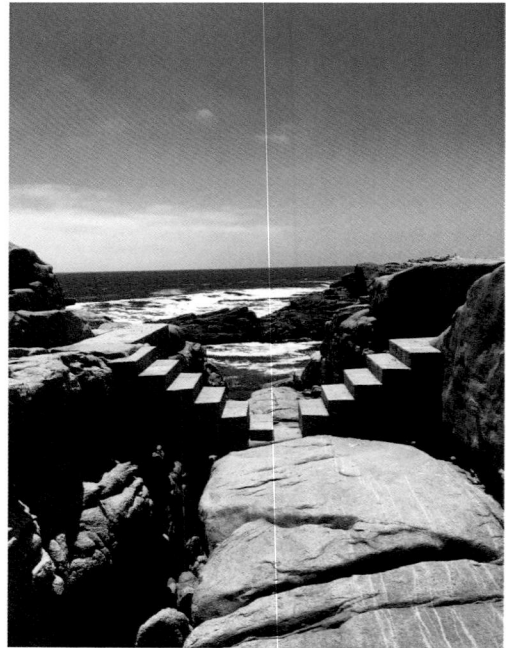

Figures 8.6 + 8.7 Teresa Moller Landscape Studio, *Punta Pite*, Papudo, Chile, 2005. Photographs by Lia Aliaga.

together with linear platforms, steps, and stairs.[39] [**Figures 8.6 + 8.7**] The use of hand-cut granite (which blends into the surrounding rocks) and of sharp platonic geometries (which set themselves apart from the rugged landscape around them) choreograph a remarkable tension, from which the coastline re-emerges in full sculptural splendor—framed, rescaled, and narrated by Moller's additions; by the wanderings of human bodies; and by the measures and paces of limbs. If the project produces a visceral and extraordinary sense of place, it is not because of its compliance with a design brief that could have produced very different results. Beyond functional uses and practical concerns, something in the built project sings. One might call it a metaphor, or think of the project as a metaphorical construct linking two objects: the intervention designed by Moller and her team, and the stretch of coastline between Zapallar and Papudo.

Harman explains that a metaphor is characterized by three key features: (1) unparaphrasability; (2) semiresemblance (the fact that, for it to succeed, the two terms it combines cannot be too similar or dissimilar); and (3) asymmetry.[40] The first one—unparaphrasability—is easily demonstrated, insofar as the built project cannot be replaced by descriptions, be they drawn (the project's construction documents, or Moller's conceptual sketches) or discursive (briefs, textual accounts, specifications). In all fairness, any real-world building resists paraphrase, so this is not of particular note. The second feature—semiresemblance—stipulates that a metaphor can only produce aesthetic effects when the two terms it connects are neither too similar nor different. Harman uses an example borrowed from Ortega y Gasset ("a cypress is like a flame") to show that the metaphor is effective because a flame is similar in shape to a cypress, and yet utterly different in kind. Excessive similarity ("a cypress is like a pine") or difference ("a cypress is like a ceramic cup") would cause the metaphor to fail. In Punta Pite, as in the flame-like cypress, the project expertly balances modes of attachment and detachment. On one side, the use of local granite (the same material found in the surrounding cliffs) anchors the project to the site, seemingly attempting to make it disappear. On the other, the project's clean outlines and sharp corners highlight its alterity, setting it apart from its context. [**Figure 8.8**]

Finally, the third feature—asymmetry—establishes that, in order to be attachable to one another, the two terms must fulfill different roles. One must behave like a sensual object (the cypress), and the other must carry sensual qualities (being flame-like). Perhaps I can now re-articulate Moller's project as follows: in

39 Teresa Moller, "Punta Pite," Teresa Moller Landscape Studio, accessed June 17, 2020.

40 Graham Harman, "A New Sense of Mimesis," in *Aesthetics Equals Politics*, 55.

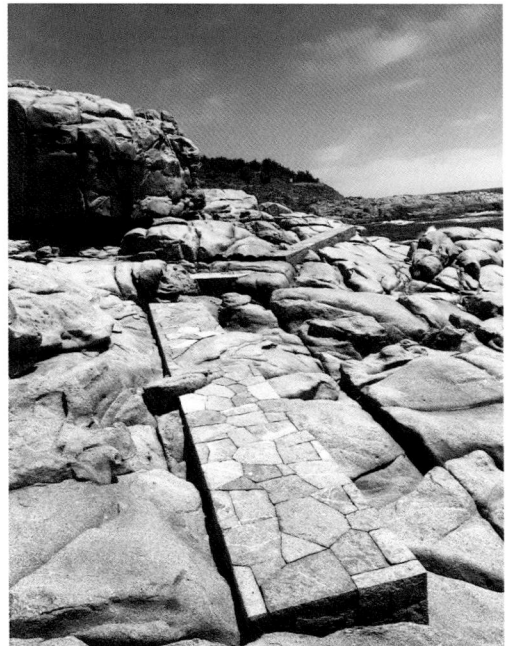

Figure 8.8 Teresa Moller Landscape Studio, *Punta Pite*, Papudo, Chile, 2005. Photograph by Lia Aliaga.

Punta Pite, the sensual qualities of sensual object D (the design project) are transferred to sensual object S (the coastline), constructing a new real object B (the built project). Accordingly, one could characterize the difference between EoIs and EoSs in the following manner: while ecologies of inception build cars, homes, walkways, stairs, writing tablets, and bathtubs; ecologies of suspension construct metaphors (the two, of course, are not mutually exclusive).

The aesthetic content of Moller's project, fueled by the tensions between her thoughtful intervention and the site into which it is woven, can be appreciated by another real object that, in this case, will be a human onlooker, rambler, or inhabitant. Similarly, Heidegger's bridge, and the emergence of the river banks in his account, rely on the role of mortals (of human beings) within his fourfold structure. And while an Andean condor or a droplet of dew can also experience the project's granite steps, it would be difficult to argue that the aesthetic content in Moller's project—or, for that matter, in any metaphor or work of art whatsoever—can be appreciated by nonhumans, and there is little point in attempting such an argument. Again, I am not aiming to shift the attention of designers away from the human, or to lower the status of human experience and delight, but to preempt their ontological priority over the delight and experiences of (and interactions between) condors, dew droplets, sea foam, and arctic foxes. Still, how do ecologies of suspension, and the metaphorical coupling of building and site discussed above, contribute to the detaxonomizing of architecture?

The answer lies in what one might call *metaphorical ethics*, or in the third requisite feature identified by Harman: asymmetry. As discussed above, in order for one term to attach to the other, and for the two to cohere into an effective metaphorical unit, their roles must be complementary: one term must serve as the bread (a sensual object), the other as the butter (sensual qualities). In more accurate terms, one must play the starring role of the cypress (the tenor or ground; a subject to which attributes are ascribed), the other the supporting role of the flame (the vehicle or figure; the object whose attributes are borrowed). Hence, setting—and committing to—a relative grammatical position (subject/object) and orientation (subject/predicate) establishes the first step in constructing a successful metaphor.[41] In the case of Punta Pite—of a three-dimensional metaphor—the Chilean coastline is certainly cast in the starring role, one that Moller's project enlivens with new and unexpected qualities. Whether one considers its metaphorical role as tenor, or its temporal preexistence and ability to steer the design, the site's rugged landscape precedes (comes before; is given priority over) Moller's intentions and authority, narrowing the scope of her choices and suggesting project-specific materials, tools, and design methodologies. It is in this sense that a metaphorical approach to design promotes a detaxonomizing ethos—one that prioritizes a context S (a preexisting site or set of materials, etc.) over a design project D (the creativity of the architect).

In this scenario, to design metaphorically is agreeing to lose a measure of subjectivity and authority; to abide by a correlational script

41 Roles cannot be changed after the fact: Shakespeare's "All the world's a stage" makes a lot more sense than its inverted form "all the stage is a world."

that casts the human (the designer, her designs) in the role of the object and the nonhuman (the coastline) in that of the subject. Moller's subtle intervention in Punta Pite illustrates how a metaphorical approach to design can combine a rejection of onto-taxonomy with a keen interest in human experience and aesthetics. Furthermore, it demonstrates that a project can be "object-oriented" without even knowing it, and certainly without parading strangeness, formal novelty, or stylistic exuberance.

To conclude this section, I should mention that while the example used above largely engaged with a site understood as physical setting (the coastline between Zapallar and Papudo), and thus implied a degree of separability between the coastline and the life of local human and nonhuman communities, a terminological shift—from *site* to *Land*—might prompt a more considered approach. Native American poet Paula Gunn Allen explains what is at stake:

> We are the land. [...] The land is not really the place (separate from ourselves) where we act out the drama of our isolate destinies. It is not a means of survival, a setting for our affairs, a resource on which we draw in order to keep our own act functioning. It is not the ever-present "Other" which supplies us with a sense of "I." It is rather a part of our being, dynamic, significant, real. [...] The land is not an image in our eyes but rather it is as truly an integral aspect of our being as we are of its being.[42]

Similarly, Indigenous scholar Sandra D. Styres and developmental psychologist Dawn M. Zinga use the capitalized word *Land* when referring to "a proper name indicating a primary relationship," and the noncapitalized *land* when referring to "landscapes as a fixed geographical and physical space."[43] This distinction is not trivial—the violence of settler colonialism could be described as the coercive transformation of the former into the latter, and as an instance of the *tabula rasa* discussed in the first part of this book.

Now, not only must a rejection of onto-taxonomy begin by recombining *I* and *world* into compound and interdependent units. As Indigenous philosopher Kyle Powys Whyte explains, the *quality* of these relationships must also change, replacing "rights, contracts (e.g. relating to private property), and consumer/commodity associations" with dynamic relationships of reciprocal responsibility.[44] He writes:

> [t]he concept of interdependence includes a sense of identity associated with the environment and a sense of responsibility to care for the environment. There is no privileging of humans as unique in having agency or intelligence, so one's identity and caretaking responsibility *as a human* includes the philosophy that nonhumans have their own agency, spirituality, knowledge, and intelligence. [...] Thus, humans ought to take responsibility to be respectful of nonhuman ways of knowing.[45]

42 Paula Gunn Allen, "IYANI: It Goes This Way," in *The Remembered Earth: An Anthology of Contemporary Native American Literature*, ed. Geary Hobson (Albuquerque: University of New Mexico Press, 1981), 191.

43 Sandra D. Styres and Dawn M. Zinga, "The Community-First Land-Centred Theoretical Framework: Bringing a 'Good Mind' to Indigenous Education Research?," *Canadian Journal of Education/Revue Canadienne de l'éducation* 36, no. 2 (July 2013): 300. Quoted in Max Liboiron, *Pollution Is Colonialism* (Durham: Duke University Press, 2021), 6.

44 Kyle Whyte, "Settler Colonialism, Ecology, and Environmental Injustice," *Environment and Society* 9, no. 1 (September 1, 2018): 136.

45 Whyte, "Settler Colonialism," 127.

The figure of the designer that emerges when Land relations and *other ways of knowing* are taken as the *object* of OOO—one centered on reciprocity, mutuality, community participation, environmental stewardship, and the forceful rejection of racism and anti-indigenous violence—is antithetical to that of the "star architect" trotting the globe to sell branded developments, and building them out of materials extracted globally and assembled according to universal or proprietary protocols. As this decadent model and its resource-hungry outputs increasingly index environmental and social injustice, and become obsolete, many exemplary practices lead the way in foregrounding local knowledges, materials, and relations as generative of *good* design (as objects and, importantly, as hyperobjects, in the sense discussed in Chapter 4).

Setting aside the question of nonhumans, which I will pursue in the next section, one might think of the work of Indian architect Anupama Kundoo, whose designs privilege local materials and regional building traditions—and the time and expertise required to build by hand—over the speed and anonymity of industrial mass production. [**Figures 8.9–8.12**]

Figure 8.9 Anupama Kundoo architects, *Wall House*, Auroville, India, 1997–2000. Photograph by Javier Callejas.

Figure 8.10 Anupama Kundoo architects, *Wall House*, Auroville, India, 1997–2000. Photograph by Javier Callejas.

Or of the *PET Lamp* project, developed by Alvaro Catalán de Ocón in collaboration with indigenous artisans and basket weavers in Colombia, Chile, Ethiopia, Japan, Australia, Thailand, and Ghana. [**Figures 8.13–8.16**] Or again, of the survey, poetically carried out by Alessandro Poli and Superstudio, that celebrates the self-sufficient life (and ingenuity) of Tuscan farmer Zeno Fiaschi. [**Figures 8.17 + 8.18**]

If these examples emphasize the situated "knowing how" of local artisans and builders, other readings of *Land* may prioritize community relations and participation, such as Theaster Gates' revitalization of cultural and public spaces in the South Side of Chicago; Bellastock's ephemeral cities [**Figures 8.19 + 8.20**]; the diversions and reactivations organized by Constantin Petcou and Doina Petrescu's atelier d'architecture autogérée (aaa); or the "urban prescriptions" and subversions ("built-up jurisprudence") curated by Santiago Cirugeda and Recetas Urbanas, among others.[46]

46 Elvira Dyangani Ose and Raúl Muñoz De la Vega, "Affection as a Subversive Architectural Form," in Kristine Guzmán, *Usted Está Aquí/You Are Here. Recetas Urbanas 2018.* (León: Museo de Arte Contemporaneo, 2019), 29. See also Nishat Awan, Tatjana Schneider, and Jeremy Till, *Spatial Agency: Other Ways of Doing Architecture* (Abingdon and New York: Routledge, 2011).

Figures 8.11 + 8.12 Anupama Kundoo architects, *Wall House*, Auroville, India, 1997–2000. Photographs by Andreas Deffner. Production of terracotta tubes and installation of vaulted roofing system.

Figures 8.13 + 8.14 Alvaro Catalán de Ocón and Bula´bula weavers (Lynette Birriran Djambarr-puyungu, Mary Dhapalany Mandhalpuy, Judith Djelirr Liyagalawumirr, Joy Gad-awarr Dabi, Melinda Gedjen Liyagalawumirr, Betty Matjarra Garwura, and Cecily Mopbarrmbrr), *PET Lamp Ramingining 1: Bukmukgu Guyananhawuy (Every family thinking forward) 1*, Arnhem Land, Northern Territory, Australia, 2016. Commissioned by NGV with the support of Vicki Vidor OAM and Peter Avery.

Figure 8.15 Alvaro Catalán de Ocón and Baba Tree Baskets, *PET Lamp Bolgatanga*, Ghana, 2020.

Figure 8.16 Alvaro Catalán de Ocón and Baba Tree Baskets, *PET Lamp Bolgatanga*, Ghana, 2020.

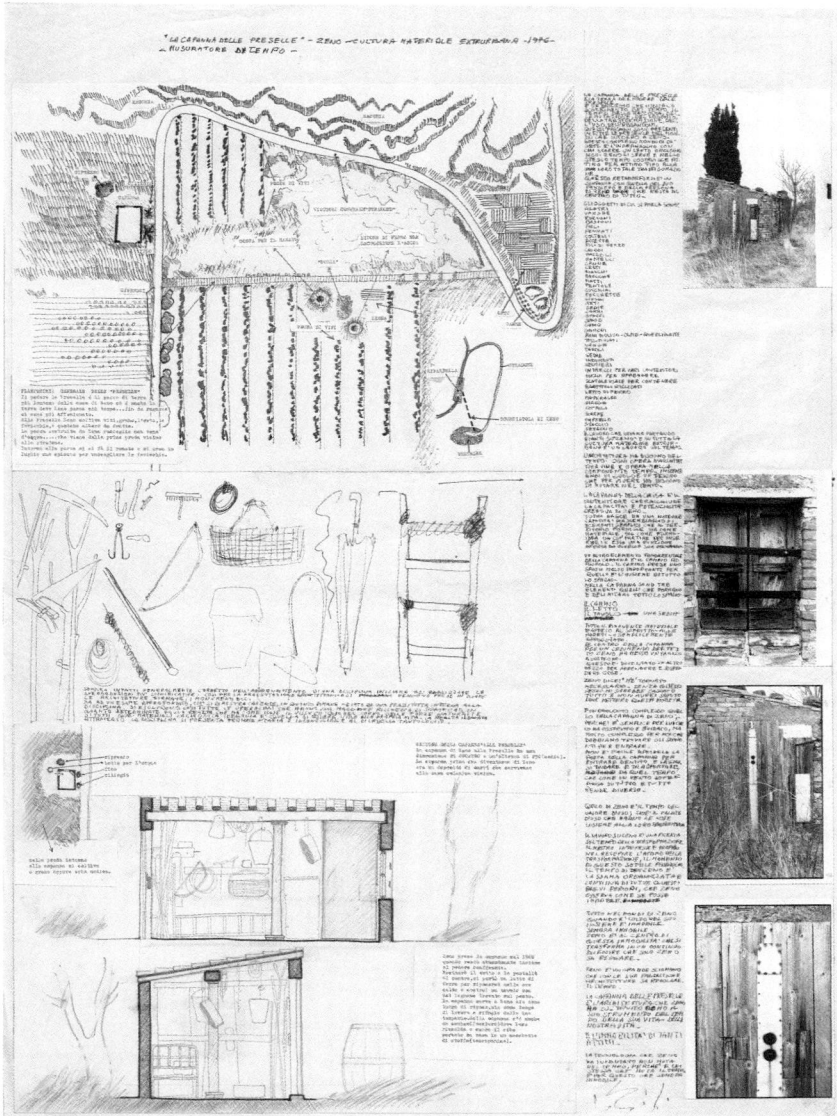

Figure 8.17 Alessandro Poli, *Collaged notes for Zeno, una cultura autosufficiente [Zeno, a self-sufficient culture]*, 1976. Ink and collage on paper, 100 x 72 cm. Alessandro Poli fonds, Canadian Centre for Architecture, Gift of Alessandro Poli, © Alessandro Poli. In the above drawing, Poli writes: "It seems generally appropriate, when learning a discipline, to begin by analyzing its most significant productions. Therefore, for architectural design, one examines monuments, the buildings signed by famous architects [*architetture firmate*], etc. But, upon further inspection, this appears to be lacking, because it remains tied to a praxis that is entirely internal to the discipline. Thus, it excludes all the operations that have a greater richness of meanings, as they are determined by a reality that has, as its base, the lived: the use of bodies, of natural forces, and of all those materials whose only ideology is to be useful to one's life. Reality, investigated through the discipline, appears fragmentary and unknowable beyond tautology." My translation.

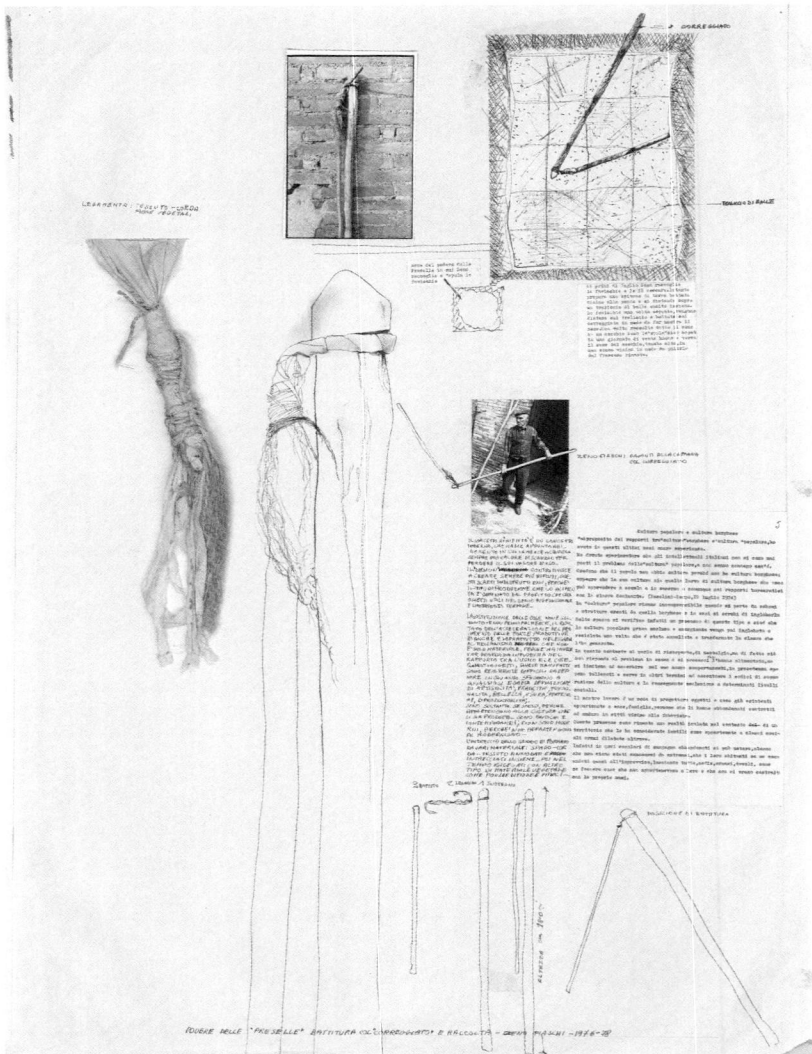

Figure 8.18 Alessandro Poli, *Collaged notes for Zeno, una cultura autosufficiente [Zeno, a self-sufficient culture]*, 1976–78. Ink and collage on paper, 100 x 70 cm. Alessandro Poli fonds, Canadian Centre for Architecture, Gift of Alessandro Poli. © Alessandro Poli. In the above drawing, Poli writes: "Waste is a modern concept, which emerges when goods acquire more and more exchange value, and lose use value. Design contributes to the creation of more and more refuse—these indestructible discards—because the kind of production that feeds it is dominated by profit, which makes objects useful in the most functional and narrow sense of the term. [...] These objects, these artefacts are really difficult to define as they elude an exact definition of artisticity, practicality, functionality, beauty, wear and tear, perfection, and reproducibility. They are only themselves because they belong to the culture that produced them." My translation.

Figure 8.19 Bellastock, *La Ville des Terres*, festival Bellastock, L'Ile-Saint-Denis, France, 2017. Photograph by Alexis Leclercq.

Figure 8.20 Bellastock, *Cime City*, festival Bellastock, Parc des Tourelles, Évry, France, 2018. Photograph by Alexis Leclercq.

8.4.2 Scenario Two: Nonhuman as Inhabitant (Ecological Ethics)

Buildings are understood to be inert. More generally, one assumes "living" and "nonliving" to be attributes that can be ascribed, with little controversy, to human inhabitants (with the additional pet or house plant) and to the structures they inhabit respectively. This attitude betrays a double taxonomical bias: on one side, only beings of a certain kind and size (human, detectable by humans, or endorsed by humans) are identified as legitimately present in interior spaces (as not pests), or even imagined to be present at all; on the other, walls and building envelopes are tasked with the separation of human beings from a feral nonhuman other beyond, preserving social space (the clearing in the forest, as narrated by Vitruvius and discussed in Chapter 3) and embodying—and thus confirming and enforcing—an onto-taxonomical division.

In this sense, the enclosing of a human interior (be it vertical, horizontal, domestic, or public) is taxonomical insofar as it assigns *zones* and geographical coordinates to humans and nonhumans, stipulating their distance and "proper place." The building of walls, fences, and concrete pavements is another instance of the technical *tabula rasa*: the appropriation, naming, and re-branding of objects, which are first marked as nonhuman (the *cow* as consigned to an inferior, and therefore consumable, ontology) and then culturalized (*beef* as the human translation of a cow, and as the only cow-format allowable within the modern home). Architectural envelopes thus perform a magic trick: crossing them, a slice of animal carcass becomes a succulent *filet mignon* and, inversely, a wasp or raccoon (one that was perfectly agreeable outside) turns into an undesirable pest and target. Here, identifying the raccoon's "proper place" is not necessary: being unwelcome is enough.[47]

In this scenario, a detaxonomized architecture might let objects roam freely and climb over fences. In practical terms, this means that: (1) boundaries lose some of their transformative and exclusionary powers, thickening to the point that separate (nonhybrid) sides are no longer

47 As Plumwood writes, "nature includes everything that reason excludes." Plumwood, *Feminism and the Mastery of Nature*, 20.

Figure 8.21 Ants of the Prairie, in collaboration with Darren Le Roux and Mitchell Whitelaw, *Life Support*, Barrer Hill, Mologo Valley, Canberra, Australia, 2019. Photograph by Mitchell Whitelaw. The project repurposes a 400-year-old dead tree, transforming it into a habitat for bats, birds, and reptiles.

48 Joyce Hwang, "My Neighbor, the Bat," *Biodesigned*, no. 8 (July 22, 2021).

49 Joyce Hwang, "Plight of the Bats," Ants of the Prairie, accessed 17 June 2020.

50 Terreform ONE, "Monarch Sanctuary: Integrated Biodiversity in Double Skin Facade," Terreform ONE, accessed June 17, 2020.

51 Stanislav Roudavski and Dan Parker, "Modelling Workflows for More-than-Human Design: Prosthetic Habitats for the Powerful Owl (*Ninox Strenua*)," in *Impact: Design With All Senses*, ed. Christoph Gengnagel et al. (Cham: Springer International Publishing, 2020).

52 Edinburgh City Council, "Swifts and Development: Information for Developers," accessed June 17, 2020.

conceivable; (2) nonhumans are elevated to the status of inhabitants (of "proper" architectural bodies).

Indeed, the erection of structures for animals is not uncommon in the history of architecture, nor is it immune to the desire to put things in their place. Not only are some spaces designed specifically for captivity and slaughter; even mutually beneficial arrangements (e.g., the dovecote, barn, chicken coop, and cat flap) depend on asymmetrical regimes of control and domestication; on human convenience (the want of guano, milk, eggs, or feline affection); and on the imposition of zones (the invention of spaces befitting nonhuman bodies). In fact, architecture has, in the Euro-Western tradition, viewed animals as enlightenment creatures—only as valuable as they are productive, useful, or amicable. Yet, a new generation of architects faces a different nonhuman body: one that is losing its natural habitats and hurtling towards extinction.

American architect Joyce Hwang has established an architectural practice, Ants of the Prairie, that facilitates conditions for animal habitability. "I am like a real estate developer looking for sites with untapped potential," she writes, "[b]ut the potential I seek has to do with increasing habitat rather than increasing capital."[48] **[Figures 8.21 + 8.22]** From 2007 onwards, Hwang's prototypes for bat pods, walls, "clouds," and towers have effectively turned bats—a species endangered by the rapid spread of White Nose Syndrome in North America—into clients, advocating their conservation and proliferation.[49] Similarly, Mitchell Joachim and Terreform ONE plan to fit an eight-story building in New York City with a double-skin façade that will serve as sanctuary, breeding ground, and way station for monarch butterflies;[50] Stanislav Roudavski and Dan Parker have developed data-driven and computational workflows for addressing nonhuman needs and senses in the design of prosthetic hollow-like nests for powerful owls in Melbourne, Australia; [51] **[Figure 8.23]** and in Edinburgh, Scotland, the local biodiversity plan has responded to declining swift numbers by encouraging the inclusion of swift nest sites (so called "swift bricks") in suitable new building developments.[52]

These few examples point the way towards structures that are designed for (and shared by) many creatures, and where control (the caged/scripted animal) is replaced by the orchestration of favorable conditions—by habitats ripe for animal occupation. This point cannot be overstated: while ecologies of inception are deterministic and predicated on certainties (on the construction of truths; on precise functions and nomenclatures), ecologies of suspension are probabilistic,

Figure 8.22 Ants of the Prairie, *Habitat Wall,* Sullivan Galleries, Chicago, IL, 2015. Photograph by Joyce Hwang. Prototype of wall structure designed for bird and bat inhabitation.

and take a weaker and more playful approach that always negotiates, *vis-à-vis* animal behavior in particular, a degree of undesignability. Therefore, taxonomy loses ground either when nonhumans are considered as primary inhabitants—for instance, in Hwang's *Bat Tower*[53] [**Figure 8.24**]—or when designers relinquish a measure of taxonomic control, puncturing the perfectly sealed envelopes that separate them from nonhumans.

If the figure of the animal client and inhabitant begins to destabilize onto-taxonomical divisions, however, these cannot be assumed to pertain to the limited sphere of human–animal relations, or reduced to creatures that are charismatic and visible to the naked eye. But how might one engage other lifeforms? Sociologist Myra Hird proposes the notion of bacterial "micro-ontologies" to promote a "microbial ethics [...] that engages seriously with the microcosmos."[54] This shift in scale immediately dissolves the presumed boundary between human and world, recognizing that our bodies, not to mention the interior of our homes, already teem with (and are inextricably bound to) nonhumans. Yet, how can the design of buildings address the microcosms that pierce and overlap the "big like us" worlds of human experience?[55]

The work of experimental architect Rachel Armstrong addresses this question, while also demonstrating, in unwavering terms, that

53 See Joyce Hwang, "Bat Tower," Ants of the Prairie, accessed June 17, 2020.

54 Myra J Hird, *The Origins of Sociable Life: Evolution after Science Studies* (Basingstoke: Palgrave Macmillan, 2009), 1.

55 By the phrase "big like us," I refer to the tendency, denounced by Lynn Margulis, to concentrate "on creatures that easily bear human ocular scrutiny." Hird, *The Origins of Sociable Life,* 21.

Figure 8.23 Dan Parker and Stanislav Roudavski, *A prosthetic nest for the powerful owl* (*Ninox strenua*), Melbourne, Australia, 2020. The hollows in large old trees that owls rely on for breeding are increasingly rare and take hundreds of years to form. Human-made structures, including conventional nest boxes, have largely failed to support powerful owl breeding. In response, this project uses digital form-making and fabrication techniques to design habitats that better suit the needs and preferences of owls. The designs draw inspiration from the natural habitat structures that owls have used for nesting: tree hollows and termite mounds.

56 See, for example: Rachel Armstrong, *Experimental Architecture: Designing the Unknown* (London and New York: Routledge, 2020); Rachel Armstrong, *Liquid Life: On Non-Linear Materiality* (Santa Barbara: Punctum Books, 2019); Rachel Armstrong, *Vibrant Architecture: Matter as a Codesigner of Living Structures* (Warsaw and Berlin: De Gruyter Open Ltd, 2015).

57 Living Architecture Consortium, "Team," Living Architecture H2020, accessed June 17, 2020.

58 Rachel Armstrong et al., "Living Architecture (LIAR): Metabolically Engineered Building Units," in *Cultivated Building Materials*, ed. Dirk E. Hebel and Felix Heisel (Birkhäuser, 2017), 168–75.

59 Rachel Armstrong, personal communication with the author.

boundaries can be radically rethought. It asks: what if building envelopes, instead of sealing interiors off from their surroundings, enhanced and augmented them? Could structures be lively and vibrant co-inhabitants, rather than inert containers? And might walls negotiate exchanges and celebrate entanglements, rather than separate, claim, and enclose? Armstrong's research seeks answers to these questions, spearheading a field she calls *Living Architecture*.[56] An EU-funded scheme of the same name, which Armstrong led alongside scientists and designers from across Europe, offers insights into what these ideas might entail.[57]

The project developed prototypes of metabolic building envelopes—active micro-organismal cities that process household waste products (urine and grey water) and transform them into fresh water, oxygen, biomass, and fertilizers, while also generating low amounts of electricity.[58] The corresponding bioreactor–partitions, which synergistically combine microbial fuel cells (anaerobic bacterial "batteries"), photo–bioreactors (photosynthetic algae), and synthetic consortia (genetically modified organisms), are described by Armstrong as sets of interconnected "stomach chambers" that process organic matter, linking the metabolism of different microbial communities—and that of human beings—in mutualistic and symbiotic relationships.[59] [**Figures 8.25 + 8.26**]

Expanding the spectrum of allowable lifeforms within the home—acknowledging (and designing with) the microbial communities that populate domestic spaces and gut microbiomes—necessarily changes the parameters for the identification of waste (from an object's position relative to a system to the temporary lack of bacterial communities suitable for processing it). Reducing the distance between sites of consumption and sites of waste collection and treatment, the project turns the discards of one species into food for another. This is not trivial: by separating buildings from their environment (by enforcing their inertia), *we* also cut off all manner of beneficial flows and interactions, requiring life-supporting systems to rely on remote, external, and energy-consuming infrastructures, largely powered by fossil fuels.

Modern architecture, as the expression of a technical and taxonomical *rasura*, is obsessed with sterilization, and the painstaking concealment of metabolic processes, as if the warm traces of our bodies (feces, urine, sweat, etc.), which evidence our animality and implicate our being in a nonhuman *taxon*, could be removed, erased, or magically disappear. As philosopher Slavoj Žižek puts it:

In human dwellings, there is an intermediate space which is disavowed: we all know it exists, but we do not really accept its existence—it

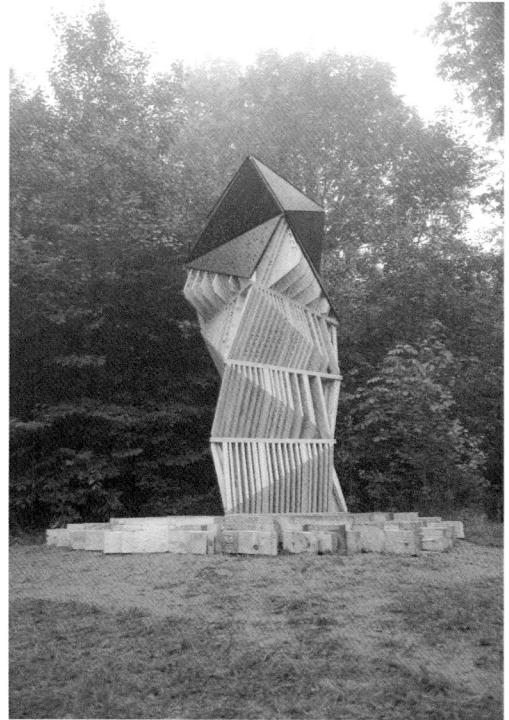

Figure 8.24 Ants of the Prairie, *Bat Tower*, Griffis Sculpture Park, East Otto, NY, 2010. Photograph by Joyce Hwang.

Figure 8.25 Living Architecture Consortium (H2020), *Bioreactor Wall*, Bristol, University of the West of England, 2019. Photograph by Rachel Armstrong.

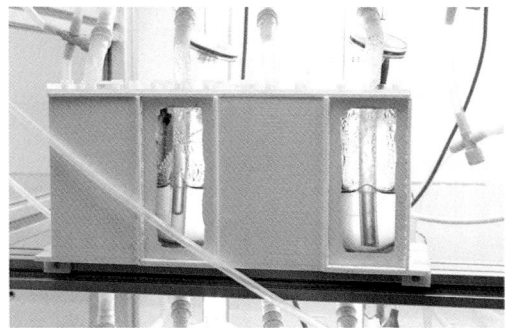

Figure 8.26 Living Architecture Consortium (H2020), *Living Brick*, Bristol, University of the West of England, 2019. Photograph by Rachel Armstrong.

remains ignored and (mostly) unsayable. The main content of this invisible space is of course excrement (in the plumbing and sewers), but it also includes the complex network of electricity supplies, digital links, et cetera—all contained in the narrow spaces between walls or under floors. Of course we know well enough how our excrement leaves the house, but our immediate phenomenological relation to it is more radical: it is as if the waste disappears into some netherworld, beyond our sight and out of our world.[60]

Timothy Morton provides a similar account: "When we flush the toilet," they write, "we imagine that the U-bend takes the waste away into some ontologically alien realm. Ecology is now beginning to tell us of something very different: a flattened world without ontological U-bends. A world in which there is no 'away.'"[61] Whereas modern architecture sanitizes all traces of digestion, hiding them in wall cavities or flushing them down drains, Armstrong celebrates the wet burning of metabolism, exposing its "soil-making ecologies" and promoting them as seeds for a new paradigm of interspecies cohabitation. Instead of the sterile cookie-cutter homes favored by real-estate developers and construction industries, Armstrong imagines a vibrant "building physiology" that is attuned to its occupants, senses changes in their habits, and shares some of their unique microbiota.[62]

Walls soften, turning into gardens, organs of a shared body, and conversational interfaces. Indeed, *Living Architecture* undermines the orthodox view that interior space is inert, controlled, reliable, and obedient—or that it must be characterized by what architectural historian and author Daniel A. Barber calls the "Comfortocene, an era defined by a global order predicated on manufactured interior consistency."[63] "Comfort," he writes, "indicates that one has risen above the inconsistencies of the natural world and triumphed, not only over nature and the weather but over chance itself."[64] Against this view, its colonial and racist implementations, and against the continued reliance on planet-destroying HVAC systems in buildings, Barber calls for an architecture of discomfort, and for a collective reimagining of the values and expectations associated with designed interiors.[65]

In a short story entitled "Bittersweet Buildings," Armstrong writes:

A canopy of tubes hung like entrails in a sausage factory from worm-infested pine beams whose excrements leaked into bags, sacks and digestors of all shapes and sizes. Under rows of containers with screw-top lids, taps and plumbing, human-sized, fluid-filled objects were suspended from a network of free-standing shelves connected by hoses and pipes that at times, appeared to possess their own pulse.

"It stinks," I said.

"Like a body," said Arvid. "You'll get used to it."[66]

60 Slavoj Žižek, *Living in the End Times* (London and New York: Verso, 2011), 259–60.

61 Timothy Morton, "Peak Nature," *Adbusters*, 2012.

62 Sean Lally, "Rachel Armstrong: Far from Equilibrium," *Night White Skies*, accessed June 17, 2020.

63 Daniel A. Barber, "After Comfort," *Log*, no. 47 (2019): 47.

64 Barber, "After Comfort," 45.

65 Ibid., 47.

66 Rachel Armstrong, "Bittersweet Building," in *Gross Ideas: Tales of Tomorrow's Architecture*, ed. Edwina Attlee, Phineas Harper, and Maria Smith (London and Oslo: Architecture Foundation and Oslo Architecture Triennale, 2019), 84.

8.4.3 Scenario Three: Object as Inhabitant (Humansnail Ethics)

Ask an architect about their work, and you may learn more about the style, form, materials, structure, and cost of a building than the bodies or minds meant to inhabit it. Examine any doorway, window, toilet, chair, or desk in that building, however, and you will find the outline of the body meant to use it. From a doorframe's negative space to the height of shelves and cabinets, inhabitants' bodies are simultaneously imagined, hidden, and produced by the design of built worlds.

Aimi Hamraie[67]

The nonhuman-as-inhabitant can be considered as a subcase of the broader object-as-inhabitant category, one according to which the architects inspired by OOO might recognize, as the mysterious and withdrawn center of a project, not their inner muses but the future occupants of their designs. While this proposition seems at first rather boring (and more so in a culture that rewards novelty above all else), it does call into question some fundamental assumptions about habitation. If designing for bats, swifts, and bacteria confronts an obvious lack of certainty and control (will these critters eventually settle in?), it also casts a critical light upon the hubristic assumption that human inhabitation is relatively straightforward, and fully codified or codifiable (the "perfect knowledge of man" touted by modernist architects).[68]

Architects, out of a degree of necessity, tend to assume a *shared* knowledge of how human beings move about, perceive, and use spaces, often borrowed from the spreadsheets of real-estate developers or the drawings and dimensions in design handbooks. The corresponding norms and standards implement ecologies of inception to such a pervasive degree that the communication and coordination between parts (between faucet and sink, door and handle, chair and table, foot and sidewalk, and so on) start to be taken for granted.

That is: when large numbers of equipmental formats join to build coherent functional constellations, the orientation of an individual unit may appear to be natural, inevitable, or given. Architects, for example, are unlikely to question whether the floors of an apartment should be flat, not least because of a vast ecology of chairs, dressers, closets, vases, sofas, dining tables, and kitchen islands designed specifically to rest upon horizontal and even surfaces. Indeed, the expansiveness of referential networks (Heidegger's "totality of equipment") breeds invincibility: if nothing can be designed in isolation (without accounting for the interactions with a myriad other objects), herding protocols have the inherent tendency to privilege and perpetuate—as well as to unmark—the status quo.

67 Aimi Hamraie, *Building Access: Universal Design and the Politics of Disability* (Minneapolis: University of Minnesota Press, 2017), 19.

68 Congrès internationaux d'architecture moderne (CIAM), "Charter of Athens," in *Programs and Manifestoes on 20th-Century Architecture*, ed. Conrads Ulrich (Cambridge: MIT Press, 1975), 142. Quoted in Hamraie, *Building Access*, 26.

In this context, the enforcement of onto-taxonomy is not active across the sole envelope dividing humans and nonhumans, but more distributed, localized, and insidious. Or rather: "enforcement" does not involve the implementation of an uncontested or predelineated boundary, but nonhumanity as a category that can be spatially renegotiated, and assigned to all manner of human and nonhuman objects. Not only is the ideal frontier between humans and nonhumans elusive and improbable when one considers that, for example and paraphrasing Myra Hird, we are bacteria and bacteria are us;[69] such a boundary is also, in its modern constitution, not neutral, and always bundled up with notions of propriety and abjection—of what (and whose bodies) can and cannot do.

69 Hird, *The Origins of Sociable Life*, 26.

Again: there isn't an objective borderline out there in the world—only a technical *tabula rasa* that, as a categorizing and re-categorizing engine, continually redraws it. Indeed, in the context of my apartment on the second floor of a hundred-year old terraced house, the cute kitten running across the living room might be more "human" than the wheelchair-using or elderly friend who is denied access by steep stairs and a narrow corridor. That is: nonhumanity—the exclusion from a human taxon and, by extension, from human space—sticks to all manner of bodies and behaviors that do not fit the relevant (spatially sanctioned) norm.[70] "A misfit," writes Rosemarie Garland-Thomson,

70 See for example the "redlining" policies that, in the US, demanded that compatible racial groups live in the same communities, and attributed high levels of risk to African American neighborhoods, making it impossible to insure mortgages. Richard Rothstein, *The Color of Law: A Forgotten History of How Our Government Segregated America* (New York and London: Liveright Publishing Corporation, 2018).

> occurs when the environment does not sustain the shape and function of the body that enters it. [...] The built and arranged space through which we navigate our lives tends to offer fits to majority bodies and create misfits with minority forms of embodiment, such as people with disabilities.[71]

Garland-Thomson traces back to Aristotle's *Generation of Animals* the idea that an inferior and aberrant *other* emerges when deviating from a norm, starting with the female body.[72] She coins the term *normate* to designate "the social figure with which people can represent themselves as definitive human beings" and "the constructed identity of those who, by way of the bodily configurations and cultural capital they assume, can step into a position of authority and wield the power it grants them."[73] Aimi Hamraie uses the phrase "normate template" to link the historical depictions of universal, average, and standard bodies (the users of buildings as imagined by Leonardo da Vinci, Le Corbusier, Ernst Neufert, Ernest Irving Freese, and others) with their implicit claim to (and prescription for) normalcy.[74] Here, the unmarked and universal *anthropos* drawing the "outline of the body meant to use" human space is largely known, white, productive, reproductively fit, able-bodied, young, neurotypical, and male (or binarily gendered). Léopold Lambert and Minh-Ha T. Pham note that even the most diversified standards—the bodies of Henry Dreyfuss' Joe and Josephine—wove a gendering bias into the fabric of everyday objects and spaces, using, for example, Joe's virtual dimensions to design the

71 Rosemarie Garland-Thomson, "Misfits: A Feminist Materialist Disability Concept," *Hypatia* 26, no. 3 (2011), 594.

72 Rosemarie Garland-Thomson, *Extraordinary Bodies: Figuring Physical Disability in American Culture and Literature* (New York: Columbia University Press, 2017), 20.

73 Garland-Thomson, *Extraordinary Bodies*, 8.

74 Hamraie, *Building Access*, 20.

seats of airplanes, armored tanks, and tractors, and Josephine's to design telephone switchboards and home appliances like ironing tables and vacuum cleaners.[75]

Yet, beyond Joe and Josephine, any normate template whatsoever—that is, any presumptive knowledge of the user or inhabitant—is bound to exert taxonomic and exclusionary pressures. Quoting Lambert and Pham at length:

> Standardized design creates violent relations between bodies and environments. The intensity of violence the standard body brings to bear on an individual's body is measured in that body's difference and distance from the standard. A chair that is too high, a beam too low, a corridor too narrow acts on the body forcefully and with a force that is unevenly distributed. [...] But to resolve this design problem does not mean that we need a more-inclusive approach to design. The very idea of inclusion, of opening up and expanding the conceptual parameters of human bodies, depends for its logic and operation on the existence of parameters in the first place. In other words, a more inclusive approach to design remains fundamentally exclusive in its logic.[76]

A diagram that, in Chapter 1, identified the boundaries of EoIs as determining of value, can now be modified to show the construction of regimes of bodily ability (the ecologically productive/communicative body). [**Figure 8.27**] In other words, the reason why notions of "inclusion" are unsatisfactory is that the inability to step over a curb, or to enter a locked door, does not precede the construction of the sidewalk, or the bolting of the door. The curb does not highlight or make visible the wheelchair user's inability to cross it. Rather, their inability is invented and violently established by the curb, in the same way that a wall establishes boundaries by forbidding access. Garland-Thomson further nuances this point:

> On the one hand, [...] it is important to use the constructionist argument to assert that disability is not bodily insufficiency, but instead arises from the interaction of physical differences with an environment. On the other, the particular, historical existence of the disabled body demands both accommodation and recognition. In other words, the physical differences of using a wheelchair or being deaf, for example, should be claimed, but not cast as lack.[77]

If any standardization or ecology of inception will—by its very constitution—put bodies in their "proper" place, and thus automatically identify *other* bodies, be they human or nonhuman, as "out of place" (and dehumanize them), considering the occupant or user as an "object" in Harman's sense—as withdrawn and unknowable—might serve as a productive counter-strategy. If the violence of taxonomy is exerted by asserting knowledge—the distillation of bodies into essentializable

75 Léopold Lambert and Minh-Ha T. Pham, "Spinoza in a T-Shirt," *The New Inquiry*, July 1, 2015.

76 Lambert and Pham, "Spinoza in a T-Shirt."

77 Garland-Thomson, *Extraordinary Bodies*, 23.

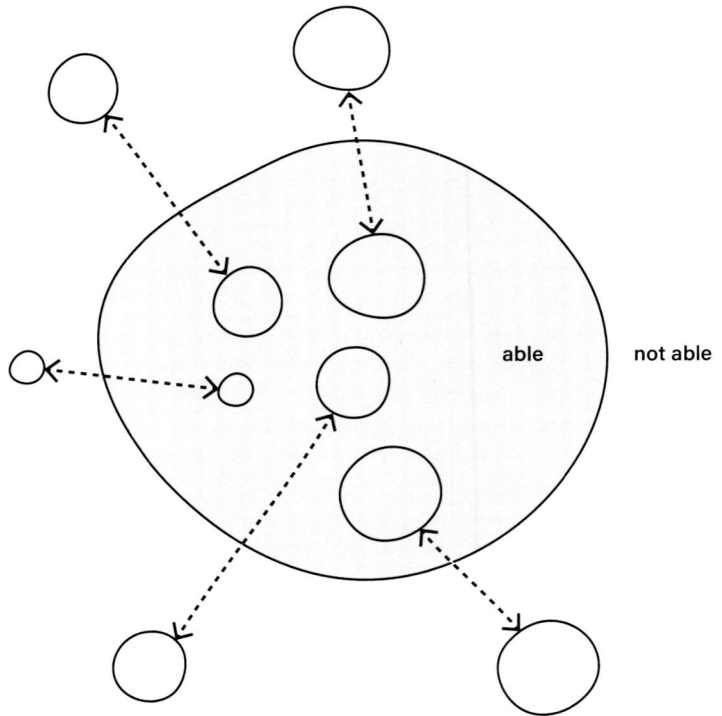

Figure 8.27 Ecologies of Inception as determining of ability and disability.

qualities and scripts—OOO, by establishing the ontological impossibility of knowledge (or, more accurately, its inherent partiality), might contribute to the neutralization and destruction of the normative body. Yet, how does one put this into practice, or learn to *unknow* the standard (and implicitly white, middle-aged, gendered, able-bodied, heterosexual, etc.) body, and to embrace a radically different—ignorant and therefore ethical—approach to design?

The object-oriented designer can learn much from the architectural practice of Shūsaku Arakawa and Madeline Gins, who regard human beings as mysterious and inscrutable "puzzle creatures."[78] The duo resists the urge to design with a specific body or perceptual apparatus in mind, rejecting the "much too hasty resolving of the indeterminate into the 'known'"[79] characteristic of standard modes of architectural design, and contesting the notion that a body could be considered apart from its environment at all.[80] "We speak of an architectural body," they write, "simply because [...] what we want to describe originates from and joins up with the physical body."[81] Not knowing what a body is or can do—deploying design to "pose questions directly to the body" and to challenge standard expectations about our senses, abilities, and modes of inhabitation—is taken as a serious point of departure, and as one capable of reframing the scope and ambitions of architectural

78 I first came across the work of Arakawa and Gins through Léopold Lambert's blog, and the following collection: Léopold Lambert, *The Funambulist Pamphlets. Volume 8, Arakawa + Madeline Gins* (Brooklyn: Punctum Books, 2014).

79 Madeline Gins and Shūsaku Arakawa, *Architectural Body* (Tuscaloosa: University of Alabama Press, 2002), 46.

80 Gins and Arakawa, *Architectural Body*, 21.

81 Ibid., 68.

design.[82] Indeed, according to Arakawa and Gins, "[a]rchitecture is the greatest tool available to our species, both for figuring itself out and for constructing itself differently."[83]

The resulting structures are breathtakingly strange, and both challenge/disorient bodies, and—by disregarding the normative body—empower them. Their *Site of Reversible Destiny—Yoro*, in Gifu Prefecture, Japan, encloses a section of Yoro Park, organizing soft and hard surfaces into undulating contours, artificial topographies, and sequences of mazes, architectural fragments, and pavilions. [**Figures 8.28 + 8.29**] The park's "directions for use" ask visitors, among other things, to "try to be more body and less person," to "renege on all geographically related pledges of allegiance," and, "[i]nstead of being fearful of losing your balance, [to] look forward to it (as a desirable re-ordering of the landing sites, formerly known as the senses)."[84]

Two residential projects, the *Reversible Destiny Lofts Mitaka—In Memory of Helen Keller*—in Tokyo, Japan, and the *Bioscleave House*

82 Ibid., 21.

83 Ibid., xx.

84 Madeline Gins and Shūsaku Arakawa, "Site of Reversible Destiny—Yoro Park," accessed 17 June 2020.

Figure 8.28 Arakawa and Madeline Gins, *Site of Reversible Destiny—Yoro Park*, 1993–95, Yoro, Gifu Prefecture, Japan. Photo courtesy of the Site of Reversible Destiny—Yoro Park. © 1997 Estate of Madeline Gins. Reproduced with permission of the Estate of Madeline Gins.

Figure 8.29 Arakawa and Madeline Gins, *Site of Reversible Destiny—Yoro Park*, 1993–95, Yoro, Gifu Prefecture, Japan. Photo courtesy of the Site of Reversible Destiny—Yoro Park. © 1997 Estate of Madeline Gins. Reproduced with permission of the Estate of Madeline Gins

Figure 8.30 Arakawa and Madeline Gins, *Reversible Destiny Lofts Mitaka—In Memory of Helen Keller*, 2005, Mitaka, Tokyo, Japan. Photo by Ken Kato. © 2005 Estate of Madeline Gins. Reproduced with permission of the Estate of Madeline Gins.

(Lifespan Extending Villa) in East Hampton, New York, locate functional living spaces (bedrooms, bathrooms, etc.) around a sunken kitchen/dining area surrounded by a large open space, with translucent windows and a bumpy, rolling floor—an interior landscape. [**Figures 8.30–8.32**] The transposition of outdoor "natural" topographies within the confines of an apartment—the deliberate confusion of landscape and building, and the interiorization of features that are typically excluded from the flattened surfaces prepared for human inhabitation—both enclose a domestic space and reject its enforcement of a neat taxonomic division. Rather, these surfaces remain loose, unclaimed; they are not defined by specific functions or *teloi*, but remain

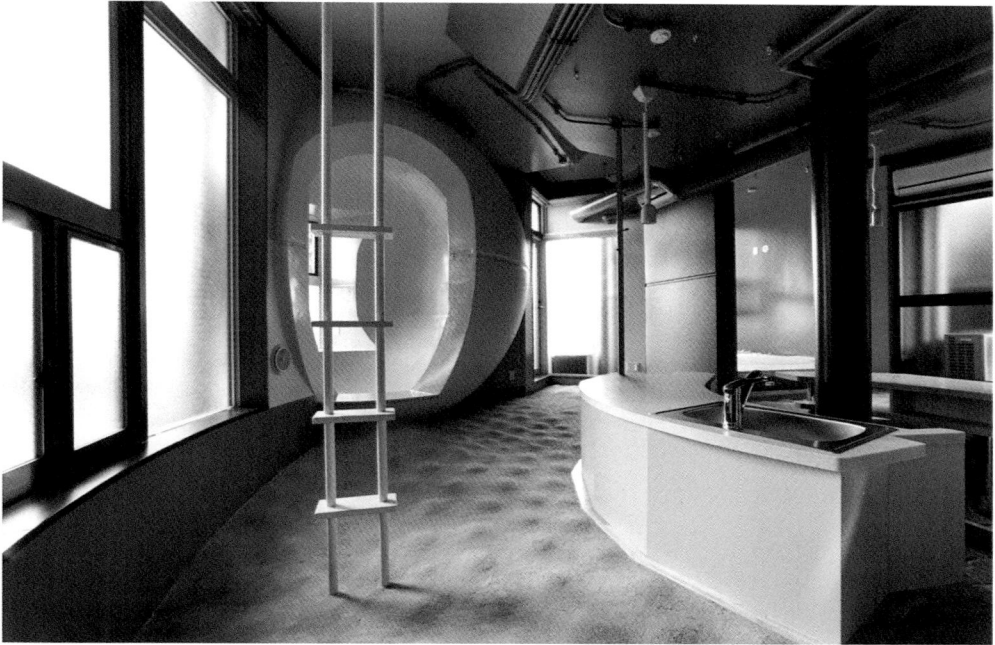

Figure 8.31 Arakawa and Madeline Gins, *Reversible Destiny Lofts Mitaka—In Memory of Helen Keller*, 2005, Mitaka, Tokyo, Japan. Photo by Masataka Nakano. © 2005 Estate of Madeline Gins. Reproduced with permission of the Estate of Madeline Gins.

open to experimentation—they are laboratories for re-inventing movement, habitation, and bodies.

Perhaps Arakawa and Gin's articulation of the difference between what they call "functional" and "procedural" architecture can clarify the distinction between ecologies of inception and ecologies of suspension. In a section of *Architectural Body* entitled "Architecture as Hypothesis," the duo imagine visiting, for the first time, a house with their clients. Once again, expectations are not met:

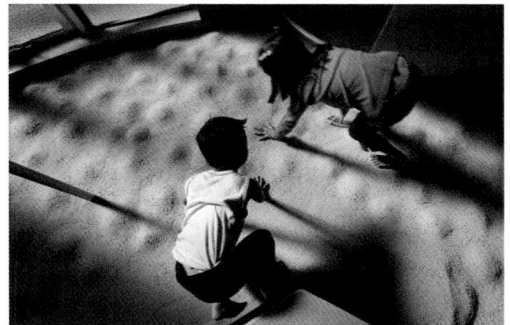

Figure 8.32 Arakawa and Madeline Gins, *Reversible Destiny Lofts Mitaka—In Memory of Helen Keller*, 2005, Mitaka, Tokyo, Japan. Photo by Masataka Nakano. © 2005 Estate of Madeline Gins. Reproduced with permission of the Estate of Madeline Gins.

ARAKAWA: Here is the house we were telling you about.

ANGELA: I don't see any house here.

GINS: Granted this is not what in our time most people dream of coming home to.

ROBERT: This heap?

GINS: Yes, a low pile of material that covers a fairly vast area.

ANGELA: Are we at a dump? This low pile covering a vast area.

GINS: What you take to be a pile of junk ranges in height from three to eleven inches. It measures close to 2,400 square feet—or 2,900 square feet if you include the courtyard.

ROBERT: Courtyard?

GINS: The shining part in the middle that has a lot of green around it.

ANGELA: That's hilarious. Your house is shorter than its shrubbery.

ARAKAWA: [Laughs] I myself find that surprising. Shall we take a walk around it?[85]

Not only is this unusual house indistinguishable from the surrounding landscape (a "low pile of material" that is "shorter than its shrubbery," as opposed to the expression of order, status, and taxonomic privilege usually performed by architectural constructs). The very figure of the pile or heap, as discussed in Chapter 1, suggests an affinity with waste, and a renunciation of order (the imposition of order, the enforcement of propriety). The shape of the house does not index clear-cut functional programs. Indeed, it can barely be recognized as a house:

ANGELA: This—this whatever it is—has a front and a back?

GINS: Of course.

ROBERT: A front door by which to enter this doormat sort of thing, this giant shower cap …[86]

This "whatever it is" resists naming, and cannot be easily paraphrased or tamed. In the above passage, the figure of the heap serves a double purpose. On one side, it identifies the house with a potential and indeterminate materiality that cannot be fully actualized or shaped (become a house, begin to have rooms) prior to inhabitation. "Rooms form," notes Angela at some point, "depending on how we move. If I bend down, I nearly lose the room."[87] On the other, the heap, apparently garbage-like and value-less when examined from the outside, reveals its (introverted and entangled) value on the inside, when the four characters (Arakawa, Gins, and their clients) begin to move about it, holding up fabric, breathing, and activating expanding mechanisms.

This is what they mean by *hypothetical architecture*: "Constructed to exist in the tense of *what if*, it presents itself as intentionally provisional, replacing definite form with tentative form, the notion of a lasting structure with that of an adaptive one";[88] not an architecture to be seen or photographed, but one to be experienced.

ANGELA: How many settings does this living space have?

GINS: Three. A zero setting that we call the snail setting. And then a medium setting, in which the material stays always at a

85 Gins and Arakawa, *Architectural Body*, 23.

86 Ibid., 24.

87 Ibid., 27.

88 Ibid., 29. It is worth noting a similar passage from Harman, which also echoes Arakawa and Gins' preoccupation with immortality: "if architecture represses all sense of what is disturbing, strange, or in excess of current knowledge and

slight remove from those within it; we have named this the close-to-snail setting. The highest setting is the one that does it all; when this is on, spine-deploying mechanisms are fully engaged; we have named it roomy.

ROBERT: At this moment … you have it on the snail setting, I think it would be fair to say. All the while … always turned to that?

ARAKAWA: Snail setting all along. This setting provides the most intense way to use this … tool … this piece of equipment. This house is a tool, a procedural one.

GINS: A functional tool, whether it be a hammer, a telephone, or a telescope, extends the senses, but a procedural tool examines and reorders the sensorium.[89]

The difference between functional and procedural equipment, as articulated by Arakawa and Gins, mirrors that between EoIs and EoSs. Ecologies of inception curate the design and construction of purposive objects, and their point of arrival tends to be an identity: the object as coextensive with (and reducible to) ecological knowledge—of how to use it, of how to name it, of how to communicate with it, of what it is, of what it does, et cetera. Ecologies of suspension, on the other hand, embrace ignorance, and always recognize the object's declared functionality or ecological role as partial, potentially violent, and open to interpretation.

If EoIs design by enclosing and fixing, EoSs do it by hypothesizing—by loosening and freeing; by speculating; by diverting, dismantling, reusing, and repurposing. The shift from ecologies of inception to ecologies of suspension—the practice of turning one into the other, time after time—corresponds with what I have been calling *exaptive design*.

8.4.4 *Scenario Four: Object as Parts (Mereological Ethics)*

With its rejection of onto-taxonomy, Harman's ontology avoids subordinating objecthood to specific kinds of beings or qualities. This does not mean that objects (e.g., people, proteins, whales, mountains, car tires) are presumed to be generic and universal—or unchanging—but that they can only be encountered through local interactions and translations. An object is real in Harman's sense when it exceeds such translations, not as an unmarked (and yet enforceable) essence, but precisely as something that can never be fully known, or essentialized.[90] In the context of design, then, an object may coincide with a plurality of entities. Architect Adam Fure writes that

[a]pplied to architecture […], OOO might designate an object to be a stair, window, roofline, or flashing detail, but also a concept, a

social practice, it will pay the same price as any field that screens out the unknown: that of falling into an actualism that risks becoming a fatalism." And again: "this is where the object-oriented approach can probably make a contribution to architecture […] by better integrating the unknown and the counterfactual into our picture of reality." Graham Harman, "Non-Relationality for Philosophers and Architects," 216–17.

89 Ibid., 30.

90 Bedford, *Is There an Object Oriented Architecture?*, 121–22.

91 Adam Fure, "Aesthetics Postdigital," in *Aesthetics Equals Politics*, 114.

92 Fure, "Aesthetics Postdigital," 119.

93 Levi R. Bryant, *The Democracy of Objects* (Ann Arbor: Open Humanities Press, 2011), 214.

94 Bryant, *The Democracy of Objects*, 214.

95 A compelling summary of these practices is offered in Nikole Bouchard, ed., *Waste Matters: Adaptive Reuse for Productive Landscapes* (Abingdon and New York: Routledge, 2021).

96 C. A. Pearson, "Material Affairs," *Architectural Record*, March 2001.

97 Romo-Melgar Carlos, "Nobody Would Visit Paris If It Looked Like Dallas: Analysis of Mark Foster Gage Architects' Proposal for the Guggenheim Museum in Helsinki," *Medium* (blog), June 25, 2021.

fictitious building, or the color "red" in a drawing. Such flexibility in signification requires those adopting an OOO framework in architecture to explicitly define the object they are addressing.[91]

If the items listed by Fure remain narrowly disciplinary, and he ends up proposing a high-modern aesthetics wherein "everything from bits to bricks can be authored,"[92] his suggestion that the adoption of OOO requires a declaration of allegiance—that it must name the objects it confronts—is compelling, and consistent with the elaboration of "scenarios" proposed here.

Now, the last such scenario reconsiders the relationship between parts and wholes, prompted by OOO's refusal to privilege the latter over the former. Levi Bryant defines this "strange mereology" as the "relation between objects where one object is simultaneously a part of another object *and* an independent object in its own right."[93] What makes this mereology strange, explains Bryant, is that "the subsets of a set, the smaller objects composing larger objects, are simultaneously necessary conditions for that larger object while being independent of that object. Likewise, the larger object composed of these smaller objects is itself independent of these smaller objects."[94] Whereas ecologies of inception—and, with them, the architectural project—curate a seamless integration of parts, subordinating their value to the integrity of a whole, a strange mereology foregrounds parts as objects in their own right, and as deserving of independent value. And if the history of architecture is not devoid of such examples—one might think of the many instances of *spolia* surviving a building or monument[95]—its more recent (author-oriented) past is characterized by a marked preference for the cohesion and integration afforded by project functions.

Again, Tod Williams' words are symptomatic of a view that most architects would readily espouse, and are worth returning to: "An important value for us," he avers, "is drawing together all of the various elements of architecture—materials, space, form, light, color—and producing a unified whole. We're not at all interested in producing a collage."[96]

Yet it is the two- and three-dimensional collage—a technique that co-opts parts from preceding objects, and that, by so doing, preempts the possibility of their seamless integration—that has inspired architects like David Ruy and Mark Foster Gage, resulting, for example, in the latter's outlandish scheme for the Helsinki Guggenheim Museum. [**Figures 8.33 + 8.34**] If Gage's proposal flaunts wastefulness (the building is imagined as constructed by stacking CNC-milled marble blocks),[97] architect Ang Li approaches the collage as a way to address the materiality of waste. Her project *Balancing Acts*, developed during a residency at RAIR Philadelphia, bales the expanded polystyrene fragments collected from the tipping yard of an industrial recycling facility,

Figure 8.33 Mark Foster Gage Architects, *Helsinki Guggenheim Museum*, Helsinki, Finland, 2014.

shrink wrapping them into large (but lightweight) building blocks.[98] [**Figure 8.35**]

There is much precedent for such operations in the arts, of course—one may think of artists like Kurt Schwitters, Tony Cragg, Elsa von Freytag-Loringhoven, Jannis Kounellis, Kcho, Nam June Paik, El Anatsui, Tara Donovan, Nancy Rubins, and Noah Purifoy, among many others. American sculptor Louise Nevelson, for example, combined found wooden objects into sophisticated assemblages that both celebrated the parts' formal exuberance and caused them to cohere into unitary monochromatic (black, white, or golden) compositions. Like the inoperative organs in the glorious body described by Agamben,[99] Nevelson's spindles, joinery offcuts, and timber fragments allude to the staircases, chairs,

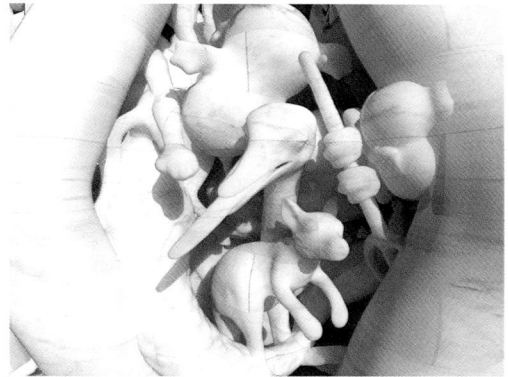

Figure 8.34 Mark Foster Gage Architects, *Helsinki Guggenheim Museum*, Helsinki, Finland, 2014.

98 Ang Li, "All That Is Solid," *Journal of Architectural Education* 74, no. 2 (July 2, 2020): 299–308.

99 See the discussion of Agamben's *Nudities* in Chapter 7.

and coffee tables they might have belonged to, yet they also proclaim a newfound independence (the suspension of previous functions, the abrogation of prior ecological scripts), all the while merging into complex compositions that challenge the viewer's ability to tell parts apart. Similarly, in Mike Kelley's *Deodorized Central Mass with Satellites*—a series of floating forms composed of stuffed animals—parts both recede into colorful masses (as large three-dimensional pixels) and simultaneously index, often quite blatantly, their autonomous (and recognizably toy-like) identity. If Kelley's *Mass* is often used

Figure 8.35 Ang Li, *Balancing Acts*, 2019. Revolution Recovery, Allentown, PA. Photo by Billy Dufala.

100 For instance, see Todd
Gannon et al., "The Object Turn:
A Conversation," *Log*, no. 33
(2015): 73–94; and Ryan Vincent
Manning, "Soft Discrete Familiars:
Animals, Blankets and Bricks,
Oh My!," in Gilles Retsin, ed.,
*Discrete: Reappraising the Digital in
Architecture*, vol. 89, Architectural
Design, 2019, 121.

101 Kurt Kohlstedt, "Interstellar
Illusions: 'Greebles' Lend Large Sci-Fi
Structures a Sense of Scale," *99%
Invisible* (blog), February 19, 2021.

102 Ryan Lambie, "Greebles: How
Tiny Details Make a Huge Star Wars
Universe," *Den of Geek* (blog), 4 May
2018.

by OOO architects as inspiration,[100] so is kit-bashing—a model-making technique that combines the components of different commercial kits (parts of miniature cars, helicopters, planes, trucks, battleships, etc.) to obtain unpredictable and futuristic designs, such as the Imperial Star Destroyer in the *Star Wars* movies.[101]

Whereas, in the sculptures by Nevelson and Kelley, ostension corresponds with the suspension of previous (recognizable) functions, the jumps in scale curated by kit-bashing erase any detectable trace of the original kits or models. Therefore, and despite being fully actualized and individuated, the kit-bashed components repel particular names or roles, merely alluding to the plausibility that these could, in a galaxy far far away, be already in place. It is worth noting that such parts are called, in special effects jargon, "greebles." Director George Lucas is reported to have coined the term to signify "something you can't otherwise define,"[102] or, in other words, a sensual object that, like a real one, resists ecological paraphrase. Whereas the stomachs of Agamben's glorious bodies continued to be stomachs (albeit freed from digestion), and the pink plush elephants in Kelley's *Mass* carry on being pink plush elephants (at least when inspected closely), greebles have irreparably lost all equipmental reference or ecological orientation. They exemplify a transitional brand of sensual object—one that, by being somewhat slippery and opaque, might be eminently co-optable. If ecologies of inception name tools (if they lock them into known and productive orientations), ecologies of suspension "unname" them, turning them into *greebles* of sorts—sites for the decoupling of form and function, objects and identities.

Versatility also characterizes recent computational approaches to tectonics that, inspired by Bryant's "strange mereology" and Bogost's "unit operations," privilege parts—discrete elements of various sizes—over wholes. Here, as explained by architect Gilles Retsin, "[b]uilding elements understood as hierarchically equal, generic units have no function or meaning prior to assembly. Meaning and function become an emergent property of the interaction between parts." [103] The scale of such elements (and the corresponding resolution) varies greatly: from the light plastic components in Alisa Andrasek and Jose Sanchez's *Bloom* project [**Figure 8.36**], which invites children to play with (and continually reshape) a flexible structure; or the standard wooden battens assembled with metallic joints in the *Folly.age* prototype by Plethora Project [**Figure 8.37**]; to the larger prefabricated timber blocks in Retsin's *Tallinn Architecture Biennale Pavilion*, or in his *Real Virtuality* installation at the Royal Academy of Arts in London. [**Figure 8.38**] And while to different component scales correspond concomitant levels of adaptability and

[103] Gilles Retsin, "Digital Assemblies: From Craft to Automation," in *Discrete*, 43.

Figure 8.36 Alisa Andrasek and Jose Sanchez, *Bloom*, London, 2012.

Figure 8.37 Jose Sanchez (Plethora Project) with Diego Pinochet and Felipe Véliz, *Folly.age prototype*, 2018.

Figure 8.38 Gilles Retsin Architecture, *Real Virtuality*, Royal Academy, London, 2019. Photo by Studio NAARO.

participation—of openness—discrete buildings are *de facto* designed to undergo permutations, and to support waves of assembly and disassembly. Accordingly, wholes loosen up and parts, with their ability to take on a range of roles, "acquire autonomy and define a system or field condition that can stand independently" of them.[104] Such a field, of course, still corresponds with an ecology of inception.

From the perspective I have developed in this book, the autonomy of parts—of Retsin's generic timber blocks; of the windows and doors reused by Flores & Prats; of the rotor blades repurposed by Superuse Studios; of the granite paving blocks tracked by Jane Hutton; of the material stock in Rotor's showroom; et cetera—begins to point to a different way of designing and describing buildings, one that foregrounds the value of embodied materials and components and refuses to consign them to single EoIs or project functions.

As for the Discrete paradigm, questions remain concerning the possibility of integrating preexisting objects and materials; the over-engineering of building blocks; and the transferability of parts across proprietary ecologies and systems.

[104] Jose Sanchez, "Architecture for the Commons: Participatory Systems in the Age of Platforms," in *Discrete*, 25.

Chapter 9
Conclusion

9.1 Design Potentials

Gilles Deleuze and Félix Guattari famously describe philosophy as "the art of forming, inventing, and fabricating concepts."[1] Indeed, over the course of this book, I have introduced—coined, borrowed, diverted, and reclaimed—several familiar and unfamiliar terms, hoping that they might begin to frame or illuminate a different view (and practice) of design. Each chapter has dusted these terms with a few additional particles, allowing concepts to evolve and accrete, page by page, across sections—and with a degree of experimental eclecticism.[2]

This conclusion will not attempt to unify or paraphrase the tentative definitions provided along the way, to consign them to a definitive glossary, or to resolve tensions and paper over contradictions. Surely, much can be gained by leaving them open for further interpretation, debate, and development. It is, however, true that after each trade and phase of construction has deposited a layer of material on a job site, and the completed building finally comes into sight, a new set of encounters becomes possible—rooms fill with light, the smell of wet concrete recedes, and one's steps no longer echo. Therefore, I will take this opportunity to reassess key terms, walk around, and snap a few photographs.

The central concept this book proposes is that of ecology of inception (EoI), followed by the related ecology of suspension (EoS). These two poles—one relational, the other nonrelational—placed at the beginning and end of the text respectively, mark gravitational fields that bend the concepts in their respective orbit. Consequently, depending on their exact position within the text, some terms may have been defined in contrasting (and even conflicting) ways, and might only be grasped by acknowledging the longer trajectory they describe (and the gradual alterations they undergo) during the course of the book. One such term is potentiality, which at the beginning of the first chapter is characterized as dependent on—and as unlocked

1 Gilles Deleuze and Félix Guattari, *What Is Philosophy?* (New York: Columbia University Press, 1994), 2.

2 I am thinking here of the opening section of Graham Harman's *Tool-being*: "A philosophy is not a private introspective diary to which the philosopher has unique access. Better to think of it as a thought experiment, a process of smashing fragments of reality together to see what emerges." Graham Harman, *Tool-Being: Heidegger and the Metaphyics of Objects* (Chicago: Open Court, 2002), 5–6.

DOI: 10.4324/9781003015444-13

by—specific encounters (between objects, within a milieu, etc.) and towards the end is understood as existing independently, outside of any specific context or relation. These two versions of potentiality—simple (internal) and pure—and the transitions between them, must be further developed. In fact, I will attempt to demonstrate that both are, in their own terms, correct, and that they do not exclude one another.

Chapter 1 sets out to describe EoIs as machines (in an abstract Deleuzian sense) capable of releasing and channeling the powers of objects, placing them within enclosures that set a context or horizon for their activation and deactivation. This requires two assumptions: that powers are not inherent (that their unlocking depends on alliances, or at least that they can be activated relationally) and that they must always be specific (not powers in general, but powers to stand up, to play the violin, to set aflame, to roll, to sweat, and to be sliced). The first assumption subscribes to Bruno Latour's critique of potentiality, according to which the term merely confuses actors with the networks through which they gain their strength.[3] Like the Megarians before him, Latour holds that stuff simply is what it is, with nothing left in reserve or *in potentia*. As Harman remarks, for Latour "a thing is only here once it is here, not sooner. To make something become actual is [...] to assemble a wide range of actors that begin in separation."[4]

Attributing powers to individual actors ("the pianist can play") certainly obfuscates the chains of association and translation required for those potentials to emerge (the ability to play as attained through alliances between the pianist's brain, nervous system, and muscles; and the piano's keys, cast-iron frames, pivots, rods, rosettes, rockers, jacks, hammers, dampers, strings, soundboards, and pedals, to name a few). With Latour, I understand these ecologies of actors and their effects to be real and, indeed, actual. Yet, if Latour dismisses potency and his method chiefly *follows* networks and their distributed action,[5] I believe assemblages and translation/mediation protocols to be firstly a question of *design*. In other words: if all the human and nonhuman actants in a piano-playing ecology *can* indeed play, mustn't this emergent and collective ability be accounted for, particularly as it might be reproduced or withheld? Ecologies of inception aim to name and retain the notions of potentiality and impotentiality as functions of ecological coordination and entanglement, and as something that can be—and often is—designed.

The second assumption (that powers are always nameable; that they must be powers to do something specific, in a given context, and between definite actors) is developed by combining Latour's actualism with James J. Gibson's theory of affordances.[6] According to the latter, as briefly discussed in Chapter 3, the physical properties of the stuff in one's environment do not bear potentials (or have meaning) per se, but acquire them when measured "relative to the animal."[7] That is: the

3 Bruno Latour, *The Pasteurization of France*, trans. Alan Sheridan and John Law (Cambridge and London: Harvard University Press, 1988), 174.

4 Graham Harman, *Prince of Networks: Bruno Latour and Metaphysics* (Melbourne: re.press, 2009), 128.

5 He writes: "If we wish to be profound, we have to follow forces in their conspiracies and translations. We have to follow them, wherever they may go, and list their allies, however numerous and vulgar these may be." Latour, *The Pasteurization of France*, 188.

6 James J. Gibson, *The Ecological Approach to Visual Perception* (New York: Psychology Press, 2011).

7 Gibson, *The Ecological Approach*, 127.

term *affordance* allows Gibson to identify powers as relational—as not strictly assignable to either one object or another, but to their complementarity and capacity for interaction. He writes:

> If a terrestrial surface is nearly horizontal (instead of slanted), nearly flat (instead of convex or concave), and sufficiently extended (relative to the size of the animal) and if its substance is rigid (relative to the weight of the animal), then the surface affords support. It is a surface of support, and we can call it substratum, ground, or floor. It is stand-on-able, permitting upright posture for quadrupeds and bipeds. It is therefore walk-on-able and run-over-able. It is not sink-into-able like a surface of water or a swamp, that is, not for heavy terrestrial animals. Support for water bugs is different.[8]

8 Ibid.

Now, removed from a disciplinary context and focus (environmental psychology), and generalized to account for the multi-directional encounters between all manner of objects (rather than the sole interactions between animal and environment), the notion of affordance describes the possible *effective* exchanges between them, ones that both rely on communication (rather than on the properties of any one term) and may persist, *in potentia*, without being actualized. On one side, potentiality becomes fluid and nomadic—attributed to the interplay between objects, rather than to the objects themselves— and on the other, the actuality of each contributing term must be capable of communication, prior to any contact. Even if the interaction between the hand, key, hammer, and string is dormant, their independent physical reality is such that the piano key is press-on-able relative to the finger, the hammer is lift-up-able relative to the upwards movement of the key, and the string is hit-against-able relative to the felted surface of the hammer. In other words, the hand–key–hammer–string assemblage *can* play (has the ability to play) because the strength of the pressing finger can be transmitted across components and produce a sound[9]—because the required translation protocols are already embodied and embedded within their individual and reciprocal (piano-wide) configurations. [**Figure 9.1**] Here, actuality and potentiality can no longer be assumed to be mutually exclusive or elusive, but appear to be interdependent and coproduced.

9 Indeed, the assemblage considered could be more expansive, including musical scripts, neurons, sound waves, human ears, and so on.

Ecologies of Inception may therefore be described as instruments for the tuning of powers—for the invention, fabrication, and continuation of affordances. In this sense, potentiality is not a mysterious ground hidden within objects (the ghost of an oak tree within the acorn), but the ability of actual forms (of acorns, cogs, hammers, strings, routers, cells, elephants, and savannas) to communicate with other actual forms. Yet, how does one know whether communication is effective? And what does "effective" mean in this context? For Latour, claiming

Figure 9.1 Exposed piano mechanisms, Pianodrome, 2018. Photograph by Chris Scott.

that "Pasteur is *designing* an actor" is to say that he "designs trials for the actor to show its mettle." He continues:

> [w]hy is an actor defined through trials? Because there is no other way to define an actor but through its action, and there is no other way to define an action but by asking what other actors are modified, transformed, perturbed, or created by the character that is the focus of attention."[10]

If, following Latour, one might assess interactions on the basis of their effects—and recognize the ability to play only when hearing music—in the context of design, music will in a sense precede the act of playing, and the "effectiveness" of outputs will strictly measure their compliance with sets of intended results. While all manner of relations and actualizations take place without being labeled, sanctioned, described, or witnessed (e.g., between atoms; between tectonic plates; between birds and tree branches; between oceanic microplastics and pathogenic bacteria; et cetera), ecologies of inception identify and name effects and outputs *in advance* (an ecology of felting, and ecology of shoe-making, and ecology of ironing, an ecology of telling time, and so on). It is only by identifying the sound of Franz Schubert's *Piano Sonata in G major* (a goal), that the work required to manufacture and play a piano can begin. Or, put

10 Bruno Latour, *Pandora's Hope: Essays on the Reality of Science Studies* (Cambridge: Harvard University Press, 1999), 122.

differently, you must know what a piano sounds like before making one. Or again, an ecology of piano manufacturing is successful in potentializing its components (in formatting them towards one another) only if their encounter yields an apposite interaction—only if the head felt hits the corresponding string with just the right amount of force.

Gilbert Ryle, whose work I touched on in Chapter 6, contributes important nuances to the present discussion, and deserves quoting at length. He writes:

> When we describe glass as brittle, or sugar as soluble, we are using dispositional concepts, the logical force of which is this. The brittleness of glass does not consist in the fact that it is at a given moment actually being shivered. It may be brittle without ever being shivered. To say that it is brittle is to say that if it ever is, or ever had been, struck or strained, it would fly, or have flown, into fragments. To say that sugar is soluble is to say that it would dissolve, or would have dissolved, if immersed in water. A statement ascribing a dispositional property to a thing has much, though not everything, in common with a statement subsuming a thing under a law. To possess a dispositional property is not to be in a particular state, or to undergo a particular change; it is to be bound or liable to be in a particular state, or to undergo a particular change, when a particular condition is realised.[11]

11 Gilbert Ryle, *The Concept of Mind* (London and New York: Routledge, 2009), 31.

Contra Latour and the Megarians, and with Aristotle, Ryle recognizes that the brittleness of glass perdures even in the absence of the corresponding (shattering) effects—or, that the ability to play does not automatically or necessarily result in music being played. "A disposition," he writes, "is a factor of the wrong logical type to be seen or unseen, recorded or unrecorded."[12] Dispositions are not potentials in an Aristotelian or hylomorphic sense: they are both already actualized (the sheet of glass as a fully individuated object here and now) and oriented (its brittleness relying on the horizon of a specific condition or encounter). And while dispositions can of course emerge without human design or intercession, EoIs function precisely by installing objects within the networks by which they will be *bound*, both in the sense of being "under a law" or enclosed (from the Old English *bindan*, to bind or make captive) and in that of being bound to "be in a particular state, or to undergo a particular change" (from the Middle English *boun*, meaning prepared or intending to do something). As Aristotle understood, being ready to play is not the same as actually playing—a difference designers cannot ignore.

12 Ryle, *The Concept of Mind*, 22.

Yet Ryle's treatment of dispositions is also relevant to this project because it steers it clear of the oversimplifications EoIs might otherwise suggest or imply. "There are many dispositions," he writes, "the actualisations of which can take a wide and perhaps unlimited variety

13 Ibid., 32.

of shapes; many disposition-concepts are determinable concepts."[13] He continues:

> When an object is described as hard, we do not mean only that it would resist deformation; we mean also that it would, for example, give out a sharp sound if struck, that it would cause us pain if we came into sharp contact with it, that resilient objects would bounce off it, and so indefinitely.[14]

14 Ibid.

In other words: even if design can be said to lock objects into set dispositional horizons—the chair as an object to sit on, with a dormant relation to human buttocks and thighs—many levels of determination (in the sense coined by W. E. Johnson, according to whom, for example, the terms "color" and "shape" are *determinables* in relation to the terms "red" and "circular," which are *determinates*)[15] may be adopted, avoiding narrow teleologies of use, or the mere execution of scripts.[16]

15 William Ernest Johnson, *Logic* (Cambridge University Press, 2014). Quoted in: Jessica Wilson, "Determinables and Determinates," ed. Edward N. Zalta, *The Stanford Encyclopedia of Philosophy*, Spring 2017.

16 When applied to design, the difference between determinables and determinates (the ability to shift from one to the other) might facilitate looser protocols for the articulation of design intentions, and for specifying materials and their performance.

Objects can occupy a wide range of coordinates within the determinable/determinate spectrum, attaining different degrees of openness and heterogeneity, and often traveling some distance from the limited preconditions and rigid assumptions that prompted their design or defined their primary use: a floor built to be walk-on-able is also dance-on-able, jump-on-able, roll-on-able; as much as the exclusive mechanical alliance between piano keys, hammers, and strings must follow a rigid operational script (K moves H, H hits S), their sum total also affords playability in general, and a high degree of freedom in the exploration of musical composition and interpretation; a human mouth evolved for breathing and eating also recites poems, sings and kisses passionately; sugar may dissolve in other (non-water-based) polar liquids; and so forth. That is: dispositions can, intentionally and unintentionally, be larger than the associated *teloi* or unlocking conditions, in the same way that boundary objects, discussed in Chapter 3, might be "plastic enough to adapt to local needs and the constraints of the several parties employing them."[17]

17 Susan Leigh Star and James R. Griesemer, "Institutional Ecology, 'Translations' and Boundary Objects: Amateurs and Professionals in Berkeley's Museum of Vertebrate Zoology, 1907-39," *Social Studies of Science* 19, no. 3 (1989), 393.

It is not by chance that, in Chapter 5, the notion of plasticity formed the basis for a rethinking of *tabula rasa* as a figure of potentiality, substituting a privileged potentializing relation (blankness; a formatting protocol; a content) with looser sets of conditions that facilitate a range of configurations (the malleability of the wax; a medium). Here, format and medium represented two models for the generation and preservation of potentials: the former operating by exclusion/rejection, the latter by inclusion/annexation; the former hardening and naturalizing ecological boundaries, the latter softening and destabilizing them. To be sure, the two are often codependent—it is because of the piano's meticulous technical assembly that one can play Chopin, or compose a sonata; and, likewise, the spontaneous powers of the bricoleur's stock are in part guaranteed by the narrow reliability of her tools.

Consequently, to be plastic is not to lack method, discipline, or know-how, or to reject formats and scripts, but to avoid their ossification—to deny their claims to purity and truth (e.g., a *proper* identity or use). Powers are not only about gaining more strength, or the ability to act and actualize, but also about dismantling and undoing (Ahmed's queer use; Bataille's formless), weakening, and withholding action (Bartleby's refusals). Potency does not privilege relation or nonrelation, but their continual dance.

9.2 Nonrelational Potentials

Up to this point, and across the first chapters of the book, I have defended a relational view that, somewhat paradoxically, locates potentials not at the heart of actual objects—as secret prefigurations and foreshadowings—but in their present ability to interact. At the same time, however, it transpired that relations are only one side of the story—there is always something left in reserve. I first encountered glimmers of nonrelationality, although not in so many words, in Chapter 1, when noticing that, while powers are indeed unlocked by relations, if the same object can acquire different powers or degrees of potency vis-à-vis specific *relata* or milieus, there must be more to the object than what is, at any time, relationally expressed or activated, either *in potentia* or *in actu*.

In Chapter 2, the introduction of impotentiality reframed potency as both capacity to do and to not do, to act and to withhold action. Nonrelationality was no longer just the flip side of the relational coin, or what relations leave over, but a fundamental ingredient in the recipe for the activation of powers: without it, potentiality would automatically pass into actuality. Following Agamben, I considered how impotentiality might survive actuality, both as the ability to suspend specific relations and as the potential for new ones to emerge. Accordingly, a crucial distinction was proposed: that between external or extrinsic impotentiality (the inability of disparate objects to communicate) and internal or intrinsic impotentiality (the privation or suspension of specific—and already actualized—communication channels). I contend that design must engage with both, aiming not only to modify objects so that they may communicate and attain the goals associated with EoIs, but also to address (and pay attention to) their suspension and possible new roles—the strange, transversal landscapes of EoSs.

Graham Harman charges the actualism of Latour and the Megarians with the inability to explain change. And whereas Aristotle resolved this problem by resorting to the potential, Harman affirms the need for a nonrelational actual. He writes:

> The problem is not that they [Latour and the Megarians] defend the actual over the potential, but that *they identify the actual with the relational*. Only a non-relational version of actuality (and not potentiality, which is relational through and through) can explain change or movement.[18]

[18] Harman, *Prince of Networks*, 130.

And again: "things must be partially separated from their mutual articulations. If this were not the case, they would never be able to enter new propositions."[19]

Now, considering these passages with the above discussion in mind, one might easily agree with the need to invest potentiality with a dose of actuality—to attribute dispositional capacities to actual forms, rather than to their ghostly projections. It is equally difficult not to recognize that the notions of nonrelationality and withdrawal, as articulated by object-oriented philosophy and discussed in Chapters 6 and 8, contribute a useful supplement to design theory and practice, both foregrounding the way in which things exceed our engagement (and, importantly, *any* engagement) with them, and demanding a vigorously detaxonomizing ethos. To understand objects as "partially separated from their mutual articulations" is to understand design as a radically partial and collaborative undertaking; to see it reconfigure and rearticulate objects across uses, users, and generations; and to definitively neutralize the hylomorphic bias against forms. Yet, if I can join Harman in inviting designers to engage with a measure of withdrawal, I cannot readily dismiss potentiality as "relational through and through." The investigations developed in this book show that a higher degree of resolution is required.

Firstly, by locating powers in actual forms (e.g., the blade's ability to cut through skin), one must grant that their *effective* existence no longer depends on direct outcomes or actualizations (e.g., on the spillage of blood), but may either produce effects or not, remaining, however, bound to do so (prompting, for instance, the careful handling of knives, or the manufacturing of leather sheaths). Furthermore, a nonrelational supplement (impotentiality) is already active within capacities, and it is this additive that allows potentials to go dormant (to suspend or withhold further actualizations) without renouncing a dispositional interior. Accordingly, an absolute separation between withdrawn (nonrelational) and sensual (relational) objects runs the risks of preempting a finer-grain inquiry into the collaborations, interdependencies, and modulations involved in their interaction—ones that the notion of impotentiality can address, for example, by articulating the difference between pure, external, and internal states.

Secondly, through the figure of the *rasura tabulae*, I have come to understand potency as predicated not on the mere expression or repression of contents—on relating, withholding relation, or not relating at all—but on the ability to switch across relational modes and positions; or to administer and mix them in a variety of dosages and combinations. Whereas internal and external impotentialities (or simple potentialities) do indeed depend on relations (they must declare in advance the terms that they connect or disconnect), pure potency describes an object's very ability to change (its autonomous plasticity; the malleable layer of wax on the wooden tablet). In Chapter 8, I have referred to this plasticity as the *wandering metaphysical surface* of objects, and developed the notion of *dynamic withdrawal* to designate the work involved in the objects' production and destruction of surfaces (of sensual objects) in response to localized contexts and stimuli. This might resemble the way that my core (naked, mostly not visible) body wears different layers of clothing or extensions in response to weather conditions or activities—layers that both conceal the body's biochemical assemblages and are shaped/articulated by them. Or perhaps it is more akin to the secretions (sweat, tears, etc.) produced by invisible and receding (and yet actual/real) glands. That is: pure potentiality is not a generic or universal potency, but one defined and constrained by the object's actuality.

Why, then, not merely do away with pure potentiality and replace it with a "non-relational version of actuality," as Harman suggests? Because a nonrelational actuality is, like a relational one, unable to explain change. It is only by positing the existence of a machine for the translation of nonrelation into relation (and vice versa) that objects can escape fixed positions, and remain neither fully concealed nor fully deployed, but able to oscillate between partial states. Pure potentiality is therefore not an ontological state comparable or complementary with actuality—in the same way that simple potentialities are—but an engine powering surface agitations, conversions, and local exchanges. Again, this is not the teleological ghost of the oak tree within the acorn, or a collection of as-yet-unexpressed properties and capacities (of potential local manifestations that are infinite because, as Levi Bryant notes, "there is no limit to the exo-relations an object can enter into"),[20] but the very mechanism that allows for the object's withdrawal to be dynamic—to translate between (and negotiate) relational and nonrelational states. If an object is a collection of withdrawn structures (organs that, like the stomachs and intestines in the glorious body discussed in Chapter 7, are fully actualized and yet fully inoperative), pure potentiality is not a blank canvas of infinite possibilities, but the mechanism whereby an object reconfigures its organs, floating them to the surface, and thus making them operative. Simple potentiality is, instead, the mere expression of the capacities thus activated.

20 Levi R. Bryant, *The Democracy of Objects* (Ann Arbor: Open Humanities Press, 2011), 121.

9.3 Ecologies of Inception and Ecologies of Suspension

Over the course of this book, ecologies of inception and ecologies of suspension have been re-formulated repeatedly, to converse with (and adjust to) a variety of contiguous terms and discourses—both gaining precision and resolution, and allowing for a degree of openness, and for responsive calibrations. Instead of ironing over the biases and framings implicit in the different accounts given—or over their nuances—I will recapitulate my key arguments, and describe how EoIs and EoSs fare in relation to the neighboring concepts encountered along the way.

I should note that these terms have, in my research, emerged with a degree of self-determination; not as ideas to be affirmed and justified, but as tools to grapple with (and think through) the question of the relationship between design and powers, and the ways in which such a relation is both structured and limited by a technical *tabula rasa*. It is only within the framework of this question that EoIs can be first articulated, or must be articulated, as potentializing enclosures, or as the territories within which potentials can become and remain active (in a dispositional sense).

9.3.1 Equipment

One of the first terms adopted and diverted to develop EoIs is equipment (*das Zeug*), with which Heidegger denotes that which one encounters in their practical dealings with chairs, planes, buoys, and pianos.[21] For the German philosopher, equipment is "given to us primarily in the unity of an *equipmental whole*, a unity that constantly varies in range, expanding or contracting" as one goes about their lives.[22] Even as one comes across and recognizes individual pieces of equipment (equipment for sitting, flying, keeping afloat, or playing music), these remain trapped within an order of significance that precedes them, and woven into a larger "totality" or "contexture"—or, as Harman puts it, "fused into a colossal web of meaning."[23]

In addition to this immersion within a vast system of references, tools are largely perceived through what Heidegger calls *circumspection* (*Umsicht*)—a special kind of "action-oriented" sight that subordinates them to their usability.[24] When one draws, for example, they hardly think of (or pay attention to) the pencil in their hand. Only when the graphite core suddenly snaps between their fingers—when the equipmental fabric momentarily tears—does the pencil come into view as present-at-hand. Therefore, the equipmental character of objects (or, more accurately, of the way one ordinarily apprehends them as ready-to-hand) is such that they are always either "in-order-to" do something (assignment) or "in-terms-of" other pieces of equipment (reference).

Now, if one turns their attention to ecologies of inception—to the way in which design unlocks or installs simple potentials—one will find striking similarities. Firstly, as discussed above, objects (for instance, a pencil) are necessarily potentialized *in relation to* other objects ("in-terms-of" hands, paper, sharpeners, erasers, desks, and so forth) and *with a functional purpose* in view ("in-order-to" draw). Secondly, both equipment and EoIs are necessarily hylomorphic, understanding production as the formation and organization of matter.[25] Elaborating on the difference between pieces of equipment (which use up matter) and works of art (which bring forth its earthly character), Heidegger writes:

> Because it is determined by usefulness and serviceability, equipment takes into its service that of which it consists: the matter. In fabricating equipment—e.g., an ax—stone is used, and used up.

21 Martin Heidegger, *Being and Time*, trans. John Macquarrie and Edward Robinson (Oxford: Basil Blackwell, 1962), 97.

22 Martin Heidegger, *The Basic Problems of Phenomenology*, trans. Albert Hofstadter (Bloomington: Indiana University Press, 1982), 163. Italics in the original.

23 Graham Harman, *Heidegger Explained: From Phenomenon to Thing* (Chicago: Open Court, 2007), 63.

24 Heidegger, *Being and Time*, 99.

25 Heidegger writes: "The currently predominant thing–concept, thing as formed matter, is not even derived from the essence of the thing but from the essence of equipment." Martin Heidegger, "The Origin of the Work of Art," in *Basic Writings: From Being and Time (1927) to The Task of Thinking (1964)*, ed. David Farrell Krell (San Francisco: HarperSanFrancisco, 1993), 163.

It disappears into usefulness. The material is all the better and more suitable the less it resists vanishing in the equipmental being of the equipment.[26]

26 Heidegger, "The Origin of the Work of Art," 170.

This disappearing act coincides with a technical *tabula rasa* and, more generally, with the violence exerted by ecological scripts. Moreover, the need to continuously comply with the latter—to continue to *properly* function—identifies the third point of overlap between equipment and EoIs: reliability. One wears shoes (or considers the shoes to be effective pieces of equipment) precisely because they can take for granted what shoes are and their ability to protect their feet from the dampness of soil, or the sharpness of gravel.[27] Yet, if for Heidegger reliability allows equipment, in its essence, to articulate the relation between world (a pragmatic system of references) and earth (the receding thingness of things), it also marks the limit or threshold between use and disuse, tools and mere stuff: "A single piece of equipment is worn out and used up," he writes, "but at the same time the use itself also falls into disuse, wears away [...]. Thus equipmentality wastes away, sinks into mere stuff. In such wasting, reliability vanishes."[28] But where might one find the boundary that, in the name of reliability, separates equipment from stuff, and useable tools from material discards? How might one approach this zone and begin to understand the transitions it negotiates and oversees?

27 Ibid., 157–58.

28 Ibid., 160.

The primary differences between EoIs and equipment begin to come into view. Even as the notion of equipment articulates a system of references that is constitutive of design as a potentializing practice (of its focus on use and operation; of the establishment of translation protocols between and across objects and parts), it remains too vague to actually engage with it. Certainly, Heidegger's predilection for phenomenology—Dasein as the horizon of all equipmental meaning—poses a first difficulty, as references will deceivingly bundle around human existence, forgetting or ignoring the relations between (other) objects.

The second difficulty has to do with the lack of an intermediate scale or unit, one capable of bridging the gap between individual pieces of equipment and the equipmental contexture within which they are suspended. In other words: whereas the latter is too large to be addressed with any degree of precision, the former is too small. Besides, from a design perspective, speaking of a piece of equipment does not contribute additional resolution or information about the individual tool—indeed, they are one and the same. Ecologies of inception must therefore occupy the intermediary position between the hammer, window, or classroom, and the contexture in which they participate, translating Heidegger's insights into conceptual tools that designers can use.

I have thus identified the main distinction between EoIs and pieces of equipment: while the boundaries of the latter match the edges of the tool, those of the former do not—an ecology of hammering is resolutely not a hammer. Rather, its edges, fuzzy as they may be, identify

Conclusion

reliability as a kind of territory, one that bounds an interior ecology within which objects can roam and communicate. In this configuration, and across a thick ecological perimeter, not only can one track objects as they lose or gain their equipmental status; one can also assign or identify detailed roles and relative positions (matter, form, herders, shearers, sheep, et cetera).

Heidegger's equipmentality also informs the notion of ecology of suspension. Ontological difference (the Heideggerian leitmotif that separates being from beings, the ontological from the ontic, concealment from unconcealment, etc.) compels one to consider the readiness-to-hand of the piece of equipment vis-à-vis its un-readiness-to-hand—the unusable tool that suddenly becomes conspicuous and "reveals itself as something just present-at-hand and no more."[29] The holistic unity of equipment suddenly cracks and, in so doing, it reveals an extra-equipmental dimension or excess (one that, in its radical OOO reinterpretation, attests to the withdrawn—and Dasein-independent—reality of objects). Introducing ecologies of suspension in Chapter 6, I wished to address and name this extra-ecological surplus—not to peer into a withdrawn reality that resists access, but to investigate what lies beyond EoIs in the sensual realm. It is here that I discovered the gaps between equipmental enclosures, those that designs leave over and forget—spaces akin to what Gilles Clément calls "the third landscape."[30]

Clément—a landscape architect, writer, and horticultural engineer—describes it as the "*undecided* fragment of the planetary garden," the sum of all the places that resist (or have been forsaken after) human exploitation.[31] He writes, not without a dose of Heideggerianism:

> If we cease to regard the landscape as an industrial object [*comme l'objet d'une industrie*] we discover [...] a number of spaces that are undecided and devoid of function, to which it is difficult to assign a name. This collection [*ensemble*] belongs neither in the realm of shadows nor in that of light. It is situated at the margins.[32]

A wide variety of microorganisms, animal and plant species find refuge in these liminal terrains. Biodiversity flourishes, wielding heterogeneity, chaos, and uncertainty against the unifying claims and organizing rhythms of equipment.[33] On a finite planet (one constrained by biophysical limits), the third landscape stands as a bastion of difference—a reserve of "planetary genetic configurations" that safeguard the future of biology and its powers of invention.[34]

Ecologies of suspension tread a similar ground, separating objects (landscapes, broken hammers, discarded rotor blades, etc.) from equipmental scripts or, rather, asserting their value apart from use, intentions, results, or effects. The lesson I learn from Clément's third landscape is therefore not, for now, that all materials can eventually renew forms of equipmental compliance (that discarded rubber tires and

29 Heidegger, *Being and Time*, 103.

30 The phrase is inspired by the political pamphlet "What Is the Third Estate?", in which Emmanuel Joseph Sieyès argued that the third estate (the common people) should replace the first and second estates (the clergy and aristocracy) in the political ordering of France.

31 Gilles Clément, *Manifeste Du Tiers Paysage*, Online, 2004, 1–3. My translation, italicized in the original. See also Gilles Clément et al., *The Planetary Garden: And Other Writings* (Philadelphia: University of Pennsylvania Press, 2015).

32 Clément, *Manifeste du Tiers Paysage*, 4. My translation.

33 "A Pangea (a unified continent)," notes Clément, "welcomes fewer species than several separate continents." Ibid., 7.

34 Ibid., 10.

246

milk cartons can become resources), or that they can do so by tuning in to different ecological frequencies, but that the attribution of value in ecologies of suspension should rely on the mere deferral of goals and orientations—on the recognition and collective affirmation of the object's bare existence.

9.3.2 Assemblage

Gilles Deleuze defines assemblages (*agèncements*) as multiplicities composed of heterogeneous terms and arranged according to a "co-functioning."[35] He writes:

> Take an assemblage of the type man–animal–manufactured object: MAN–HORSE–STIRRUP. [...] This is a new man-animal symbiosis, a new assemblage of war, defined by its degree of power or "freedom," its affects, its circulation of affects: what a set of bodies is capable of. Man and the animal enter into a new relationship.[36]

Following this passage, and despite their considerably narrower scope, EoIs would clearly fit the designation of assemblage, coordinating, as they do, diverse sets of actors toward common functions and new collective powers (ecologies of horse riding, of glass blowing, of plastering, et cetera).

Now, according to Deleuze, the man–horse–stirrup assemblage is not the immediate result of a technological invention (the stirrup), but rather mediated by "a social machine or collective assemblage" that unlocks its viability and widespread use (in this case, land grants associated with feudalism).[37] Similarly, EoIs exist within larger ecologies that prepare and contextualize their activation or invention, as well as maintain and protect their continued operation. *More* ecologies are always entangled with—nested in, propping up, intersecting, or comprising—the ones under consideration, often remaining unseen or taken for granted. In other words: EoIs draw boundaries not only by establishing the parameters used to determine ecological compliance—and by rejecting noncompliant items and behaviors—but by submitting them to processes of supra-ecological reference and validation.

Yet, if these references form a Heideggerian "totality of equipment," how does one think about (or draw) their boundaries? One might imagine them as the space between two envelopes: one expanding outwards and leaning on external objects; the other contracting into precise dioramas. It would then be possible to measure the edge of EoIs (their width) by determining the distance between their ecological and supra-ecological equipmentalities. Indeed, this complicates notions of *inside* and *outside*: if towards the innermost envelope these relative positions can be straightforwardly identified, as one moves towards the periphery, they become hazy and increasingly difficult to pinpoint.

35 Gilles Deleuze and Claire Parnet, *Dialogues*, trans. Hugh Tomlinson and Barbara Habberjam (New York: Columbia University Press, 1987), 69.

36 Deleuze and Parnet, *Dialogues*, 69–70.

37 Ibid., 70. Deleuze and Guattari write in *A Thousand Plateaus*: "Even technology makes the mistake of considering tools in isolation: tools exist only in relation to the interminglings they make possible or that make them possible. The stirrup entails a new man–horse symbiosis that at the same time entails new weapons and new instruments. [...] a society is defined by its amalgamations, not by its tools." Gilles Deleuze and Félix Guattari, *A Thousand Plateaus: Capitalism and Schizophrenia*, trans. Brian Massumi (Minneapolis: University of Minnesota Press, 1987), 90.

38 Deleuze and Parnet, *Dialogues*, 70.

39 Ibid., 70–71.

Returning to assemblages, Deleuze reminds the reader that they combine *effectuation* (machinic assemblages; bodies that "interpenetrate, mix together, transmit affects to one another")[38] and *enunciation* (collective assemblages; "regimes of utterances: signs [...] organized in a new way, new formulations [...] new gestures [...]").[39] That is to say, the interactions between objects (the increased lateral stability of the horse-riding knight; the transmission of forces from feet to stirrup to saddle) would not be as relevant without a corresponding—and collective—reorganization of signs (e.g., the knight's emblems, "the juridical regime of heraldry," oaths, and codes of conduct).[40]

40 Deleuze and Guattari, *A Thousand Plateaus*, 89.

Now, how are these linguistic or expressive regimes accounted for in EoIs? In order to respond, I will revisit and clarify two terms introduced in Chapters 1 and 6 respectively: codes and thresholds. The first one is taken directly from assemblage theory. Here, coding refers, following DeLanda, "to the role played by language in fixing the identity of a social whole," such as the rituals and regulations that are put in place to legitimize authority structures.[41] In the context of EoIs, I have described decoding and recoding mechanisms as the discursive operations needed to implement a technical *tabula rasa*, both in the transition from natural objects to culturalized materials (from *tree* to *timber*) and in the transformation from matter to form (from *timber* to *plank*). In a more general sense, coding refers to the expressive operations associated with the *proper* functioning of EoIs, either through inward-facing protocols (e.g., workflows, schedules, specialized jargon, internal policies, regulations, charts) or outward-facing broadcasts (e.g., advertisements, branding, user manuals, certifications, lifecycle assessments).

41 Manuel DeLanda, *Deleuze: History and Science* (New York: Atropos, 2010), 13.

I have used the second term—*threshold*—to identify the steps that precede coding. Before a *cow* can become *beef*, a collective translation apparatus (customs, values, laws) must have ripened, allowing for the cow to be viewed as meat-reserve, and for its killing to be classified as slaughter and not murder. If one were to situate these operations alongside the thick ecological border identified above, one would find that codes graze the ecology's innermost envelope, and are curated from within, while thresholds stretch towards its outermost limits, exposing it to a socio-historical world beyond. In any case, what the doubling of ecological boundaries makes clear is that EoIs (and, by extension, design) can never be preoccupied with just one layer—both have to be considered, engaged with, and wrought (although not necessarily by designing things).

I must now consider what Deleuze and Guattari call territorialization, or rather the processes that, through deterritorializations and reterritorializations, stabilize or destabilize boundaries, increasing or decreasing an aggregate's degree of organization and homogeneity.[42] Following DeLanda, I am not going to use this term to separate rigid aggregates (strata) from supple ones (assemblages), but as

42 Deleuze and Guattari, *A Thousand Plateaus*, 88.

a tool for measuring the degree to which constellations in general are segmented, or subject to relations of interiority.[43] I introduced cycles of deterritorialization and reterritorialization in Chapter 1 to describe the operations in a technical *tabula rasa*, which both undo and reassign boundaries (from tree to log; from forest to lorry) and rewire the associated networks (from solar energy, mineral nutrients, and mycorrhizal webs, to timber trusses, purlins, and rafters). The use of the prefixes *de-* and *re-* helpfully evokes a persistent and continually shifting physical substrate, one where "what is deterritorialized is not just what comes before what is territorialized."[44] In addition, the philosophers' emphasis on relations of exteriority suggests, in the context of this book, a shift from the design of wholes to the design of components that can be easily reused, assembled, disassembled, and moved from one ecology to the next. [**Figures 9.2–9.4**] The future of design, as imagined here, is one in which parts survive their relations of interiority or, better yet, one in which the survival of components (e.g., bricks, window frames, toilet bowls, screws, wall panels, glass bottles, and computer chips) is valued more than either relations of interiority or relations of exteriority—one in which an object's value (as an embodiment of labor, energy, and carbon) is not subordinated to relations.

To be clear, when discussing EoIs, *relations of interiority* designate the performance of an equipmental role or script—the relations that contribute to the emergence of an ecological whole. Instead, with the phrase *relations of exteriority* I refer to the roles that components take up autonomously, or to relations that are independent of (external to) a native ecological enclosure. Within the second type, one must further differentiate between *relations of interior exteriority* and *relations of exterior exteriority*. This verbose addition is useful to distinguish between parts that enter new relations by maintaining their previous role and ecological identity (the tire moved from car A to car B) and those that enter new relations by disregarding their previous role (the tire turned into roofing surface and gutter, or into post-consumer leather). [**Figures 9.5 + 9.6**]

These differences notwithstanding, and as already discussed in Chapters 4 and 6, another striking feature of EoIs and of their strange boundaries is the fact that they are not mere constellations of synchronous parts, or separable from the historical life of their components—nor is their emergence neatly zoned according to the abstract outlines or deliberate effects of a here-and-now whole. An ecology of

[43] DeLanda, *Deleuze: History and Science*, 103.

[44] Ibid., 105.

Figure 9.2 Flores & Prats, *Sala Beckett*, Barcelona, Spain, 2016. Reconditioning existing windows, and reusing existing carpentry fragments to fabricate new ones. Photographs by Judith Casas.

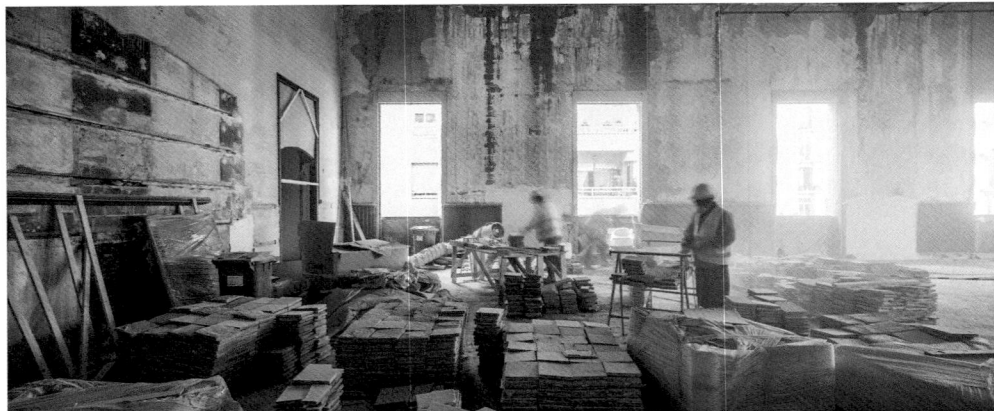

Figure 9.3 Flores & Prats, *Sala Beckett*, Barcelona, Spain, 2016. Dismantling and storing existing floor tiles. Photograph by Adrià Goula.

Figure 9.4 Anupama Kundoo architects, *Volontariat Homes for Homeless Children*, Pondicherry, India, 2008–10. Glass bottles used as structural units for masonry.

Figures 9.5 + 9.6 Refunc in cooperation with Architecture Sans Frontières UK (ASF-UK), *Fringerator*, England, 2010.

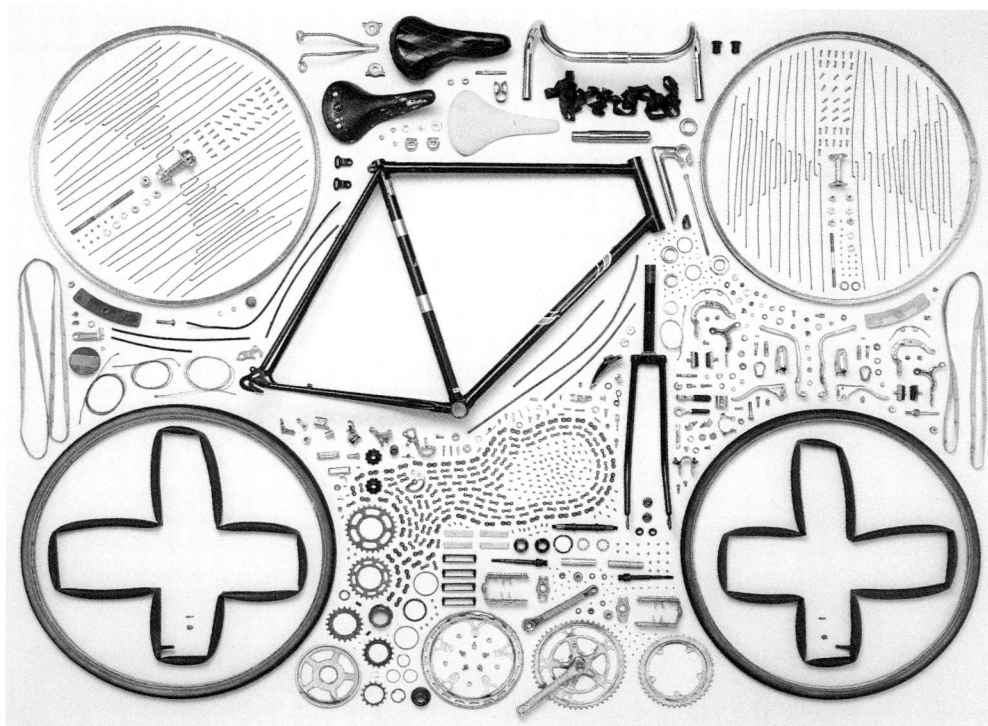

Figure 9.7 Todd McLellan, *Things Come Apart*, Disassembled Bicycle, 2013.

biking, for example, is not just a bicycle, a human–bike–road assemblage, or a collection of bike parts—not even one as neatly displayed as those in Todd McLellan's photographic series.[45] **[Figure 9.7]** It encompasses the material trajectories of each component, from the mining of bauxite ore to the extraction of latex sap, from the extrusion and welding of aluminum parts to the vulcanization of rubber, from the expansion of polyurethane shells to the gluing of microfibre seat coverings—across people, geographies, petrochemicals, supply chains, and seasons.

An example of what an EoI, in this extended material sense, might entail, or of what sensibilities it might invite, is offered by designer Thomas Thwaites. As a student at the Royal College of Art in London, Thwaites set out to build an electric toaster from scratch—by himself and using only preindustrial tools and methods.[46] **[Figures 9.8-9.10]** Under the assumption that a low cost would correspond to fewer parts, he selected the cheapest electric toaster on the market (costing only £3.94) and attempted the impossible task of reverse-engineering it, remaking (in principle) its 404 components.[47] **[Figure 9.11]** His close encounters with iron ore, mica, propylene, copper, and nickel yielded an unorthodox (and not particularly reliable) toaster, yet the project

45 Todd McLellan, *Things Come Apart 2.0: A Teardown Manual for Modern Living* (London: Thames & Hudson, 2019).

46 Thomas Thwaites, *The Toaster Project: Or a Heroic Attempt to Build a Simple Electric Appliance from Scratch* (New York: Princeton Architectural Press, 2011).

47 Thwaites, *The Toaster Project*, 19.

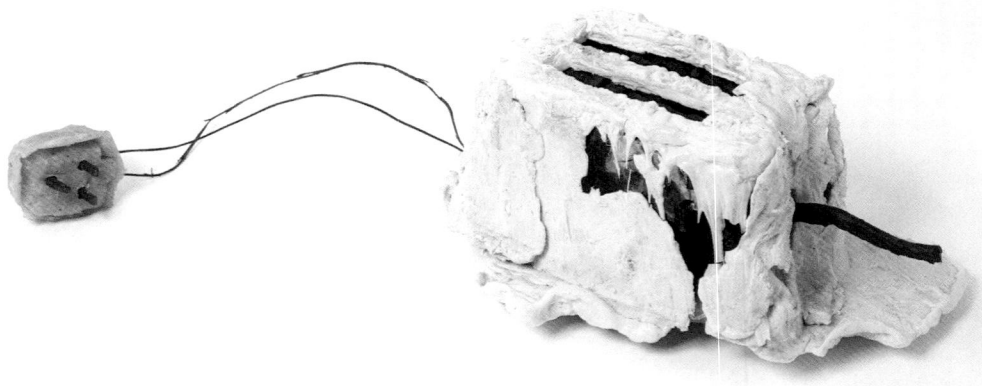

Figures 9.8 + 9.9 Thomas Thwaites, *The Toaster Project*, 2010. Photographs by Daniel Alexander.

is exemplary for its ability to question consumer expectations, and to communicate the staggering gap between the appliance's cost (what Annie Leonard calls an "impossibly low price tag")[48] and the complex, environmentally destructive, and carbon-intensive combination of raw materials, labor, and technical processes required to build it. Thwaites writes:

> £3.94 for a toaster that is entirely made from stuff that a few months ago was rocks and sludge distributed in giant holes all over the world, then brought together in an elaborate series of processes and exchanges, gradually assembled by many people, wrapped, and boxed and then somehow shipped to that shop, which is heated and lit and has people being paid to assist you in your purchase: Somehow £3.94 for all of this doesn't seem to quite add up.[49]

48 Annie Leonard and Ariane Conrad, *The Story of Stuff: How Our Obsession with Stuff Is Trashing the Planet, Our Communities, and Our Health – and a Vision for Change* (London: Constable, 2010), 16.

49 Thwaites, *The Toaster Project*, 170.

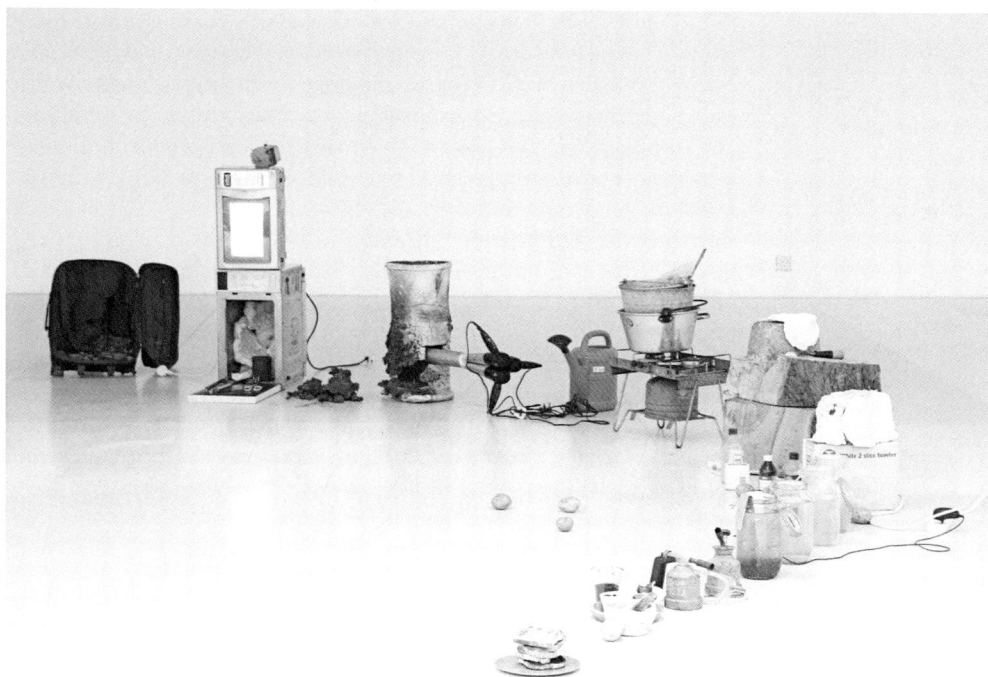

Figure 9.10 Thomas Thwaites, *The Toaster Project*, 2010. Photograph by Nick Ballon.

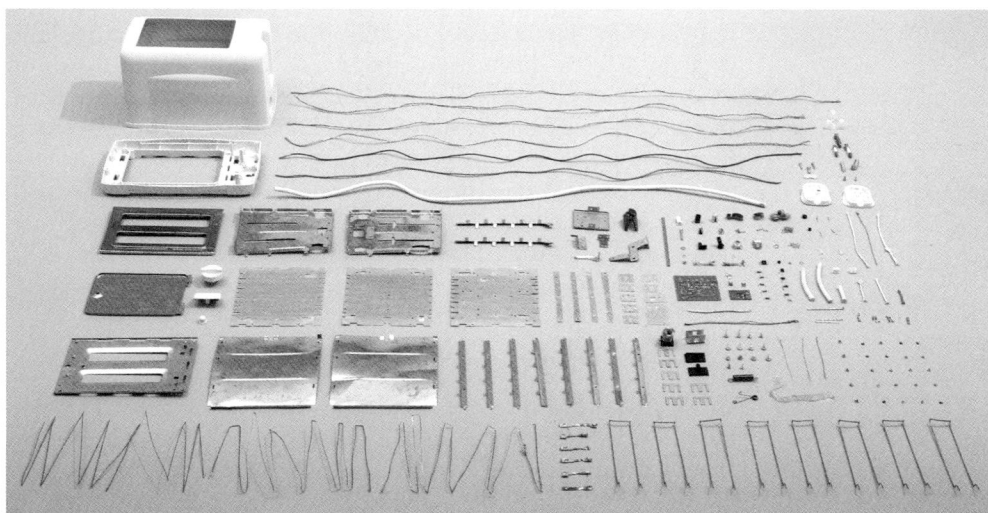

Figure 9.11 Thomas Thwaites, *The Toaster Project*, 2010. Photograph by Daniel Alexander. Deconstructed toaster.

The project raises many important questions: is toasting bread really worth it? Are all the other cheap appliances and gadgets in *our* lives necessary? And who ends up paying the price for their toxic and environmentally damaging extraction, production, distribution, consumption, and disposal? Yet, *The Toaster Project* also provides a hopeful glimpse into what it means for designers to consider the production and sourcing of materials (and the associated responsibilities) as coextensive with their projects. Furthermore, Thwaites' toaster, with its poorly melted plastic casing and scruffy look, is a reminder that the appearance of objects (or, more broadly, their aesthetic content) can never be separated from the way they were made—not because individuation trumps individuals, but because it abides by design decisions.

If, as the pencil in Leonard E. Read's story claims, "not a single person on the face of this earth knows how to make" it,[50] that is not (or not only) because the process is blind, utterly uncoordinated, or too complex to fathom, but because we (architects and designers) have been accustomed to think that *it does not matter*—that what we bring into the world are pencils (objects; outputs; the stuff we design) and not, as is the case, ecologies of pencil-making and graphite mining, of cedar milling, drawing, and underlining, alongside other ecologies that intersect and contain them. I will clarify this point in the following section, when discussing *hyperobjects*. For now, and in conclusion, I should return to the question of boundaries.

As indicated above, two lines can be identified by cutting across the edges of EoIs: an interior one that fixes and oversees the execution of precise equipmental scripts, discarding and rejecting noncompliant items and behaviors, and a supra-equipmental one that identifies and curates exchanges with the *externalities* upon which the EoI depends. Now, a similar doubling can be found by cutting EoIs longitudinally: an inner envelope narrowly defines the perimeter of its forms (a constellation of parts), and an outer one extends to wrap and unite the preparatory stages, technical chains, and individuating (matter-to-form) conversions that, progressively and across geographies, forced them into their current configurations.

If one squints a little, they might see, growing at ninety degrees from this second skin, a thicket of hairy tendrils to which other objects, willingly or unwillingly, stick.

9.3.3 Hyperobject

The last term I must return to is *hyperobject*—with which Timothy Morton denotes entities that, like global warming, hydrocarbons, or plutonium, are "massively distributed in time and space."[51] I first put this definition to use (albeit brutally excised from Morton's own arguments) in Chapter 3, invoking it as a figure with which to name and interrogate hypermaterials—the silent streams of petroleum, sand,

50 Leonard E. Read, *I, Pencil: My Family Tree as Told to Leonard E. Read*, Online (The Library of Economics and Liberty, 1959).

51 Timothy Morton, *Hyperobjects: Philosophy and Ecology after the End of the World* (Minneapolis: University of Minnesota Press, 2013), 47.

aluminum, and lithium (just to mention a few) that fuel the global materials economy. In this simplistic interpretation, the above definition does not refer to the vast spatiotemporal networks required to extract, process, distribute, and dispose of material stocks, but to how these are translated by industrial and economic machines, and both granted ubiquity (the ability to be or appear everywhere at once) and condemned to absence (their substitution by universal avatars and placeholders). This is how designers and architects largely encounter materials—replaced by standards, averages, formulas, spreadsheets, performance specifications, photographs, samples, hatches, digital textures, and certificates.

Rejecting these abstract approximations (the undermining of material objects; their reduction to known strings of deployable code; the erasure of the processes, people, and land involved in their progressive transformation, maintenance, and eventual disposal), and understanding them as dependent on (and fueling of) extractive economies and environmental injustices, *exaptive design* proposes an alternative approach that accounts for (and learns from) the strange reality of objects and their histories—the fact that they always precede and exceed the attentions showered upon them. Or, one that refuses to call non-humans *materials*[52] and that demands, in Morton's terms, "a *tuning* to the object,"[53] or, following Jane Bennett, a "special sensory access to the call of things."[54] Besides, my study of the technical *tabula rasa* has confirmed the nonexistence of a generic and reifiable materiality, showing that *matter* and *form* are not ontological categories, but the equipmental roles that are assigned to objects as they enter and exit ecologies of inception. As Morton sums it up: "I've seen wood, I've seen photographs of atoms, I've seen clouds in diffusion chambers, I've seen drawings of wave packets. Sure. But have I ever seen matter?"[55]

The implicit answer to this rhetorical question is, of course, no. Yet if matter (as a generic, formless, and placeless goop) does not exist, isn't the sole purpose of its hypermaterial avatars to lubricate the quantification, accumulation, and exchange of capital? Indeed, Morton claims that "OOO begins to see beyond capitalism, if by that economic process we mean the positing of value in some mystical, ethereal beyond: the shadow world of capital."[56]

Recognizing, with Marx and Engels, that "[m]odern bourgeois society [...] is like the sorcerer who is no longer able to control the powers of the nether world whom he has called up by his spells,"[57] an exaptive approach to design—prioritizing the encounter with a pre-existing material substrate and decoupling value from equipmental scripts—begins to unravel capitalist orthodoxies and modern procedures. By reclaiming the ability to allocate and re-allocate value (locally, contingently, *ad hoc*, but also virally, by contagion, at scale); to socially construct materials (to not assume that they are natural or given, but dependent on knowledges, tools, and skills); to reset equipmental scripts

52 Morton, *Hyperobjects*, 172.

53 Ibid., 174.

54 Jane Bennett, "Powers of the Hoard: Further Notes on Material Agency," in *Animal, Vegetable, Mineral: Ethics and Objects*, ed. Jeffrey Jerome Cohen (Washington: Oliphaunt Books, 2012), 244.

55 Morton, *Hyperobjects*, 150.

56 Ibid.

57 Karl Marx and Friedrich Engels, "Manifesto of the Communist Party," in *Marx/Engels Selected Works*, vol. One (Moscow: Progress Publishers, 1969), 98–137.

and parameters; and to dismiss the imperatives of productivity (of eco-logical fitness) and growth, exaptive design aspires to become a political form of material resistance and diversion, one that privileges encounters over ideas, storage over extraction, and persistence over novelty—and where a human or nonhuman *other* is always invited as codesigner, client, neighbor, or patient.

What if we banned toxicants and planned obsolescence, and committed—through regimes of maintenance, repair, and reuse—to the continued survival and adaptation of buildings, electric toasters, bricks, springs, copper wires, and plastic toys? What if we used our advanced computational technologies not to generate senseless algorithmic forms, but to repurpose the ones lying dormant in layer upon layer of landfilled refuse? What if we curtailed the extraction of raw materials and learnt to design not forms but *with* forms? Could architects and designers become the harbingers of a society in which, like in the Japanese practice of *kintsugi*, value increases upon successive uses and generations? Could we forcefully re-internalize the costs (environmental, ecosystemic, in human health, etc.) that the economy externalizes by dint of homicidal and ecocidal self-interest? Or, how might one expand the purview of design so that these longer causal chains become visible, and even obvious? To begin answering these questions, I must return to ecologies of inception and suspension.

Admittedly, the notion of hypermateriality made poor use of its reference to hyperobjects, calling on their powerful definition—"massively distributed in time and space"—to illustrate obedient and rarefied flows of materials rather than the sticky and invasive giants that inhabit Morton's text. A more faithful reading was reintroduced in Chapters 4 and 7 as I attempted, with difficulty, to draw an outline around EoIs. As in the discussion of ecological boundaries above, I found that ecologies of inception project shadows far and in many directions, and that, no matter how distant or disconnected in space and time, these shadows do indeed originate from the same source. For this reason, it seems useful to compare EoIs to hyperobjects or, in other words, to think of them not as constellations of objects but as objects in their own right.

Morton provides a compelling case for this argument. He recounts the class action lawsuit brought by five Amazonian tribes against Texaco/Chevron in the 1990s.[58] During its operations in the Lago Agrio oil field in Ecuador, the company had dumped 68 billion liters of toxic waste water and 77 million liters of crude oil into the rainforest, contaminating the soil and polluting sources of drinkable water.[59] Following these events, residents had started to experience an upsurge in cancer cases and birth defects. Morton notes that while Chevron's strategy was to continue to study how hydrocarbons in the soil correlated with the health problems confronted by the local population (to exactly identify and quantify their mutagenic and carcinogenic effects), a judge finally

[58] Morton, *Hyperobjects*, 182.

[59] "Chevron Wins Ecuador Rainforest 'Oil Dumping' Case," *BBC News*, September 8, 2018.

decided to "suspend the endless construction of (necessarily incomplete statistical) data" and to "act as if the threat were real."[60] This implied that the oil should be viewed, as Morton puts it, "not as assemblages of relations but as a unit, as an entity with unknown powers, a unique entity consisting of all kinds of other entities."[61]

In Morton's example, the judgment represents a shift to an object-oriented paradigm: instead of assuming that the oil spill can be fully translated—that it can be exhaustively mapped and, therefore, known—the lawsuit reaches a point where the evidence presented ("its appearance as cancer; its appearance as sores covering the body of a newborn baby")[62] is sufficient, and further studies would primarily serve, in this context, as excuses to delay proceedings. In other words: the exact toxicological mapping of hydrocarbons—or, the chimera of definitive results—would not inform or substantiate a legal resolution of the case, but slow it down or prevent it from being adjudicated.[63]

In any case, comparing ecologies of inception to hyperobjects, or viewing them as spatiotemporal *units*, can be similarly useful. Certainly, monitoring actors and alliances, analyzing resources and life cycles, investigating supply chains and outputs, and mapping EoIs would all be necessary pursuits. Yet, what is powerful about Timothy Morton's *hyperobjects* or Jane Hutton's *reciprocal landscapes* is that they introduce a metaphorical reading of these networks, one to which one can relate.

In our quotidian dealings, we (human beings) don't consider human bodies to be assemblages or equipment, nor do we view them as clusters of organs, networks transmitting electric and biochemical signals, or strings of life-sustaining reactions and conversions. We don't see them as vessels filled with oxygen, blood, urine, and faeces; as systems, or as factories processing proteins, sugars, fats, and carbohydrates. We see neither repositories of genetic information nor squishy bioreactors brimming with microorganisms—we see *persons*.

Indeed, human bodies are all of the things listed above and more, but in our lives as architects, teachers, students, farmers, sons, citizens, car mechanics, grandmothers, and poets, we don't meaningfully relate to each other's neurons, cells, circulatory systems, or lymph nodes—we relate to personalities, facial expressions, jokes, hugs, tears, compassion, insults, and stories. We don't care for enzymes, feet, or spleens—we care for people. And we would find laughable the suggestion that a person—any person—can be paraphrased or known in their entirety. Now, if one translates this commonsensical insight into a tentative definition of person or, following Arakawa and Gins, of "puzzle creature"— that which we don't presume to be able to replace with knowledge—it becomes clear that OOO extends a measure of personhood to nonhumans. The object is no longer a vector for the radial extension of (and exploitation by) a subject, but a relative that one must attend to with humility and patience—one that might periodically throw a punch or

60 Morton, *Hyperobjects*, 182.

61 Ibid.

62 Ibid.

63 This is also why I have largely avoided the use of figures to support my argument. While architects are usually keen to remind the public that, for example, the construction industry accounts for a staggering 40% of global carbon emissions, I cannot imagine the call for decarbonization being any less convincing or urgent if that figure dramatically fell.

overstay their welcome, but that we are generally inclined to care about, or listen to. It is in this extended sense that EoIs cohere into hyperobjective units.

To be clear, I am not claiming that our engagement with person A reveals their true being—person B, a rain drop, a bacterium, an electrocardiogram, and a timber floor will all come into contact with different translations of person A, none of which is more authentic than the last. And yet, when we hear their tone of voice, fight off their muscular strength, or ask for their advice, we are not experiencing disconnected fragments of sense data—we are experiencing person A. Similarly, when one encounters the many sensual objects that partake in ecologies of inception, or the Latourian "freeze-frames" that identify partial constellations along a material trajectory, one is reminded of the vast withdrawn monster lurking behind the surface—one that can finally be named. By *naming* I don't mean knowing, or the imposition of an identity or purpose (the chair as object to sit on), but the recognition of (and responsibility towards) nonhuman personhood—a being that is *other* and not in one's control.

How might one begin to represent or conceptualize these vast durational creatures? As seen above, the outer boundaries of ecologies of inception are blurry, irregular, and difficult to pin down. Ecological scripts, spatiotemporally extruded as they may be, are equally limited, as they remain woefully blind to the many steps, actors, and losses preceding (and issuing from) them. One must therefore set, as the central spine and origin of EoIs, the spatiotemporal reality of the objects they divert, modify, use up, and release. To avoid "ontological U-bends" and the reductive framings of creative, economic, industrial, or socio-political attention regimes, I will follow Locke and consider these objects on the strict basis of a common origin (e.g., the mine, the forest, the lab) and of numerical identity—also tracking all manner of conversions, byproducts, and emissions. These elongated cores thus appear as chronophotographic skeletons—splitting, branching out, merging, touching, intersecting, forming joints and knuckles, bending, and dispersing. A dense *flesh* of subecologies (of extraction, processing, distribution, consumption, disposal, and maintenance scripts) clusters around them—translating, steering transformations, and funneling effects.[64]

I should mention that my appeal to chronophotography (to Etienne-Jules Marey's flying gull as a metaphor for EoIs, particularly in its sculptural bronze rendition) is markedly different from the one proposed by Bruno Latour and Albena Yaneva in "'Give Me a Gun and I Will Make All Buildings Move': An ANT's View of Architecture."[65] In the well-known text, the authors argue that a building is dynamic ("a continuous flow") and that, both before and after completion, it should be understood not as "a static object but a moving *project*"—continually renegotiated by architects, clients, foam models, zoning regulations, inhabitants, construction permits, and so forth.[66]

64 One could perhaps think of these objects also as "quasi-objects" in the sense, described by Serres, of the ball during a game of soccer, which is "the centre of the referential" and, "when being passed, makes the collective, if it stops, it makes the individual." Michel Serres, *The Parasite*, trans. Lawrence R. Schehr (Baltimore: Johns Hopkins University Press, 1982), 225–26.

65 Bruno Latour and Albena Yaneva, "'Give Me a Gun and I Will Make All Buildings Move': An ANT's View of Architecture," *Ardeth* 01, no. 08 (2017): 102–11.

66 Latour and Yaneva, "Give Me a Gun," 103.

In their account as in Marey's images, the dynamism of a building is constructed by layering, one after the other, the "freeze-frames" that capture specific instances of its movement (design phases, revisions, construction sequences, change orders, refurbishments, et cetera). In the case of EoIs, instead, adding up individual frames does not paint a picture of the whole object; freeze-frames are not partial or incomplete in a spatiotemporal sense, but in an ontological one—they are sensual objects, with a real hyperobject lurking beneath them.

Another difference in my approach is that Latour and Yaneva limit existence (what is worth following) to trials, alliances, negotiations, actors, and effects, neglecting anything that is not knowable, not changing (either affecting or being affected; translating or being translated), or part of a *project* that, while accounting for many stakeholders, revolves around the architect's office.[67] What EoIs describe is, instead, a hyperobjective core that is only partially translated by the projects floating upon its surface.

Clearly, one notable feature of this EoI-as-hyperobject is that it discounts the difference between ecologies of inception and ecologies of suspension as articulated until now, insofar as the hyperobject (the reality of a tree as it is progressively modified, turned into chair and A4 sheets, broken, folded, etc.) is indifferent to (not exhausted by) the scripts, names, and values associated with the equipmental clouds orbiting around it at any given point. I could resolve this confusion by adopting an intermediate term—for example, by collapsing EoIs and EoSs into the phrase *design ecologies*. This move might usefully decouple real objects from their common names: whereas OOO philosophers usually speak of withdrawn chairs, plant pots, cotton balls, and paving slabs, and EoIs describe ecologies of sitting, planting, disinfecting, and walking, a focus on *design ecologies* might detach hyperobjects from their equipmental labels, thus recognizing the latter's role in the object's sensual existence-for-us (while also refusing to reduce them to preindividual or formless streams of materials).

Yet the ambiguity arising between the term EoI (understood as potentializing sets of objects coordinated by design scripts) and the identical term EoI (understood as the real hyperobject of which equipmental constellations are mere sensual cross sections) is worth maintaining and nourishing, as it forcibly connects the two, denying the possibility that one could be considered apart from the other, or that designers could continue to view components or materials as distinct from the environmental injustices, toxic and polluting emissions, ecocidal and homicidal violence, dehumanizing labor practices, carbon expenditures, inequality, and racist, sexist, and colonial hubris that often fuel and sustain them.

In this sense, EoIs display the main traits in Morton's hyperobjects: viscosity, nonlocality, temporal undulation, interobjectivity, and phasing. *Viscosity* refers to the impossibility of pressing an *off* switch, or of displaying an *away* sign ("Out of sight," writes Morton, "is no longer

67 Indeed, this is also consistent with Yaneva's ethnographic method ("to follow architects at work"). Albena Yaneva, *Made by the Office for Metropolitan Architecture: An Ethnography of Design* (Rotterdam: 010 Publishers, 2009), 23.

68 Morton, *Hyperobjects*, 36.

out of mind").**68** Binding EoIs to hyperobjects necessarily attaches them to those instances of violence and injustice that architects and designers could previously pretend not to be party to (or to be outside of). Distance is thus revealed to be "only a psychic and ideological construct designed to protect me from the nearness of things."**69**

69 Ibid., 27.

Nonlocality addresses the spatiotemporal distribution of hyperobjects. Morton writes that

> global warming, like all hyperobjects, is nonlocal: it's massively distributed in time and space. What does this mean? It means that my experience of the weather in the *hic et nunc* is a false immediacy. It's *never the case* that those raindrops only fall on my head!**70**

70 Ibid., 48.

One could say something similar about toasters, carpet tiles, and buildings—not only in the sense that these items *rain* through industrial chains of reproduction, spreading across the globe (e.g., the Billy bookcase having entered millions of living rooms worldwide), but also that the contact with designed objects always triggers a proximity with factory and mine workers, resins and glues, contaminated waters, microplastics, et cetera. *One is never just using a toaster.* When one touches the local manifestations of hyperobjects, they necessarily come into some degree of contact with a diffused and squid-like beast that spans geographies and temporalities.

Temporal undulation refers to Einstein's theory of relativity and the invention of spacetime—where space and time cease to be empty containers (another instance of the *tabula rasa*) but rather become emergent properties (and emissions) of the objects themselves.**71** Hyperobjects are therefore both historical ("When you look at oil," writes Morton, "you are looking at the past")**72** and futural ("an object could exert a backward causality on other entities").**73** In both cases, hyperobjects complicate a linear understanding of time, and elicit questions concerning the temporality and directionality of one's designs (and the associated stakes and responsibilities).

71 Ibid., 61, 67.

72 Ibid., 58.

73 Ibid., 67.

The term *interobjectivity* describes how interconnectedness, natural or designed as it may be, always involves intermediate steps or translations—or, in OOO terms, the mediation of sensual objects. This is not only true in real time (the wind as revealed by the rustling of leaves) but across longer durations. Morton writes:

> We see the footprint of a dinosaur left in some ancient rock that was once a pool of mud. The dinosaur's reality exists interobjectively: there is some form of shared space between the rock, ourselves, and the dinosaur, even though the dinosaur isn't there directly. The print of a dinosaur's foot in the mud is seen as foot-shaped hole

in a rock by humans sixty-five million years later. There is some sensuous connection, then, between the dinosaur, the rock, and the human, despite their vastly differing timescales.[74]

74 Ibid., 86.

Strikingly, the connection between dinosaur and mud (or some other creature living alongside it in the Cretaceous) is not ontologically different from that between the dinosaur and a human being experiencing the fossilized footprints today. In both cases, real objects send off sensual emissaries that translate one object for another. Yet if one takes this seriously—and renounces the expectation that a *mark* should be as literally traceable as a footprint or hand cast—any chaise longue, raincoat, teapot, or curtain wall (anything that has been made) is also a point of sensual contact with carpenters, textile designers, and cotton harvesters; with sewing machine operators, factory stylists, and polyester carders; with ceramicists, silica sand miners, aluminum extruders, acid electrolyte baths, and powder coaters. And, of course, anything one does is also a translation of them projected into the future.

Finally, *phasing* refers to the fact that hyperobjects "occupy a high-dimensional phase space that makes them impossible to see as a whole on a regular three-dimensional human-scale basis."[75] Indeed, when one toasts bread, they don't usually take the toaster apart à la Thwaites; they don't see its nickel-chromium element exposed; or the New Caledonian opencast mines the ore is extracted from; or the way mining sediments release hexavalent chromium into the waters of a downstream village;[76] or the welders risking exposure by working with high chrome alloys; or the cancers and damage inflicted by the toxic chemicals to noses, lungs, eyes, and skin. And yet we—miners, welders, villagers, rivers, aquatic animals, designers, and toasters of bread—all experience the same hyperobject, albeit in carefully segregated sensual "slices."[77] The reintegration of these slices into a unified (and identifiable) picture remains—in a political and ethical sense that informs both forensic investigation and proactive proposals—an urgent task, and one of the greatest challenges for design in the twenty-first century.

75 Ibid., 70.

76 Peggy Gunkel-Grillon et al., "Toxic Chromium Release from Nickel Mining Sediments in Surface Waters, New Caledonia," *Environmental Chemistry Letters* 12, no. 4 (December 2014): 511–16.

77 Morton, *Hyperobjects*, 73.

To *design hyperobjects* is to collapse the colossal creatures described by Morton (giants such as global warming, oil, and uranium) with the cozy artifacts (tiles, lamp posts, motorbikes, and pianos) that designers presume to shape and control. While this is partially a provocation—the system boundaries of one's designs never match those of the corresponding outputs—it also acknowledges that architecture and design have been actively feeding these vast creatures and, indeed, that they can stop doing so.

My hope is that the lens of ecologies of inception, in both its equipmental and hyperobjective renditions, will provide architects and designers with a novel conceptual and methodological toolset; that viewing design not as the production of outputs but as the engagement with lengthy (and monstrous) spatiotemporal extrusions will force them to admit that these precede and exceed the projects and signatures of any one generation, and prompt a collective reconsideration of potentials and value, radically prioritizing practices of maintenance, reuse, care, and exaptive co-option.

Bibliography

Abramson, Daniel M. *Obsolescence: An Architectural History*. Chicago and London: The University of Chicago Press, 2016.

Agamben, Giorgio. *Nudities*. Translated by David Kishik and Stefan Pedatella. Stanford: Stanford University Press, 2010.

———. *Potentialities: Collected Essays in Philosophy*. Translated by Daniel Heller-Roazen. Stanford: Stanford University Press, 1999.

———. *The Man without Content*. Translated by Georgia Albert. Stanford: Stanford University Press, 1999.

———. *"What Is an Apparatus?" And Other Essays*. Translated by David Kishik and Stefan Pedatella. Stanford: Stanford University Press, 2009.

Ahmed, Sara. *What's the Use? On the Uses of Use*. Durham: Duke University Press, 2019.

———. "Declarations of Whiteness: The Non-Performativity of Anti-Racism." *Borderlands E-Journal* 3, no. 2 (2004). https://webarchive.nla.gov.au/awa/20050616083826/http://www.borderlandsejournal.adelaide.edu.au/vol3no2_2004/ahmed_declarations.htm.

Akrich, Madeleine. "The De-Scription of Technical Objects." In *Shaping Technology/Building Society: Studies in Sociotechnical Change*, edited by Wiebe E. Bijker and John Law, 205–24. Cambridge: MIT Press, 2010.

Alberti, Leon Battista. *On the Art of Building in Ten Books*. Translated by Joseph Rykwert, Neil Leach, and Robert Tavernor. Cambridge and London: MIT Press, 1997.

Alberts, Elizabeth Claire. "'Our Life Is Plasticized': New Research Shows Microplastics in Our Food, Water, Air." *Mongabay*, July 15, 2020. https://news.mongabay.com/2020/07/our-life-is-plasticized-new-research-shows-microplastics-in-our-food-water-air/.

Allen, Paula Gunn. "IYANI: It Goes This Way." In *The Remembered Earth: An Anthology of Contemporary Native American Literature*, edited by Geary Hobson, 191–93. Albuquerque: University of New Mexico Press, 1981.

Allen, Stan. "Field Conditions." In *Constructing a New Agenda: Architectural Theory 1993–2009*, edited by Krista Sykes, New York: Princeton Architectural Press, 2010.

Altman, Rebecca. "The Myth of Historical Bio-Based Plastics." *Science* 373, no. 6550 (July 2, 2021): 47–49. https://doi.org/10.1126/science.abj1003.

Anstey, Tim, Katja Grillner, and Rolf Hughes, eds. *Architecture and Authorship*. London: Black Dog Publishing, 2007.

Architectural Association. "Design & Make: 2014–15: Wood Chip Barn." *AA 2016* (blog). Accessed December 29, 2020. https://pr2016.aaschool.ac.uk/2014-15--Woodchip-Barn.

Aristotle. *Aristotle in Twenty-Three Volumes. 17: The Metaphysics: books I–IX*. Translated by Hugh Tredennick. Cambridge: Harvard University Press, 2003.

———. *Categories*. Translated by E.M. Edghill. The Internet Classics Archive. Accessed April 14, 2019. http://classics.mit.edu/Aristotle/categories.1.1.html.

———. *On the Generation of Animals*. Translated by Arthur Platt. Vol. Book II. Accessed May 30, 2020. https://en.wikisource.org/wiki/On_the_Generation_of_Animals/Book_II.

———. "On the Soul." Translated by J.A. Smith. In *The Complete Works of Aristotle: The Revised Oxford Translation*, edited by Jonathan Barnes, 1–64. Princeton: Princeton University Press, 1984.

———. "Physics." Translated by R.P. Hardie and R. K. Gaye. In *The Complete Works of Aristotle: The Revised Oxford Translation*, edited by Jonathan Barnes, 1–161. Princeton: Princeton University Press, 1984.

Armstrong, Rachel. "Bittersweet Building." In *Gross Ideas: Tales of Tomorrow's Architecture*, edited by Edwina Attlee, Phineas Harper, and Maria Smith. London and Oslo: Architecture Foundation and Oslo Architecture Triennale, 2019.

———. *Experimental Architecture: Designing the Unknown*. London and New York: Routledge, 2020.

———. *Liquid Life: On Non-Linear Materiality*. Santa Barbara: Punctum Books, 2019.

———. *Vibrant Architecture: Matter as a CoDesigner of Living Structures*. Warsaw: De Gruyter Open, 2015. https://doi.org/10.1515/9783110403732.

———, Andrew Adamatzky, Gary S Caldwell, Simone Ferracina, Yannis Ieropoulos, Gimi Rimbu, José Luis Garcia, et al. "Living Architecture (LIAR): Metabolically Engineered Building Units." In *Cultivated Building Materials*, edited by Dirk E. Hebel and Felix Heisel, 168–75. Birkhäuser, 2017.

Augustsson, Anna, Louise Sörme, Anna Karlsson, and Jennie Amneklev. "Persistent Hazardous Waste and the Quest Toward a

Circular Economy: The Example of Arsenic in Chromated Copper Arsenate-Treated Wood: Arsenic Flows with CCA-Treated Wood, Sweden." *Journal of Industrial Ecology* 21, no. 3 (June 2017): 689–99. https://doi.org/10.1111/jiec.12516.

Awan, Nishat, Tatjana Schneider, and Jeremy Till. *Spatial Agency: Other Ways of Doing Architecture*. Abingdon and New York: Routledge, 2011.

Ayres, Robert U., and Allen V. Kneese. "Production, Consumption, and Externalities." *American Economic Review* 59, no. 3 (1969): 282–97.

Bahrani, Ramin. *Plastic Bag*. Noruz Films and Gigantic Pictures, 2009. www.youtube.com/watch?v=stqyjxRmW30.

Baker-Brown, Duncan. *The Re-Use Atlas: A Designer's Guide Towards the Circular Economy*. London: RIBA Publishing, 2017.

Ballantyne, Andrew. *Deleuze and Guattari for Architects*. London and New York: Routledge, 2007.

Banham, Reyner. "Chairs as Art." *New Society*, April 20, 1967. Quoted in Nigel Whiteley, *Reyner Banham: Historian of the Immediate Future*. Cambridge: MIT Press, 2002.

Barad, Karen. *Meeting the Universe Halfway: Quantum Physics and the Entanglement of Matter and Meaning*. Durham: Duke University Press, 2007.

Barassi, Sebastiano. "The Modern Cult of Replicas: A Rieglian Analysis of Values in Replication." *Tate Papers*, no. 8 (Autumn 2007). www.tate.org.uk/research/publications/tate-papers/08/the-modern-cult-of-replicas-a-rieglian-analysis-of-values-in-replication.

Barber, Daniel A. "After Comfort." *Log*, no. 47 (2019): 45–50.

Bartow J., Elmore. *Citizen Coke: The Making of Coca-Cola Capitalism*. New York: W. W. Norton & Company, 2014.

Bataille, Georges. *Œuvres Complètes*. Paris: Gallimard, 1970.

———. "Formless." In Yve-Alain Bois and Rosalind E. Krauss. *Formless: A User's Guide*. New York and Cambridge: Zone Books, 1997.

Baudrillard, Jean. *The System of Objects*. Translated by James Benedict. London and New York: Verso, 1996.

Bauman, Zygmunt. *Wasted Lives: Modernity and Its Outcasts*. Cambridge: Polity, 2011.

BBC News. "Chevron Wins Ecuador Rainforest 'Oil Dumping' Case." *BBC News*, September 8, 2018. www.bbc.co.uk/news/world-latin-america-45455984.

Bedford, Joseph, ed. *Is There an Object Oriented Architecture?: Engaging Graham Harman*. London and New York: Bloomsbury Academic, 2020.

Beiser, Vince. "Sand Mining: The Global Environmental Crisis You've Probably Never Heard Of." *The Guardian*, February 27, 2017, Online edition. www.theguardian.com/cities/2017/feb/27/sand-mining-global-environmental-crisis-never-heard.

————. "Why the World Is Running out of Sand." *BBC Future*, November 18, 2019. www.bbc.com/future/article/20191108-why-the-world-is-running-out-of-sand.

Benedikt, Michael, and Kory Bieg, eds. *The Secret Life of Buildings*. Austin: Center for American Architecture and Design at the School of Architecture, University of Texas at Austin, 2018.

Bennett, Jane. "Powers of the Hoard: Further Notes on Material Agency." In *Animal, Vegetable, Mineral: Ethics and Objects*, edited by Jeffrey Jerome Cohen, 237–69. Washington: Oliphaunt Books, 2012.

————. *Vibrant Matter: A Political Ecology of Things*. Durham: Duke University Press, 2010.

Benyus, Janine M. *Biomimicry: Innovation Inspired by Nature*. New York: Morrow, 1997.

Bhandar, Brenna. *Colonial Lives of Property: Law, Land, and Racial Regimes of Ownership*. Global and Insurgent Legalities. Durham: Duke University Press, 2018.

Billiet, Lionel, Michaël Ghyoot, and Maarten Gielen. "Le Cerisier et La Plaque de Plâtre." *Criticat* 9 (March 2012): 102–13.

Blum, Andrew. *Tubes: Behind the Scenes at the Internet*. London: Viking, 2012.

Bouchard, Nikole, ed. *Waste Matters: Adaptive Reuse for Productive Landscapes*. Abingdon and New York: Routledge, 2021.

Brand, Stewart. *Clock of the Long Now: Time and Responsibility: The Ideas Behind the World's Slowest Computer*. New York: Basic Books, 2008.

————. *How Buildings Learn: What Happens after They're Built*. New York: Penguin Books, 1995.

Braungart, Michael, and William McDonough. *Cradle to Cradle: Remaking the Way We Make Things*. New York: North Point Press, 2002.

————, and with a foreword by President Bill Clinton. *The Upcycle: Beyond Sustainability--Designing for Abundance*. New York: Farrar, Straus & Giroux, 2014. E-book.

Brooker, Graeme, and Sally Stone. *Rereadings: Interior Architecture and the Design Principles of Remodelling Existing Buildings*. London: RIBA Publishing, 2017.

Bryant, Levi R. *The Democracy of Objects*. Ann Arbor: Open Humanities Press, 2011.

Byles, Jeff. *Rubble: Unearthing the History of Demolition*. New York: Three Rivers Press, 2006.

Calvino, Italo. *The Road to San Giovanni*. Translated by Tim Parks. Boston: Mariner Books, 2014. E-book.

Carcas, Carlos, and Norberto López Amado. *How Much Does Your Building Weigh, Mr. Foster?* Documentary, 2011.

Carson, Rachel. *Silent Spring*. Boston: Houghton Mifflin, 1962.

Chapman, Jonathan. *Emotionally Durable Design: Objects, Experiences and Empathy*. London and New York: Routledge, 2015.

———. "Product Moments, Material Eternities." In Duncan Baker-Brown, *The Re-Use Atlas*, 161–165. London: RIBA Publishing, 2017.

Chertow, Marian R. "Waste, Reuse, and Symbiosis: Closing Material Loops." Presented at Discarded: Unmasking & Understanding the Waste Stream, Connecticut College, March 6, 2021.

Clément, Gilles. *Manifeste Du Tiers Paysage*. Online, 2004. www.gillesclement.com/fichiers/_tierspaypublications_92045_manifeste_du_tiers_paysage.pdf.

———. *The Planetary Garden: And Other Writings*. Translated by Sandra Morris, and with a foreword by Gilles A. Tiberghien. Philadelphia: University of Pennsylvania Press, 2015.

Cole, Nicki Lisa, and Alison Dahl Crossley. "On Feminism in the Age of Consumption." *Consumers, Commodities & Consumption* 11, no. 1 (December 2009). https://csrn.camden.rutgers.edu/newsletters/11-1/cole_crossley.htm

Congrès internationaux d'architecture moderne (CIAM). "Charter of Athens." In *Programs and Manifestoes on 20th-Century Architecture*, edited by Conrads Ulrich. Cambridge: MIT Press, 1975. Quoted in Aimi Hamraie. *Building Access: Universal Design and the Politics of Disability*. Minneapolis: University of Minnesota Press, 2017.

Corvellec, Hervé, Steffen Böhm, Alison Stowell, and Francisco Valenzuela. "Introduction to the Special Issue on the Contested Realities of the Circular Economy." *Culture and Organization* 26, no. 2 (March 3, 2020): 97–102. https://doi.org/10.1080/14759551.2020.1717733.

Cradle to Cradle Products Innovation Institute. "Material Health Certificate: The Cradle to Cradle CertifiedTM Products Program." Accessed February 18, 2020. https://s3.amazonaws.com/c2c-website/resources/media_kit/print_collateral/MHC_Overview_and_Sample_07102018.pdf.

Cramer, Ned. "The Day MoMA Died." *Architect Magazine*, May 1, 2013. www.architectmagazine.com/design/the-day-moma-died_o.

Cuff, Dana. *Architecture: The Story of Practice*. Cambridge: MIT Press, 1991.

Cullen, Jonathan M. "Circular Economy: Theoretical Benchmark or Perpetual Motion Machine?" *Journal of Industrial Ecology* 21, no. 3 (June 2017): 483–86. https://doi.org/10.1111/jiec.12599.

Darwin, Charles. *On the Origin of Species*. London: J. Murray, 1859.

Daston, Lorraine, ed. *Biographies of Scientific Objects*. Chicago: University of Chicago Press, 2000.

De Decker, Kris. "How Circular Is the Circular Economy?: Why This Proposed Solution Is Little More than a Magic Trick." *Uneven Earth* (blog), November 27, 2018. http://unevenearth.org/2018/11/how-circular-is-the-circular-economy/.

De la Durantaye, Leland. "Readymade Remade: Pierre Pinoncelli and the Legacy of Duchamp's 'Fountains.'" *Cabinet*, Fall 2007. www.cabinetmagazine.org/issues/27/durantaye.php.

DeLanda, Manuel. *Assemblage Theory*. Speculative Realism. Edinburgh: Edinburgh University Press, 2016.

———. *Deleuze: History and Science*. New York: Atropos, 2010.

———. "Homes: Meshwork or Hierarchy?" In *Nomadic Trajectories*, edited by John Sellars. Coventry: Department of Philosophy, University of Warwick, 1998.

Deleuze, Gilles. *Essays Critical and Clinical*. Translated by Daniel W. Smith and Michael A. Greco. London and New York: Verso, 1998.

———, and Giorgio Agamben. *Bartleby: Gilles Deleuze, George Agamben*. Macerata: Quodlibet, 2012.

Deleuze, Gilles, and Félix Guattari. *A Thousand Plateaus: Capitalism and Schizophrenia*. Translated by Brian Massumi. Minneapolis: University of Minnesota Press, 1987.

———. *What Is Philosophy?* European Perspectives. New York: Columbia University Press, 1994.

Deleuze, Gilles, and Claire Parnet. *Dialogues*. Translated by Hugh Tomlinson and Barbara Habberjam. New York: Columbia University Press, 1987.

Descalzo, Ricardo. *Annea Lockwood—RCSC*. Alicante: NEUMA Records & Publications, 2014. www.youtube.com/watch?v=wc96e9K_gV4&t=243s.

Devlieger, Lionel. "Architecture in Reverse." *Volume* 51: Augmented Technology. Studio Rotor: Deconstruction (October 2017).

Douglas, Mary. *Purity and Danger: An Analysis of Concepts of Pollution and Taboo*. London and New York: Routledge, 2002.

Druot, Frédéric, Anne Lacaton, Jean-Philippe Vassal, and Susana Landrove. *Plus: La vivienda colectiva, Territorio de excepción; Les grandes ensembles de logements, Territoire d'exception; Large-scale housing developments, An exceptional case*. 2G Books. Barcelona: Ed. Gustavo Gili, 2007.

Durmisevic, Elma. *Green Design and Assembly of Buildings and Systems: Design for Disassembly a Key to Life Cycle Design of Buildings and Building Products*. Saarbrücken: VDM Verlag Dr. Müller, 2010.

Dyangani Ose, Elvira, and Raúl Muñoz De la Vega. "Affection as a Subversive Architectural Form." In *Usted Está Aquí / You Are Here. Recetas Urbanas 2018*, edited by Kristine Guzmán. León: Museo de Arte Contemporaneo, 2019.

Easterling, Keller. *Extrastatecraft: The Power of Infrastructure Space*. London and New York: Verso, 2014. E-book.

———. *Medium Design*. Moscow: Strelka Press, 2018. E-book.

———. *Medium Design: Knowing How to Build the World*. London: Verso, 2021.

———. *Subtraction*. Edited by Nikolaus Hirsch and Markus Miessen. Berlin: Sternberg Press, 2014.

Eckelman, Matthew J., and Marian R. Chertow. "Quantifying Life Cycle Environmental Benefits from the Reuse of Industrial Materials in Pennsylvania." *Environmental Science & Technology* 43, no. 7 (April 2009): 2550–56. https://doi.org/10.1021/es802345a.

Eco, Umberto. "Function and Sign: The Semiotics of Architecture." In *Rethinking Architecture: A Reader in Cultural Theory*, edited by Neil Leach, 173–86. New York: Routledge, 2005.

Edinburgh City Council. "Swifts and Development: Information for Developers." Accessed June 17, 2020. www.edinburgh.gov.uk/downloads/file/24591/swifts-and-development.

Eisenman, Peter. "The End of the Classical: The End of the Beginning, the End of the End." *Perspecta* 21 (1984): 154. https://doi.org/10.2307/1567087.

———. *The Formal Basis of Modern Architecture*. Zürich: Lars Müller Publishers, 2018.

Ellen MacArthur Foundation. "Towards a Circular Economy: Business Rationale for an Accelerated Transition." Ellen MacArthur Foundation, November 2015. www.ellenmacarthurfoundation.org/assets/downloads/publications/TCE_Ellen-MacArthur-Foundation_26-Nov-2015.pdf.

———. "Homepage." Accessed June 7, 2020. www.ellenmacarthur foundation.org.

Escobar, Arturo. *Designs for the Pluriverse: Radical Interdependence, Autonomy, and the Making of Worlds*. Durham: Duke University Press, 2018.

European Commission. "Eurostat: Waste Statistics," 2021. https://ec.europa.eu/eurostat/statistics-explained/index.php?title=Waste_statistics#Total_waste_generation.

Fellner, Johann, Jakob Lederer, Christoph Scharff, and David Laner. "Present Potentials and Limitations of a Circular Economy with Respect to Primary Raw Material Demand." *Journal of Industrial Ecology* 21, no. 3 (June 2017): 494–96. https://doi.org/10.1111/jiec.12582.

Ferracina, Simone. "Exaptive Architectures." In *Unconventional Computing: Design Methods for Adaptive Architecture*, edited by Rachel Armstrong and Simone Ferracina, 62–65. Toronto: Riverside Architectural Press, 2013.

———. "Exaptive Design: Radical Co-Authorship as Method." In *Experimental Architecture: Designing the Unknown*, edited by Rachel Armstrong, 121–43. London and New York: Routledge, 2019.

———. "Unit 2: Radical Co-Authorship." ESALA, MA (Hons) & BA Architecture Programs, 18–19, September 17, 2018.

Ferro, Sérgio. "Concrete as Weapon." Translated by Silke Kapp and Alice Fiuza, and with an introduction by Silke Kapp, Katie Lloyd Thomas, and João Marcos de Almeida Lopes. *Harvard Design Magazine*, Fall/Winter 2018.

Fink, Bruce. *The Lacanian Subject: Between Language and Jouissance*. Princeton: Princeton University Press, 1995.

Flores & Prats, Agustina Bersier, Mariela Allievi, and Judith Casas. *44 Doors and 35 Windows for the New Sala Beckett*. 15-L FILMS, 2016.

Flusser, Vilém. *The Shape of Things: A Philosophy of Design*. London: Reaktion, 1999.

Foucault, Michel. *Power/Knowledge: Selected Interviews and Other Writings, 1972–1977*. Edited by Colin Gordon. New York: Pantheon Books, 1980.

———. "What Is an Author?" In *The Foucault Reader*, edited by Paul Rabinow, 101–20. New York: Pantheon Books, 1984.

Franta, Benjamin. "Shell and Exxon's Secret 1980s Climate Change Warnings." *The Guardian*, September 19, 2018, Online edition. www.theguardian.com/environment/climate-consensus-97-per-cent/2018/sep/19/shell-and-exxons-secret-1980s-climate-change-warnings.

Frichot, Hélène. *Dirty Theory: Troubling Architecture*. Baunach, Germany: Spurbuchverlag, 2019.

Frosch, Robert A., and Nicholas E. Gallopoulos. "Strategies for Manufacturing." *Scientific American* 261, no. 3 (September 1989): 144–52.

Fure, Adam. "Aesthetics Postdigital." In *Aesthetics Equals Politics: New Discourses across Art, Architecture, and Philosophy*, edited by Mark Foster Gage, 99–125. Cambridge: The MIT Press, 2019.

Furth, Montgomery. *Substance, Form, and Psyche: An Aristotelean Metaphysics*. Cambridge and New York: Cambridge University Press, 1988.

Gabrys, Jennifer. "Salvage." In *Depletion Design: A Glossary of Network Ecologies*, edited by Carolin Wiedemann and Soenke Zehle, 137–39. Amsterdam: Institute of Network Cultures, 2012.

Gage, Mark Foster, ed. *Aesthetics Equals Politics: New Discourses across Art, Architecture, and Philosophy*. Cambridge: The MIT Press, 2019.

———. "Killing Simplicity: Object-Oriented Philosophy in Architecture." *Log*, no. 33 (2015): 95–106.

Gambetta, Curt. "Throwaway Houses: Garbage Housing and the Politics of Ownership." In *The Culture of Nature in the History of Design*, edited by Kjetil Fallan, 221–36. London and New York: Routledge, 2019.

Gannon, Todd, Graham Harman, David Ruy, and Tom Wiscombe. "The Object Turn: A Conversation." *Log*, no. 33 (2015): 73–94.

Garelli, Jacques. "Introduction à la problématique de Gilbert Simondon." In Gilbert Simondon, *L'individuation à la lumière des notions de forme et d'information*, 9–19. Grenoble: Millon, 2005.

Garland-Thomson, Rosemarie. *Extraordinary Bodies: Figuring Physical Disability in American Culture and Literature*. New York: Columbia University Press, 2017.

———. "Misfits: A Feminist Materialist Disability Concept." *Hypatia* 26, no. 3 (2011): 591–609.

Georgescu-Roegen, Nicholas. *Analytical Economics: Issues and Problems*. Cambridge: Harvard University Press, 1967.

———. *The Entropy Law and the Economic Process*. Cambridge: Harvard University Press, 1971.

Ghyoot, Michaël, Lionel Devlieger, Lionel Billiet, and André Warnier. *Déconstruction et réemploi: Comment faire circuler les éléments de construction*. Lausanne: Presses Polytechniques et Universitaires Romandes, 2018.

Gibson, James J. *The Ecological Approach to Visual Perception*. New York: Psychology Press, 2011.

Gielen, Maarten. "Lecture at CCA." Canadian Centre for Architecture (CCA), February 4, 2016. www.cca.qc.ca/en/events/38078/rotor-deconstruction.

Gins, Madeline, and Shūsaku Arakawa. *Architectural Body*. Tuscaloosa: University of Alabama Press, 2002.

———. "Site of Reversible Destiny—Yoro Park." Accessed June 17, 2020. www.yoro-park.com/pdf/hantenchi-guidemap_english.pdf.

Giovannini, Joseph. "American Folk Art Museum." *New York Magazine*, December 24, 2001.

Gissen, David. *Subnature: Architecture's Other Environments*. New York: Princeton Architectural Press, 2009.

Gordillo, Gastón. *Rubble: The Afterlife of Destruction*. Durham: Duke University Press, 2014.

Gould, Stephen Jay, and Elisabeth S. Vrba. "Exaptation: A Missing Term in the Science of Form." *Paleobiology* 8, no. 1 (1982): 4–15.

Groys, Boris. *On the New*. Translated by G. M. Goshgarian. Brooklyn: Verso, 2014.

Gunkel-Grillon, Peggy, Christine Laporte-Magoni, Monika Lemestre, and Nicolas Bazire. "Toxic Chromium Release from Nickel Mining Sediments in Surface Waters, New Caledonia." *Environmental Chemistry Letters* 12, no. 4 (December 2014): 511–16. https://doi.org/10.1007/s10311-014-0475-1.

Hamraie, Aimi. *Building Access: Universal Design and the Politics of Disability*. Minneapolis: University of Minnesota Press, 2017.

Haraway, Donna. "Situated Knowledges: The Science Question in Feminism and the Privilege of Partial Perspective." *Feminist Studies* 14, no. 3 (1988): 575–99. https://doi.org/10.2307/3178066.

———. *When Species Meet*. Minneapolis: University of Minnesota Press, 2008.

Harman, Graham. "A New Sense of Mimesis." In *Aesthetics Equals Politics: New Discourses across Art, Architecture, and Philosophy*, edited by Mark Foster Gage, 49–63. Cambridge: The MIT Press, 2019.

———. *Bells and Whistles: More Speculative Realism*. Winchester: Zero Books, 2013.

———. *Circus Philosophicus*. Winchester: Zero Books, 2010.

———. *Dante's Broken Hammer: The Ethics, Aesthetics and Metaphysics of Love*. London: Repeater Books, 2016.

———. *Guerrilla Metaphysics: Phenomenology and the Carpentry of Things*. Chicago: Open Court, 2005.

———. *Heidegger Explained: From Phenomenon to Thing*. Chicago: Open Court, 2007.

———. "Object-Oriented Ontology (OOO)." In *Oxford Research Encyclopedia of Literature*, by Graham Harman. Oxford University Press, 2019. https://doi.org/10.1093/acrefore/9780190201098.013.997.

———. *Prince of Networks: Bruno Latour and Metaphysics*. Anamnesis. Melbourne: re.press, 2009.

———. *The Quadruple Object*. Winchester and Washington: Zero Books, 2011.

———. "The Real Problem Is Taxonomy, Not Anthropocentrism." *Object-Oriented Philosophy* (blog), May 22, 2019. https://doctorzamalek2.wordpress.com/2019/05/22/the-real-problem-is-taxonomy-not-anthropocentrism/.

———. "The Third Table." In *Documenta: 100 Notes-100 Thoughts*, edited by Katrin Sauerländer, 4–15. Documenta, 2012.

———. *Tool-Being: Heidegger and the Metaphysics of Objects*. Chicago: Open Court, 2002.

———. "Architecture and Objects." Unpublished manuscript, June 9, 2021, typescript.

Harney, Stefano, and Fred Moten. *All Incomplete*. With a foreword by Denise Ferreira da Silva, photos and an afterword by Zun Lee. New York: Minor Compositions, 2021.

Hartman, Saidiya. "The End of White Supremacy, An American Romance." *Bomb*, June 5, 2020. https://bombmagazine.org/articles/the-end-of-white-supremacy-an-american-romance/.

Hawthorne, Christopher. "Elizabeth Diller Defends MoMA Plan to Demolish Folk Art Building." *Los Angeles Times*, January 16, 2014, Online edition. www.latimes.com/entertainment/arts/culture/la-et-cm-elizabeth-diller-defends-demolition-of-folk-art-building-20140115-story.html.

Hecht, Gabrielle. "Human Crap." *Aeon*, March 25, 2020. https://aeon.co/essays/the-idea-of-disposability-is-a-new-and-noxious-fiction.

Heidegger, Martin. *Basic Writings: From Being and Time (1927) to The Task of Thinking (1964)*. Edited by David Farrell Krell. San Francisco: HarperSanFrancisco, 1993.

———. *Being and Time*. Translated by John Macquarrie and Edward Robinson. Oxford: Basil Blackwell, 1962.

———. "Building Dwelling Thinking." In *Poetry, Language, Thought*, translated by Albert Hofstadter, 141–60. New York: Perennial Classics, 2001.

———. *The Basic Problems of Phenomenology*. Translated by Albert Hofstadter. Bloomington and Indianapolis: Indiana University Press, 1982.

———. "The Origin of the Work of Art." In *Basic Writings: From Being and Time (1927) to The Task of Thinking (1964)*, edited by David Farrell Krell, 80–101. San Francisco: HarperSanFrancisco, 1993.

———. "The Thing." In *Poetry, Language, Thought*, translated by Albert Hofstadter, 165–82. New York: Perennial Classics, 2001.

Hill, Jonathan. *Actions of Architecture: Architects and Creative Users*. London and New York: Routledge, 2003.

Hird, Myra J. *The Origins of Sociable Life: Evolution after Science Studies*. Basingstoke: Palgrave Macmillan, 2009.

Holland, Eugene W. *Deleuze and Guattari's "A Thousand Plateaus": A Reader's Guide*. London and New York: Bloomsbury Academic, 2013. E-book.

Hooke Park—AA School's Woodland Campus. "Wood Chip Barn." Accessed May 31, 2020. http://hookepark.aaschool.ac.uk/woodchip-barn/.

Hustvedt, Siri. "A Woman in the Men's Room: When Will the Art World Recognise the Real Artist behind Duchamp's Fountain?" *The Guardian*, March 29, 2019. www.theguardian.com/books/2019/mar/29/marcel-duchamp-fountain-women-art-history.

Hutton, Jane. *Reciprocal Landscapes: Stories of Material Movements*. Abingdon and New York: Routledge, 2020.

Hwang, Joyce. "Bat Tower." Ants of the Prairie. Accessed June 17, 2020. www.antsoftheprairie.com/?page_id=203.

———. "My Neighbor, the Bat." *Biodesigned*, no. 8 (July 22, 2021). www.biodesigned.org/joyce-hwang/my-neighbor-the-bat.

———. "Plight of the Bats." Ants of the Prairie. Accessed June 17, 2020. www.antsoftheprairie.com/?page_id=1085.

Iliadis, Andrew. "Two Examples of Concretization." *Platform: Journal of Media and Communication* 6 (2015): 86–95.

Ingold, Tim. *The Perception of the Environment: Essays on Livelihood, Dwelling & Skill*. London and New York: Routledge, 2000.

IPCC. "Chapter 3: Impacts of 1.5° of Global Warming on Natural and Human Systems." In *Special Report: Global Warming of 1.5°*, 2020. www.ipcc.ch/sr15/.

———. "Special Report: Global Warming of 1.5°," 2020. www.ipcc.ch/sr15/.

Jackson, Steven J. "Rethinking Repair." In *Media Technologies: Essays on Communication, Materiality, and Society*, edited by Tarleton Gillespie, Pablo J. Boczkowski, and Kirsten A. Foot. Cambridge: The MIT Press, 2014.

Jencks, Charles. "The Style of Eureka." In Jencks, Charles, and Nathan Silver. *Adhocism: The Case for Improvisation,* vii–xviii. Cambridge: MIT Press, 2013.

———, and Nathan Silver. *Adhocism: The Case for Improvisation*. Cambridge: MIT Press, 2013.

Johnson, William Ernest. *Logic*. Cambridge University Press, 2014. Quoted in Jessica Wilson, "Determinables and Determinates." Edited by Edward N. Zalta. The Stanford Encyclopedia of Philosophy, Spring 2017. https://plato.stanford.edu/archives/spr2017/entries/determinate-determinables/.

Jørgensen, Finn Arne. *Recycling*. Cambridge: The MIT Press, 2019.

Jullien, François. *The Propensity of Things: Toward a History of Efficacy in China*. New York: Zone Books, 1999.

Kafka, Franz. "The Cares of a Family Man," trans. Willa and Edwin Muir. In *The Complete Stories*, edited by Nahum N. Glatzer, 469–470. New York: Schocken Books, 1988.

Kallipoliti, Lydia. "History of Ecological Design." In *Oxford Research Encyclopedia of Environmental Science*. Oxford University Press, 2018. https://doi.org/10.1093/acrefore/9780199389414.013.144.

Kelly, Annie. "Apple and Google Named in US Lawsuit over Congolese Child Cobalt Mining Deaths." *The Guardian*, December 16, 2019, Online edition. www.theguardian.com/global-development/2019/dec/16/apple-and-google-named-in-us-lawsuit-over-congolese-child-cobalt-mining-deaths.

Khalili, Nader, and Iliona Outram. *Emergency Sandbag Shelter and Eco-Village: Manual-How to Build Your Own with Superadobe*. Hesperia: Cal-Earth Press, 2008.

Kimmelman, Michael. "Defending a Scrap of Soul against MoMA." *The New York Times*, May 13, 2013, Online edition. https://archive.nytimes.com/query.nytimes.com/gst/fullpage-9507E4DB173BF930A25756C0A9659D8B63.html.

Kimmerer, Robin Wall. *Braiding Sweetgrass: Indigenous Wisdom, Scientific Knowledge and the Teachings of Plants*. Minneapolis: Milkweed Editions, 2013.

Kohlstedt, Kurt. "Interstellar Illusions: 'Greebles' Lend Large Sci-Fi Structures a Sense of Scale." *99% Invisible* (blog), February 19, 2021. https://99percentinvisible.org/article/interstellar-illusions-greebles-lend-large-sci-fi-structures-a-sense-of-scale/.

Korhonen, Jouni, Antero Honkasalo, and Jyri Seppälä. "Circular Economy: The Concept and Its Limitations." *Ecological Economics* 143, no. C (2018): 37–46.

Kurokawa, Kishō. *Metabolism in Architecture*. London: Studio Vista, 1977.

Lally, Sean. "Rachel Armstrong: Far from Equilibrium." *Night White Skies*. Accessed June 17, 2020. https://seanlally.net/2019/03/14/night-white-skies/.

Lambert, Léopold. "Simondon/Episode 03: Topological Life: The World Can't Be Fathomed in Plans and Sections." *The Funambulist* (blog). Accessed April 14, 2019. https://thefunambulist.net/architectural-projects/simondon-episode-03-topological-life-the-world-cant-be-read-in-plans-and-sections.

———. *The Funambulist Pamphlets. Volume 8, Arakawa + Madeline Gins*. Brooklyn: punctum books, 2014.

———, and Minh-Ha T. Pham. "Spinoza in a T-Shirt." *The New Inquiry*, July 1, 2015. https://thenewinquiry.com/spinoza-in-a-t-shirt/.

Lambie, Ryan. "Greebles: How Tiny Details Make a Huge Star Wars Universe." *Den of Geek* (blog), May 4, 2018. https://www.denofgeek.com/movies/greebles-how-tiny-details-make-a-huge-star-wars-universe/.

Laporte, Dominique. *History of Shit*. Translated by Nadia Benabid and Rodolphe el-Khoury. Cambridge: MIT Press, 2000.

Latour, Bruno. *Pandora's Hope: Essays on the Reality of Science Studies*. Cambridge: Harvard University Press, 1999.

————. *Science in Action: How to Follow Scientists and Engineers through Society*. Cambridge: Harvard University Press, 1987.

————. *The Pasteurization of France*. Translated by Alan Sheridan and John Law. Cambridge and London: Harvard University Press, 1988.

————. *We Have Never Been Modern*. Translated by Catherine Porter. Cambridge: Harvard University Press, 1993.

Latour, Bruno, and Emilie Hermant. "Paris: Invisible City." Translated by Liz Carey-Libbrecht. Bruno-Latour.fr. Accessed October 19, 2018. www.bruno-latour.fr/sites/default/files/downloads/viii_paris-city-gb.pdf.

————. *Paris Ville Invisible*. Paris: Les Empêcheurs de Penser en Rond & La Découverte, 1998.

Latour, Bruno, and Albena Yaneva. "'Give Me a Gun and I Will Make All Buildings Move': An ANT's View of Architecture." *Ardeth* 01, no. 08 (2017): 102–11. https://doi.org/10.17454/ARDETH01.08.

Lavin, Sylvia. "Architecture In Extremis." *Log*, no. 22 (2011): 51–61.

Law, John. "What's Wrong with a One-World World?" *Distinktion: Journal of Social Theory* 16, no. 1 (January 2, 2015): 126–39. https://doi.org/10.1080/1600910X.2015.1020066.

Lazell, Jordon, Solon Magrizos, and Marylyn Carrigan. "Over-Claiming the Circular Economy: The Missing Dimensions." *Social Business* 8, no. 1 (May 31, 2018): 103–14. https://doi.org/10.1362/204440818X15208755029618.

Le Corbusier. *Towards a New Architecture*. Translated by Frederick Etchells. New York: Dover Publications, 1986.

————. *When the Cathedrals Were White*. Translated by Francis E. Hyslop Jr. New York, Toronto and London: McGraw-Hill Book Company, 1964.

LEED. "Regional Materials." USGBC, 2009. www.usgbc.org/credits/new-construction-schools/v2009/mrc5.

Lefebvre, Henri. *The Production of Space*. Translated by Donald Nicholson-Smith. Malden: Blackwell, 2011.

León, Ana María, and Quilian Riano. "About #FolkMoMA." *FolkMoMA*. Accessed October 18, 2018. https://folkmoma.tumblr.com/about.

Leonard, Annie, and Ariane Conrad. *The Story of Stuff: How Our Obsession with Stuff Is Trashing the Planet, Our Communities, and Our Health - and a Vision for Change*. London: Constable, 2010.

Leroi-Gourhan, André. *Gesture and Speech*. Cambridge: MIT Press, 1993.

————. *L'homme et la matière: évolution et techniques*. Paris: Éditions Albin Michel, 2013.

Le Roux, Hannah, and Gabrielle Hecht. "Bad Earth." *E-Flux Architecture*, Accumulation, August 21, 2020. www.e-flux.com/architecture/accumulation/345106/bad-earth/.

Lévi-Strauss, Claude. *The Savage Mind (La Pensée Sauvage)*. London: Weidenfeld and Nicolson, 1966.

Li, Ang. "All That Is Solid." *Journal of Architectural Education* 74, no.2 (July 2, 2020): 299–308. https://doi.org/10.1080/10464883. 2020.1790940.

Liboiron, Max. "Modern Waste as Strategy." *Lo Squaderno: Explorations in Space and Society*, no. 29 (2013): 9–12. https://maxliboiron. files.wordpress.com/2013/08/liboiron-modern-waste-as-strategy-extracted.pdf.

———. *Pollution Is Colonialism*. Durham: Duke University Press, 2021.

———. "Waste Is Not 'Matter out of Place.'" *Discard Studies* (blog). Accessed May 23, 2020. https://discardstudies.com/2019/09/09/ waste-is-not-matter-out-of-place/.

Living Architecture Consortium. "Team." Living Architecture H2020. Accessed June 17, 2020. https://livingarchitecture-h2020.eu/ partner-profiles/.

Lloyd Thomas, Katie. "Building Materials: Conceptualising Materials via the Architectural Specification." PhD dissertation, Middlesex University, 2010.

———. "Specifications: Writing Materials in Architecture and Philosophy." *Architectural Research Quarterly* 8, no. 3–4 (December 2004): 277–83. https://doi.org/10.1017/S1359135504000296.

———. "The Architect as Shopper: Women, Electricity, Building Products and the Interwar 'Proprietary Turn' in the UK." In *Architecture and Feminisms: Ecologies, Economies, Technologies*, edited by Hélène Frichot, Catharina Gabrielsson, and Helen Runting, 54–65. London and New York: Routledge, 2018.

Locke, John. *An Essay Concerning Human Understanding*. Edited by Jonathan Bennett. Vol. Book II: Ideas, 2004. www.earlymoderntexts. com/assets/pdfs/locke1690book2.pdf.

———. *Second Treatise of Government*. Edited and with an introduction by C. B. McPherson. Indianapolis and Cambridge: Hackett Publishing Company, 1980. www.gutenberg.org/files/7370/7370-h/7370-h.htm.

———. *Political Writings*. Edited and with an introduction by David Wootton. London: Penguin, 1993.

Lynch, Kevin. "Environmental Adaptability." *Journal of the American Institute of Planners* 24, no. 1 (March 31, 1958): 16–24. https://doi. org/10.1080/01944365808978262.

———. *The Image of the City*. Cambridge: MIT Press, 2005.

MacBride, Samantha. "Does Recycling Actually Conserve or Preserve Things?" *Discard Studies* (blog), February 11, 2019. https://discard-studies.com/2019/02/11/12755/.

———. *Recycling Reconsidered: The Present Failure and Future Promise of Environmental Action in the United States*. Cambridge: MIT Press, 2013.

———. "The Fungibility of Carbon Waste: Plastics, Organics & Thermal/Biological Treatments." Jean Thomas Lambert Environmental Lecture presented at Discarded: Unmasking & Understanding the Waste Stream, Lear-Conant Symposium, Connecticut College, March 6, 2021.

Malm, Andreas. *How to Blow up a Pipeline: Learning to Fight in a World on Fire*. Brooklyn: Verso Books, 2020.

Maloney, Jennifer. "MoMa Rethinks Plan to Raze Former Home of Folk Art Museum." *The Wall Street Journal*, May 9, 2013. www.wsj.com/articles/SB10001424127887324744104578473402294516878.

Manning, Ryan Vincent. "Soft Discrete Familiars: Animals, Blankets and Bricks." In *Discrete: Reappraising the Digital in Architecture*. Vol. 89. Architectural Design, edited by Gilles Retsin, 118–23. John Wiley & Sons, 2019.

Martin, Chris. "Wind Turbine Blades Can't Be Recycled, So They're Piling Up in Landfills." *Bloomberg Green*, February 5, 2020. www.bloomberg.com/news/features/2020-02-05/wind-turbine-blades-can-t-be-recycled-so-they-re-piling-up-in-landfills.

Marx, Karl. *Capital: Volume One*. Translated by Samuel Moore and Edward Aveling. Ware: Wordsworth Editions Ltd, 2013.

———. *Karl Marx: A Reader*. Edited by Jon Elster. Cambridge and New York: Press Syndicate of the University of Cambridge, 1986.

———, and Friedrich Engels. "Manifesto of the Communist Party." In *Marx/Engels Selected Works*, 98–137. Moscow: Progress Publishers, 1969.

Mattern, Shannon. "Maintenance and Care." *Places Journal*, November 2018. https://placesjournal.org/article/maintenance-and-care/.

McDonough Braungart Design Chemistry (MBDC). "Cradle to Cradle CertifiedTM: Product Standard, Version 3.1." Cradle to Cradle Products Innovation Institute, 2016. https://s3.amazonaws.com/c2c-website/resources/certification/standard/STD_C2CCertified_ProductStandard_V3.1_082318.pdf.

McLellan, Todd. *Things Come Apart 2.0: A Teardown Manual for Modern Living*. London: Thames & Hudson, 2019.

McLuhan, Marshall. *Understanding Media: The Extensions of Man*. Cambridge: MIT Press, 1994.

———, and Eric McLuhan. *Laws of Media: The New Science*. Toronto: University of Toronto Press, 1999.

Melville, Herman. "Bartleby." In *The Piazza Tales*. New York: Dix & Edwards, 1856.

Moe, Kiel. *Empire, State & Building*. New York: Actar, 2017.

———. *Unless: The Seagram Building Construction Ecology*. New York: Actar Publishers, 2020.

Moller, Teresa. "Punta Pite." Teresa Moller Landscape Studio. Accessed June 17, 2020. http://teresamoller.cl/portfolio/punta-pite/.

Moreau, Vincent, Marlyne Sahakian, Pascal van Griethuysen, and François Vuille. "Coming Full Circle: Why Social and Institutional

Dimensions Matter for the Circular Economy." *Journal of Industrial Ecology* 21, no. 3 (June 2017): 497–506. https://doi.org/10.1111/jiec.12598.

Moreno, Gean, and Ernesto Oroza. "Generic Objects." *E-Flux Journal*, no. 18 (September 2010). www.e-flux.com/journal/18/67456/generic-objects/.

Morton, Timothy. *Being Ecological*. UK: Pelican, 2018.

———. "Frankenstein and Ecocriticism." In *The Cambridge Companion to Frankenstein*, edited by Andrew Smith, 143–57. Cambridge: Cambridge University Press, 2016. https://doi.org/10.1017/CBO9781316091203.012.

———. *Hyperobjects: Philosophy and Ecology after the End of the World*. Minneapolis: University of Minnesota Press, 2013.

———. "Peak Nature." *Adbusters*, 2012. www.adbusters.org/magazine/98/peak-nature.html.

———. *The Ecological Thought*. Cambridge: Harvard University Press, 2012.

Mulrow, John, and Victoria Santos. "Moving the Circular Economy beyond Alchemy." *Discard Studies* (blog), November 13, 2017. https://discardstudies.com/2017/11/13/moving-the-circular-economy-beyond-alchemy/.

Muschamp, Herbert. "Fireside Intimacy for American Folk Art Museum." *The New York Times*, December 14, 2001.

Naess, Arne. *Ecology, Community and Lifestyle: Outline of an Ecosophy*. Cambridge: Cambridge University Press, 1998.

NASA. "Blue Marble—Image of the Earth from Apollo 17," November 30, 2007. www.nasa.gov/content/blue-marble-image-of-the-earth-from-apollo-17.

Nėjė, Julija. "Coca-Cola Invents 16 Bottle Caps to Give Second Lives to Empty Bottles." *BoredPanda* (blog). Accessed April 14, 2019. www.boredpanda.com/coca-cola-ogilvy-mather-2nd-lives-bottles/.

Nesbit, Molly. "What Was an Author?" *Yale French Studies*, no. 73 (1987): 229–57. https://doi.org/10.2307/2930205.

Nietzsche, Friedrich Wilhelm. *Philosophy in the Tragic Age of the Greeks*. Translated by Marianne Cowan. Washington: Regnery Publishing, 1998.

Norman, Donald A. *The Design of Everyday Things*. New York: Doubleday, 1990.

Norwood, Bryan E. "Metaphors For Nothing." *Log*, no. 33 (2015): 107–19.

O'Donnell, Caroline, and Dillon Pranger, eds. *The Architecture of Waste: Design for a Circular Economy*. New York: Routledge, 2021.

Odum, Howard T. *Environmental Accounting: EMERGY and Environmental Decision Making*. New York: Wiley, 1996.

OgilvyAsia Admin. "2nd Lives." Ogilvy's Asia, May 7, 2015. www.ogilvyasia.com/forceforgood/2nd-lives/.

O'Neill, Kate. *Waste*. Cambridge and Medford: Polity Press, 2019.

Opalis EU. Accessed May 31, 2020. https://opalis.eu/en.

Oppenheimer Dean, Andrea, and Timothy Hursley. *Proceed and Be Bold: Rural Studio after Samuel Mockbee*. New York: Princeton Architectural Press, 2005.

Oroza, Ernesto. "Technological Disobedience." *MKSHFT.ORG* (blog), July 7, 2020. https://mkshft.org/2012/07/technological-disobedience/.

———. "Technological Disobedience: From the Revolution to Revolico." *Technological Disobedience Archive* (blog), March 30, 2016. www.technologicaldisobedience.com/2016/03/30/technological-disobedience-from-the-revolution-to-revolico-com/.

Otero-Pailos, Jorge. "Experimental Preservation." *Places Journal*, September 2016. https://doi.org/10.22269/160913.

PA DEP (Pennsylvania Department of Environmental Protection). "Background Paper on Residual Waste." Philadelphia: PA DEP, 2001. Quoted in Samantha MacBride, *Recycling Reconsidered: The Present Failure and Future Promise of Environmental Action in the United States*. Cambridge: MIT Press, 2013.

Packard, Vance. *The Waste Makers*. New York: Pocket Books, 1969.

Pawley, Martin. *Garbage Housing*. London: Architectural Press, 1975.

Paz, Octavio. *Marcel Duchamp: Appearance Stripped Bare*. Translated by Rachel Phillips and Donald Gardner. New York: Arcade Publishing, 2014.

Pearce, Fred. "The Hidden Environmental Toll of Mining the World's Sand." *Yale Environment 360*, February 5, 2019. https://e360.yale.edu/features/the-hidden-environmental-toll-of-mining-the-worlds-sand.

Pearson, C. A. "Material Affairs." *Architectural Record*, March 2001.

Perez, Adelyn. "American Folk Art Museum/Tod Williams + Billie Tsien." *ArchDaily* (blog). Accessed October 19, 2018. www.archdaily.com/61497/american-folk-art-museum-tod-williams-billie-tsien.

Peters, John Durham. *The Marvelous Clouds: Toward a Philosophy of Elemental Media*. Chicago and London: University of Chicago Press, 2015.

Plumwood, Val. *Feminism and the Mastery of Nature*. London: Routledge, 2003.

Pogrebin, Robin. "Ambitious Redesign of MoMA Doesn't Spare a Notable Neighbor." *The New York Times*, January 8, 2014, Online edition. www.nytimes.com/2014/01/09/arts/design/a-grand-redesign-of-moma-does-not-spare-a-notable-neighbor.html.

———. "Architects Mourn Former Folk Art Museum Building." *The New York Times*, April 15, 2014, Online edition. www.nytimes.com/2014/04/16/arts/design/architects-mourn-former-folk-art-museum-building.html.

———. "Options Dim for Museum of Folk Art." *The New York Times*, August 24, 2011, Online edition. www.nytimes.com/2011/08/25/

arts/design/american-folk-art-museum-weighs-survival-strategies. html.

Posner, Miriam. "Seeing like a Supply Chain." UCLA, February 11, 2021.

Potting, José, Marko Hekkert, Ernst Worrell, and Aldert Hanemaaijer. "Circular Economy: Measuring Innovation in the Production Chain." Policy Report. The Hague: PBL Netherlands Environmental Assessment Agency, January 2017.

Rancière, Jacques. *The Politics of Aesthetics: The Distribution of the Sensible*. Edited by Gabriel Rockhill. London: Bloomsbury, 2013.

Ranganathan, Malini. "Property, Pipes, and Improvement." *Power (Buell Center for the Study of American Architecture)*, July 16, 2019. https://power.buellcenter.columbia.edu/essays/property-pipes-and-improvement.

Read, Leonard E. *I, Pencil: My Family Tree as Told to Leonard E. Read*. Online. The Library of Economics and Liberty, 1959. www.econlib. org/library/Essays/rdPncl.html?chapter_num=2#book-reader.

Reday-Mulvey, Geneviève, Walter R. Stahel, and Commission of the European Communities. "The Potential for Substituting Manpower for Energy: Final Report 30 July 1977." Study (Battelle Geneva), 1977.

Retsin, Gilles, ed. *Discrete: Reappraising the Digital in Architecture*. Vol. 89. Architectural Design. John Wiley & Sons, 2019.

Reuter, Markus, Antoinette Schaik, and Miquel Ballester. "Limits of the Circular Economy: Fairphone Modular Design Pushing the Limits." *World of Metallurgy—ERZMETALL* 71 (March 19, 2018): 68–79.

Riegl, Alois. "The Modern Cult of Monuments: Its Essence and Its Development." In *Historical and Philosophical Issues in the Conservation of Cultural Heritage*, edited by Nicholas Stanley-Price, Mansfield Kirby Talley, and Alessandra Melucco Vaccaro, translated by Karin Bruckner and Karen Williams, 69–83. Los Angeles: Getty Conservation Institute, 1996.

Right to Know Network, "Toxics Release Inventory database." www. rtknet.org/db/tri/tri.php?database. Search term "331314: Secondary Smelting and Alloying of Aluminum"; search conducted 4 May 2015. Quoted in Carl A. Zimring, *Aluminum Upcycled: Sustainable Design in Historical Perspective*. Baltimore: Johns Hopkins University Press, 2017.

Riofrancos, Thea. "What Green Costs." *Logic Magazine*, December 7, 2019. https://logicmag.io/nature/what-green-costs/.

Rogers, Heather. *Gone Tomorrow: The Hidden Life of Garbage*. New York and York: New Press, 2006. Ebook.

Romo-Melgar, Carlos. "Nobody Would Visit Paris If It Looked like Dallas: Analysis of Mark Foster Gage Architects' Proposal for the Guggenheim Museum in Helsinki." *Medium* (blog), June 25, 2021. https://medium.com/@c31913/nobody-would-visit-paris-if-it-looked-like-dallas-696e7a403035.

Rothstein, Richard. *The Color of Law: A Forgotten History of How Our Government Segregated America*. New York and London: Liveright Publishing Corporation, 2018.

Rotor. "Rotor DC: Reuse Made Easy." Rotor. Accessed May 31, 2020. http://rotordb.org/en/projects/rotor-dc-reuse-made-easy.

Roudavski, Stanislav, and Dan Parker. "Modelling Workflows for More-than-Human Design: Prosthetic Habitats for the Powerful Owl (*Ninox Strenua*)." In *Impact: Design With All Senses*, edited by Christoph Gengnagel, Olivier Baverel, Jane Burry, Mette Ramsgaard Thomsen, and Stefan Weinzierl, 554–64. Cham: Springer International Publishing, 2020. https://doi.org/10.1007/978-3-030-29829-6_43.

Rowe, Colin, and Fred Koetter. *Collage City*. Cambridge: MIT Press, 1978.

Ruy, David. "Returning to (Strange) Objects." *Tarp Architecture Manual*, Spring 2012.

———. "Returning to (Strange) Objects." RuyKlein.Com. www.ruyklein.com/essays/Returning%20to%20(Strange)%20Objects%20-%20Ruy.pdf

Ryle, Gilbert. *The Concept of Mind*. London and New York: Routledge, 2009.

Sachez, Jose. "Architecture for the Commons: Participatory Systems in the Age of Platforms." In *Discrete: Reappraising the Digital in Architecture*. Vol. 89. Architectural Design, edited by Gilles Retsin, 22–29. John Wiley & Sons, 2019.

Said, Edward W. *Culture and Imperialism*. New York: Vintage Books, 1994.

Scanlan, John. *On Garbage*. London: Reaktion Books, 2005.

Schwabsky, Barry. "MoMA's Demolition Derby." *The Nation*, May 1, 2013. www.thenation.com/article/archive/momas-demolition-derby/.

Scott Brown, Denise. "The Redefinition of Functionalism." In *Architecture as Signs and Systems: For a Mannerist Time*, by Robert Venturi and Denise Scott Brown. Cambridge and London: Belknap Press of Harvard University Press, 2004.

SCP/RAC. "Plastic's Toxic Additives and the Circular Economy," September 2020. https://ipen.org/sites/default/files/documents/plastics_and_additives_final-low-o-en.pdf.

Self, Martin. "Hooke Park: Applications for Timber in Its Natural Form." In *Advancing Wood Architecture: A Computational Approach*, edited by Tobias Schwinn and Oliver David Krieg, 141–53. London and New York: Routledge, 2017.

Serres, Michel. *Le Mal Propre: Polluer pour s'approprier?* Paris: Pommier, 2008.

———. *Malfeasance: Appropriation through Pollution?* Translated by Anne-Marie Feenberg-Dibon. Stanford: Stanford University Press, 2011.

———. *The Parasite*. Translated by Lawrence R. Schehr. Baltimore: Johns Hopkins University Press, 1982.

Sessions, George, ed. *Deep Ecology for the Twenty-First Century*. Boston: Shambhala, 1995.

Shelley, Mary Wollstonecraft. *Frankenstein: Or, The Modern Prometheus*. Vol. 1. London: Lackington, Hughes, Harding, Mavor & Jones, 1818.

Shonfield, Katherine. "Two Architectural Projects about Purity." In *Architecture: The Subject Is Matter*, edited by Jonathan Hill, 29–43. London and New York: Routledge, 2001.

Siever, Raymond. *Sand*. Scientific American Library Series, no. 24. New York: Scientific American Library, 1988.

Simard, Suzanne. *Finding the Mother Tree*. New York: Alfred A. Knopf, 2021.

Simondon, Gilbert. *L'individu et sa genèse physico-biologique; l'individuation à la lumière des notions de forme et d'information*. Paris: Presses universitaires de France, 1964.

———. *L'individuation à la lumière des notions de forme et d'information*. Grenoble: Millon, 2005.

———. *On the Mode of Existence of Technical Objects*. Translated by Ninian Mellamphy and with a preface by John Hart. University of Western Ontario, 1980.

———. *L'invention dans les techniques, Cours et conférences*. Paris: Seuil, 2005.

Slater, Duncan, and Roland Ennos. "Interlocking Wood Grain Patterns Provide Improved Wood Strength Properties in Forks of Hazel (*Corylus Avellana* L.)." *Arboricultural Journal* 37, no. 1 (January 2, 2015): 21–32. https://doi.org/10.1080/03071375.2015.1012876.

Smith, Roberta. "Downsizing in a Burst of Glory." *The New York Times*, May 12, 2011, Online edition. www.nytimes.com/2011/05/13/arts/design/quilts-at-the-american-folk-art-museum-review.html.

Smuts, Barbara. "Encounters with Animal Minds." *Journal of Consciousness Studies* 8, no. 5–7 (May 2001): 293–309.

Sofia, Zoë. "Container Technologies." *Hypatia* 15, no. 2 (2000): 181–201.

Sohn-Rethel, Alfred. "The Ideal of the Broken Down: On the Neapolitan Approach to Things Technical." *Hard Crackers: Chronicles of Everyday Life* (blog), February 15, 2018. https://hardcrackers.com/ideal-broken-neapolitan-approach-things-technical/.

Soper, Kate. *What Is Nature? Culture, Politics, and the Non-Human*. Oxford and Cambridge: Blackwell, 1998.

Srinivasan, Ravi, and Kiel Moe. *The Hierarchy of Energy in Architecture: Energy Analysis*. London: Routledge, 2015.

Stahel, Walter R. *The Performance Economy*. Houndsmille and New York: Palgrave Macmillan, 2010.

———, and Geneviève Reday-Mulvey. *Jobs for Tomorrow: The Potential for Substituting Manpower for Energy*. New York: Vantage Press, 1981.

Star, Susan Leigh. "The Structure of Ill-Structured Solutions: Boundary Objects and Heterogeneous Distributed Problem Solving." In *Distributed Artificial Intelligence*, edited by Les Gasser and Michael N. Huhns, II:37–54. Elsevier, 1989. https://doi.org/10.1016/B978-1-55860-092-8.50006-X.

———, and James R. Griesemer. "Institutional Ecology, 'Translations' and Boundary Objects: Amateurs and Professionals in Berkeley's Museum of Vertebrate Zoology, 1907–39." *Social Studies of Science* 19, no. 3 (1989): 387–420.

Strasser, Susan. *Waste and Want: A Social History of Trash*. New York: Owl Books, 2000.

Styres, Sandra D., and Dawn M. Zinga. "The Community-First Land-Centred Theoretical Framework: Bringing a 'Good Mind' to Indigenous Education Research?" *Canadian Journal of Education/Revue Canadienne de l'éducation* 36, no. 2 (July 2013): 284–313.

Sun, Monic, and Remi Trudel. "The Effect of Recycling versus Trashing on Consumption: Theory and Experimental Evidence." *Journal of Marketing Research* 54, no. 2 (April 2017): 293–305. https://doi.org/10.1509/jmr.15.0574.

Taylor, Kate. "Folk Art Museum Considers Closing." *The New York Times*, August 19, 2011, Online edition. www.nytimes.com/2011/08/20/arts/design/american-folk-art-museum-considers-final-options.html.

Terreform ONE. "Monarch Sanctuary: Integrated Biodiversity in Double Skin Facade." Terreform ONE. Accessed June 17, 2020. www.terreform.org/projects_butterfly.html.

Thill, Brian. *Waste*. Object Lessons. New York: Bloomsbury Academic, 2015. E-book.

Thompson, Michael. *Rubbish Theory: The Creation and Destruction of Value*. London: Pluto Press, 2017.

Thwaites, Thomas. *The Toaster Project: Or A Heroic Attempt to Build a Simple Electric Appliance from Scratch*. New York: Princeton Architectural Press, 2011.

Tillman Lyle, John. *Regenerative Design for Sustainable Development*. New York: Wiley, 1994.

TWBTA. "American Folk Art Museum." Tod Williams Billie Tsien Architects Partners. Accessed October 18, 2018. http://twbta.com/work/american-folk-art-museum.com.

Uexküll, Jakob von. *A Foray into the Worlds of Animals and Humans: With a Theory of Meaning*. Translated by Joseph D. O'Neil, with an introduction by Dorion Sagan, and an afterword by Geoffrey Winthrop-Young. Minneapolis: University of Minnesota Press, 2010.

UN Environment and International Energy Agency. "Towards a Zero-Emission, Efficient, and Resilient Buildings and Construction Sector," Global Status Report, 2017.

Valenzuela, Francisco, and Steffen Böhm. "Against Wasted Politics: A Critique of the Circular Economy." *Ephemera: Theory & Politics in Organization* 17, no. 1 (2017): 23–60.

Valero, Antonio, and Alicia Valero. "Thermodynamic Rarity and Recyclability of Raw Materials in the Energy Transition: The Need for an In-Spiral Economy." *Entropy* 21, no. 9 (September 8, 2019): 873. https://doi.org/10.3390/e21090873.

Van der Ryn, Sim, and Stuart Cowan. *Ecological Design*. Washington: Island Press, 1996.

Van Hinte, Ed, Césare Peeren, and Jan Jongert. *Superuse: Constructing New Architecture by Shortcutting Material Flows*. Rotterdam: 010 Publishers, 2007.

Vidler, Anthony. "The Ledoux Effect: Emil Kaufmann and the Claims of Kantian Autonomy." *Perspecta* 33 (January 1, 2002): 16–29. https://doi.org/10.2307/1567293.

Viney, William. *Waste: A Philosophy of Things*. London and New York: Bloomsbury Academic, 2014.

Vitruvius. *The Ten Books on Architecture*. Translated by Morris Hicky Morgan. New York: Dover, 1960.

Watson, Julia, and Wade Davis. *Lo-Tek: Design by Radical Indigenism*. Taschen, 2020.

Whitman, Walt. "This Compost." In *Leaves of Grass*, edited by Jim Manis. PSU-Hazleton, Hazleton PA. Accessed June 5, 2020. https://edisciplinas.usp.br/pluginfile.php/3985648/mod_resource/content/1/LEAVES%20OF%20GRASS.pdf.

Whyte, Kyle. "Settler Colonialism, Ecology, and Environmental Injustice." *Environment and Society* 9, no. 1 (September 1, 2018): 125–44. https://doi.org/10.3167/ares.2018.090109.

Wilde, Oscar. *The Soul of Man under Socialism and Selected Critical Prose*. Edited by Linda C. Dowling. London and New York: Penguin Books, 2001.

Wiscombe, Tom. "A Specific Theory of Models: The Posthuman Beauty of Weird Scales, Snowglobes and Supercomponents." *Architectural Design* 89, no. 5 (September 2019): 80–89. https://doi.org/10.1002/ad.2483.

———. "Discreteness, or Towards a Flat Ontology of Architecture." *Project: A Journal for Architecture*, no. 3 (Spring 2014): 34–43.

Wong, Liliane. *Adaptive Reuse: Extending the Lives of Buildings*. Basel: Birkhäuser, 2017.

Yaneva, Albena. *Made by the Office for Metropolitan Architecture: An Ethnography of Design*. Rotterdam: 010 Publishers, 2009.

———. *The Making of a Building: A Pragmatist Approach to Architecture*. Oxford and New York: Peter Lang, 2009.

Zimring, Carl A. *Aluminum Upcycled: Sustainable Design in Historical Perspective*. Baltimore: Johns Hopkins University Press, 2017.

Zink, Trevor, and Roland Geyer. "Circular Economy Rebound." *Journal of Industrial Ecology* 21, no. 3 (June 2017): 593–602. https://doi.org/10.1111/jiec.12545.

———. "Material Recycling and the Myth of Landfill Diversion." *Journal of Industrial Ecology* 23, no. 3 (June 2019): 541–48. https://doi.org/10.1111/jiec.12808.

Žižek, Slavoj. "First as Tragedy, Then as Farce." Online lecture, the RSA, London. Accessed February 18, 2020. https://vimeo.com/8073858.

———. *Living in the End Times*. London and New York: Verso, 2011.

Zummer, Thomas. "Essay on Potatoes." In *Text Messaging: September 17 – November 16, 2008*, edited by Karen Shaw. Islip Art Museum, 2008. www.islipartmuseum.org/pdf/IslipTextMessaging Catalogue.pdf.

Acknowledgments

This book has accreted, across continents, over a long period of time, and many have contributed—knowingly and unknowingly, directly and indirectly—to its evolution. I am indebted to all the friends, teachers, students, and colleagues whose shoulders I stand on.

I am grateful to Brian for his continuing love, patience, and encouragement (and for his helpful notes on the manuscript); and to Lauren Jade Martin, who took me seriously as I started writing and thinking about an academic career. Without their support, I might not be here today.

I would also like to thank my family (Belosis, Ferracinas, and Fords). My niblings Carlotta, Martina, and Tommaso are on my mind when thinking about the impacts of climate change on future generations, as are the students I met along the way.

At the European Graduate School and beyond, I am thankful to Thomas Zummer for his wisdom and kindness, and for convincing me to "stop sharpening pencils"; to Federico Ruberto and Andrea Perunović for their infectious intelligence and friendship; to Giorgio Agamben, whose seminars changed the trajectory of my research; and to Graham Harman, whose thoughtful comments and unwavering support as my doctoral supervisor, even as I reinterpreted or criticized his work, were consistently forthcoming, generous, and helpful—as were the insights offered by Christopher Fynsk and Timothy Morton during the doctoral defense.

At Newcastle University, my gratitude goes to Rachel Armstrong for her contagious enthusiasm and boundless generosity—and for telling me, when a violent allergic reaction had left me feeling (and looking) monstrous, that "there is no better company than that of a monster." Because of her, I had the fortune to share many adventures with the Experimental Architecture Group (Rachel Armstrong, Rolf Hughes, Andrew Ballantyne, and Pierangelo Scravaglieri), from whom I have learnt—and continue to learn—a lot.

Katie Lloyd Thomas organized the "Sparks of Life: Frankenstein & Regeneration at Carliol House" event to which I contributed, with Pierangelo Scravaglieri, the first instance of the *Memory of Parts* project, with support from the Architecture Research Collaborative (ARC). I am thankful to her, and to Andrew Ballantyne, Adam Sharr, Zeynep Kezer, Christos Kakalis, and others, for their warm welcome to the School. Christos' invitation to write a collaborative paper, and a call from the *Edinburgh Architecture Research* (EAR) journal, prompted my reflections about formats and media (Chapter 5), a preliminary fragment of which appears in the paper "Notating Not Knowing: The Oceanic Challenge to Format and Medium."[1] The collaboration eventually resulted in the chapter "Notating Silences and Absences" published in Christos' book *Architecture and Silence*.[2] The early thoughts about suspension and refusal published there were modified and further developed for Chapter 6. Finally, Rachel Armstrong's invitation to contribute a chapter in her book *Experimental Architecture* provided a chance to write about exaptive design and the story of the Folk Art Museum.[3] The resulting text was revised and expanded in Chapter 7.

At the University of Edinburgh, I am indebted to the students and colleagues who have, over the years, contributed to the Radical Coauthorship unit—Asad Khan (my brilliant teaching partner), Michelle Bastian, Moa Carlsson, Susan Falconer, Laura Harty, Joyce Hwang, Sepideh Karami, Angus MacDonald, Samantha MacBride, Brett Mommersteeg, Sonakshi Pandit, Remo Pedreschi, Giorgio Ponzo, and Liam Ross. Cameron Angus, Jamie Begg, Skye Brownlow, Cindy Chananithitham, Alannah Marie Cumming, Hannah Davis, Myrto Efthymiadi, Esther Fletcher, Elida Harjo Hansen, Mimi Hattori, Kaja Isobel Hellman-Hayes, Sarah Kemali, Rachel Leong, Ryan Liu, Rana Tabatabaie, Andrew Stuart Wyness, Ivy Yan, and Tenny Zhang graciously agreed to have their work featured in this book.

In 2019, Mark Dorrian invited me to contribute to the ESALA Research Seminar Series.[4] There and elsewhere, I am grateful for the questions, comments, and suggestions offered by colleagues at the university: Richard Anderson, Michelle Bastian, Richard Coyne, Mark Dorrian, Suzanne Ewing, Laura Harty, Francisca Lima, Lisa MacKenzie, Lisa Moffitt, Remo Pedreschi, and Liam Ross, among others. Teaching a studio on deconstruction and on the rehabilitation of soon-to-be-demolished buildings with Moa Carlsson has been, and continues to be, a privilege—I have learnt a lot from her, from the invited guest speakers, and from our trailblazing students. I am grateful for Moa's emotional and intellectual support, for her careful reading of this manuscript, and for her thoughtful comments. I am also thankful to Craig Martin, who took the time to read the manuscript and provided numerous insights and helpful suggestions, and to the ESALA Climate Action group—and to Michelle Bastian, Kate Carter, Anaïs Chanon, Lewis Evans, Laura Harty, W. Victoria Lee, and Anna

1 Rachel Armstrong, Simone Ferracina, Christos Kakalis, and Rolf Hughes, "Notating Not Knowing: The Oceanic Challenge to Format and Medium," ed. Sarah Borree, Laura Bowie, and Nikolia Kartalou, *Edinburgh Architecture Research* (EAR), no. 36 (2020). I am also thankful to the peer reviewers, who provided helpful feedback.

2 Rachel Armstrong, Simone Ferracina, Christos Kakalis, and Rolf Hughes, "Notating Silences and Absences," in Christos Kakalis, *Architecture and Silence* (Abingdon and NewYork: Routledge, 2019).

3 Simone Ferracina, "Exaptive Design: Radical Co-Authorship as Method," in Rachel Armstrong, *Experimental Architecture: Designing the Unknown* (London and New York: Routledge, 2019), 121–43.

4 Simone Ferracina, "Towards a Glossary of Exaptive Design" (Edinburgh School of Architecture and Landscape Architecture, November 20, 2019).

Rhodes in particular—for the hours spent discussing how the education of architects and landscape architects can (and must) change in response to the climate emergency. Finally, this book would not have been possible, in its current form, without the support of the Research and Knowledge Exchange Committee at the Edinburgh College of Art, which provided indispensable funds for the acquisition of images—a process that was guided, with much patience and kindness, by Jasmine Fyfe at the RKEI Office.

Back in New York, Samantha MacBride challenged my designerly optimism and introduced me to the field of Discard Studies. Had our paths not crossed, this book would be very different (and much more naive).

My gratitude goes to Césare Peeren, Alessandro Poli, Tim Vincent-Smith, Matt Wright, and Thomas Zummer, who took the time to discuss their exemplary work with me; to Arne Vande Capelle and Gaspard Geerts from Rotor, who offered numerous insights on re-use, deconstruction, and the reclamation market during their Geddes Fellowship at ESALA in March 2022; and, in order of appearance, to the artists, scholars, architects, and designers who have contributed images for this book: Raumlabor, Richard-Max Tremblay, Everitt Clark, Helen Kirkum, Rachel Dray, Catie Newell/Alibi Studio, Greg Lynn FORM, Brian Forrest, David Erdman, Benjamin Rasmussen, Superuse Studios, Denis Guzzo, the Elisha Whittelsey Collection, Barbara Smuts, Todd McLellan, Zachary Mollica, Valerie Bennett, Evgenia Spyridonos, Lacaton & Vassal, Philippe Ruault, Iwan Baan, Timothy Hursley, Adrià Goula, Flores & Prats, Rotor, Lionel Devlieger, Olivier Béart, James Henkel, Tim Vincent-Smith, Matt Wright, Chris Scott, Olivier Bardina, Lucas Muñoz, Ernesto Oroza, John Habraken, the Heineken Collection Foundation, Thomas Zummer, Richard Anderson, Scott Norsworthy, Koh Noguchi, Roger Jardin, Refunc, Ishka Michocka, BakerBrown Studio, Tom Wiscombe Architecture, Teresa Moller Landscape Studio, Lia Aliaga, Anupama Kundoo architects, Javier Callejas, Andreas Deffner, Alvaro Catalán de Ocón, Alessandro Poli, the Canadian Centre for Architecture, Bellastock, Alexis Leclercq, Joyce Hwang/Ants of the Prairie, Darren Le Roux, Mitchell Whitelaw, Dan Parker, Stanislav Roudavski, Rachel Armstrong, Arakawa and Gins, Miwako Tezuka, the Estate of Madeline Gins, Ken Kato, Masataka Nakano, Mark Foster Gage Architects, Ang Li, Billy Dufala, Alisa Andrasek, Jose Sanchez, Diego Pinochet, Felipe Véliz, Gilles Retsin, Studio NAARO, Judith Casas, Thomas Thwaites, Daniel Alexander, and Nick Ballon.

At Routledge, I'd like to thank the peer reviewers for their constructive comments, Jane Fieldsend for her expert copyediting, and Fran Ford, Trudy Varcianna, and Alanna Donaldson for their responsiveness, patience, and guidance.

Index